Makarios Drousiotis

Cyprus 1974:

Greek Coup and Turkish Invasion

PELEUS

STUDIEN ZUR ARCHÄOLOGIE UND
GESCHICHTE GRIECHENLANDS UND ZYPERNS

BAND 32

Makarios Drousiotis

Cyprus 1974:

Greek Coup and Turkish Invasion

BIBLIOPOLIS
Mannheim und Möhnesee 2006

PELEUS
Studien zur Archäologie und Geschichte Griechenlands und Zyperns
Herausgegeben von Reinhard Stupperich und Heinz A. Richter
Band 32

Umschlagvignetten:
Umschlagbild: Flüchtende Mutter mit ihren Kindern
Gegenüber Titelblatt: Innenbild einer Schale des Peithinosmalers, Berlin, Pergamonmuseum (CVA Berlin 2, Taf. 61).

Gesamtherstellung: Druck Partner Rübelmann GmbH, Carl-Benz-Str. 11, 69 502 Hemsbach

BIBLIOPOLIS
D - 59519 Möhnesee-Wamel, Schulpatt 13
Tel. 02924/2781, Fax 02924/2757, e-mail: bibliopolis@web.de

ISBN 3-933925-76-2

Table of Contents

Foreword

Two important events occurred in the summer of 1974 - the collapse of the military junta in Greece and the Turkish invasion of Cyprus. In Greece democracy returned, while in Cyprus 36 percent of its territory was occupied by an invading army. The Greek inhabitants in the north of the island were forced to flee, turning one third of the population into refugees, and the island was partitioned. Ever since then, each UN Secretary General, each US President, the EU and others have tried to find a solution to re-unite the island. In vain.Turkey set up a regime in the north of the island and allowed it to form a state, the "TRNC", recognised only by Turkey. Thus Cyprus became the last divided country in Europe.

This book tells the background story of these developments. It begins with a description of the first Cyprus crisis in 1963/4 when the paramilitaries of both camps provoked a civil war, making Cyprus an apple of discord between East and West. It describes how the US stepped in and some bright fellows developed all kinds of models for a solution, including a radical solution called "enosis by putsch". This involved a Greek Central Intelligence Agency (KYP) plot to kill the President of Cyprus, Archbishop Makarios, the Greek Government declaring Enosis (union of Cyprus with Greece), the US-Government influencing the Turks to remain calm telling them that they would get territorial compensation when things had cooled down. This plan became the blueprint for the 1974 coup by the Athens junta. Another bright idea was the Acheson plan, proposing double enosis, in other words partition and enosis.

Makarios Drousiotis meticulously describes the dramatic developments between the first crisis in 1963 and the 1974 catastrophe. His study is based on extensive archival research in the US where he consulted the National Archives in Maryland and various collections of oral history. He had access to the archives of the Cypriot Central Intelligence Agency. He interviewed 16 former high ranking eyewitnesses and evaluated testimonies to the Cypriot parliamentary committee researching the 1974 events. His bibliography is comprehensive and comprises all publications in Greek and English.

This comprehensive English account is a compilation from his five earlier books in Greek covering the time between the beginning of the liberation struggle in Cyprus and the coup of the Greek junta and the Turkish invasion.

Makarios Drousitis is a journalist by profession, who became a historian over the years, and a good one. He combines investigative journalism with the strict rules of the historian. Belonging to the younger generation of Cypriots (born 1959) he knows that a possible re-unification of the island and a cooperation of the two communities on it is only possible if the past and the mistakes committed by both sides are no longer buried in the basement but openly discussed and evaluated. Only the truth can pave the way to a happier future for this beautiful island, which saw so many nightmares; historians have an obligation to help overcome these.

I read the book by Makarios Drousiotis with great interest. Sometimes the story was heartstoppingly painful to read. His language is that of a journalist and makes for easy reading. This study is full of new evidence and I must congratulate the author for the splendid job he has done. I can only wish him many readers.

Heinz Richter

Introduction

The Greco-Turkish 'Para-State' and Cyprus (1947 – 1970)

At the beginning of 1947, civil war was raging in Greece between government forces supported by the British and those of the Democratic Army controlled by the Greek Communist Party (*Kommounistikon Komma Ellados* – KKE). Britain was facing serious economic difficulties, and her role as the leading power in the Balkans and the Middle East was being put to the test. In an effort to maintain her influence in Greece and to bring the war with the communists to a close, Britain, together with the Greek government, turned to the United States for economic assistance. America seized the opportunity to penetrate Greece economically, politically and militarily – but also Turkey, whose regime Britain was likewise unable to prop up – and to take on a dominant role in the region.

On 12 March 1947, American President Harry Truman promulgated in Congress the Truman doctrine, a programme of economic aid to Greece and Turkey amounting to $400 million. "It is necessary only to glance at a map to realise that the survival and integrity of the Greek nation are of grave importance in a much wider situation. If Greece should fall under the control of an armed minority, the effect upon its neighbour, Turkey, would be immediate and serious. Confusion and disorder might well spread throughout the entire Middle East",[1] President Truman told Congress, heralding the onset of the Cold War.

On 20 June, the governments of Greece and the United States signed a cooperation protocol that determined the method of payment and the use of the American aid, according to which general responsibility for its management was assigned to the American Mission for Aid to Greece (AMAG). The first head of AMAG was Dwight Griswold, who arrived in Greece on 14 July and was endowed with powers equivalent to those of a colonial governor. Indicative of the control exerted by the AMAG over the Greek government is an extract from one of its memoranda, dated 17 November 1947: "We have established practical control…over national budget, taxation, currency issuance, price and wage policies, and state economic planning, as well as over imports and exports, the issuance of foreign exchange and the direction of military reconstruction and relief expenditures."[2]

The greatest portion of American aid to Greece concerned the complete re-organisation of the country's armed forces. The Greek army acquired bombers, airports, naval vessels and communications systems. Docks, railway lines, roads and bridges were built. Infantry units became more mobile, with greater quantities of ammunition. By the end of 1947, the Greek army relied exclusively on American assistance, even for its food and clothing.[3] At the end of the year, however, a separate American mission was set up, the Joint U.S. Military Advisory and Planning Group, Greece – JUSMAPG – which took away from the Greek generals the responsibility for drawing up the battle plans against the guerrillas of the Democratic Army. With all this military power and under the guidance of American officers, the government forces eventually won the war against the Democratic Army. The Civil War ended in the summer of 1949, leaving in its wake 154,000 dead and wounded. Tens of thousands of members of the Democratic Army went into exile in Eastern Europe and the Soviet Union. Of those who stayed behind, many were executed while the others

---

1 Speech by US President Harry Truman to Congress, 12 March 1947. *The Avalon Project at Yale Law School, Documents in Law, History and Diplomacy*, http://www.yale.edu/lawweb/avalon/trudoc.htm.

2 William Blum, Killing Hope: U.S. Military and CIA Interventions Since World War II (Monroe, Maine: Common Courage Press, 1995), p. 38.

3 *Ibid.*, p. 37.

suffered relentlessly persecution through banishment, imprisonment, torture and displacement to arid islands.

Based on the experience it had gained through its intervention in Greece, the US at the end of the 1940s set up a network of semi-legal paramilitary organisations in Europe, within the framework of a defence plan against the 'communist threat'. The mission of these organisations was to continue the fight against the communists in the eventuality of any country being occupied by the Soviet Union – and for this reason, the network of organisations was named 'Stay Behind'. Each national organisation had a different name. In Italy it was the Gladio, in Belgium SDRA-8, in France Rose des Vets, in Holland P-26, in Greece it was called Sheepskin, in Switzerland Schwert, in Britain the Secret British Network and in Turkey Special Warfare Department.[4] A body named Super NATO, based in the Alliance's headquarters in Brussels, coordinated the work of the organisations.[5]

Members of the network, mainly fascists and fanatical anti-communists, were recruited, their mission to prevent the rise of the left to power anywhere in Western Europe, and to impose the domination of the United States through psychological warfare and terrorism. The US National Security Council had ordered that operations of psychological warfare be designed to be "deniable", meaning, "planned and executed (so) that any US government responsibility for them is not evident to unauthorised persons and that if uncovered, the US government can positively disclaim any responsibility."[6]

In its decision 10/2 of 1 September 1948, the National Security Council assigned the responsibility for psychological warfare operations to the Office of Policy Coordination (OPC),[7] which was the covert action arm of the CIA. As Marcus Ruskin, member of the National Security Council staff, wrote to Senator George McGovern, "we were involved in assassinations, assassination attempts. We were operating paramilitary operations with mercenary forces hired in other people's countries with no knowledge on the part of our own Congress, our press or the American people."[8] And, referring to the methods employed by the United States, Christopher Simpson, one of the most authoritative researchers on post-war American policy, wrote: "The role of the United States in world affairs during our lifetime has often been rapacious, destructive, tolerant of genocide and willing to sacrifice countless people."[9]

The members of the organisations in the Stay Behind network were trained using special manuals written by American specialists in guerrilla warfare. One such handbook, which was used by the Turkish organisation, mentions the following operational methods: "Assassinations, bombings, armed robbery, torture, attacks, kidnap, threats, provocation,

---

4 Ertugrul Kurkcu, "Turkey. Trapped in a Web of Covert Killers" *Covert Action Quarterly*, 61 (Washington: Summer 1967). Desmond Fernandes and Iskender Ozden, "United States and NATO Inspired 'Psychological Warfare Operations' against the 'Kurdish Communist Threat' in Turkey" *Variant*, 12 (Glasgow: Spring 2001).

5 "Staying Behind: NATO's Terror Network" *Fighting Talk*, 11 (London: May 1995).

6 NSC 10/2, June 18, 1948, Foreign Relations of the United States, 1945-1950, Emergence of the Intelligence Establishment, Document 292, http://www.state.gov/www/about_state/history/intel/290_300.html.

7 *Ibid.*, Document 300.

8 As quoted in Lewis Lapham's investigative documentary "American Power: Episode 4 – Omnipotence" screened on Discovery Channel, 1999, Fernandes and Osden, *Art. Cit.*

9 Christopher Simpson, Science of Coercion: Communication Research and Psychological Warfare, 1945-1960 (New York: Oxford University Press, 1996).

militia training, hostage-taking, arson, sabotage, propaganda, disinformation, violence and extortion."[10]

The existence of the Stay Behind network was revealed for the first time in 1976, in a Senate report on the CIA, prepared by Frank Church,[11] without, however, revealing the extent of its operations. Only in 1990, with the collapse of the Soviet Union and the end of the Cold War, was the existence of the Italian Gladio (Latin for 'sword') organisation disclosed. It emerged that Gladio had cooperated with the Mafia and the neo fascists, its mission being to prevent the Italian communists from taking power, either through revolution or legitimate elections. Prime Minister Giulio Andreotti, in his testimony before a parliamentary committee on 2 August 1990, acknowledged the existence of Gladio and admitted that Italy employed "a strategy of tension" to undercut the influence of the legal communist party.[12] The Gladio revelations were among the causes of the acute political crisis that rocked Italy in the early 1990s. Disclosures followed concerning the operations of sister organisations in other European countries. Although each organisation of the Stay Behind network had its individual name, they all came to be called Gladio because the Italian organisation was the only one about which so much evidence was disclosed.[13]

By the end of the 1940s, the Americans had imposed their complete suzerainty over Greece, displacing all the props that the British had established in the country by 1947. The Joint U.S. Military Aid Group, Greece (JUSMAG Greece), which had succeeded AMAG, employed 5,000 people, many of whom were agents of the CIA.[14] The local CIA station in Greece was founded in 1949 by the agency's Tom Karamesinis, a Greek American and former cadre in the OSS,[15] and was housed in the Army Fund's premises, together with the American Military Mission.

Part of CIA operations was the organisation, guidance and funding of the local Stay Behind organisation *Provia* (Sheepskin). Some sources refer to it as 'Red Sheepskin'. The *Provia* organisation was dependent on the Sacred League of Greek Officers (*Ieros Desmos Ellinon Axiomatikon* - IDEA), which had been founded with the assistance of the OSS immediately after the liberation, with the aim of rehabilitating those officers who had collaborated with the Germans during the occupation.[16] Among the cadres of the IDEA was the subsequent dictator George Papadopoulos, who had served in the Security Regiments in Patra.[17] After the liberation, the members of the Security Regiments were absorbed into National Defence Regiments (*Tagmata Ethnikis Aminis* - TEA), which were established by

---

10 Serdar Celik, "Turkey's Killing Machine: The Contra-Guerrilla Force" *Kurdistan Report*, 17 (February/March 1994).

11 Fernandes and Osden, *art. cit.*

12 Lucy Komisar, "Turkey's Terrorists: a CIA Legacy Lives on" *The Progressive* (Madison, Wisconsin: April 1997).

13 For the activities of Gladio in Italy, see "Operation Gladio, Statewatch", http://users.westnet.gr/~cgian/gladio.htm.

14 Philip Agee, "Ο 'νέος αμερικανικός παράγοντας' και η 'συγκαλυμμένη δραστηριότητα' της CIA στην Ελλάδα" [The 'New American Factor' and the 'Hidden Activities' of the CIA in Greece] in *Anti* (Athens: May 1997).

15 *Ibid.*

16 The first IDEA leader Georgios Karayiannis writes about it in his book *1940-1952: Το δράμα της Ελλάδας, έπη και αθλιότητες* (1940-1952: The tragedy of Greece, epics and wretchedness). The book was withdrawn shortly after publication with the author's consent. It has been republished in its entirety as part of the series *The Junta Trials*, published by Democratic Times, p. 1547.

17 Demetris Paralikas, *Ι.Δ.Ε.Α. και Α.Σ.Π.Ι.Δ.Α. (ρίζες και πλοκάμια), 1944-1974* [I.D.E.A. and A.S.P.I.D.A. (Origins and Spread), 1944-1974] (Athens, 1978), p. 56.

the Greek government and used in operations against communists throughout the civil war. IDEA played a leading role in the founding of the National Defence Regiments,[18] as did the 'X'[19] organisation, whose leader was the Cypriot Lieutenant Colonel, George Grivas It was during this period that IDEA member George Papadopoulos made the acquaintance of Grivas.[20]

According to Christopher Simpson, secret Pentagon papers now in the United States National Archive show that the US pumped millions of dollars into the IDEA, aiming at the creation of a 'Secret Army Reserve' made up of selected Greek military, policemen and anti-communist militia officers. With this aim, sufficient money, arms and supplies were shipped to Greece to equip a fighting force of 15,000 men as part of this programme alone.[21]

The German magazine *Der Spiegel* wrote in November 1990 that in Greece there were over 800 hiding places containing weapons, wirelesses and other equipment – in caves, in the cellars of public buildings, in covered wells, even under remote country churches. *Der Spiegel* mentions that one of the officers of the secret services that knew the men serving in the secret army of IDEA and their duties was Colonel George Papadopoulos. The IDEA army was enlisted in the *Provia* organisation of the Stay Behind network. In 1955, an agreement was signed for cooperation between the network and the Mountain Commando Regiments (*Lochoi Orinon Katadromon* - LOK). The CIA, together with the Special Forces Command of the Pentagon, had taken on the training of the commando officers and supplied them with tents, special lorries and fighting equipment.[22] The LOK had a mission to participate in guerrilla warfare operations in the mountains of Greece in the event of a Soviet invasion and occupation, together with the National Defence Regiments. The *Provia* organisation was behind the many operations of Greek paramilitaries during the fifties and sixties, which culminated in the coups of 21 April 1967 in Greece and 15 July 1974 in Cyprus.

Just as in Greece, the United States used financial aid to create an infrastructure to control political developments in Turkey. The same legislation that created the American Mission of Aid for Greece in 1947 also created the American Mission for Aid to Turkey – AMAT. At the end of 1949, the Joint American Military Mission for Aid to Turkey – JAMMAT – was established, through which the armed forces, the police and the country's secret services were organised. By the end of 1950, Turkey had received $200 million in economic assistance, while 1,200 American military advisers had arrived in the country. From 1950 until 1979, the USA officially granted Turkey military aid amounting to $5.8 billion.[23] Turkey joined NATO with Greece on 4 April 1952. That same year, the local organisation of the Stay Behind network was founded. The name of the organisation was the Tactical Mobilisation Group (*Seferberlik Tetkik Kurulu* – STK). In 1965, the STK changed its name to the Special Warfare Department (*Ozel Harp Dairesi* - OHD). It was

---

18 Christopher Simpson, *Blowback: America's Recruitment of Nazis and its Effects on the Cold War* (New York: Weidenfeld and Nicholson, 1988), p.81. Paralikas, *op. cit.*, p. 55.

19 'X' was a monarchist organisation set up in 1943 with the help of British members serving in the Allies' Military Mission to act as a counter balance to the KKE-controlled ELAM/ELAS.

20 Biographical note on Papadopoulos, http://www.geocities.com/Pentagon/Base/4343/

21 Simpson, *op. cit.*, p. 81.

22 Alexis Papahelas, *Ο βιασμός της ελληνικής δημοκρατίας - Ο αμερικανικός παράγων, 1947-1967* [The Rape of Greek Democracy – the American Factor, 1947-1967] (Athens: Estia, 1997), p.25.

23 Fernandes and Osden, *art. cit.*

organised and funded by the CIA and had its administrative centre in the same building as that of JAMMAT.[24]

Just as elsewhere in Europe, the existence of the organisation was kept secret from Turkey's political leadership. Until 1990, Turkey categorically denied it had an organisation equivalent to the Italian Gladio. Only when a former CIA chief, William Colby, revealed its existence, did the authorities admit it. On 3 December 1990, General Dogan Beyazit, President of the Operations Department of the General Staff, and General Kemal Yilmaz, commander of the Special Forces, revealed that the title of the special department of the Stay Behind network in Turkey was the Special Warfare Department and that its task was "to organise resistance in the case of a communist occupation".[25]

Bulent Ecevit admitted in an interview to researcher Lucy Komisar that he had learned of the existence of the Special Warfare Department in 1974. He was Prime Minister at the time, and a request was submitted to him from the Chief of the General Staff, Semih Santzar, to pay from the prime minister's secret fund for the erection of new buildings for the organisation. Santzar told him that the Americans had funded the Special Warfare Department from the start, but now they were allegedly pulling out. From another military source, Ecevit was informed that the members of the organisation were lifelong "volunteer patriots", whose names were kept secret.[26]

The "volunteer patriots" were none other than the Grey Wolves, a paramilitary organisation established in the sixties. They formed the militant arm of the Nationalist Action Party, which was founded by Colonel Alparslan Turkes, of Cypriot extraction, who during the Second World War had been the leader of the Pan-Turkish movement that backed Hitler in exchange for financial support from Berlin. They had hoped the victory of the Nazis would enable Turkey to annex those regions of the Soviet Union with Turkic populations.[27]

Imitating Nazi practices, the CIA used Pan-Turkish organisations to foment anti-Soviet feelings among Muslim minorities in the Soviet Union. Despite the fact that the Pan-Turks were just as anti-Western as they were anti-Soviet, the CIA's strategy strengthened the ties of the American agencies with Turkish ultra-nationalists.[28]

The Grey Wolves are held responsible for bombings and the murder of hundreds of people in Turkey, including civil servants, journalists, students, leftist trade unionists and Kurds.[29] They played a significant part in three coups in Turkey – on 27 May 1967, on 12 March 1971 and on 12 September 1980.

After 1974, the Turkish Gladio created a base in occupied Cyprus. The organisation laundered money that it received for its activities through banks and casinos in the occupied territories. The Grey Wolves murdered a journalist, Kutlu Adali,[30] who had attempted to investigate the activity of the Turkish Gladio in occupied Cyprus.

The relations of the Special Warfare Department with Turkish para-governmental entities and the Grey Wolves were revealed after a car accident on 3 May 1996 near the village of Susurluk, 100 miles southwest of Istanbul. The accident killed a top police official, Husseyin Kocadag, and Abdullah Catli, a criminal wanted for drug trafficking and

---

24 Celik, *art. cit.*

25 *Ibid.*

26 Komisar, *art. cit.*

27 Fernandes and Osden, *art. cit.*

28 "The War against the People: the Contra-Guerrilla. Turkey's 'Cointelpro' Scandal", *ANTIFA Info-Bulletin*, translated from *Kurtulus* weekly, http://www.ozgurluk.org/contrind/brochu/part1.html.

29 Martin A. Lee, "Turkish Dirty War revealed, but Papal Shooting still Obscured", *Los Angeles Times*, April 12, 1998.

30 "Cyprus, from Occupation to Annexation?", *Kurtulus*, 1 August, 1998.

murder. Catli had been imprisoned in France and Switzerland for drug trafficking in 1980, but escaped in 1990 and fled to Turkey, where he undertook to fight Kurdish separatists on behalf of the Turkish state.

After the accident, it was revealed that Catli was under the protection of Interior Minister Mehmet Agar, who was forced to resign. He had links with the secret police, who offered him protection and supplied him with diplomatic passports and other documents, which he used in his activities as a drug trafficker or to organise criminal activities at the expense of members of the Turkish opposition.

One of Catli's associates, Mehmet Ali Agca, had been jailed for the murder of journalist Abti Ipeksi on 1 February 1979. Catli helped him escape from prison, and supplied him with forged identities and travel documents. On 13 May 1981, Agca shot and nearly killed the Pope in St. Peter's Square in the Vatican[31]

The CIA set up a whole propaganda machine and fed public opinion with false evidence that Agca was a secret agent of the Soviet Union and Bulgaria,. who had trained him to assassinate the Pope.[32] On 24 May 2002, the Bulgarian president's office announced that Pope John Paul II, in a conversation with President Parvanov, had stated that he had never believed that Bulgaria was involved. With this announcement, which is considered to have been made with the assent of the Pope, Bulgaria has been absolved from the false charge.[33] As Lucy Komisar writes, the attempt on the Pope's life was probably the result of cooperation between the Italian Gladio and the Grey Wolves, to create tension and prevent the rise to power of the left.[34]

When in 1947 Britain had invited the United States to contribute economically so she could maintain her presence in Greece and Turkey, she had not been disposed to cede her dominance to the rising superpower. Britain's intention was to secure help from the United States, without losing influence in the two countries. Very soon, however, America displaced Britain, and after her successful intervention in Greece and Turkey, imposed her power across Europe through the Marshall Plan.

Britain nevertheless retained much of the Middle East under its influence, and worked hard to maintain its decisive role in the region. As a British colony, Cyprus was a key bulwark in the Eastern Mediterranean. The population of the island was about half a million, of which 80 per cent were Greeks and 18 per cent Turks. Most were farmers and workers in mines exploited by foreign companies. The only organised political force was the communist party AKEL (*Anorthotikon Komma Ergazomenou Laou*), which controlled the trade unions and was the mouthpiece for about half of the population, Greeks and Turks.

In its effort to curb the 'Communist Peril', the British Colonial government in the late 1940s helped in the reorganisation of the Church and in bolstering right-wing trade unions.[35] However, in the early 1950s, the Church proclaimed a struggle for the union of Cyprus with Greece (*Enosis)*, and began to pose a problem for Britain. It was then that the right in Cyprus acquired a political and religious leader, Archbishop Makarios III.

---

31 Kurkcu, *art. cit.* Lee, *art.cit.*

32 Komisar, *art. cit.*

33 "Πάπας: 'Δεν είχε ανάμιξη η Βουλγαρία στην απόπειρα εναντίον μου'" [The Pope: Bulgaria was not Involved in the Attempt on my Life], *Eleftherotypia*, 25 May, 2002.

34 Komisar, *art. cit.*

35 Xenophon Kallis, "Η Αγγλία και οι δύο μητέρες πατρίδες" [Britain and the two motherlands], *Eleftheroptypia*, 13 July 2000.

Charismatic and ambitious, Makarios made self-determination for Cyprus his life's ambition, and undertook an international campaign to promote the demand for *Enosis*, which had been a centuries-long passion for the majority of Greek Cypriots.

Ignoring the harsh realities of international politics and unaware of the rivalries of the Cold War, Makarios believed *Enosis* could be promoted through the United Nations, pressuring Greece to raise the Cyprus issue at the UN. Greece, which was then in the process of joining NATO, was not willing to come into conflict with Britain over Cyprus. Making use of the great attraction that the demand for *Enosis* had for the Greek public, and of the warm support he enjoyed from the Archbishop of Athens, Spyridon, Makarios pressured the Greek government through speeches, rallies and other means of raising popular support.

In contrast to Britain, the United States looked on the Cypriot demand for *Enosis* with sympathy, supporting the principle of self-determination for British colonies after the Second World War in order to further their own interests. In the midst of the Anglo-American rivalry for dominance of the Middle East, a decision was reached to organise an armed struggle for *Enosis* in Cyprus. Two Cypriot exiles in Greece played a leading role in implementing this goal, the brothers Savvas and Socrates Loizides, who had close ties with the Church and contacts in the Greek establishment. The Loizides brothers brought Makarios into contact with the former Army Minister during the Civil War, Georgios Stratos, who in turn proposed the former leader of the 'X' Organisation, Georgios Grivas, as the military leader of the movement.[36]

Those in Greece behind the initiative for an armed struggle in Cyprus, which led to the formation of the National Organisation of Cypriot Fighters (*Ethniki Organosi Kyprion Agoniston* - EOKA), stemmed from the nationalist right and from the Church, and had initially worked together with the British and later the Americans in the war against the communists. Most of these were cadres in, or dependent on, the Greek para-state:

- Georgios Stratos, Army Minister from January to November 1948 at a time when the army in Greece was under the complete control of JUSMAG Greece.
- Nicolas Papadopoulos (Grandfather), "freshly crowned with the laurels of a national victory over the leftists rebels," according to Savvas Loizides.[37]
- Dimitrios Bezanis, associate of Grivas in the 'X' Organisation, head of counter espionage.[38]
- Gerasimos Konidaris, cadre of 'X'.
- Ilias Alexopoulos, veteran Colonel in the intelligence department of 'X'.
- Antonis Avgikos, extreme right wing lawyer, friend of Georgios Stratos.
- Zafiris Balbis, political advisor to Grivas in the 'X' Organisation.
- Michalis and Constantinos Efstathopoulos, in charge of ideological guidance in 'X'. From 1943 they were in contact with Force 133, a special British intelligence agency.[39]
- Georgos Gazouleas, member of 'X'.
- Cosmas Mastrokolias, one of Grivas' closest associates in 'X'. Twenty years later he played a leading part in the founding of EOKA B.

---

36 Savvas Loizides, *Άτυχη Κύπρος* [Unlucky Cyprus] (Athens: Bergadis Publications, 1980), p. 97. Interview with Socratis Loizides in Papademetris, Panayiotis, Petros Petrides, *Ιστορική Εγκυκλοπαίδεια της Κύπρου, 1878-1978* [Historical Encyclopaedia of Cyprus, 1878-1978], vol. 10, pp. 363-366.

37 Loizides, *op. cit.*, p. 99.

38 Charles Foley and W.I. Scobie, *The Struggle for Cyprus* (Stanford, California: Hoover Institution Press, 1975), p. 15.

39 *Ο άγνωστος πόλεμος της Χ* [X's Hidden War], p. 22.

Given the degree of dependency that the Greek government, the army and the IDEA had on the American military mission and the US intelligence services in the 1950s, the Americans were able to exercise complete political control over Greece through JUSMAG

Therefore, it would be plausible to argue that the American Mission in Greece was aware of the founding of EOKA. As Socrates Loizides writes regarding the setting-up of EOKA, the pioneers of the organisation were in contact with the Greek establishment at the highest possible level. "In the course of the setting-up of the struggle here, we have come into contact here in Athens with the Greek government, and with the King. I do not know if Grivas came into direct contact with the King, but in any case the King was informed by the then archimandrite, and later Archbishop, Kotsonis."[40] According to Grivas, the Chief of the General Staff, General G. Kosmas, had called him to his office on 27 January 1951 and "announced to me that he was in full agreement with my view concerning a military solution to the Cyprus issue and that he would offer me his unreserved support".[41] Archbishop Spyridon of Athens, who had ties with the IDEA, also warmly supported the setting-up of the movement in Cyprus. When in 1951 IDEA made its first coup attempt in Greece, Archbishop Spyridon was mentioned during the interrogations that followed as being the leader of the movement; indeed, he was destined to become regent.[42]

As a result of the pressure from the Cypriots for *Enosis*, the Greek Prime Minister, Alexandros Papagos, proclaimed in March 1954 the willingness of Greece to make recourse to the United Nations and to demand self-determination for Cyprus. Reacting to the Greek demands, Britain formed an alliance with Ankara, elevating Turkey to the status of a country having direct interest in the Cyprus issue. On 28 April, Under Secretary for the Colonies Henry Hopkinson presented to the British Cabinet a plan for a joint Anglo-Greco-Turkish government in Cyprus, which would provide for self-government and for rights over the use of the ports and the airports of the island by both Greece and Turkey.[43] British recognition of Turkish rights in Cyprus coincided with the formation of the Pan-Turkish movement, whose stated goal was the reintegration of the island – which had been an integral part of the Ottoman Empire – into Turkey. On 21 April 1954, the Pan-Turkish Association 'Cyprus is Turkish' was founded in Istanbul. The association was set up in the course of a meeting organised by the National Federation of Turkish Students to discuss the Cyprus issue, in which owners and publishers of major Turkish newspapers took part. The President of the Association was the publisher of *Hürriet*, Hikmet Bil, and its general secretary was Kamil Onan, an infantry lieutenant, who had been decommissioned and worked as a journalist. Onan had been recruited to the National Intelligence Agency (*Milli Istihbarat Teskilati* - MIT) of Turkey from the early 1950s.[44]

The 'Cyprus is Turkish' Association had the personal backing of Turkish Prime Minister Adnan Menderes and of the Turkish opposition leader Ismet Inonu. Its main strength lay in its access to the mass circulation newspapers in Turkey. Four of the seven members of its central committee were publishers or journalists. The press supported the Pan-Turkish position that if Britain decided to pull out of Cyprus, the island, should revert

---

40 Loizides interview in Papademetris, Panayiotis, Petrides, *op. cit.*, vol. 10, pp. 363-366.

41 Georgios Grivas-Dighenis, *Απομνημονεύματα Αγώνος ΕΟΚΑ 1955-1959* [Memoirs of the EOKA Struggle, 1955-1959] (Athens, 1984), p. 15.

42 Paralikas, *op. cit.*, p.42.

43 Angelos Vlachos, *Δέκα Χρόνια Κυπριακού* [Ten Years of the Cyprus Problem] (Athens: Estia, 1980), p. 78.

44 Christos P. Ioannides, *Νεο-οθωμανικός ιμπεριαλισμός, 1955-1995* [Neo-Ottoman Imperialism, 1955-1995], (Athens: Karatzias/Trochalia, 1995), p. 109.

to Turkey. Through intense anti-Greek propaganda, articles against Greece, the Patriarchate of Constantinople and Archbishop Makarios, the press aroused Turkish public opinion and maintained it in a continual state of nationalist euphoria.[45]

With the help of the newspapers, the Pan-Turks conveyed the message that the *Enosis* struggle in Cyprus was a communist plot. They maintained that by regaining Cyprus, not only would Turkey take what was rightfully hers, but she would also be offering a valuable service to the free world.

On 28 July 1954, Henry Hopkinson, speaking to the House of Commons, made clear Britain's refusal to discuss the issue of self-determination for the people of Cyprus: "...There are some territories in the Commonwealth which, owing to their particular circumstances, can never expect to be fully independent."[46]

This position came into direct conflict with the policy of the United States in favour of the abolition of colonies and the self-determination of peoples. Speaking during the tenth anniversary of the foundation of the United Nations, American President Dwight Eisenhower called upon all member states to reaffirm their commitment to the principles of the Organisation: "Every people has the inherent right to select in full freedom the individuals who conduct that government," he stated. Eisenhower's speech caused unease in Britain's representative at the United Nations, Sir Pierson Dixon, who warned his government that the United States would support the Greek recourse to the UN.[47]

Despite the concerns of the British diplomat, the United States did not want the internationalisation of the problem, and were opposed to any discussion of the Cyprus issue at the United Nations. On 28 June, US Secretary of State Foster Dulles had sent a personal message to Field Marshal Papagos, stating that he "considered a public debate on the Cyprus problem in the United Nations to be untimely".[48] The United States favoured bipartite negotiations and undertook to exercise their influence on Britain to accept a discussion on the future of Cyprus. The Greek government, however, had publicly committed itself to recourse to the UN, and could no longer draw back. On 22 August, Greece's permanent representative at the UN, Christianos Xanthopoulos-Palamas, lodged the first Greek recourse with the secretariat of the Organisation.

Whether the Greek recourse on Cyprus would be accepted depended on the judgement of the General Assembly, which was to begin its sessions on 19 September. Makarios went to New York to support Greece's demand and exerted his influence on the Greek delegation so they would not buckle under pressure from Britain. Prompted by the colonial administration in Cyprus, a delegation of the Turkish Cypriot community also went to New York. On its way to New York, the delegation, which was headed by Faiz Kaymak, President of the Federation of Turkish Cypriot Organisations, stopped off in Ankara and London. In Turkey, they had a meeting with Prime Minister Menderes, who informed them that he had written guarantees from America that *Enosis* was not feasible, while President Celal Bayer urged them: "Demand that the British remain on the island. Support the British or they will collapse!"[49] This exhortation was a great surprise to the Turkish Cypriot delegation. Up to that moment, the position they were adopting was the return of Cyprus to Turkey.

---

45 *Ibid.*, pp. 99 and 111.

46 Robert Holland, *Η Βρετανία και ο κυπριακός αγώνας* [Britain and the Revolt in Cyprus, 1954-1959] (Athens: Potamos, 1999), p. 80.

47 Brendan O'Malley and Ian Craig, *Η Συνωμοσία της Κύπρου* [The Cyprus Conspiracy] (Athens: I. Sideris, 2002), p. 63.

48 Vlachos, *op. cit.*, p. 78.

49 Anonymous, *Πώς φτάσαμε στην ΕΟΚΑ* [How we got to EOKA] (Nicosia: Archeio/3, Diafaneia, 2000), p. 79.

From Ankara the delegation went to London, and on 17 September met with the Under Secretary for Colonial Affairs, Henry Hopkinson. As Kaymak writes, in the talks, "we stressed that we are against *Enosis* and are content with the British administration on the island. And we asked for British sovereignty to continue!"[50]

In New York, an official from the British delegation received the Turkish Cypriot delegation, and they made arrangements for the meetings they would have with the delegations from various countries.

Greece's demand for the Cyprus question to be put on the agenda at the ninth General Assembly was discussed on 24 September. Despite Britain's fierce resistance, the Cyprus issue was registered with 30 votes in favour, 19 against and 11 abstentions. Among those that abstained were the United States. The Greek side saw America's abstention as an encouraging development. Prime Minister Papagos tried to persuade President Eisenhower that the USA should maintain a neutral position throughout the discussion; but Washington's answer was that, "despite their anti-colonial stance, they would support Britain".[51]

Under pressure from Makarios, the Greek government gave orders to its delegation at the United Nations to introduce a draft resolution that would call for the principle of self-determination to be applied in Cyprus. Under the circumstances, this was the best that Athens could achieve. In reaction, Britain introduced through New Zealand another draft resolution, which asked the General Assembly not to follow up on the Cyprus debate. In the impasse that followed, the USA intervened as a *Deus ex machina*. They indicated to El Salvador and Columbia that they should propose the addition of the phrase "for the time being" to the New Zealand resolution. As Greek diplomat Angelos Vlachos writes, "these three words, whose addition was accepted even by Greece, Britain and Turkey, was a crumb that nourished the propaganda of all three interested parties".[52] Britain put forward the argument that the General Assembly did not have the authority to discuss the Cyprus issue. Turkey stated triumphantly that the Cyprus question was now "closed". And Greece that the General Assembly was in principle entitled to discuss the Cyprus problem and that it had merely postponed the discussion to a later date. The only winner was the USA, which now began to take on a balancing role among the parties directly involved.

After the failure of the Greek recourse to the UN General Assembly, Makarios gave Grivas the green light to come secretly to Cyprus and to organise a liberation movement. After Grivas' arrival in November 1954, and the beginning of EOKA action on 1 April 1955, the colonial government appeared incapable of dealing with the situation, and failed to crack the organisation before it reached maturity. Historian Robert Holland, who has studied archive material of the period, attributes this failure to "deficiencies in the intelligence gathering mechanisms, which proved that it was one of the critical weaknesses of the British during the State of Emergency" in Cyprus.[53]

However, the lack of intelligence material cannot be advanced as a serious argument, given that the British secret services had infiltrated the organisation. For example, the information that Grivas was in Cyprus had reached the Special Branch of the Cyprus police

---

50 *Ibid.*
51 Vlachos, *op. cit.*, p. 79.
52 *Ibid.*, p. 80.
53 Holland, *op. cit.*, 72.

immediately after his arrival.[54] Grivas had made two other trips before this one, on 5 July 1951 and on 3 October 1952. During his second trip, he had stayed on the island for five whole months, and on both occasions he reached Cyprus through normal channels, having secured a visa from the British embassy in Athens. The third time, the British refused him a visa, because they had information that his previous two visits had been connected with the setting-up of a movement against the colonial regime. This information is provided in the book *Grivas and the history of EOKA* by British Colonel Byford Jones – who served in Greece in December 1944 and had saved Grivas when he was surrounded by ELAS guerrillas in the Thisio area of Athens. Jones argues the British refusal to grant Grivas a visa was a very serious mistake: "If they had granted it and then shadowed Grivas from the moment he disembarked there would not have been four years of murder and terrorism."[55]

Another British writer, Dudley Baker, who wrote the history of EOKA based upon British sources, says: "It is astonishing that although the British authorities in Cyprus knew quite a lot of what was going on, they did so little to counter it that Grivas was able, for at least six months after his clandestine arrival, to travel openly about the island, taking few precautions to conceal himself."[56]

This complacency is most clearly demonstrated by the way in which the British handled the seizure of the ship, the *Ayios Georgios*, found loaded with explosives off the coast near Chlorakas village, and of the arrest of its crew, on the evening of 25 January 1955. From the interrogations that followed, the British gathered significant intelligence on the preparations for the EOKA struggle. Despite all this, they failed to take drastic measures and to strike the movement at the root before it even began.[57] Referring to the unexpectedly mild reaction after the seizure of the *Ayios Georgios*, Grivas wrote in his memoirs: "Fortunately, the authorities were not able, or did not attempt, seriously to investigate the matter and to determine who were the real instigators of the movement in Cyprus."[58]

In reality, the British knew a lot about Grivas, since they had one of their men planted in his close entourage, the construction sector secretary of the right wing trade union (SEK), Paschalis Papadopoulos, who had rented the house where Grivas stayed and whom the EOKA leader used as his chauffeur in all his travels. Later, it was revealed that he was in the pay of the British, and he fled to Britain, where he lived in self-imposed exile until his death.[59] In order to provide an interpretation for the complacency shown by the British in the first phases of EOKA, Robert Holland lends credence to an argument advanced quite cautiously as early as 1960 by Doros Alastos: "that the Cyprus [colonial] Government 'might even welcome a showdown in order to strike at the extremists on both sides'," that is against the Right and the Left.[60]

If the British tolerated the arrival of Grivas in Cyprus, and did not crack down on EOKA before it got organised and gathered strength, they did so in order to exploit the *Enosis* struggle and to arouse Turkish nationalism. As we have seen from 1954, before the establishment of EOKA, the Pan-Turkish movement in Turkey with the association 'Cyprus is Turkish' at its head, undertook a national mobilisation of public opinion against *Enosis.*

---

54 The information was contained in a report sent to Grivas by Pavlos Stokkos, who was serving in the Special Branch at the time, which was quoted by Grivas in his *Χρονικόν Αγώνος ΕΟΚΑ 1955-1959* [Chronicle of the EOKA Struggle, 1955-1959] (Nicosia, 1997), p. 46.

55 W. Byford-Jones, *Grivas and the Story of EOKA* (London: Robert Hale Limited, 1959), p. 47.

56 Dudley Barker, *Grivas – Portrait of a Terrorist* (London: The Cresset Press, 1959), p. 73.

57 Makarios Droushiotis, *Η 'εισβολή' της χούντας στην Κύπρο* (Athens: Stachi, 1996), pp. 68-78.

58 Grivas, *Απομνημονεύματα*, p. 31.

59 Droushiotis, *op. cit.*, p. 87.

60 Holland, *op. cit.*, p. 72.

At the beginning of 1955, the association had founded about 50 local branches in various parts of the country.[61] The seizure of the *Ayios Georgios*, and later the onset of EOKA action, was like oil on the fire of Turkish nationalism. The association organised protest rallies against "Greek expansionist aims", in which over 100,000 people took part. Speakers alleged attacks by Greek Cypriots against Turkish Cypriots, stirring up anti-Greek sentiments.[62] Turkish irredentism and anti-Greek feelings were transferred to Cyprus. On 21 July 1955, the president of the 'Cyprus is Turkish' Association, Hikmet Bil, came to the island and helped in the reorganisation of the Turkish National Association of Cyprus, which was a weak political party under the doctor Fazil Kutchuk, which he renamed 'Cyprus is Turkish'. The new party was organically linked with its equivalent Turkish association and funded through large sums of money from Turkey.[63]

In the climate of conflict that had been created over discussion of the future of Cyprus, Britain in mid-1955 invited Greece and Turkey to a tripartite conference in London to discuss "matters concerning policy and defence in the Eastern Mediterranean, including Cyprus".[64] Despite the disagreement of the Cypriot Ethnarchy, the Greek government accepted the invitation and sent a representative to the conference, which began on 29 August. The mere convocation of the conference was a great success for Britain. Turkey was recognised as an interested party in the Cyprus issue, something that changed the status quo in the international arena, as well as on the island itself. As a result of Pan-Turkish activities, the Cyprus problem had become an issue of prestige among the Turkish population.

On the eve of the conference, rumours circulated in Turkey about bloodshed against Turkish Cypriots in Cyprus, and about a possible massacre of the entire Turkish population of the island. "During the last days of August and the first days of September in 1955, Turkey resembled a powder magazine of chauvinism and anti-Greek sentiments."[65] In reality, up to that time there had been no conflict or quarrel between Greek and Turkish Cypriots. The only disturbance was from so far limited EOKA activity, mainly bombings of government targets.

On 5 September, and while the London conference, which had started without any preparatory work, was heading towards collapse, there was a small explosion in the grounds of the Turkish consulate in Salonica. It was proved later that the bomb had been set by Oktay Engin, a student from Komotini, who had close ties with 'Cyprus is Turkish'. Oktay was later given a prison sentence by a Greek court, but escaped to Turkey and was taken on by the Turkish Secret Services (MIT).[66]

News of the explosion in Salonica was broadcast in Turkey, blown up by the media and linked with the information about "imminent massacres of Turks in Cyprus". On the evening of 6 to 7 September, violent incidents broke out against the Greek minority in Istanbul and Izmir. The mob spilled out onto the streets and launched into an orgy of destruction of Greek properties in Istanbul. They looted hundreds of Greek shops, desecrated churches and cemeteries and set fire to Greek schools. The international press spoke of a pogrom against the Greek population in Turkey.[67] The provocation in Salonica and the

---

61 Ioannides, *op. cit.*, p. 105.
62 *Ibid.*, pp. 106-110.
63 *Ibid.*, p. 127.
64 Vlachos, *op. cit.*, p. 102.
65 Ioannides, *op. cit.*, p. 142.
66 *Ibid.*
67 *Ibid.*, pp. 147-156.

incidents that followed were the first operation planned and executed by the Turkish Gladio.[68]

EOKA's armed action against the British coincided with important changes in the Middle East. The pro-British government of Jordan was overthrown by a coup backed by Egypt. Egyptian President Gamal Abdul Nasser had a vision of creating a pan-Arab federation that would extend from North Africa to the heart of the Middle East. This region provided Britain with 70 per cent of her needs in oil. These developments suddenly established Cyprus as an exceptionally important military bridgehead for the needs of a future military operation in the Middle East to control sources of energy.

On 26 July 1956, Nasser nationalised the Suez Canal. British Prime Minister Anthony Eden feared that if Nasser's coup went unchallenged, British interests in the region would crumble. Harold Macmillan, Eden's Chancellor of the Exchequer, believed that if the Canal was surrendered to Egypt, Europe's fate would be left in the hands of 'satellites of Russia'.[69]

The United States, which did not worry about Nasser's plans, saw the Suez crisis as an opportunity to dislodge the British from the Middle East once and for all. Britain formed an alliance with Israel and France, the latter seeing its own interests in North Africa in jeopardy. The three countries prepared for an assault on Egypt. The United States reacted against these plans, and Eisenhower sent a secret mission to Eden, warning him not to proceed to military action. "I am afraid, Anthony, that from this point onward our views on the situation diverge," he wrote to him.[70]

Despite America's warnings, the three allies countries went ahead with their plans. In the autumn of 1956 substantial British and French forces were transferred to Cyprus and the island became an administrative and assault centre for a Suez landing. On the evening of 21 October, 200 British and 40 French planes took off from Cyprus, Malta and aircraft carriers and bombed 12 Egyptian airfields with 2,000 bombs. On 29 October, Israeli troops penetrated inside Egypt. In the Security Council, the Americans introduced a motion that demanded an immediate Israeli withdrawal and an end to hostilities. Britain and France exercised their veto, but an emergency meeting of the UN General Assembly overwhelmingly voted it down, and called for an immediate ceasefire. The allies ignored the UN decision and continued their operations. At dawn on 5 November, French and British transport planes that took off from Cyprus landed 1,000 parachutists in Egypt. The Americans reacted and punished the British, selling off their reserves in sterling. At the same time the Soviets threatened rocket attacks on London, Paris and Tel Aviv. But the colonial powers were defiant, and at dawn on 6 November Anglo-French naval forces landed at Port Said. Even if the operation, from a military point of view, was going very well, with Anglo-French troops only 75 miles from Suez, the allies were forced to agree to a ceasefire. While Eden refused to withdraw troops from Egypt, Washington continued the frantic sale of sterling, blocked British rights to loans from the International Monetary Fund and refused to help London with its shortfall in oil supplies. In November 1956, the British economy was on the verge of collapse. Chancellor Macmillan feared Britain's foreign exchange reserves would be drained within weeks, and that the economy would be paralysed for want of oil. Eden sent his Foreign Secretary John Selwyn Lloyd to Eisen-

---

68 "The War against the People: the Contra-Guerrilla. Turkey's 'Cointelpro' Scandal", *ANTIFA Info-Bulletin*, translated from *Kurtulus* weekly, http://www.ozgurluk.org/contrind/brochu/part1.html.

69 O'Malley and Craig, *op. cit.*, p. 92.

70 *Ibid.*, p. 96.

hower and asked for support, but the American President refused to meet him and banned all communication with Eden's government until Britain and France pulled their forces out of Suez.[71]

Macmillan, without informing the ailing Eden, contacted Eisenhower, requesting understanding to enable Britain to get out of the impasse. The Americans were willing to release Britain's loan rights in the International Monetary Fund only after an immediate and unconditional withdrawal of French and British troops from Suez. Macmillan committed himself to work in this direction. The secret understanding between Macmillan and Washington paved his way to the premiership. On 1 December 1956, the British Cabinet conceded defeat in Egypt and troop withdrawals started in mid-December. Immediately afterwards, the United States approved a British request to the International Monetary Fund for the immediate withdrawal of $561 million. On 9 January 1957, Eden resigned and Macmillan succeeded him as Prime Minister.[72]

Britain's defeat at Suez marked the end of her domination in the Middle East. The British Empire of old no longer had any influence in the region and was economically dependent on the USA. President Eisenhower announced in a radio broadcast that the United States was asserting its leadership in the Middle East.[73]

While the British Empire was crumbling, the United States were drawing up their own plans to penetrate the last significant British bulwark in the Eastern Mediterranean, Cyprus. Initially, the US-dependent Greek government supported EOKA action. Grivas' associate, Andreas Azinas, who took refuge in Athens shortly before the seizure of the *Ayios Georgios* and acted as EOKA's representative in the Greek capital, linked up with Greek Foreign Minister Evangelos Averoff, who offered him every possible facility for sending arms to Cyprus.[74] Averoff corresponded with Grivas, and the movement of EOKA messages to and from Cyprus was ensured through the diplomatic bag of the Greek consulate in Nicosia.[75]

In order to send arms to Cyprus, Azinas worked closely with the head of the IDEA and Director of the Greek Central Intelligence Agency (KYP), Alexandros Natsinas, as well as with the Chief of Police of Athens-Piraeus, Theodoros Rakintsis.[76] The assistance given by the Greek KYP for the arming of EOKA is an indication that the American services were in favour of its armed activities.

At the same time, the Turkish Resistance Movement (*Turk Mukavemet Teskilati* - TMT) was founded in Cyprus. TMT was established in mid-November 1957 by the then attorney in the colonial government Rauf Raif Denktash, the administrative attaché to the Turkish consulate in Nicosia Mustafa Kemal Tanrisevdi, and the Turkish Cypriot doctor Burhan Nalbantoglu.[77]

At the end of December, Denktash, together with the political leader of the Turkish Cypriots, Fazil Kutchuk, went to Ankara on an important mission: to link up TMT with the

---

71 *Ibid.*, pp. 99-102.
72 *Ibid.*, pp. 106-107.
73 *Ibid.*, p. 108.
74 *Ibid.*, p. 110.
75 Andreas Azinas, *50 χρόνια σιωπής* [Fifty Years of Silence] (Nicosia: 2001), vol. 2, p. 554.
76 *Ibid.*, p. 468.
77 Yusuf Kanli, interview with Rauf Denktash, *Turkish Daily News*, 28 July 1997.

Turkish Gladio. Denktash and Kutchuk met with General Danis Karabelen and his associate, Colonel Ismail Tansu, at the Modern Palace Hotel.[78]

General Karabelen had served in Korea in 1952–53. When he returned to Cyprus, he was placed in a branch of the Stay Behind network called the Council for the Supervision of Mobilisation. Selected officers that knew the tactics of secret operations staffed the department, and some had been trained in the Commando academy. According to Tansu, who was a leading member of TMT in Turkey, the officers who served in the Council for the Supervision of Mobilisation "were all capable of establishing secret services, training their staff, and taking on the leadership of these organisations".[79]

In 1958, Karabelen was decommissioned, taken on as a civilian in the General Staff and assigned the responsibility for TMT. In May 1958, the administration of TMT Turkey was established, followed in July by that of TMT Cyprus. TMT's organisation was based on the American model and officers were employed who had been trained in guerrilla warfare in the United States. The chief of the Cyprus administration was lieutenant Colonel Riza Vuruskan, who at the time worked with the Special Planning Department of the Joint US Military Mission for Aid to Turkey (JUSMMAT J3).[80] Vuruskan undertook to implement in Cyprus a plan hatched by the Council for the Supervision of Mobilisation, which was named Plan for the Recapture of Cyprus (*Kibris Istirdat Plani*).[81] Before leaving for Cyprus on 22 July 1958, Vuruskan met Turkish Foreign Minister Fatin Zorlu. As he himself states, Zorlu told him that his mission was the occupation of Cyprus by Turkey in its entirety.[82] Vuruskan reached the island with the identity of inspector in the Labour Bank. Together with him came a staff of 11 serving officers and 14 reservists, who appeared as teachers, school inspectors and imams.

Vuruskan was also called Bozkurt – 'Grey Wolf'. The grey wolf is also depicted in the emblem of TMT, proving the group's link with the Pan-Turks. The pecking order of the organisation was led by the *bairaktaris* (standard bearer), who had his headquarters in Nicosia. Throughout Cyprus, 10 sub-administrations were established, the so-called *sanjaks* with the *santzakarides* (standard bearers). Each sub-administration had at its command ten regiments, and 40-50 trained individuals served in each regiment.

To keep the group supplied with arms, warehouses were set up in Mersin and Anamur with every type of weapon, ammunition and other provisions, which could be shipped to Cyprus in small boats. From the autumn of 1958, the small boat *Elmas* began systematically transporting weaponry, making trips from Anamur to the Turkish Cypriot village of Kokkina on the north coast of the Paphos district. Denktash received the first shipment of weapons, and distributed them personally.[83]

After acquiring footholds in EOKA through the Greek regime and controlling TMT through the Turkish Gladio, the United States embarked on a behind-the-scenes diplomatic initiative to find a solution to the Cyprus problem. Washington was now in favour of the British leaving Cyprus while maintaining important military rights and the control of the island through the two mother countries. With this aim in mind, the United States encouraged Greece and Turkey to begin behind-the-scenes negotiations. The first Greco-

---

78 "TMT", *Agon*, 14 July, 1997.
79 *Agon*, 11 October, 1997.
80 *Agon*, 29 June, 1997.
81 *Agon*, 28 August, 1997.
82 *Agon*, 30 June, 1997.
83 *Agon*, 3 July, 1997.

Turkish contacts on the Cyprus issue took place between Averoff and the Turkish ambassador in Athens Settar Iksel in two meetings they had on 6 and 7 October 1956. During those meetings, Averoff sounded out the Turkish government concerning the 'proportional solution', his term for partition.[84]

The American view on the future of Cyprus, as Macmillan noted in his diary on 15 March 1957, was that Britain could make do with an airfield, whether on long lease or with sovereignty, as with Gibraltar. "Then the Greeks and the Turks could divide the rest of the island up between themselves."[85]

In March 1957, Macmillan had talks with Eisenhower in Bermuda, discussing Anglo-American relations after London's acceptance of the leading role of the United States. The United States was already tending in the direction of a solution of conditional independence. The creation, that is, of an independent Cypriot state under the guardianship of Greece and Turkey, with Makarios as President – who would guarantee its anti-communist leaning.

During his talks with Macmillan, Eisenhower extracted a promise to release Makarios, who had been exiled to the Seychelles.[86] A few days later, Makarios was set free, but was not allowed to return to Cyprus and established himself in Athens. At the urging of the US, Makarios accepted the solution of independence and proclaimed his position publicly.[87]

While the future of Cyprus had largely been predetermined, on the island Grivas had opened up a front against the communists, accusing the Communist Party AKEL of betraying the struggle. Initially, AKEL had come out against the EOKA armed struggle. However, Grivas left no room for cooperation. The communists, he wrote, should from the beginning be directly "smashed and humiliated to the point that they would not be able to project themselves on either the political or the military level".[88]

In January 1958, EOKA carried out a series of murders of leftist cadres in the Famagusta district, starting with that of Elias Tofaris in Koma tou Yialou on 21 January. That same evening in Lysi, Michalis Petrou was murdered. The most shocking murder was that of Savvas Menikou, who was stoned to death. The stoning of Menikou sparked angry reactions, even from the Greek Consul, Angelos Vlachos: "I was indignant, and wrote to Grivas in reproof," he writes. "He responded in a very natural tone that stoning was an authentically Greek tradition."[89]

AKEL, in protest at Grivas' methods, mobilised public opinion. In reply, Grivas published a proclamation maintaining that those murdered were traitors. "Now that AKEL's cries of hysteria have ceased, as well as the mourning for its dead, it is time for us to speak out," he wrote,[90] and announced the publication of the *Black Book of AKEL Treachery*. The *Black Book* was a booklet of 67 pages, which recorded various accusations against AKEL members. The allegations of treachery were based on whispers by anonymous witnesses, and referred mainly to disagreements concerning the form of the EOKA struggle.[91]

---

84 Droushiotis, *op. cit.*, p. 185.
85 O'Malley and Craig, *op. cit.*, p. 112.
86 *Ibid.*, p. 113.
87 *Ibid.*, p. 144.
88 Spyros Papageorgiou, *ΑΚΕΛ το άλλο ΚΚΕ* [AKEL, the other KKE] (Athens: G. Ladia Publications, 1984), p. 335.
89 Vlachos, *op. cit.*, p. 348.
90 Papageorgiou, *op. cit.*, p. 337.
91 Published in full in Spyros Papageorgiou, *Αρχείον των παρανόμων εγγράφων του κυπριακού αγώνος 1955-1959* [Archive of Unofficial Documents of the Cyprus Struggle, 1955-1959] (Nicosia: K. Epiphaniou Publications, 1984)

Makarios disagreed with Grivas' tactics, and sent a letter from Athens. Grivas attributed the views of Makarios to misinformation received through contacts with AKEL members. "If we let go of the reins, they will screw us," he wrote to him.[92] In another of his letters at the end of January 1958, he said: "The communists are our adversaries, whether we want it or not. It is advisable that we eliminate them as a political entity, so that they are no longer to be reckoned with and capable, through their decisions, of influencing the national issue, as has happened until now, for example."[93]

During the same period, the TMT blackmailed the Turkish Cypriots into withdrawing from AKEL's trade unions. The starting point of this persecution was May Day 1958, when Greek Cypriots and Turkish Cypriots paraded together in the towns, as they had done ever since the founding of the Pancyprian Labour Federation (*Pankypria Ergatiki Omospondia* - PEO), which was controlled by AKEL. This time, TMT announced that Turkish Cypriots should resign from the leftist trade unions or pay a high price. After executions and terrorist attacks, the Turkish Cypriot newspapers were flooded with announcements of resignations from PEO. The case of Ahmed Yahya, a barber from Famagusta, is typical: on 29 May 1958 he went to the offices of PEO in Nicosia and conveyed his resignation. Next, he went to the newspaper *Halkin Sesi* and made the relevant announcement. In the evening, now free of care, he spent the night in a hotel in Seray Square. The next day *Halkin Sesi* wrote: "Crime in a hotel room." In the same issue were the news of his murder and the announcement of his resignation from PEO.[94]

In parallel to their anti-communist activities, the two nationalist organisations began indiscriminately to murder ordinary Greek and Turkish Cypriots. A pretext was given by an act of provocation by TMT. On 7 June 1958, a bomb exploded at the entrance of the Press Office of the Turkish Consulate in Nicosia. At the time of the blast, Turkish Cypriots were gathered in the area, and they swarmed out into the Greek quarters, looting houses, destroying property and causing incidents. On 26 June 1984, Rauf Denktash, in an interview for British ITV television, admitted that Turks had planted the bomb with the aim of creating tension.[95]

Over the next few days, there was an orgy of arson and looting, resulting in deaths, injuries and extensive material damage, the victims both Greek and Turkish Cypriots. The incidents lasted three months, from June until August, and 107 people were killed, 56 Greeks and 51 Turks.[96] The victims were ordinary citizens, their only 'guilt' their ethnic background. Indicative of the climate is the experience of the Turkish Cypriot TMT executioner, Mehmet Ali Tremeseli: "We listened to the radio. As soon as we heard of the murder of a Turkish Cypriot, we immediately responded in kind. One day we heard that the Greek Cypriots had killed a Turkish Cypriot. We were upset. We found a friend who was a very good motorcycle rider, changed the number plate, and went into action. We shot four people who were in Kaimakli Square. At the same time we fired at a person who was running in the Hantaka area in Kaimakli. In the end, he turned out to be a Turk. Yetka, who was aware of our operation, told us "Greek Cypriots have shot a Turkish Cypriot, who is in Nalbandoglu's clinic". We realised what had happened. We found out that this Turkish Cypriot did not die. He was later given a fighter's pension."[97]

---

92 Papageorgiou, *AKEΛ*, p. 343.
93 *Ibid.*, p. 336.
94 "TMT", *Αγών*, 1 September, 1997.
95 End of Empire: Cyprus, Britain's Grim Legacy", ITV, 26 June, 1984.
96 Nancy Crawshaw, *The Cyprus Revolt*, (London: George Allen & Unwin, 1978).
97 Testimony recounted by Mehmet Ali Tremeseli, *Ortam*, 20-27 April, 1992.

AKEL argued the victims of the situation were the innocent population, Greeks and Turks, and mainly the working class. Grivas spoke of treachery, and in a proclamation stated that, "the AKEL leadership is embracing even Turks, and is betraying our people who kill Turks".[98] Grivas was basing himself on a report prepared for him by the President of the Pancyprian Committee for the Cyprus Struggle (*Pankypria Epitropi Kypriakou Agona* - PEKA), Tassos Papadopoulos, which stated that the leadership of AKEL, "blinded by its doctrine of 'internationalism' and 'brother Turks', was betraying yet again the struggle of our people, putting the blame for the events that occurred 'on the mistaken tactic of the EOKA armed struggle, a tactic that led to the uprising of the Turks'."[99]

While in Cyprus Greeks and Turks were killing each other, the foreign ministers of Greece and Turkey, Averoff and Zorlu, continued with their talks and ended up with a solution of conditional independence, which satisfied the specifications laid down by the Americans. The new state would ensure the dominance of the United States through the two mother countries, while Britain would maintain sovereign bases in Cyprus. With their presence in Cyprus, the Greek and Turkish para-states would ensure the anti-communist character of the new state.

Prime Ministers Karamanlis and Menderes ratified the agreements in Zurich on 11 February 1959. On the basis of these agreements, Cyprus would acquire a constitution that distorted the principle of majority rule to the point where it became unrecognisable. The Turks of Cyprus, who formed 18% of the population, were to rule jointly with the majority of 82%, and would have a 30-50% share in power. A part of the agreement was also the Treaty of Alliance between Greece, Turkey and Cyprus, according to which military contingents from Greece (*Elliniki Dynami Kyprou* – ELDYK) and Turkey (*Tourkiki Dynami Kyprou* - TURDYK) would be stationed on the island. Furthermore, the signing of a Treaty of Guarantee was agreed on the basis of which Britain, Greece and Turkey undertook the obligation to guarantee the security, independence and territorial integrity of the Republic of Cyprus. A basic provision of this treaty gave the right to the guarantor powers, jointly or separately and observing some preconditions, to intervene in the event of constitutional order being overturned, with the aim of restoring the status quo as provided for in the agreement. After many hesitations, Makarios signed the agreements on 19 February in London. Cyprus was declared an independent state on 15 August 1960.

Despite the fact that the EOKA struggle brought results that were the opposite of those it had aspired to, it was projected in Cyprus and Greece as a victorious revolution. The British had located Grivas' hideout and could have arrested him, but they allowed him to flee to Greece, where he was received with great honours.[100] The EOKA struggle became a legend that touched the hearts of all Greeks. The climate that had been created was such that those who had liberated Cyprus rightfully sought power in the new state. Makarios was the undisputed political leader. As a man of the Church, an anti-communist, and identified with the EOKA struggle, he was acceptable to the West as suitable to lead the new state. The left, bearing the stigma of "betrayal" of the struggle, was squeezed to the sidelines of political life.

Immediately after the signing of the London-Zurich Agreements, the intelligence services of Greece, Turkey, Britain and the United States began networking at all levels of

---

98 Papageorgiou, *AKEΛ*, p. 351.

99 *Ibid.*

100 Droushiotis, *op. cit.*, pp. 235-244.

power in the new state in order to prevent Cyprus from sliding to the left. From the first days of independence, the Greek KYP began to implement a plan to set up in Cyprus an organisation like those that were involved in the Stay Behind network. Antonis Georgiades, Grivas' adjutant during the EOKA struggle, testifies that in the middle of March 1959, while he was Minister of Communications and Works in the interim government, he was approached by the head of the Greek Secret Services (KYP) and the then head of IDEA, Alexandros Natsinas, who proposed that he lead a secret army group that would be the executive organ of the Greek government. Georgiades already had in his possession a large quantity of EOKA weaponry that had not been handed over in the course of the plan for the decommissioning of the organisation. The Greek KYP would send additional weapons to Cyprus.

Georgiades said he had been lukewarm about the proposal, and asked Makarios for clarification. "Makakarios said he had heard something of such a unit, but had no details as to the numbers or extent of support being offered by the Greeks." Georgiades said he later discovered that the group was to have been organised with the aim of controlling the Left and those elements of the Right that might oppose Makarios' plans. He passed on this information after many years to US ambassador Taylor Belcher, judging that Makarios had been fully informed, but for some reasons was trying to delude him. Georgiades told Belcher that later he was informed by an Athens source that the weapons for this secret army had been sent to Cyprus by air. As the minister in charge of airports, he investigated the matter and verified the arrival of the shipment, which was delivered to the Ministry of the Interior. "It was at this time that he found out that Georgadjis had been given the position originally offered him," Belcher writes in a note.[101] Georgadjis, who was Minister of Labour in the interim government, with the help of the Greek KYP, created an unofficial intelligence service, whose mission was anti-communist propaganda and counter-espionage.[102] With the proclamation of the Republic of Cyprus, the official Central Intelligence Agency (*Kentriki Ypiresia Pliroforion* – KYP) was set up. The establishment of Cyprus KYP came about with the assistance and support of the later Greek dictator Colonel George Papadopoulos, who came to Cyprus in 1960 at the head of a large group of officers.[103]

Georgadjis, who was moved to the Interior Ministry after the proclamation of the Republic, had direct links to the CIA. Employing the funds and assistance in technology he received from the United States, he tracked the movements and activities of the Left and gave the information to the CIA. At the Head of this network was Georgios Lagodontis, former head of counter-espionage in EOKA and at the same time an agent of the British.[104] According to Lagodontis, the CIA supplied money for the maintenance of the surveillance network in cash, and he handled them himself. Lagodontis at that time funded several small organisations, such as the Organisation for the Protection of the Greeks of Cyprus (*Organosis Prostasias Ellinon Kyprou* - OPEK) of Nicos Sampson, and the National Youth Anti-communist Association (*Antikikommounistikos Sindesmos Ethnikis Neoleas* - ASEN).

101 Written note by Belcher regarding his meeting with Antonis Georgiades on 31 October, 1966, "Arming the Underground Army in 1959". NARA, RG59, Cyprus 1964-1966, Lot #68D356.102.

102 Droushiotis, *op. cit.*, p. 353.

103 Georgios Lagodontis, interview with the author, Athens, 10 March 1996. Nicos Ioannou-Psoma, testimony before the Committee on the 'Cyprus File' of the Cyprus House of Representatives, 14 December 1999.

104 Droushiotis, *op. cit.*, p. 276.

Lagodontis used these organisations for anti-communist activity, as well as to impose himself as the protector of the underworld through extortion, threats, beatings and murders.[105]

Makarios, who approved of the anti-communist activities of the US in Cyprus, tolerated the creation of a para-state by Georgadjis. As an antidote to the all-powerful Georgadjis, he allowed Sampson to set up small armed units, as well as Vassos Lyssarides, who appears to have been the leader of an armed pro-Makarios group from 1960. At the same time, he offered a political haven to the left wing, which was in political limbo, on account of the 'betrayal' of the EOKA struggle. The Cyprus left was initially in opposition to Makarios and in the first presidential elections led the anti-Zurich front, which put up as candidate the moderate right wing politician Ioannis Clerides. Clerides obtained 33% of the vote, of which the 30% was from AKEL and the remaining 3% from right-wingers who disagreed with Makarios. The left's opposition to Makarios lasted only for some months. In January 1960, Makarios took AKEL into his coalition. The pretext was given by the first parliamentary elections, which were set to take place in January 1959. On the initiative of Makarios, the elections did not take place and the seats were divided up. Although AKEL represented more than 30% of the population, it got only five of the 35 seats in the house. The Patriotic Front, which was a transient pre-election set-up that housed EOKA fighters, took the remaining 30 seats.[106]

The 'transgression' of AKEL and the support it offered Makarios moderated the intense criticism it received from the Right for not having participated in the Struggle, and helped the party to get on its feet. The price, however, was a heavy one.

AKEL was the only Greek Cypriot party to have links with Turkish Cypriots. The party's collaboration with Makarios made left-wing Turkish Cypriots easy game for TMT. Despite the signing of the London-Zurich Agreements, the TMT, unlike EOKA, was not disbanded; it immediately began a policy of heavy intimidation of Turkish Cypriots so they would break off all relations with Greek Cypriots. Known as 'From Turk to Turk', this policy ordered that Turkish Cypriots were to have exchanges only between themselves and not with Greeks. Those Turkish Cypriots who did not conform were forced to pay heavy fines.

After the signing of the agreements, TMT was significantly reinforced by men from within Turkey. According to Ismail Tansu, the aim of TMT was to create by the end of 1959 an organisation of 5,000 armed men, rising to 10,000 by the end of 1960.[107]

As previously mentioned, TMT arms were shipped to Cyprus on board the *Deniz* (codename *Elmas*). On the night of 17 to 18 October 1959, nine whole months after the signing of the Agreements, a British patrol boat spotted the *Elmas*; faced with the danger of having the cargo revealed, the crew were instructed from Turkey to scuttle it. The British arrested the captain, Resat Yavuz, the engineer Uluz Kontoglu and the mate Murat Gunduz. Two of these three men had been trained in guerrilla warfare in the United States.[108] A Cypriot court sentenced each of the prisoners on 11 November to prison terms of one year. The next day, the British Governor ordered them sent to Turkey, ostensibly to serve out their sentences over there.

In 1960, Menderes was toppled by a coup in Turkey. For some time, the Council for the Supervision of Mobilisation and its offshoot in Cyprus, the TMT, went through a period of crisis. The new Turkish government, which had not been informed about the activities of

---

105 *Ibid.*, p. 354.
106 *Ibid.*, p. 342.
107 "TMT", *Agon*, 20 July, 1997.
108 *Ibid.*, 27 June, 1997.

the Turkish Gladio and its relationship with NATO, had the impression it was a secret army of the previous regime. They even described the organisation as "the Menderes Gestapo", and tried to disband it.[109] Eventually, the leader of the Pan-Turkish movement, Alpaslan Turkes, who was involved with the leaders of the coup, intervened and restored the channels of communication between the TMT and the new government. However, the leaders of TMT in Turkey and Cyprus, Karabelen and Vuruskan, were expelled.[110]

Turkish dissenters today vehemently maintain that there was cooperation between the Greek Cypriot and Turkish Cypriot para-states, and that Georgadjis actually channelled part of the American aid he received for anti-communist propaganda to the Turkish Cypriot side. At the head of the Turkish Cypriot para-state was the political leader of the TMT, Rauf Denktash, who had been elected president of the Turkish Cypriot Communal Assembly.

The creation of the Cypriot para-state, with the assistance of the Greek secret services and the CIA and the strengthening of TMT, an offshoot of the Turkish Gladio, combined with the influence of Greek and Turkish Cypriot nationalism to drive matters to a head. The problematic nature of the Agreements and the absence of good will for their implementation were creating opportunities for another round of bloody conflict.

Reacting to continuous problems over the implementation of the Agreements, Makarios took the political decision at the beginning of 1962 to proceed to a phased revision of the constitution, with the aim of achieving true independence, the final goal being *Enosis*. Makarios did not consult with the Greek government, which was opposed to any attempt to disturb the balance achieved in Zurich. However, he had the encouragement and support of the Greek army through its contingent in Cyprus.

On the other hand, the leadership of the Turkish Cypriots, which made no serious attempt to make the solution work, reacted furiously against Makarios' plans. Relations between the two communities entered a phase of continual conflict. Nationalist euphoria had carried everyone away. No voices were raised in support of common sense, and, almost in its entirety, the press, whether Greek Cypriot or Turkish Cypriot, left wing or right wing, added grist to the mill of conflict. Although AKEL was somewhat restrained, it remained haunted by the 'betrayal' syndrome from the EOKA struggle, and also supported Makarios' initiative. The only exception was the small Turkish People's Party of the doctor Ihsan Ali. The main associates of Ihsan Ali were the lawyers Ayhan Hikmet and Ahmed Gurkan from Nicosia. These two lawyers and politicians were publishers of the weekly newspaper *Cumhürriyet*, which was in circulation on the first day of the founding of the Republic, and a passionate supporter of co-existence between Greeks and Turks, while harshly critical of the president of the Turkish National Assembly, Rauf Denktash.

The climate of tension and conflict became even more charged when, on the dawn of 25 March 1962, there were explosions at the Bayraktar and Omeriye mosques in Nicosia. Georgadjis blamed the Turkish Cypriots and Denktash the Greek Cypriots. On 27 March, Gurkan went to the Turkish embassy to meet the ambassador and to ask him to intervene so the evil would not spread. At that time Denktash's relations with the Turkish Government were hostile, as a result of the suspicion with which Inonu viewed the TMT, which he still saw as Menderes' private army. The consequence of this relationship was the public squabble between the Turkish ambassador in Nicosia, Emin Dirvana, and Denktash. The

---

[109] *Ibid.*, 29 August, 1997.
[110] *Ibid.*, 18 October, 1997.

Turkish ambassador being absent, Gurkan met with the press attaché, who was also Director of the Turkish Intelligence Services, Mehmet Pamir, who told him the explosions were the work of Denktash. Pamir's motives are as yet undetermined. However, Gurkan, ignoring the intrigues behind the scenes, turned to Interior Minister Polycarpos Georgadjis to obtain the information. With the help of Lagodontis and his associate Nicos Ioannou-Psomas. Georgadjis taped his conversation with Gurkan[111].

In the meanwhile, an investigative committee was set up to find out the causes of the explosions, and the two Turkish Cypriot journalists were summoned to testify. On 27 April, they published in their paper that they would unmask the perpetrators. The next day they were both murdered. Gurkan in the garage of his house, and Hikmet in his bedroom, while sleeping with his wife and two children. The murders were immediately blamed on TMT. In the Turkish Cypriot collective consciousness, the moral instigator was Denktash. On 21 May 1962, Georgadjis was summoned to testify before the committee investigating the explosions at the two mosques. There, to the surprise of all, he handed to the committee the tape of his conversation with Gurkan. The committee heard the tape, and its contents were published in all the newspapers.[112] The climate within the Turkish Cypriot community changed immediately. The two victims, from being martyrs for freedom, were seen as stool pigeons of Georgadjis. The murder of the two Turkish Cypriots, like almost all the politically motivated crimes of the decade 1960-70, remain unsolved.

Unsolved also are the circumstances surrounding the explosion at the mosques. Ihsan Ali, quoting information from a reliable source, wrote in his memoirs that the explosions as well as the murder of the two lawyers were in fact the work of Lagodontis.[113] Denktash also attributes the murders to Lagodontis. In contrast, Turkish Cypriot opposition newspaper *Avrupa* quotes testimony suggesting that it was TMT that murdered the two journalists.[114] One reliable source – who spoke on condition of anonymity – said there was a plan by Lagodontis to blow up the mosques. The source added that after the explosions, policemen serving under Lagodontis, as well as his collaborator Takis Melodias, planned to target them again with the aim of levelling them to the ground.[115]

Today, it is of little importance whether the bombers spoke Greek or Turkish. What is more or less certain is that the blowing up of the mosques and the murders of the journalists was the work of one of the offshoots of the Stay Behind network in Cyprus.

While the climate of bitterness between the two communities was intensifying, Makarios gave his consent to Georgadjis for the setting-up of an organisation equivalent to the Turkish TMT. The aim of the 'Organisation' (that was its name) was to train citizens in the use of weapons so as to neutralise the Turkish Cypriots in the event they should try to provoke incidents and break away from the Cyprus Republic, using the pretext of Makarios' decision to modify the constitution.

The founding, training and ideological orientation of the Organisation had been undertaken by officers from the Greek Contingent, who were cadres of the IDEA. A leading cadre of IDEA and of the Organisation was the subsequent dictator Dimitrios Ioannides,

---

111 Georgios Lagodontis, interview with the author.

112 "Εις νέας συνταρακτικάς αποκαλύψεις προέβη ο υπουργός κ. Πολ. Γιωρκάτζης" [Startling new Revelations from from Minister Polycarpos Georgadjis], *Philelftheros*, 22 May 1962.

113 Ihsan Ali, *Τα Απομνημονεύματά μου* [Memoirs], (Nicosia, 1980), p. 34.

114 "Lawyers Hikmet and Gurkan Killed by TMT", *Avrupa*, Cyprus Press and Information Office bulletin, 4 June 1999.

115 Interview with the author, on condition of anonymity.

who was refining plans for operations against Turkish Cypriot civilians. Ioannides had a close relationship with Nicos Sampson, who had founded his own organisation and was a rival of Georgadjis.

On the Cypriot side, the leadership of the Organisation was composed of its chief, Polycarpos Georgadjis, who had the pseudonym 'Akritas' (for this reason the Organisation was usually called Akritas), with deputy leaders Glafcos Clerides and Tassos Papadopoulos. It had a staff that included the political leaders of the right wing, and government ministers ran the Organisation. Each staff member had as his 'adviser' the corresponding staff officer in the Greek Contingent. Georgadjis had as his adviser the commander of the Greek Contingent, deputy leader Tassos Papadopoulos the deputy commander, the man in charge of propaganda and information, Christodoulos Christodoulou, had the Head of the 2nd Bureau, and so forth.[116]

Journalist Spyros Papageorgiou describes how, in a gathering at the house of Georgadjis associate and subsequent diplomat Andros Nicolaides, where the training took place of those who would staff the Office of Information, Propaganda and Psychological Warfare, Greek Contingent Colonel Gragiskos proposed that the Organisation be called the Sacred League of Greek Cypriot Fighters (*Ieros Desmos Ellinokyprion Agoniston* - IDEA in its Greek acronym, just like the mainland Greek organisation).[117]

Despite the fact that the Organisation was ostensibly created to defend against an eventual Turkish threat, its anti-communist orientation permeated all its proclamations.[118] According to Papageorgiou, in a two-day map exercise conducted with the participation of Greek Contingent officers at the presidential residence in the Troodos mountains in December 1962, the possibility was raised of armed resistance by the Turkish Cypriots against legitimate state authorities. When the exercise ended, a senior Greek officer, came to the following conclusion: "We did OK, though I believe there will never be any need to fight against the Turks, since the real danger does not come from them, but from the communists!..."[119]

In the spring of 1963, Makarios negotiated with Britain a revision of the Agreements. Makarios promised Britain an important role in Cyprus if she helped to free the island from the guarantees of Greece and Turkey. From the diplomatic correspondence in the British public record office, it is clear that the Colonial Office looked positively on Makarios' initiative, in contrast to the Foreign Office, which had reservations. There are indications that the Colonial Office, which had lost its role after the United States won out in the Middle East (it was shortly after dissolved and its departments merged with the Foreign Office) hoped Britain could regain some of its influence in Cyprus.

With encouragement from Britain, and ignoring the opposition of Greek Foreign Minister Evangelos Averoff, Makarios decided to proceed to a revision of the constitution. In the autumn of 1963 he had ready a written proposal for vice-president Kutchuk for the modification of 13 points. British diplomacy was actively involved in the process, and the British High Commissioner, Arthur Clark, after written instructions from London, took receipt of the Makarios proposal and entered into handwritten corrections to the draft.[120]

---

116 Chrysafis Chrysafi, interview with the author, Nicosia, 25 November 2000.

117 Dionysios Kardianos (Spyros Papageorgiou), *Ο Αττίλας πλήττει την Κύπρο* [Attila Strikes in Cyprus], (Athens: G. Ladia publications, 1976), p. 108.

118 Spyros Papageorgiou, *Τα κρίσιμα ντοκουμέντα του Κυπριακού (1959-1967)* [Critical Documents of the Cyprus Problem], (Athens: G. Ladia Publications, 1983), 'Archive Material of the Organisation', vol. 1.

119 Kardianou, *op. cit.*, p. 108.

120 Makarios Droushiotis, *Η Πρώτη Διχοτόμηση* [The First Division]. (Nicosia: Alfadi publications, 2004), p. 105

At the same time, the British Foreign Office was also in contact with the Turkish Government, sounding out its reactions. In his note to the Foreign Office dated 16 September 1963, envoy Morgan Man recorded the conversation he had had with the Director General of the First Department of the Turkish Foreign Ministry, Turan Tuluy: "The most important point to emerge from our talk was that the Turkish Government not only appear to be resigned to, but actually to welcome, the fact that Archbishop Makarios may attempt to change the existing 'regime' (as Tuluy calls it) unilaterally. According to the Turkish view, such action may well create conditions favourable for the execution of a Turkish plan for partition."

Tuluy told Man that the irony of fate was leading Makarios to push the Turks by stages into a position where they would have to take matters into their own hands and thus do the very thing that Makarios wanted to avoid, namely partition the island. Commenting, Man wrote that "Makarios was in fact playing into Turkish hands by making this possible".[121]

At the same time as they prepared diplomatically, the Greek Cypriots were also taking appropriate military measures, intensifying the training in the Organisation. Greek Contingent officers brought weapons from the army camp stores to train members of the Organisation in their use before returning them. The training programme and the arrangements for providing means for training came from Ioannides.[122] The Organisation itself had a limited amount of arms at its disposal. Some belonged to EOKA, and Georgadjis illegally brought in others from abroad. The weaponry was of mixed type and there was a shortage of ammunition. However, the Organisation was expecting a large quantity of arms from Greek army stores.

Arrangements for the sending of arms from Greece were made under the following conditions: in the spring of 1963, Georgadjis and his deputy in the organisation, Tassos Papadopoulos, went to Greece and requested the dispatch of arms to Cyprus from the then Foreign Minister Evangelos Averoff. As one of the architects of the Zurich Agreements, Averoff was opposed to armed confrontation with Turkey and was furious. According to Papadopoulos, "he pressed his office bell and his bodyguards entered. Then he told us that we had two minutes to leave, or he would have us thrown out."[123]

Nicos Ioannou-Psomas related the same incident, describing Averoff's reaction: "Why should we provide you with arms to fight the Turks? I won't do so." Finally, Ioannou states, "we had to ask for help from the subsequent dictator George Papadopoulos, and he had to come to Cyprus to discuss the matter then go back to Athens, from where he told us 'Fine, gentlemen, I am sending you the first 1,000 weapons with ELDYK, and don't tell either Averoff or Karamanlis, and I shall send you about a 1,000 weapons at a time.'"[124] During his visit to Cyprus, George Papadopoulos, who was the link between the Greek Secret Services (KYP) and the CIA, established contact with leading personalities. Among others, he met with Vassos Lyssarides, who had founded an armed group of his own, which acted independently from the Organisation, but in conjunction with the Greek Contingent.[125]

---

121 Morgan Man, note on his conversation with Turan Tuluy, 18 September, 1963. British Public Record Office, F.O. 371/16897 30261.

122 Nicos Koshis, testimony before the Committee on the 'Cyprus File' of the Cyprus House of Representatives, 11 January 2000.

123 Tassos Papadopoulos, interview with the author, Nicosia, 27 August 2001.

124 Nicos Ioannou-Psoma, testimony before the Committee on the 'Cyprus File' of the Cyprus House of Representatives.

125 Vassos Lyssarides, interview with the author, Prodromos, 21 August 2001.

In July of 1963, Papadopoulos duly sent 1,000 weapons to Cyprus, using as an excuse the replacement of troops who had served their tour of duty. However, these arms were not handed to the Organisation, but were stashed away in army stores. With the next change-over of Greek troops, which was to take place in six months, another 1,000 weapons were to be dispatched. The Organisation was not to go into action before January 1964. "There was an order to the effect that we should not start things before the arms arrived," recalls Chrysafis Chrysafi, who served in the Cyprus army and was posted to the staff of the Organisation.[126]

In November 1963, Makarios submitted his proposals for a reworking of the Constitution. The Turks exploited the opportunity and brought on a political crisis. As Turan Tuluy revealed to Morgan Man, it was a strategic decision by the Turks in order not to give the impression that it was they who had started off armed conflict. "Tuluy," writes Man, "hoped of course, that it would never come to this, and stressed that it would not be the Turks who fired the first shot; indeed, Turkey was prepared to accept that the first casualties in the fighting should be Turks, in order to demonstrate to world opinion that all subsequent Turkish reactions were purely defensive; accordingly the Turkish community in Cyprus had been 'instructed' to ensure that it was not Turks who started the fighting."[127]

On 3 December, on the order of Georgadjis, members of the Organisation blew up the statue of EOKA hero Marcos Drakos near Paphos Gate in Nicosia.[128] The action was attributed to the Turks. Spirits were already aroused, and a general clash seemed unavoidable. On 21 December, an armed patrol of Georgadjis clashed with Turkish Cypriots. Shots were exchanged, and Zeki Halil and Cemaliye Emirali were killed. Although the official version was that the patrol was on a designated mission and that members of TMT provoked it, in reality the incident was no more than a usual quarrel between members of the underworld, which had nothing to do with ethnic disputes. However, Nicosia, which was ready to explode, was not in a position to make such a distinction. Members of TMT, who were on stand-by and spread out all along the dividing line of the Turkish quarter waiting for the Organisation to make a mistake, exploited the incident and opened fire. The Organisation responded and in a few hours Nicosia was turned into a battlefield from end to end. Despite appeals by Makarios and vice-president Kutchuk for self-restraint, the situation got out of control and the clashes spread to other parts of Cyprus.

Finally, on the initiative of British Colonial Secretary Duncan Sands, who came post haste to Cyprus, agreement was reached on 30 December to draw up the Green Line between the two quarters of Nicosia, which has since then divided the capital.[129]

Using the intercommunal clashes as a pretext, the Turkish Cypriots implemented a plan for partition of their own. The Turkish Cypriot ministers walked out of the government and the deputies from Parliament. Together with the members of the Turkish Communal Assembly, they formed their own House of Representatives, while beginning to lay the foundations of a state with separate services. Under the guidance of TMT, the Turkish Cypriots who lived in Turkish villages or those of mixed communities, moved to areas that had a purely Turkish population and created enclaves.

The largest enclave was north of Nicosia and was put under the protection of the Turkish Contingent, which was moved from its army camp and occupied the strategically

126 Chrysafis Chrysafi, interview with the author.

127 Morgan Man, note on his conversation with Turan Tuluy, 18 September, 1963. British Public Record Office, F.O. 371/16897 30261.

128 Confession by a member of the Organisation to the author, under the condition of anonymity.

129 Glafcos Clerides, *Η κατάθεσή μου* [My Deposition], (Nicosia: Alithia, 1988-1991), vol. 1, p. 248.

important heights of St. Hilarion in the Pentadactylos mountain range. Thus, for the first time, the Turkish Cypriots acquired complete control in a mainland area. Reacting, the Greek Cypriots began to implement limited measures, such as control of the movement of produce and the banning of supply of specific materiel to the enclaves, with the justification that they would be used for military purposes. In the first phases of the Turkish withdrawal into enclaves there were interruptions in the water and electricity supply. These measures had the result of rallying the population around TMT.

Attacks on unarmed civilians by Greek Cypriot extremists gave the pretext for moving the Turkish Cypriots into enclaves. The most extreme of the groups was that of Nicos Sampson, which was in action in the Omorphita area of Nicosia around Christmas of 1963, killing and taking hostage dozens of Turkish Cypriots, mainly women and children, and looting their property.[130] According to *The Washington Post*, Sampson was from that time an instrument of the CIA and received financial aid from the agency's funds earmarked for anti-communist activities, via Savvas Constantopoulos, publisher of the Athens newspaper *Eleftheros* Cosmos.[131] Sampson's relationship with the CIA is also confirmed by a former agent of the American National Security Agency (NSA), Winslow Peck. According to Peck, the CIA man in Cyprus that supported Sampson was the first victim of the Greek 'November 17' terrorist organisation, Richard Wells. When the crisis broke out in 1963, Wells was serving in Cyprus. According to Peck, Wells was behind the intercommunal troubles of 1963, in which both Ioannides and Sampson had leading roles. "I remember specifically that when I sometimes met with Wells in Washington, he told us proudly: 'Did you see what I did in Cyprus in '64?'"[132]

In January 1964, at the suggestion of the CIA, there were negotiations between the Americans and Grivas concerning his direct involvement in the Cyprus crisis. On the American side, the negotiator was the attaché of the American embassy in Athens, Norbert Anschutz, while Socrates Eliades represented Grivas. "Our secret services," the Secretary of State George Ball writes in his memoirs, "had reported the growing antipathy between Makarios and General George Grivas, the famous leader of EOKA. Though Grivas was, of course, a passionate advocate of *Enosis*, he might, I thought, be easier to work with than Makarios, so we established an underground contact with Socrates Eliades."[133]

At the end of January, preparations for Grivas' return to Cyprus intensified. Interior Minister Polycarpos Georgadjis, who had a leading role in the affair, invited the British Deputy Commander of the United Nations Peacekeeping Force in Cyprus, General Michael Carver, to spend a Sunday on Troodos, where he maintained a governmental country residence. Georgadjis informed him of the imminent arrival of Grivas, and told him that it was with the approval of Makarios. Carver recalls: "Georgadjis asked me to persuade the British not to object. In the light of subsequent events and of Georgadjis' ultimate fate, I have doubts about whether the Archbishop had approved. I had doubts then, but passed his request on both to the UN and the British authorities, neither of whom did raise any objections."[134]

---

130 Testimony by a member of the Sampson gang. Vassos Lyssarides, testimony before the Committee on the 'Cyprus File' of the Cyprus House of Representatives, 11 February 2000. Lyssarides, interview with the author.

131 "Greek Army Weak, NATO memo says", *Washington Post*, 24 July, 1974.

132 "Η Αθήνα, το νέο στρατηγείο της CIA για τη Μέση Ανατολή" [Athens, the CIA's New Headquarters for the Middle East], *Anti*, 17 April, 1976.

133 George W. Ball, *The Past Has Another Pattern* (New York: WW Norton and Company, 1982), p. 357.

134 Field Marshal Lord Carver, "Peacekeeping in Cyprus", in: John Koumoulides (eds.), *Cyprus in Transition 1960-1985*, (London: Trigraph, 1986), p. 30.

In February, Grivas established himself at Armed Forces Headquarters in Athens. He created the Cyprus Special Mixed Staff (*Eidikon Mikton Epiteleion Kyprou* - EMEK) and drew up plans for his return to Cyprus. In March, after George Papandreou won the elections in Greece and became prime minister, Defence Minister Petros Garoufalias informed Cyprus' ambassador in Athens Nicos Kranidiotis, about the intentions of the Greek Government "concerning the immediate dispatch to Cyprus of 1,000 to 2,000 well-trained men from the mountain commando regiment"[135]

While preparatory work for sending Grivas and Greek troops to Cyprus continued, a spate of articles appeared in the international and Greek press, according to which the United States had made a dramatic about-turn on the Cyprus issue in support of *Enosis*. This re-kindled *enotist* (unionist) feelings among the Greek Cypriots. The newspapers predicted a successful outcome to national aspirations; students took to the streets in demonstrations and various organisations made declarations in favour of union.

In May the secret dispatch of the first Greek troops to Cyprus began, with the consent of the Cyprus government. Greek officers and troops came to Cyprus on cruise ships owned by the ship owner Andreas Potamianos, equipped with forged civilian identities and Cypriot names.

The conspiratorial means by which the Greek troops were transferred to Cyprus created the impression that it was a top secret operation at the behest of the Greek government, carried out without the Turks or British realising what was going on. In reality, the dispatch of Greek troops to Cyprus was with the knowledge of the United States and Britain and was tolerated by Turkey, which did not protest at the rapid change in the balance of forces in Cyprus.

Grivas got the green light to go to Cyprus from Greek Defence Minister Petros Garoufalias and Foreign Minister Stavros Costopoulos, and left the same night on board the ship *Eleftheria*, owned by Potamianos. He landed in Limassol on 12 June and was received on the pier by Georgadjis and Nicos Koshis.[136] Makarios was not aware of Grivas' arrival. He was later informed by Georgios Karayiannis, who had a few weeks earlier become the Commander of the National Guard.[137] Also unaware of the departure of Grivas was Greek Prime Minister George Papandreou, who, fearing Turkish and American intervention, sent a message demanding his immediate return to Greece. Grivas refused to comply,[138] while in a letter to Garoufalias, Georgadjis wrote: "Yesterday I had a meeting with American circles in Nicosia, which knew from Athens about the arrival of Leader Georgios Grivas-Dighenis in Cyprus. (...) They believe that the General's stay here brings many advantages to Cyprus."[139] As with the arrival of Greek troops, there was no Turkish reaction over the arrival of Grivas. The Turks had received assurances from the Americans that Grivas was coming as a counterweight to Makarios, so that the Greek government would be facilitated in proceeding to an agreement on 'double *Enosis*' with Turkey. "The fact that the Grivas Plan also called for the ouster of Makarios enhanced its attractiveness," wrote George Ball in his memoirs.[140]

---

135 Nicos Kranidiotis, *Ανοχύρωτη πολιτεία, Κύπρος 1960-1974*, [The Undefended State, Cyprus 1960-1974], (Athens: Estia, 1985), vol. 1, p. 177.

136 "Είναι και πάλι ανάμεσά μας" [He is Among us Again], *Η Μάχη*, 24 June 1964.

137 Georgios Karayiannis, "Ο Στρατηγός Γρίβας αναλαμβάνει την ηγεσίαν" [General Grivas Takes the Ledership], *Εθνικός Κήρυκας*, 17 June 1965.

138 Spyros Papageorgiou, *Τα κρίσιμα ντοκουμέντα*, *op. cit.*, vol. 2, p. 15.

139 *Ibid.*, p. 19.

140 Ball, *op. cit.*, p. 357.

The climate created was such that Makarios was obliged to accept the presence of Grivas on the island. In fact, he presented him in person to the Cyprus people, in a rally that took place in Nicosia on 28 June. Makarios and Grivas appeared as the symbols of unity for a new struggle for *Enosis*, the latter now supported by political forces in Cyprus, even including AKEL. On the initiative of Makarios, the AKEL leadership met with Grivas at the Presidential Palace on 1 July and agreed, "it is essential for a successful waging of the struggle for self-determination that there be general unity among the people, irrespective of ideological or personal differences".[141] Five years after the end of the EOKA struggle, the 'betrayal' syndrome continued to direct the decisions of AKEL.

In the meantime, large amounts of Greek troops continued to arrive in Cyprus throughout July. Makarios had given his consent to the arrival of just 2,000 officers and men, but by the beginning of August 1964 there were 7,328 Greek troops and 957 officers in Cyprus. By the end of the month a whole brigade had disembarked, with enough material to equip an army corps. The Greek Brigade was installed in camps on Troodos, Pentadactylos, Stavrovouni and Nicosia.[142]

Some of the cadres of IDEA served in both the Greek Brigade and the National Guard. Grivas' staff was composed entirely of IDEA officers. Chief of staff was Petros Kefalas, later a member of the Junta. The assistant to Kefalas was the subsequent minister in the Junta, Costas Karydas. The Head of the 1st Bureau was Major Dimitrios Papadopoulos, who billeted each officer that arrived, making sure that all the key posts went to cadres of IDEA. The Head of the 2nd Bureau was Colonel Lambros Stathopoulos, who enjoyed the complete trust of George Papadopoulos. He subsequently played an active part in the April coup and was Head of the Greek KYP during the critical days of July 1974. The Head of the Third Bureau was Yiannis Davos, another leading member of the Junta. The following core members of the Junta also served in Cyprus: Nicos Dertilis, Petros Costellis and Georgios Carousos, subsequently the deputy of Grivas in EOKA B. Many lower ranking officers were also hard-core IDEA cadres, mostly captains, such as the Commander of the General's Regiment and subsequently chief torturer of the Junta, Theophilos Theofiloyiannakos. Grivas' adjutant was Athanasios Sklavenitis, whom Ioannides made Leader of EOKA B in 1974, with his headquarters at the Armed Forces Headquarters.[143]

At the same time as the Greek troops arrived in Cyprus, there was a reinforcement of Turkish forces. The only Turkish enclave with access to the sea was that of Mansoura. The TMT off-loaded supplies in the evenings from Turkish ships anchored off the coast. In July 1964, they began to land troops in Mansoura, mainly Turkish Cypriot students who had been trained in the use of weapons by the administration of the Turkish TMT. A representative of the United Nations stated on 11 July to the French Press Agency that during the previous five days the Turks had landed 500 men a day at Mansoura. A representative of the Turkish government, who said that the landing of troops was a counter measure to the sending of Greek military forces to Cyprus, confirmed this information the same day in statements to a London radio station.[144]

---

141 "Οι βουλευτές της Αριστεράς είχαν συνάντηση με τον στρατηγό Γρίβα" [The Deputies of the Left Held a Meeting with General Grivas], *Χαραυγή*, 2 July 1964.

142 Organisation chart of ELDYK/M in: Ioannis G. Bitos, *Από την πράσινη γραμμή στους δύο Αττίλες* [From the Green Line to the two Attilas], (Athens, 1997), p. 357.

143 Aris G. Bouloukos, *Υπόθεση Ασπίδα* [The 'Shield' Case], (Athens: O. Typos A.E., 1989), p. 240.

144 "Η Άγκυρα ομολόγησε χθες ότι Τούρκοι στρατιώτες απεβιβάσθησαν στη Μανσούρα" [Ankara Admits Turkish Soldiers Landed in Mansoura], *Haravghi*, 12 July 1964.

In the summer of 1964, Cyprus was under the occupation of 'Super NATO', the co-ordinating agency of the Stay Behind network. On the one side was the Greek Brigade under the control of IDEA and the Greek Gladio, and on the other was TMT, controlled by the Council of Supervision of Mobilisation and the Turkish Gladio.

During the same period the US made an important diplomatic initiative, aiming at the union of Cyprus with Greece, while offering territorial concessions to Turkey. During the last third of June, President Lyndon Johnson called the prime ministers of Greece and Turkey to Washington for talks, with a view to persuading them to accept a plan for double *Enosis* prepared by his Secretary of State, George Ball. Further talks took place behind Makarios' back in Geneva. The coordinator was a former US Secretary of State, Dean Acheson.

Acheson proposed the union of Cyprus with Greece, ceding to Turkey a large military base in the Karpass peninsula. The Turkish Cypriots would have a self-governing regime in two districts of the northern part of Cyprus, while a mechanism would be set up to protect minorities throughout the island. Makarios, who was unofficially informed through his own sources, reacted with fury to the Acheson Plan, which he termed disguised partition, and obliged Papandreou to reject it.[145]

In the meanwhile, the Cyprus government assigned to Grivas the task of wiping out of the Mansoura-Kokkina enclave, through which TMT was channelling arms from Turkey. As the poorly-planned operation headed for failure, the Turkish air force went into action, bombing military and civilian targets.

After the Mansoura events, Acheson submitted a second plan, according to which the area to be ceded to the Turks for a military base would not be sovereign but on a 50-year lease. The Greek island of Kastellorizo would also be ceded to Turkey. Papandreou at first accepted the second plan, considering it a bargain. "They are offering us an apartment block in return for a penthouse," was his characteristic comment.[146] Subsequently, he changed his mind and rejected it, despite intense pressure from the United States.

President Johnson summoned Greek ambassador Alexandros Matsas to the White House and urged him to convey to Athens the view of the United States that the Greek government ought to accept union with territorial concessions to Turkey, including Kastellorizo. Matsas reminded Johnson of the position set out by Papandreou, that "no Greek parliament could accept such a plan" and that "the Greek constitution does not allow a Greek government to give away a Greek island". Johnson was furious and replied to Matsas: "Then listen to me, Mr. Ambassador. Fuck your Parliament and your Constitution. America is an elephant. Cyprus is a flea. Greece is a flea. If those two fleas continue itching the elephant, they may just get whacked by the elephant's trunk, whacked good. (...) We pay a lot of good American dollars to the Greeks, Mr. Ambassador. If your Prime Minister gives me talk about democracy, parliament and constitutions, he, his Parliament and his Constitution may not last very long."[147]

Indeed, within less than a year the Americans, through IDEA, carried out their political coup of 15 July 1965 and toppled George Papandreou. On the pretext of a conflict between Papandreou and the Palace, deputies of the Centre Union Party were bought out and defected from the government. This opened the way for the military coup by IDEA on 21

---

145 Makarios Droushiotis, "Το πάρε δώσε για την Κύπρο" [The Give-and-take on Cyprus], *Elephtherotypia*, 19 August, 2002.

146 Makarios Droushiotis, "Ο βομβαρδισμός του '64 και τα σχέδια της διχοτόμησης" [The Bombings of '64 and the Plans for Partition], *Elephtherotypia*, 20 August, 2002.

147 Philip Deane, *I Should have Died*, (New York: Atheneum, 1977), p. 113.

April 1967. As Charles Foley wrote in *The Observer*, Papadopoulos was the first paid agent of the CIA to become the prime minister of a state.[148]

On the first day of the coup, nobody in Nicosia knew what was happening in Greece. Telephone communications had been cut and there was no information about the identity of the new regime. The first Cypriot to be informed that the leader of the coup was Papadopoulos was Georgadjis. Papadopoulos himself telephoned Georgadjis and told him: "It's me here, don't worry, you'll have whatever help you need."[149]

Makarios' first reaction was positive, in the sense that the new regime would be preoccupied with the internal problems of the country and would allow freedom of manoeuvre on the Cyprus issue.[150] His expectations were soon dashed, as the Junta began to intervene in Cyprus.

A few months after its rise to power, the Junta, using the excuse of a military operation by the National Guard against the Turkish Cypriot village of Kofinou, recalled Grivas to Greece and withdrew the Greek Brigade from Cyprus. There remained, however, about 600 officers on the island to staff the National Guard. Through these officers, the Junta and the Greek para-state continued to indoctrinate the Cyprus community with nationalism and to undermine Makarios, stating in its propaganda that he was the only reason that *Enosis* had not been implemented.

The officers' propaganda found a foothold in the decision by the Cyprus government to abandon the policy of the 'desirable', i.e. *Enosis*, and to focus on the policy of the 'feasible', i.e. an independent state. From the beginnings of 1968, consultations were in full swing for the beginning of intercommunal negotiations for a solution to the Cyprus problem within the framework of an independent state.

As a result of political developments, the situation in Cyprus was normalised. Barricades outside the Turkish Cypriot enclaves were dismantled, the Turkish Cypriots were allowed freedom to move without constraints throughout Cyprus and the law of economics began to solve everyday problems between the two communities.

This peace on the domestic front was disturbed by the nationalist organisation, the National Front, which was directed by the Commander of Mountain Commando Regiment (*Lohoi Orinon Katadromon* – LOK) in Greece, Constantinos Aslanides, who was a cadre of IDEA and of the Junta. This organisation undertook terrorist actions, its slogan being *Enosis* and a purge of the internal front of "anti-nationalist elements". Through bomb attacks, attempted assassinations and sabotage, it tried to abolish the state. Ultimately, the organisation self-destructed.[151]

At the same time as the National Front was active, the Commander of LOK in Cyprus, Dimitrios Papapostolou, together with Makarios' aide de camp, who was an agent of the Greek KYP, Athanasios Poulitsas, formed an alliance with Georgadjis. A group of Georgadjis' men and one of Grivas supporters who had links with the echelon of the Greek KYP in Nicosia and LOK, attempted to assassinate Makarios. On 8 March 1970, the helicopter that was to take him from the Archbishopric to Machairas Monastery to perform the memorial service for EOKA hero Gregoris Afxentiou, was shot down. The attempt on

---

148 The Observer, 1 July, 1973, "*Greek dictator in CIA's pocket*".

149 Nicos Ioannou-Psoma, testimony before the Committee on the 'Cyprus File' of the Cyprus House of Representatives.

150 Makarios to British journalist Michel Wall, May 1967, in: "Δεν έπρεπε να συνεχιστεί ο διάλογος" [The Dialogue Should not have Continued], *Ta Nea*, 7 October 2000.

151 Makarios Droushiotis, *Η 'εισβολή' της χούντας στην Κύπρο* [The Junta's 'Invasion' of Cyprus] (Athens: Stachi, 1996), pp. 88-119.

Makarios' life was part of a wider plan, which provided for the overturning of the government by a coup and Turkish intervention.[152]

Makarios was miraculously saved and the plans were thwarted. Later, Papapostolou and the son of junta cadre Constantinos Aslanides, Captain Georgios Aslanides, trapped Georgadjis and murdered him, thereby silencing him. Makarios, fearing the worst, covered Papapostolou and allowed Poulitsas to flee Cyprus. The unfinished work was destined to be continued by another organisation that was in the pipeline: the EOKA B of Georgios Grivas, who was preparing his third visit to the island.

---

[152] *Op. cit.*, pp. 122-240.

1. The Creation of EOKA B

When the 21 April 1967 coup took place in Greece, George Grivas was military commander of Cyprus, heading the National Guard as well as the Greek Brigade and the Greek Contingent. Nonetheless, he had no part in the coup. Later the same year, immediately after the Kofinou affair, he was recalled to Greece for consultations and was not allowed to return to Cyprus. His confinement was the result of a 'gentleman's agreement' reached between Athens and Ankara. Grivas took up residence in his house in Halandri, which was guarded by security forces on the pretext that his life was in danger.[1] Grivas was bitter at the way the regime had treated him, angry at having been made the scapegoat for the tragic outcome of the operation in Kofinou and the subsequent recall of the Greek Brigade from Cyprus. Similar sentiments were harboured by those Cypriot officers loyal to Grivas, who served in the Greek army and were stationed in Cyprus, whether in the Greek Brigade or the National Guard. Indeed, a group of Cypriot officers, among whom were Croesus Christodoulides, Michael Kalogeropoulos-Diakos, Stavros Stavrou-Syros, Andreas Achillides, Kikis Constantinou and Andreas Avgoustis, decided to disobey orders from the Armed Forces Headquarters and to refuse to follow the Brigade in its recall from Cyprus. All those serving in the National Guard were to refuse their transfer from Cyprus to Greece. Ultimately, however, only Croesus Christodoulides and Michael Kalogeropoulos remained in Cyprus. These two, together with other, non-military, elements loyal to Grivas (among whom was the lawyer Panicos Soteriou), formed an alliance that they sought to infuse with the spirit of the '*Filiki Eteria*' of the 19th century Greek revolution against Ottoman rule, with the aim of starting a new struggle for *Enosis*.[2]

In early 1968, following the failed attempt against the military by King Constantine, which culminated in his self-imposed exile, Grivas - who was a fanatical monarchist - tried unsuccessfully to create guerrilla units on the EOKA model in order to overthrow the Junta of Colonels and bring the King back to Greece. He invited to Athens some of his Cypriot contacts so they could train Greeks in guerrilla warfare techniques. Among these were Lefteris Papadopoulos, Costas Nikitas and Panicos Soteriou. Nikitas and Soteriou had seen intensive action in EOKA and were experienced in sabotage operations. According to Soteriou, Greek army officers Nicolas Lytras and Spyros Moustaklis, with whom Grivas worked in gathering war material and training men, also took part in his movement.[3] A small quantity of arms and explosives was sent from Cyprus to Greece to meet the needs of the organisation, with the help of ship owner Andreas Potamianos.

On two occasions, in August and November 1968, Grivas approached the royalist colonel of commandos, George Carousos, for help in a movement against the Junta. According to Carousos, Grivas would instruct his men to say if they were arrested that their aim was not to cause problems for the regime but to prepare a new *Enosis* struggle in Cyprus, and that their enemy was Makarios.[4] According to Soteriou, many of the important cadres of the movement did not take things seriously.[5] Before the organisation even got off the ground, the security forces in September 1968 arrested some of Grivas' men and locked them up in the cells of the Greek Military Police (*Elliniki Stratiotiki Astinomia* - ESA). The ESA

---

1 This information was given by Grivas himself, in a statement released on 28 September 1973.

2 Panicos Soteriou, interview with the author, Limassol, 2000.

3 *Η ζωή και το έργο του Γεωργίου Γρίβα Διγενή* [The Life and Works of George Grivas Dighenis] proceedings of conference held in Nicosia, 1995, p. 110.

4 George Carousos, interview with the author, Athens, 13 June 2000.

5 Panicos Soteriou, interview with the author.

commander at the time was Dimitrios Ionnides, one of the leading members of the Junta. Among those arrested were officers Lytras and Moustaklis, the Cypriot Lefteris Papadopoulos and the Greek Cosmas Mastrokolias, an associate of Grivas' from the days of the 'X' organaisation. A search of Lystras' house brought to light papers and notes, as well as the oath taken in Grivas' organisation.[6] However, while Lytras and Moustaklis remained in prison until the end of the dictatorship, Papadopoulos was released and returned to Cyprus. Mastrokolias was also set free. The regime did not touch Grivas.

Carousos has since claimed that, during their detention, Lefteris Papadopoulos and Cosmas Mastrokolias came into contact with Ioannides and accepted to cooperate with him, luring Grivas into his camp.[7] Mastrokolias, who had worked with Grivas since the German occupation, had also since had links with the secret services. Ioannides, as a cadre of the Greek Gladio, was a hard-core member of the Junta, which was responsible for most of the conspiratorial activities of the Greek officers in Cyprus, which culminated in EOKA B's activities and the coup of 15 July 1974. Throughout those years, Mastrokolias was Ioannides' line of communication with Grivas; and Lefteris Papadopoulos was for a long time the compliant tool of Mastrokolias.

After the arrests of his associates, Grivas' efforts against the Junta gradually slackened to the point where they completely lapsed. His focus switched back to Cyprus and he began to draw up plans against Makarios. Towards the end of 1969, he asked Captain Christodoulides[8] to make suggestions for the creation of an organisation in Cyprus, whose aim would be to overthrow Makarios and implement *Enosis*. Christodoulides prepared a written memo and submitted it to Grivas. The memo said the situation in Cyprus was "highly entangled, unclear, chaotic, with suspect, weak tendencies, full of enormous and obvious dangers, both as regards the correct handling of our national question, as well as the future survival of Hellenism on the island." According to Christodoulides, in order to "provide a realistic possibility of facing and putting right this unacceptable situation", there had to be radical change, with the sole objective of "*Enosis* with the mother country, without any intermediate stage or the slightest concession."

The strategic aim of the nascent movement, as described in Christodoulides' memo, was as follows: "Perfectly organised, trained and armed, in the utmost secrecy, so as to carry out at the right moment a surprise operation, swift and powerful, with a view to the seizure of power and radical abolition of the existing government under Makarios, as well as of all the political parties and organisations of any guise, whatsoever, should such appear on the scene."[9]

At the beginning of 1970, Grivas began publicly to declare his intentions for a new, armed *Enosis* struggle. On 5 April he spoke at a large gathering in Athens, on the occasion of the anniversary of the EOKA uprising and defined the aims and targets of the projected campaign in Cyprus.

---

6 Vasilis Philias, *Τα αξέχαστα και τα λησμονημένα* [The Unforgettable and the Forgotten] (Athens: Papazisi Publications, 1997), p. 123.

7 Andreas Athanasiou, *Ο άγνωστος πόλεμος Αθηνών – Λευκωσίας* [The Unknown War between Athens and Nicosia] (Athens: Tzionis Publications, 1989), p. 179. Carousos, interview broadcast on CyBC1, 16 July 1994. Carousos, interview with the author.

8 After their refusal to follow the Greek Brigade to Greece, Christodoulides and Kalogeropoulos resigned from the Greek army and were appointed by Makarios as trainers to the Cyprus police.

9 'Davakis' (Croesus Christodoulides), note to Grivas, submitted by former head of KYP Georgios Tombazos to the Committee on the 'Cyprus File' of the Cyprus House of Representatives, 16 November 1999.

In his speech:

a) He bitterly criticised the signing of the London-Zurich Agreements.
b) He accused the Cyprus leadership of having several times rejected *Enosis* as a solution to the Cyprus problem.
c) He announced indirectly, but distinctly, his decision to start a struggle for *Enosis*: "… I declare that I shall not rest, as long as I live, until the struggle I have set as my life's goal is brought to a successful conclusion. Young men of Cyprus, close your ears to the siren of the 'feasible' and unfurl the flag of *Enosis*. … The times will not wait. The fruit has ripened long ago. Unfortunately, we have not taken it. If we leave it still, it will fall and rot. It is now or never! … Many have called me mad because I took on the Cyprus struggle in 1955. But great works and heroic deeds require foolish daring, which some, if they so wish, may call madness. However, we are determined to repeat this insanity, if need be, for the sake of Cyprus".[10]

The *Enosis* question was beginning to stir again in Cyprus. In March 1970, the weekly paper *Patris* (Homeland) re-appeared, funded by Andreas Potamianos and managed by Socratis Eliades, one of Grivas' closest associates in Nicosia. The newspaper was the mouthpiece of the Grivas faction and was prominent in its devastating criticism of Makarios, whom it labelled as the sole obstacle to *Enosis*. In Nicosia, an anti-Makarios faction had already been formed, but its popular support was limited. In the presidential elections of 1968 Makarios gained 97% of the vote and his opponent, president of the Democratic National Party (*Dimokratiko Ethniko Komma* - DEK), Takis Evdokas, only 3%. Apart from DEK, the anti-Makarios faction was made up of former EOKA fighters loyal to the principles of Grivas, who believed Makarios had betrayed the vision of *Enosis*; there were also those who considered they had been unfairly treated in the distribution of power in the newly founded Republic, as well as those loyal to Kyprianos, Bishop of Kyrenia.[11]

All these tendencies came together to compose the Grivas front. An unofficial preparatory committee, in which representatives of all tendencies took part, began to hold meetings in Nicosia and planned Grivas' return to Cyprus. The main protagonist was Socratis Eliades, and important roles were played by the journalist Spyros Papageorgiou, later a theoretician of EOKA B, and also by Takis Evdokas, teachers Gabriel Mina, Thassos Sophocleous, Photis Papaphotis and Ioannis Kasinis, as well as by the associate of the Bishop of Kyrenia, Polycarpos Ioannides and his son Costakis Ioannides, director of the DEK newspaper, *Gnomi (Oppinion)*.

Meanwhile, Croesus Christodoulides, to whom Grivas had entrusted military preparations for the organisation, began to set up armed groups. He began contacts with Greek army officers serving in active units of the National Guard and mainly in the armoured corps. The armoured units were one of the most battle-ready and best organised, and their participation in any future coup was considered essential.

Similar activities were undertaken by Socrates Eliades, who in early 1970 approached cadres of the National Front, offering them financial incentives to join the new movement. This initiative was to prove fruitless, with the leadership of the National Front wary of Eliades' intentions. In any case, the organisation was on the verge of dissolution, and Grivas felt it lacked seriousness.[12]

---

10 Kranidiotis, *op. cit.*, vol. 2, p. 21.

11 Kyprianos had been in continual conflict with Makarios since 1950, when the latter was elected Archbishop – a position on which he had his own eye.

12 Droushiotis, *Η 'εισβολή' της χούντας*, pp. 287-288.

In March, came the failed attempt on Makarios' life, organised by the Commander of the Mountain Commando Regiment, Dimitris Papapostolou, and Polycarpos Georgadjis. Shortly after, Eliades met with Papapostolou at the house of second lieutenant Sotiris Gambroudis as part of his contacts aimed at setting up the new organisation. According to Spyros Papageorgiou, "the conversation was basically a rabid monologue by the diminutive colonel, who, among hysterical outbursts, repeatedly said: 'such a traitor (Makarios) should not be alive!'"[13]

During the same period, work began on the first hideouts in the Pentadactylos mountain range, to be used as refuges for Grivas' men. In a statement made to police, Andreas Georgios Drakos, confessed to his part in digging out the hideouts. Drakos was taken to Makarios, and confessed to him that members of a new organisation were being recruited under Grivas. Drakos said he took orders from Papaphotis, who had told him, "Makarios got away once, and lightly at that, but this time he will not escape".[14]

In the autumn of 1970, the plotters looked for a suitable headquarters for Grivas. Elli Christodoulidou[15] was responsible for finding one. Finally, the house of Diana Mavros was chosen, an upper floor at 4, Sparta Street, near the commercial Eleftheria Street in Limassol. Mavros travelled to Athens at Christmas 1970 and met Grivas, who gave her instructions for the construction of his hideout.[16]

On Sunday 4 April 1971, a year after his speech at the 'Orpheas', Grivas again spoke in Athens on the anniversary of 1st April, at the 'Akropol' Theatre. According to *Patris*, Grivas "uttered a highly significant and very revealing speech" and demanded that Makarios resign "so that the struggle for *Enosis* might successfully proceed". The audience of 2,000, almost entirely made up of Cypriot students, was addressed by the president of the National Association of Cypriot Students (*Ethniki Fititiki Enosis Kyprion* – EFEK), Nicos Koutsou, who called on Grivas to continue the struggle of EOKA for Enosis.[17]

While Grivas was preparing his arrival in Cyprus, relations between Athens and Nicosia were going through another period of strain. The Greek government revived its interest in cooperating with Turkey for a solution to the Cyprus problem on the basis of the principles laid down in the Acheson Plan, and was pressing Makarios to go along with this. Makarios, who refused to buckle under pressure, believed the Greek regime was behind the actions that Grivas was preparing on the island, with the aim of undermining the domestic front in Cyprus and so ease the imposition of a solution. In early 1971, Makarios acted to secure the widest possible domestic support to face the expected pressure from Athens. On 27 January, he called a meeting at the Presidential Palace of political party leaders, members of the Council of Ministers, former ministers, members of the House of Representatives and former deputies, in order bring them up to date with developments in the Cyprus problem and to ask for their support. Makarios gave an extensive analysis of the Cyprus problem from

---

13 Spyros Papageorgiou, *Μακάριος - Πορεία διά πυρός και σιδήρου* [Makarios – the Path through Fire and Brimstone] (Athens: Ladia Publications, 1967), p. 38.

14 Cyprus KYP report entitled 'Προετοιμασίαι και δημιουργία προϋποθέσεων αφίξεως Γρίβα εις Κύπρον, συνωμοτικαί και άλλαι πολιτικαί δραστηριότητες, έργα και ημέραι Χουντικών αξιωματικών, ματαιωθέν πραξικόπημα Φεβρουαρίου 1972 και πραξικόπημα Ιουλίου 1974' [Preparations and creation of conditions for the arrival of Grivas to Cyprus, conspiracies and other political actions, activities of Junta officers, the thwarted coup of February 1972 and the coup of July 1974]; the report is based on evidence gathered from intercepted telephone conversations, author's personal archive, p. 1.

15 Grivas had stayed in her house throughout the EOKA struggle and had a close personal relationship with her.

16 Droushiotis, *Η 'εισβολή' της χούντας*, p. 297.

17 *Ibid.*, p. 298.

1960 to that time, and concentrated on the 1964 Acheson Plan, which he believed was being revived. Makarios referred indirectly to Grivas' plans to return to the island, and asked those present to work with him in forming a strong internal front: "The degree of our national resistance will depend on the state of the domestic front, which presents, as I have stated, dangerous cracks. However, I do not believe the cracks are unbridgeable."[18]

According to a briefing obtained by the American Embassy in Nicosia describing what happened at the Presidential Palace, Makarios "was successful to a surprising degree in his aim, which was to appease and bring together the leadership of the many dissimilar political groupings of the Greek Cypriot community." However, as American ambassador David Popper noted in his report, this did not refer to the pro-*Enosis* factions – which in any case did not attend the meeting – nor was it likely that the spirit of unity would last for long. Nevertheless, according to Popper, "the meeting's outcome demonstrates once again the Archbishop's enormous political astuteness". As one observer expressed to Popper, "most of those who went to the Palace were disillusioned and suspicious of the Archbishop, but they left eating out of his hand".[19]

At the same time as Makarios was arguing against the Acheson Plan, which he viewed as anathema, Grivas appeared to support it, considering it a historic opportunity that had been missed. According to Spyros Papageorgiou, Grivas sent the two Acheson plans to those newspapers favourable to him, with the following note: "Give it a high profile. It is on this that we shall base our policy."[20] Thus, on 8 February 1971, the newspapers *Patris* in Nicosia, *Ellinikos Voras* (The Greek North) of Salonica and *Estia* in Athens, published an identical text with different headlines, according to which the Acheson Plan was a unique opportunity for the union of Cyprus with Greece, one which had been lost due to the anti-*Enosis* stance of Makarios. *Estia* ran the headline: "The Acheson Plan: a Vindication of Greek demands over Cyprus. Unpatriotic Rejection of it by Makarios."[21]

In reaction to the articles in the pro-Grivas press, Makarios began to speak publicly in favour of "pure *Enosis*", making it clear he would not consider territorial concessions to Turkey, as provided for in the Acheson Plan. In a speech on 14 March 1971, in Yialousa in the Karpass region, which the Acheson Plan would have ceded to Turkey for a military base, Makarios said: "Cyprus has been Greek since the dawn of her history and will remain Greek. Greek and undivided we inherited her, Greek and undivided we shall keep her, and Greek and undivided we shall hand her over to Greece…"[22] This speech provoked furious reaction from Turkey and Turkish Cypriot leader Rauf Denktash, and was put forward as proof of the lack of will by Makarios for achieving a solution to the Cyprus problem that would preclude *Enosis*.

Makarios believed the revival of the demand for *Enosis* and Grivas' attempt to resurrect the Acheson Plan served Greek government policy for rapprochement with Turkey. In a political manoeuvre, Makarios proposed to Grivas that they form a common anti-Junta front. On 14 February 1971, he invited to the Presidential Palace Anthimos, the Bishop of Kitium, whom he knew had contacts with Grivas' entourage. He told him that he expected

---

18 Miltiades Christodoulou, *Η πορεία μιας εποχής* [The Course of an Era] (Athens: I. Floros, 1987), p.538.

19 Note from Popper to the State Department, 4 February 1972, "CYPRUS: Relations to Makarios' National Unity Meeting", NARA, RG59, CFPF, 1970-1973, Cyprus.

20 Papageorgiou, *Μακάριος*, p. 77.

21 In 1964, when the Acheson Plan was under discussion, *Estia* – perhaps uniquely in the Greek press – condemned it as partitionist.

22 Makarios III, Archbishop of Cyprus, Άπαντα [Complete Works] (Nicosia: Archbishop Makarios III Foundation), vol. IB, p. 281

conflict with the Junta, that there was a need for a strong domestic front, and he asked him to mediate with Grivas with a view to cooperation, which would not exclude his return to Cyprus.

The next day, the Bishop of Kitium called Socrates Eliades to the bishopric in Limassol and briefed him on the Makarios proposal. On 18 February, Eliades went to Athens and gave Grivas the information. On 22 February, Eliades wrote to his friend, Greek army major Stavros Stavrou-Syros, who was ready to come to Cyprus as a staff officer in Grivas' organisation: "When I transmitted the proposals of Makarios to the Leader, he correctly observed: 'Twice he has cheated me over Cyprus. I want Mr. M(akarios) to tell us what he wants, and if he will commit himself etc etc. The Bishop of Kitium undertakes to carry out the necessary work. Let us wait and see and I believe that something will come out of this, because this time M(akarios) does not know what to do. Care and secrecy are needed'."[23]

In the negotiations that followed through the good offices of Bishop Anthimos, Grivas laid down a basic condition: Makarios was to make a public announcement, in which he would invite him to return to Cyprus that they may unite in a common struggle for *Enosis*. Makarios replied that the *Enosis* struggle was unfeasible at that stage of the Cyprus problem, and that what took precedence was to confront the Junta's plans to solve the Cyprus problem in collusion with Turkey. Grivas agreed that the danger from the Junta did indeed exist, and accepted the reconciliation, but only under the irrevocable precondition that his terms be met. However, Makarios was not disposed to accept such a thing. As he explained to Grivas' associates with whom he was negotiating, he did not for tactical reasons want to come into open conflict with the Athens regime. In reality, Makarios hesitated to enter into an equal partnership with Grivas because he feared he would be lured by his entourage into actions that would soon undermine whatever partnership they had. Makarios' fears were not groundless. Such an enterprise had already been attempted in 1964, and had failed.

In Turkey, the army's intervention removed Suleyman Demirel from the post of Prime Minister; on 12 March 1971, Nihat Erim, the architect of Turkish policy on Cyprus since 1955, took over. The new government reviewed its strategy on the Cyprus issue and aimed at political rapprochement with Greece rather than political confrontation, with the aim of jointly dealing with the "intransigence" of Makarios.

Speaking to American officials shortly before taking over as prime minister, Erim said he considered cooperation with Greece one of the keystones of Turkish policy. He said he did not wish to see Greece isolated within the European Community or in NATO, since in the long term that would be harmful to the security of Turkey. "Greece is not only a neighbour of Turkey's in the Eastern Mediterranean, but is her natural ally," he said.[24]

In April 1971, Erim, together with Denktash, shaped the final text of a comprehensive proposal for the solution of the Cyprus problem, through internal Cyprus talks. This text was submitted by Denktash to Glafcos Clerides on 27 April 1971 and was the response to proposals submitted by Clerides on 30 November 1970.

When the Republic of Cyprus was established in 1960, the earliest bone of contention between the two communities had concerned the powers and responsibilities of local administrations. The Turks demanded separate municipalities, which would have a significant degree of autonomy. Makarios considered the Turkish demands tantamount to

---

23 Athanasiou, *op. cit.*, p. 155.

24 Handley to Secretary of State, "Cyprus: Possible Greek-Turkish bilateral agreement". NARA, NPMS, NSC, Cyprus/Greece, telegram 2608, Ankara, 16 April 1971.

degree of autonomy. Makarios considered the Turkish demands tantamount to federation, which, with the passing of time, would result in full geographical separation and partition.

In the proposals submitted by Clerides in 1970 there was a provision for the laws for the municipalities being voted by the House of Representatives, while the local administrations would have the right to issue regulations on administrative matters. However, in no case could they legislate. For Makarios, this was the limit to the concessions he could make. In its counterproposals, the Turkish side accepted most of the Greek suggestions on other matters, but asked in exchange precisely what Makarios most feared: a significant degree of autonomy for local administrative bodies, the responsibilities and powers of which would have to be incorporated in the constitution.

Makarios considered the Turkish Cypriots' proposals unacceptable, but the Greek government saw them as positive. The Cyprus government was moving in favour of rejection, of ending the talks and searching for a solution through another procedure, via the United Nations. The Greek government, however, pressured the Cypriots not to reject the Turkish proposals, to keep the dialogue going, and above all not to involve the United Nations.

The governments of Greece and Turkey agreed to work together to impose a solution to the Cyprus problem. Thus was arranged a meeting between Turkish Foreign Minister Osman Olcay and Greek deputy Foreign Minister Christianos Xanthopoulos Palamas in Lisbon at the beginning of June 1971, on the sidelines of the spring session of the NATO Council, in order to discuss the content and form of their mutual cooperation. Palamas, a supporter of Greco-Turkish rapprochement, told US ambassador to Athens Henry Tasca on 18 May that "the Greek government had decided to enter into direct talks with Turkey", and that he felt strongly that an "understanding between Greece and Turkey was of basic importance" in the solution of the Cyprus problem through peaceful means.

As to Makarios' reaction, Palamas told Tasca that the Greek government "found it intolerable that its foreign policy was at the mercy of the Archbishop", that "it was worrisome that Makarios possessed such potential for causing trouble" and that "Prime Minister Papadopoulos had taken a final decision not to return to Cyprus to find himself squeezed between the two sides".

Commenting on the content of his discussion with Palamas, Tasca noted in the telegram he sent to Washington that he found it interesting that the deputy Foreign Minister of Greece "expressed much warmer feelings towards the Turks than towards his compatriot, President Makarios", to the point, according to Tasca, of describing Denktash's response to the Clerides proposals as "a good letter".

Tasca again commented that Greece desired good relations with Turkey and peace in Cyprus, and blamed Makarios for the fact that "it could secure neither the one nor the other." He also reported that Greek government's policy was to support internal Cyprus talks, and that, in the event of no result, "the direct talks with Turkey could be used for other purposes..."[25]

While Makarios was fretting at the proposals submitted by the Turkish side, from Athens, Papadopoulos unleashed a charm offensive on Turkish Prime Minister Nihat Erim. On 29 May, the Turkish newspaper *Milliyet* published an interview with Papadopoulos, in which he attributed Greco-Turkish difficulties to a "psychological crisis" that prevailed between the two peoples. Addressing his interviewer, Papadopoulos said: "I would request a favour from you. Would it be possible for you to assure the honourable Prime Minister

---

[25] Tasca to Secretary of State, "Cyprus: Meeting with Palamas", NARA, RG59, CFPF, 1970-1973, Cyprus, telegram 2431, Athens, 18 May 1971.

Mr. Erim that in Athens there are friends who desire a close, absolute cooperation with Turkey? It is my personal conviction that developments are leading towards a federation of Greece and Turkey. This may not occur until 20 or 50 years later. But it will happen."

In the same interview, Papadopoulos promised Erim that he would not allow the stronger party (the Greek Cypriots) to mistreat the weaker (the Turkish Cypriots). He also assured Ankara that if needs be, he would use force to intervene in Cyprus: "If it comes to conflict, we shall not hesitate to proceed to intervene anew among our people. And we shall not tell them 'do as you please'."

Taking further steps in his overtures to Turkey, Papadopoulos added: "Mr. Erim should know that whatever Mr. Papadopoulos says, that is what he thinks and what he does. I categorically state that we shall act according to what we say. And Mr. Papadopoulos will be just as sure concerning Mr. Erim. It would be pleasing to us if a similar statement could come from Ankara."[26]

Erim replied to Papadopoulos on the idea of a Greco-Turkish federation, suggesting that a start could be made with Cyprus. Erim says in his memoirs how he argued to Papadopoulos that it was unacceptable that a nineteeth century priest, who "wishes to rule a chauvinist country", should manipulate relations between the two countries. He continues, "in Cyprus two communities live side by side in a de facto federation. How good it would be if they managed to make it workable. Turkey and Greece have many points of common interest and have many reasons to be friends and allies... it would be very sad if they were to overlook all this merely to please Makarios." Papadopoulos' reaction, Erim writes, was positive, with an assurance that he "agreed and harboured similar thoughts".[27]

Just a few days after the Papadopoulos interview in *Milliyet*, the meeting between Turkish Foreign Minister Olcay and Greek deputy Foreign Minister Palamas took place in Lisbon. On 1 June 1971 the two ministers met alone for three hours, without the presence of interpreters, while the following day they had a working lunch. The American reporter Laurence Stern published the testimony of the Turkish diplomat on the talks:

"We did not reach any written preliminary agreement, but the meeting seemed very promising indeed. (...) Both sides made an enormous effort to eliminate misunderstandings. We insisted that the Greeks had to abandon the illusion of creating a unified state in Cyprus that bore no relationship with the initial perception of a sovereign state. The Greeks indirectly suggested that if matters went from bad to worse, instead of breaking off relations between Greece and Turkey, we could come to an agreement on some kind of division, it would be possible to find some territorial arrangement that would involve the concession of a large base to Turkey, so that the Turks should feel greater security. The population would remain as it is."[28]

Another official of the Turkish foreign ministry, who briefed the US ambassador in Ankara on the content of the meeting, told him "the Turkish government was heartened by the very forthcoming attitude adopted by Palamas in his meeting with Olcay". According to the same official, Palamas revised the position that the Greek government had limited options for exerting pressure on Makarios and was now convinced that "Clerides would present proposals at the next session of talks which would be acceptable to the Turkish side." The two ministers agreed that the Cyprus talks had long been deadlocked, and Palamas suggested a timescale be set, until September 1971, for a solution to be found. If by then there

---

26 Droushiotis, *Η 'εισβολή' της χούντας*, p. 269.

27 Extracts from Nihat Erim, "Recollections about Cyprus", quoted in Christodoulou, *op. cit.*, p. 525.

28 Laurence Stern, Λάθος άλογο [Wrong Horse] (Nicosia: Tamasos Publications, 1978), p. 115.

was no solution, they would meet in September when they would be at the United Nations, in order to decide what measures Greece and Turkey should take to achieve a solution.[29]

Agreement on the timeframe was confirmed by Palamas, in a conversation with Tasca about the outcome of the talks with Olcay. Palamas told the American ambassador that Denktash's proposals were negotiable and that they could reach a mutually acceptable agreement by September. Otherwise, they would seek another solution in the meeting they would have in New York.[30]

Even more revealing was a conversation Palamas later had with Leonidas Papagos, chamberlain to King Constantine. According to Papagos, Palamas told him he had submitted to Olcay a proposal from George Papadopoulos for a federal solution in Cyprus.[31] Palamas' "magnanimity" was accepted with enthusiasm in Ankara. As Turkish President Sunay remarked to King Constantine when they met in October 1971, "Turkey found an unhoped for assistance personally from Mr. Palamas and from the Greek government," but "the resistance of the Cypriots" had to be overcome.[32]

On 12 June, following the Palamas-Olcay understanding, the Greek government, in a diplomatic note urged Makarios to accept the proposals submitted to Clerides by Denktash. On the thorny issue of local self-government, the Greek note said: "…the Turkish demand concerning safeguarding in the constitution that which is agreed on the powers of Turkish local administration is well-grounded." Beyond the adoption of the Turkish position on local self-government, the Greek government submitted to the Cyprus government a suggestion concerning the "appointment of a Turkish minister or deputy who would be responsible for affairs of local administration in both communities and who would have decisive powers in specific matters." According to the note, the presence of the Turkish "superminister" would safeguard the unity of the state.[33] No sooner had Makarios read the note than he exploded. "They committed themselves to accepting them (the Turkish proposals) and now they are trying to present them to me in a prettified fashion as if I were a little child and they could cheat me," he told his secretary.[34]

On 15 June, the Cypriot Cabinet unanimously rejected the content of the Greek note. Makarios explained to US ambassador David Popper that acceptance of the Greco-Turkish proposals would be tantamount to partition. "I am known to be stubborn, and as long as my head is on my shoulders, I will not yield to divisive Turkish Cypriots or Turkish demands," he said.[35]

On the evening of 19 June, the director of the Fourth Political Bureau of the Greek Foreign Ministry, ambassador Angelos Chorafas, arrived hurriedly in Cyprus on a mission from his government. Makarios was in his summer residence in the Troodos Mountains and Chorafas, accompanied by the Greek ambassador to Nicosia, Constantine Panayiotakos, immediately went there. Chorafas tried to persuade Makarios to accept the proposals and

---

29 Handley to Secretary of State, "Cyprus: Olcay - Palamas meeting", NARA, RG59, CFPF, 1970-1973, Cyprus, telegram 4076, Ankara, 11 June 1971.

30 Tasca to Secretary of State, "Cyprus: meeting with Palamas", NARA, RG59, CFPF, 1970-1973, Cyprus, telegram 2886, Athens, 10 June 1971.

31 Leonidas Papagos, *Σημειώσεις 1967-1977* [Notes 1967-1977] (Athens: Goulandri-Horn Institute), pp. 403-405.

32 *Ibid.*, p. 389.

33 Clerides, *op. cit.*, vol. 3, p. 72.

34 Nitsa Christodoulou, Μακάριος - Ένα προσωπικό ημερολόγιο [Makarios – A Personal Diary] (Published illegally without the author's permission), p. 33.

35 Popper to Secretary of State, "Cyprus: Makarios digs in", NARA, RG59, CFPF, 1970-1973, Cyprus, telegram 1236, Nicosia, 16 July 1971.

insisted that the presence of the Turkish minister would safeguard the unity of the state. However, Makarios continued to consider this arrangement unacceptable. "Thanks to the unity of the state, which is put forward as an excuse, we shall be turkified, the lot of us. In the end, we shall have a unified turkified state,"[36] he replied to Chorafas, and told him to report to Athens that he preferred the Zurich solution to the Greek proposal.

Having been rebuffed, Chorafas pulled out a letter from Papadopoulos and gave it to Makarios. In the letter, Papadopoulos crudely threatened Makarios with harsh measures. In his letter, the Greek Prime Minister refuted reports of a secret Greco-Turkish agreement to remove Makarios from power, adding: "The soundness of judgement for which you are known give me hope that even at the eleventh hour you will wish to revise your decisions. If the opposite occurs, if you insist on shattering our common front, I am obliged to inform you that you bear the heaviest responsibility vis-à-vis the Greeks of Cyprus, the Greek nation generally and history itself. In such an eventuality, the Greek government will find itself faced with the harsh necessity of taking those measures demanded by the national interest and the well-understood interest of Cyprus Hellenism, however bitter these may be."[37]

Makarios gave a written response to Athens on 24 June, in which he focussed on the question of the appointment of a Turkish minister or deputy minister who would have responsibility for local government affairs. Rejecting the Greek government's assertion regarding the safeguarding of the unity of the state, he wrote: "I disagree with this view. The determination of areas of local administration on the basis of race already shatters at its core the unity of the state, or, through the appointment of a Turkish minister for local government, leads to that very thing.

"A Turkish minister, taking into consideration that he will exercise authority and control over already separate authorities of first and second degree local government, will in form and substance represent the central vehicle of local government. Moreover, I find nationally unacceptable the subordination of the local government affairs of Greeks to a Turkish minister, for the sake of superficial unity of the state (...) The Greek government believes that the present, existing enclaves will vanish merely by satisfying the Turkish Cypriots on the matter of local government in the above way (...) but the enclaves, through the preceding acceptance of local government, do not go away. On the contrary, they are made permanent and legitimised."

Commenting on the threats of "bitter" measures, Makarios wrote in his answer: "The content of this paragraph gives the impression of the utterance of a threat, although I find it difficult to accept as accurate the ensuing interpretation and impression. If, however, the paragraph in question does indeed constitute a threat, it pains me to state that it creates an unacceptable situation, which, as the representative of Cyprus Hellenism, I am unable to ignore. Consequently, it would be desirable to have the requisite clarifications, so as to be able to pursue harmonious cooperation to the benefit of our common national cause."[38]

On 6 July, in an interview with the newspaper *Ellinikos Voras* Malarios was asked if he felt life was in danger, and if such a threat came from "a conspiracy instigated from abroad". He replied: "I find it difficult to give a positive answer as to what degree there is a threat against my life. I believe, however, that if there are plans being hatched against Cy-

---

36 Nitsa Christodoulou, *op. cit.*, p. 34.

37 Constantinos Panayiotakos, *Στην πρώτη γραμμή αμύνης...* [On the First Line of Defence...] (Athens, 1979), p. 345.

38 Makarios III, Archbishop of Cyprus, Άπαντα [Complete Works] (Nicosia: Archbishop Makarios III Foundation), vol. IB, p. 699.

prus, in any circles whatsoever, I cannot be very popular in such circles... I have survived thirteen prime ministers of Greece. I shall survive the fourteenth also."[39]

Apart from the Greco-Turkish alliance, Makarios by mid-1971 also had to face the threat of George Grivas, who was preparing to come to Cyprus to initiate military action against him. In an attempt to close down this front, Makarios tried to approach Grivas once more to make him review his plans. He therefore opened contacts with the *Enosis* faction, briefing its leadership on the Greco-Turkish approach to the Cyprus issue. In one such encounter with the president of DEK, Takis Evdokas, the latter suggested he invite Grivas to return to Cyprus. Makarios left the door ajar, though this caused difficulties given the confrontation he had had with the Greek government: "When you see Grivas, tell him we shall see what we can do," he told him.[40] Evdokas informed the pro-Grivas Member of Parliament, George Tjirkotis, and asked him to transmit Makarios' message to Grivas. Tjirkotis went to Athens and met Grivas at his house in Chalandri, on 28 May 1971. Grivas repeated the condition he had laid down on the previous occasion, that Makarios should publicly call on him to return to Cyprus.[41]

On 14 June, Tjirkotis met Makarios, and reported Grivas' conditions. What was said during that meeting is reported in a letter that Tjirkotis sent to Grivas the following day:

1. His Beatitude sincerely wishes to meet you. This may be because he fears the imminent crisis, and because at that moment he will face it alone.
2. He is aware that a solution to the Cyprus problem is looming that is against the national interest.
3. He calculates that the crisis will break out in September.
4. He is determined to reject any solution that is against the national interest.
5. Until the crisis, he is bound by the line he has laid down with the Greek government.[42]

Pursuing his contacts with Grivas' entourage, Makarios met with Socratis Eliades, who at that time had a strong interest in seeing progress in the effort to reconcile Makarios and Grivas. The reason was that he had submitted an application the Ministry of Commerce and Industry for a long-term lease of Snake Island in Kyrenia, aiming at its tourist development in cooperation with Crown Agents, a British organisation. Eliades raised the matter with Makarios during their encounter. Makarios was disposed to cede the island to him on condition he achieved his own aim.

Eliades discussed the matter with Bishop Anthimos of Kitium, in a telephone conversation on 24 June:

"Eliades: I have had a misunderstanding with the guys in England (the men from Crown Agents) because they want to come to Cyprus to meet with our government, and I cannot tell them to come.

Anthimos: I urged Lefteris [Papadopoulos] to write to them to wait for a more appropriate time, given the situation.

E: But is the situation so critical? You know the situation well, since you are going up to see Grivas, you see, my journey did a lot of good.

A: Yes, right.

E: I don't think they'll force a solution on us.

A: You'll see, and soon too. In 15 days at most.

---

39 Droushiotis, *Η 'εισβολή' της χούντας*, p. 276.

40 Athanasiou, *op. cit.*, p. 159.

41 *Ibid.*

42 Ibid, p. 166

E: As quickly as that? They [the Junta] are bastards and we'd better get moving. Does Makarios accept the thoughts we spoke of?

A: Yes, yes, he accepts a reconciliation, because he is sitting on hot coals.

E: Why don't you go to Athens, then?

A: I told him [Makarios] that if he does not authorise me, I shall go by myself. He told me to wait for him to brief me first about the situation and then we'd see. I am telling him, if events overtake you, that's it, the affair is done for this time, because there is the probability that [George] Papadopoulos will react.

E: So he wants the old man [Grivas to return to Cyprus]?

A: Of course he does.

E: Since he does, let him tell us so, and we have a way of bringing him secretly at night without anyone being the wiser.

A: It's not so simple, my dear man; he is being followed step by step, and will not be able to get out of there.

E: We've got a way of getting him here immediately, as long as Makarios presents no obstacle; as for the matter of responsibility, we'll let them off the hook and say it was done without his knowledge. But if he does not object, as I said, he's got to make a deal, all legal, etc.

A: Let me see him on Sunday and afterwards we'll meet and talk it over."[43]

While Socratis Eliades pressed for cooperation between Makarios and Grivas, Lefteris Papadopoulos wrote an article against Makarios in *Patris*. Eliades was indignant, but could not curb him. He tried, therefore, to limit his role, sending a letter to Grivas in which he accused Papadopoulos and Papaphotis of being fanatics and extremists. As is reported in a note from the Cyprus Central Intelligence Agency (KYP), Eliades had a telephone conversation with Spyros Papageorgiou informing him of the contents of his letter, and saying:

1. The situation prevailing in Cyprus is absolutely critical.
2. It is imperative to isolate the fanatical elements, Photis Papaphoti and Lefteris Papadopoulos, who put suggestions to Grivas that are inspired by hate and passion, not caring about whether Cyprus is destroyed - as long as Makarios is snuffed out.
3. Cyprus must be saved in view of the serious dangers it faces, even if Makarios survives.[44]

Makarios thought Eliades was playing a double game. Eliades tried to communicate with him, in order to explain that he had nothing to do with the attacks in *Patris*. On 28 June, the questions of Snake Island, the *Patris* article and the eventual cooperation between Makarios and Grivas were all discussed in a telephone conversation between Eliades and businessman Stavros Galatariotis, who played the role of intermediary with Makarios:

"Eliades: About the island, he's got to give me a permit because the country will benefit a lot. I can understand he is against me because he thinks that I am behind all these plots.

Galatariotis: The Archbishop has never accused you. I think those who are spreading rumours are hypocrites.

E: I changed the day after the Greeks left [he is referring to the departure of the Greek Brigade from Cyprus]. But I told myself not to make my bed where I was spitting the day before. I keep up appearances. Take *Patris* today, it stinks. It is put out by some

---

43 Telephone conversation between Socratis Eliades and Bishop Anthimos of Kitium, recorded by Cyprus KYP.

44 Telephone conversation between Socratis Eliades and Spyros Papageorgiou, recorded by Cyprus KYP.

patriots, guerrillas etc who come here too, but I can't kick them out because they'd go to the old man [Grivas] and I don't want to upset him.

G: I've said many times you can help Makarios and your country.

E: I've come out in favour of reconciliation, even if it is just a formal one, and the Archbishop knows it.

G: He wants it, but they don't let him, neither here nor in Athens.

E: I did what I could with your friend the Bishop of Kitium, and I went to see the old man. But unfortunately, with his speech to EFEK [National Association of Cypriot Students], he blew it all. Hey, old man, I told him: we're trying to cool things down, and you fire off a five-page speech against Makarios, blow out the window panes and pull up the pegs. After that, of course Makarios quite rightly thinks I'm playing a double game because he tells the Bishop of Kitium, where's your friend Socratis now? That's why I want to see him, to put him straight.

G: OK, I'll fix it so you see him.

E: I am anti-Makarios, I admit it, but not to that extent.

G: If it weren't for Makarios, we'd all be wearing a fez, assuming we'd got a head left, that is, and you can see that after Grivas' speech it's quite understandable that he should get you wrong.

E: It's Makarios' fault a bit too, though, because on two occasions he took us for a ride, while the old man is honest, since when you tell him something about Cyprus, he cries.

G: You've got to admit that the old man is also a bit shallow, because anyone who cares about Cyprus has to keep cool and not believe whatever someone happens to tell him."[45]

At that time, the prerequisites for a wider front against the Junta were theoretically in place, since the position of the pro-*Enosis* factions on the Cyprus issue were substantially the same as those of Makarios. The *Enosis* faction, though suspicious of Makarios, believed Papadopoulos was ready to sell Cyprus out to Turkey. In fact, Spyros Papageorgiou at that time published a series of highly critical articles in *Patris* against Papadopoulos' overtures to Turkey. The Athens newspaper *Acropolis* published a commentary on 1 July 1971, in which it reported growing unity in Cyprus around the figure of Makarios, a fact which the newspaper called "a consolation, and encouraging". The picture of Cypriots rallying round Makarios bothered Grivas, who, according to Papageorgiou, "...furiously cut out the commentary, marked the lines concerning unity with red ink and wrote in his own hand his observation in the margin, sending it to his associates in Cyprus: "See what you've done!"[46]

Makarios again discussed the domestic situation with the President of DEK, Takis Evdokas, who pointed out the danger of open conflict with the Athens regime, which controlled the National Guard. In order to avert this danger, Evdokas proposed to Makarios: "Bring Grivas therefore, so that then we can all rally round you." Makarios, however, was negative: "That would be a direct challenge to Papadopoulos and I do not want a confrontation." Evdokas briefed Socratis Eliades on his conversation with Makarios, and the two of them went to Athens on 4 July 1971, met with Grivas and set out the latest developments, Makarios' position and their appraisal of the situation. However, their attempt to bring

45 Telephone conversation between Socratis Eliades and Stavros Galatariotis, recorded by Cyprus KYP.

46 Papageorgiou, *Μακάριος*, p. 78.

Makarios and Grivas together was in vain. "The General was already determined to return to Cyprus and he was now working on various plans."[47]

What were Grivas' plans for Cyprus? At that time he sent an order to Croesus Christodoulides, who was organising EOKA B, to draw up a plan to occupy the Karpass and to tie down government forces in the peninsula. The exact content of Grivas' order is unknown, but the above is deduced from Christodoulides' answer, which came into the hands of the Director of Cyprus KYP, Georgios Tombazos. In his "top-secret" reply concerning "the order to study the occupation of the Karpass", Christodoulides, who wrote under the pseudonym "Davakis", said the "above action should perhaps not be carried out" because of a lack of manpower, means and an organised system of administrative supervision. Christodoulides also mentioned that the mooted operation was untimely, "because until now I was in the stage of organising, and Famagusta especially is making no progress as far as placing cadres is concerned. Secondly, there would be no tactical or strategic gain, because it is not possible to maintain occupied areas or focal points, due to the lack of strength in guerrilla numbers, precisely because of the issue of their organisation and composition." Christodoulides suggested that the ground should be well prepared beforehand, "in accordance with the rules of subversive warfare (...) with the later aim being a coup against the government".[48]

What purpose would such an action in the Karpass have served? There was a Turkish enclave in the area, Gallinoporni, and the peninsula had moreover since 1964 had been earmarked for a military base for Turkey. Its occupation by Grivas' organisation would certainly have provoked Turkish reaction and handed Turkey the pretext for military intervention to liberate the Turkish Cypriots in the enclave. Combining this element with the setting in motion of the Acheson Plan, which made provision for the cession of the Karpass to Turkey, Tombazos calculates that Grivas was driven by unknown circles towards a limited coup that would create the preconditions for a Turkish intervention, and a de facto implementation of the Acheson Plan.[49]

Tombazos' assessment is backed by the parallel activities undertaken at the same time by the Turkish paramilitary organisation TMT, together with the Turkish military contingent in Cyprus. In July 1971, alarm bells at the US State Department were set ringing by a telegram from their ambassador in Nicosia David Popper, which included information that Turkey was preparing military action in Cyprus, with the aim of expanding Turkish enclaves and creating a purely Turkish zone.

The Turkish *chargé d'affaires* in Cyprus, Tunabas, had told his American counterpart William Crawford that what was needed on the island was "a line defining the zone of Turkish occupation and control, within the state of Cyprus." This line, according to the Turkish diplomat, would not have the character of international borders, but would be as visible as the administrative boundaries dividing districts. "The administration of the Turkish Cypriot zone will have a federal relationship with that of the Greek Cypriot zone, forming a single sovereign government." After defining the line's boundaries, the Greek Cypriots living in the Turkish zone would have the choice of leaving, while the same would apply to the Turkish Cypriots in the Greek zone.

---

47 Athanasiou, *op. cit.*, p. 174.

48 'Davakis' (Croesus Christodoulides), note to Grivas, submitted by former head of KYP Georgios Tombazos to the Committee on the 'Cyprus File' of the Cyprus House of Representatives, 16 November 1999.

49 Georgios Tombazos, testimony before the Committee on the 'Cyprus File' of the Cyprus House of Representatives, 16 November 1999.

Expressing his "personal" opinion, Tunabas mentioned that the Turkish zone would embrace, as a minimum, Kyrenia, North Nicosia and Northern Famagusta. Replying to a question by Crawford as to Makarios' likely reaction, he answered that "a few extremists, such as Makarios, would have to go." As to the danger of bloodshed and the consequences of such an operation, the Turkish diplomat said the difficulties would be minimal if, as they hoped, "Greece (and the Greek officers in Cyprus) acted in accordance with the public pronouncements of the Greek government, i.e. that her good relations with Turkey were the most important consideration."

Popper wrote in his telegram that the US embassy would not have taken the Turkish diplomat's words seriously if it had not been for specific information from the UN peacekeeping force (UNFICYP) concerning Turkish military movements:

- In the three preceding months, elite Turkish forces in new uniforms had dropped out of their accustomed positions and had been trained in offensive operations. Thus were created three or four units, each consisting of 300-400 men. These units took up positions in areas controlled by the Turks in the Pentadactylos mountain range, from St. Hilarion up to the beginning of the Karpass Peninsula. The movements and training of the units took place in wooded areas, only at night.
- The Turkish enclaves situated outside the northwestern region of Cyprus had been for some days in a state of high alert.
- The Turkish Cypriots had taken up positions, with the aim of speedily occupying, and being able to hold, a line along Myrtou-Skylloura-Northern Nicosia-Tymbou airfield-Northern Famagusta, while needing only minimum support from mainland Turkey. Moreover, the force of the Turkish military contingent was more numerous and more heavily armed than ever before.

According to UNFICYP's calculations, resistance from the National Guard was certain, but not necessarily from the Greek military contingent; for such an operation to be crowned with success in 24 to 36 hours, support from Turkey would be needed. This was estimated to be 48 aircraft for air cover and an air bridge to transport 4,000 men. UNFICYP also estimated that it would itself have to face the movement of 100,000 persons to and from the Turkish zone.[50]

The above information was confirmed to some extent by the commander of the Turkish contingent, Colonel Dogu, who told a US embassy official that Turkey's military contingency plans in Cyprus would be put into action if the stalemate in the talks continued. He added that Turkey could impose a military solution on Cyprus within three days, with minimum difficulty. Dogu said Makarios was trying to turn Cyprus into the Cuba of the Mediterranean, and that Turkey would not allow such a thing. "We do not care what the civilian politicians say. There is a deadline for the intercommunal talks. Of course, Turkey will not allow the negotiations to drag on for another three years," he told the American diplomat. As to the danger of casualties among the Turkish Cypriots, Dogu replied: "In every national struggle there have to be some sacrifices."

Popper linked Dogu's comments with similar positions taken by Brigadier Sol, representing the Turkish general staff at a NATO conference in London. Sol specifically stated

[50] Popper to the State Department, "Cyprus: partition talk", NARA, RG59, CFPF, 1970-1973, Cyprus, telegram 1214, Nicosia, 14 July 1971.

that "the Turkish general staff is prepared to accept high casualties among the Turkish Cypriot community, to protect Turkey's strategic interests in Cyprus".[51]

In July 1971 the situation was dangerously unstable. According to an analysis by the State Department, the Turkish government had decided that the status quo in Cyprus was working against its interests. "It appears that the Turks have made a judgment (in our view a correct one) that with the passage of time the Turkish Cypriot enclaves have been weakened as more Turkish Cypriots re-enter Greek Cypriot economic life, and more emigrate," the report states. In addition, the economic cost in hard currency to Turkey of maintaining the Turkish Cypriots in their enclaves amounted to $20 million a year and was unbearable. Ankara therefore had serious reasons to precipitate matters towards a speedy arrangement. The circumstances, according to the State Department analysis, were in Turkey's favour:

- After Nihat Erim's rise to power, "the military had greater influence in the decision-making process. And the Turkish general staff was more inclined towards taking immediate action on Cyprus than were the politicians."
- Prime Minister Erim "had a long and intimate association with the Cyprus problem, and was chief Turkish negotiator in the period 1963-64, when the solution of the Cyprus problem by geographical partition of the island, giving one part to Greece and the other to Turkey (the essence of the 1964 Acheson Plan), was very much in vogue".

Makarios, however, remained stubborn in his refusal to countenance any solution that would satisfy Turkish aspirations. As the State Department analysis sets out, "the unyielding position of the Archbishop concerning partition and the clear orientation of the Turkish government during the recent months towards the position that partition may be the only acceptable solution, give rise to real concern." The conclusion of the State Department was that, given the estimation that "the Turks and Turkish Cypriots are not disposed to put up with the continuation of the status quo, we may foresee increased pressure for a 'solution' through a successful outcome to the talks (for the Turks), or, if the talks were to fail, through the imposition by Greece and Turkey of an agreed arrangement, or through unilateral action on the part of Turkey by means of a dismemberment of the island by force."[52]

Such was State Department's analysis of the situation in Cyprus in mid-summer 1971, just as Grivas was preparing to return secretly to Cyprus in order to overthrow Makarios. At the end of July, Fletcher, a British Secret Service agent, discussed the situation with Member of Parliament George Tjirkotis. Tjirkotis was a fanatic anti-communist and enthusiastic supporter of Grivas. He wrote to Grivas how he met with Fletcher every two or three months and discussed "the communist threat and its expansion in Cyprus". In a meeting they had on 29 July, Fletcher expressed his pessimism to Tjirkotis, and "stressed the critical nature of the situation after the non-acceptance by the entire Cypriot people of the Papadopoulos proposals" for the solution of the Cyprus problem. In view of Makarios' expected refusal to accept the solution of the Cyprus issue as envisaged by the West, Fletcher asked Tjirkotis to sound out Grivas concerning the following: "I understand that in the past General Grivas had accepted one of the variations of the Acheson Plan. If in the future this plan is reintroduced, or another similar one, would General Grivas be disposed to accept it? I would ask you, if you could, to give me a specific answer as soon as possible, because I am

---

51 Popper to Secretary of State, "Cyprus: Turk contingent commander on military intervention and partition", NARA, RG59, CFPF, 1970-1973, Cyprus, telegram 1232, Nicosia,16 July 1971.

52 Rogers to American Embassy Ankara, Athens, Nicosia, "Cyprus: current situation", NARA, NPMS, NSC, Cyprus/Greece, telegram 131443, State Department, 20 July 1971.

drawing up a report for my government. Naturally, there will still be difficulties, because I surmise that even if General Grivas, the Greek and Turkish governments accept such a plan, Makarios would again reject it."

Tjirkotis told Fletcher he would communicate with Grivas and would give him an answer. Previously, however, he had told him that, if "General Grivas accepts such a plan, and if the Greek and Turkish governments jointly come to an agreement after General Grivas does, then you should not fear a possible refusal by Makarios, because all you have to do is to send General Grivas to Cyprus and there will be no problem at all."[53]

Grivas instructed Tjirkotis to meet Fletcher once more and ask him for Britain's help for his coming to Cyprus. The second Tjirkotis-Fletcher meeting took place on 6 August. Tjirkotis briefed Lefteris Papadopoulos on the exchanges. Papadopoulos then sent Grivas a detailed note in which he mentioned that Tjirkotis had told Fletcher that "the General would not refuse to discuss the efforts for a solution that would lead towards *Enosis*, now more necessary than ever because of the support Russia had obtained through Makarios' policies, but that this would not be possible for as long as he remained in Greece." And he added: "if you wish for talks with him you must find a way of bringing him over." He ended: "you must bear in mind, Mr. Fletcher, that the General is not anti-British, even if we have been in conflict. The General, like me, is anti-communist."

The British agent replied: "I am delighted that the General is flexible. Ever since he left, communism in Cyprus has increased three hundred times." Fletcher pledged to give a favourable briefing to his government.[54]

The above correspondence was found in EOKA B archives confiscated by the police, and was published, together with a photocopy of the hand-written note by Lefteris Papadopoulos, in *Phileftheros* newspaper in November 1973, while Grivas and Tjirkotis were still alive. Neither of the two, nor Lefteris Papadopoulos himself, put its authenticity in doubt.

---

53 "Γρίβας - Ιντέλιτζενς Σέρβις" [Grivas – Intelligence Service], *Phileftheros*, 28 November 1973.

54 "Προκάλεσε σάλον η αποκάλυψις διά συνεργασίαν Γρίβα - Ιντέλιτζενς Σέρβις" [Revelation of Grivas-Intelligence Service Collaboration Sparks Commotion] *Phileftheros*, 29 November 1973.

2. The Grivas Campaign and Double *Enosis*

In August 1971, Grivas was making final arrangements for his clandestine return to Cyprus. He had set August 28 as the date for his departure from Athens. His escape was organised by Cosmas Mastrokolias, while the lawyer and former member of the 'X' organisation, Constantinos Efstathopoulos, played an important part.

The operation began at 2.15pm. Efstathopoulos, in a car driven by his son, arrived outside the apartment block in Chalandri, which was being watched by the security forces and where Grivas was staying. Grivas described the manner of his escape in his personal diary[1]: "14.15, as arranged. C. Efstathopoulos gave the signal that all was ready and that the escape route was free of policemen, so that I could get away by car.

"I went down immediately to the basement of the apartment block, where I suddenly found myself facing the concierge in the basement apartment through which I was to escape. I managed to mislead him as to the reason for my descent to the basement, as I opened up a storehouse that was there, full of food provisions and other things of mine. On which he left, and I immediately got out via the chosen route through the basement and got into the car waiting for me, as did Constantinos Efstathopoulos, Costas (my chauffeur) and the Efstathopoulos' son, Spyros, driver of the car."[2] Grivas arrived with his entourage at the marina in Glyfada, where a caique called the *Dolphin* was waiting for him. The boat had been chartered by Mastrokolias, who accompanied Grivas on his journey to Cyprus.

From the contents of his diary, it seems that Grivas left his house in a conspiratorial manner. Nevertheless, as Adonis Kiros (editor of *Estia* newspaper, long the mouthpiece of Grivas in Athens) wrote after the Cyprus tragedy of 1974, "the return of Grivas to Cyprus is shrouded in mystery. It was said he left Athens clandestinely, without the knowledge of the military regime, which was keeping a vigilant watch over him in his house in Chalandri. However, such a scenario is hard to believe, and the most likely is that the only one to be convinced that he left in secret was Grivas himself."[3]

Kiros suggests Grivas left with the knowledge of the regime, which chose to look the other way. Most written sources are in agreement that the decision for Grivas' mission to Cyprus had not been taken by the Greek government, but by the Aslanides-Ioannides group, the hard-core members of the junta. After the success of the 21 April coup, Papadopoulos took on a political role and broke off from the body of the Greek army. Ioannides, however, remained an active officer, and his group were in charge at the time of operation 'Provia', the Greek arm of the 'Stay Behind' network that the US secret services had set up across Europe, ostensibly to face the communist threat.

Many sources show Prime Minister George Papadopoulos declaring ignorance of Grivas' intentions. Deputy Foreign Minister Xanthopoulos Palamas writes that his ministry was only informed after Grivas' departure, and that Papadopoulos had assured him that he had not been informed in time and that Grivas and his friends had conspired together.[4] The later minister of Foreign Affairs, Phedon Kavaleriatos, told Leonidas Papagos, chamberlain

---

1 Grivas was a prolific writer and kept a detailed daily diary. The ultimate whereabouts of his full diary are unknown. A part of it is in the possession of the lawyer Panicos Soteriou, who, during a banquet in Nicosia on 4 June 1995, made public those of its pages that refer to his escape from Greece.

2 Η ζωή και το έργο του Γεωργίου Γρίβα Διγενή, op. cit., p. 129.

3 Droushiotis, *Η 'εισβολή' της χούντας*, p. 304.

4 Christianos Xanthopoulos-Palamas, *Διπλωματικό τρίπτυχο* [Diplomatic Triptych] (Athens: Ekdoseis ton Filon, 1979), p. 236.

to King Constantine, that Papadopoulos had repeatedly told him that it was not he who had sent Grivas to Cyprus.[5] Further, the then head of the National Guard General Staff, Lieutenant General Charalambopoulos, used to say "Ioannides fooled Grivas into going down there [to Cyprus], with false promises".[6] The Cyprus government had information from the beginning that hard-core officers in the junta were involved in the return of Grivas, but failed to judge the degree of involvement of Dimitrios Ioannides.

According to a confidential briefing to foreign journalists by Cyprus Government Spokesman Miltiades Christodoulou, as well as to information leaked to the United Nations from the Cyprus Foreign Ministry, Grivas' return to Cyprus was the work of junta officers Antonios Lekas, Antonios Mexis and Petros Kostellis. Also mentioned were the names of Constantinos Karydas and Ioannis Ladas. All these officers were members of IDEA and among the instigators of the 21 April coup. Lekas, Mexis and Karydas had served in Cyprus and had come into conflict with Makarios.[7]

The *Dolphin*, carrying Grivas and Ioannides' agent Mastrokolias, approached the coast west of Limassol after an eventful journey, on Monday evening, 31 August 1971. Grivas recalled the events in his diary: "At about 19.00 hours we arrived at Pissouri jetty, where I made contact with our people, who were waiting, Lefteris (Papadopoulos) and Panicos (Soteriou), and at about 20.00 hours I disembarked, after saying farewell to the crew and to Mastrokolias, who had accompanied me." From there, he was taken to Panicos Soteriou's house, and later to that of Diana Mavrou, which was his hideout.

There, he met Elli Christodoulidou, who supplied him with clothes and other personal effects, and he immediately began to issue orders: "Let area leaders be appointed. What have Diakos and Rossides done about the mission entrusted to them (tank and artillery unit, heavy infantry weapons)?"[8] Of course, EOKA B was not a regular army and did not have tank and artillery units under its command. As a consequence, the previous year's plans, which had been drawn up by Croesus Christodoulides, seemed to have moved on, and officers of the National Guard had been drawn into the organisation to the extent that Grivas took it for granted that he had at his disposal organised army units with heavy weapons.

Military action was one of Grivas' priorities. Forty-eight hours after his arrival, on 2 September, he wrote in his diary: "I ordered Lefteris Papadopoulos to organise two DEATH squads, with five men in each, operating independently and taking direct orders from me, fully armed with automatic weapons and pistols."[9] In the same diary entry, he wrote that he had named his organisation EOKA B.

Makarios was informed of Grivas' arrival the day after his landing, through a telephone call from the Greek embassy. The Council of Ministers was in session. Makarios interrupted the meeting and called Socratis Eliades to the Presidential Palace to ask him for whatever information he had. Eliades expressed his surprise, and told him he hadn't a clue.

Makarios was to leave that day for Athens, on a prearranged, formal visit – his first contact with the Greek government since the latest crisis over the Cyprus issue. He went ahead

---

5 Papagos, *op. cit.*, p. 486.

6 Charalambos Charalambopoulos, *Περιμένοντας τον «Αττίλα»* [Waiting for 'Attila'] (Athens: Estia, 1992), p. 157.

7 Crawford to Secretary of State, "Cyprus – Grivas". NARA, RG59, CFPF, 1970-1973, Cyprus, telegram 1685, Nicosia, 15 September 1971.

8 Η ζωή και το έργο του Γεωργίου Γρίβα Διγενή, op. cit., p. 131.

9 Ibid.

with the trip despite the developments, and the Grivas question was raised during his talks. George Papadopoulos protested that he was completely in the dark.

Nevertheless, despite the assurances given by Athens that it had no involvement in Grivas' plans, it made absolutely no attempt to disassociate itself from them. On the contrary, deputy Foreign Minister Palamas, in comments to the press, indicated that the Greek government was anything but upset about this development.[10]

Therefore, although Grivas' campaign may not have been at Papadopoulos' behest, Greece accepted the development as a counterbalance to Makarios' refusal to accept a compromise solution on the Cyprus issue.

Turkey was officially informed of Grivas' arrival by the representative of the UN Secretary General, Ozorio Tafal, who, on 8 September, passed on the information to Inhan, the Turkish envoy in Nicosia. The Turkish Foreign Ministry issued a statement broadcast on Turkish radio, which asserted Turkey "could not tolerate" Grivas' return to Cyprus.[11] This announcement was Turkey's only reaction, despite the fact that after the Kofinou events in November 1967, there had been a gentleman's agreement between Athens and Ankara to recall Grivas from Cyprus and confine him to Greece.[12]

According to Inhan, Turkish policy on this issue was:

a) Quietly but firmly to remind the governments of Cyprus and Greece that Turkey would not indefinitely accept the return of Grivas.
b) Stay cool and keep propaganda at a low level.[13]

Moreover, according to a telegram from the American ambassador in Ankara, "Since the flight of Grivas from Athens, the officials in the Turkish Foreign Ministry, including those unconnected with the Cyprus problem, have occasionally commented that his presence on the island could eventually turn out to Turkey's benefit, by bringing about a double *Enosis* solution with the cooperation of the Greek and Turkish governments."[14]

Turkey's accommodating stance caused anxiety among sectors of the Turkish Cypriot community. Turkish Cypriot opposition politician Midhat Berberoglu asked Denktash for explanations. According to an article in *Yeni Duzen*, Berberoglu asked Denktash: "Why have you accepted the return of Grivas, and why have you kept silent and turned a blind eye to his preparations for a new round of terrorist acts?" Denktash replied: "They gave their

---

10 Palamas always nurtured a liking for Grivas. In a letter dated 27 March 1974 to Adamantios Androutsopoulos, prime minister of the Ioannides regime, Palamas said of Grivas: "The Greek government did not send General Grivas to Cyprus. He went there inspired by nationalist instincts. He knew very little. He had underestimated the influence of the Cyprus authorities. He raised the flag of *Enosis*. ...Dighenis offered his services as a patriot to Cyprus. A first reaction made itself felt; a first halt in the slide down the slippery slope." In the same letter, Palamas urged Androutsopoulos to cooperate in the abolition of the Cyprus state and the declaration of *Enosis*, irrespective of the consequences. "*Enosis* would transform Cyprus, or at least four fifths of Cyprus, into a Greek administrative district." (Adamantios Androutsopoulos, *Η μαρτυρία ενός πρωθυπουργού* [A Prime Minister's Testimony] (Athens, 1993), p. 220.)

11 Cuthell to Secretary of State, "Cyprus: Turk reactions to Grivas disappearance and Makarios trip", NARA, RG59, CFPF, 1970-1973, Cyprus, telegram 6112, Ankara, 8 September 1971.

12 Tasca to Secretary of State, "Cyprus: Grivas disappearance", NARA, RG59, CFPF, 1970-1973, Cyprus, telegram 4732, Athens, 8 September 1971. Cuthell to Secretary of State, "Cyprus: Turk reactions to Grivas disappearance and Makarios trip", NARA, RG59, CFPF, 1970-1973, Cyprus, telegram 6112, Ankara, 8 September 1971.

13 Crawford to Secretary of State, "Cyprus/Turkey: GOT posture regarding Grivas' return", NARA, RG59, CFPF, 1970-1973, Cyprus, telegram 1651, Nicosia, 10 September 1971.

14 Handley to Secretary of State, "Cyprus: Grivas situation", NARA, RG59, CFPF, 1970-1973, Cyprus, telegram 8207, Ankara, 2 December 1971.

word that, for as long as Grivas remains in Cyprus, there will be no bloody nose for as much as a single Turk."[15]

Furthermore, Berberoglu told an Ankara newspaper in September 1973 that Denktash had assured him that "Turkey was silently in collusion over the secret arrival of Grivas in Cyprus, and had come to an agreement with Greece over the partition of Cyprus".[16]

Connected with the Turkish reaction to Grivas' arrival was the information leaked by British Intelligence to the president of the London Federation of Cypriot Organisations, Homer Habibis, who communicated it in writing to Makarios, in a note dated 29 October 1971:

"This is a message communicated verbally by a person well known to me for many years. I set down the substance of what he told me with the greatest possible accuracy.

"A few days ago (about 10), the Greek ambassador to London, Sorokos, met with his Turkish counterpart. The Turk said little, while Mr Sorokos was extremely voluble.

"Mr Sorokos told his Turkish colleague that the Greeks and the Turks should be friends and brothers, but this is difficult on account of the Cyprus problem, which has become a thorn in relations between the two countries.

"His government, continued Mr Sorokos, has every reason to hope that soon the problem will be solved. General Grivas has now got powerful support on the island and soon will sweep the Archbishop aside and take power.

"He added that a solution would then be possible. And the only solution that the Greek government considers possible is the partition of Cyprus and the *Enosis* (union) of the two parts with Turkey and with Greece.

"When the Turkish ambassador asked him about (the Cyprus Communist Party) AKEL, he was told that it was a minority and that, 'when we will be in the driving seat' it will be possible to limit its activities and come to an arrangement with it. At one stage of the conversation Mr Sorokos said that this was taking place with the blessing of the Americans."[17]

Secure in the backing of the Greek government, the acquiescence of Turkey and the full support of officers in the National Guard loyal to Ioannides, Grivas began to forge plans to overthrow Makarios.

Ioannides was the only member of the Junta to refuse political office. He remained a serving officer, and as Commander of the Military Security Police (*Elliniki Stratiotiki Astynomia* - ESA), he created his own network for the control of the Greek army and, through it, of the National Guard in Cyprus.

According to the former chief of the National Guard General Staff, Charalambos Charalambopoulos, "Ioannides or his minions" kept all the officers who were posted in Cyprus informed.[18] Thus, the officers holding key posts in the National Guard were pent up against Makarios, whom they considered pro-communist and hostile to *Enosis*.

Ioannides' number one man in Cyprus was his personal friend, Brigadier General Pavlos Papadakis, who arrived on the island on 25 September 1971, a little after Grivas, and was made Commander of the Greek Military Contingent. Papadakis was in regular contact with Ioannides, making frequent trips to Athens for consultations. He also forged links with

---

15 Papageorgiou, *Μακάριος*, p. 108.

16 "Εδόθη διαβεβαίωσις στον Ντενκτάς ότι ο Γρίβας δεν θα βλάψη Τούρκους" [Denktash Given Assurances that Grivas will not Harm the Turks], *Phileleftheros*, 16 September 1973.

17 Papageorgiou, *Μακάριος*, p. 110.

18 Charalambopoulos, *op. cit.*, p. 155.

Grivas' confidant in Nicosia, Socrates Eliades, through whom he communicated messages from Ioannides.

In the General Staff, matters concerning EOKA B were handled by the Second Staff Bureau. Its head at the time when Grivas arrived in Cyprus was Colonel Pantelis Lalaounis, who set up an EOKA B support network in the National Guard, using the Second Bureau of the Supreme Tactical Commands, as well as the Second Bureau of the units. These bureaux functioned as virtual administrative centres for EOKA B. The Second Bureau also infiltrated reserve officer associations[19], promoting people who had been thoroughly vetted. Lalaounis recruited many of the members of the associations as agents.

The work of the Second Bureau of the National Guard General Staff was complemented by the local section of the Greek Central Intelligence Agency (KYP), which had its headquarters in a building adjacent to the Greek embassy. The man who pulled the strings in Greek KYP was Vasilis Vintzileos, who was in Cyprus as a consular official, but in reality was the brain behind the local section of the agency for eight successive years, from 1966 until 1974. Through officers loyal to Ioannides and Greek KYP, which was an extension of the CIA, EOKA B came under the control of the Greek Gladio.

The complete identification of the National Guard General Staff with the Grivas faction and the infiltration of the Association of Reserve Officers by Lalaounis provoked reactions even among Grivas supporters, on account of the frostiness felt towards George Papadopoulos as a result of his Cyprus policy. Among those who reacted was journalist Spyros Papageorgiou, who discussed the issue on the telephone with Lefteris Papadopoulos:

Papageorgiou: "I have been informed that the reserve officers were, without exception, established on arrival on the island as the Praetorian Guard of the Greek regime and have been infiltrated.

Papadopoulos: No, come on. OK, there are some bastards in their ranks but I think we're unfair on them.

Papageorgiou: I wanted to tell you something about [Spyros] Arotis, because I see him in all pro-Junta demonstrations, either in anti-Lyssarides demonstrations or in demonstrations in Kiti, or elsewhere.

Papadopoulos: Was he at Kiti?

Papageorgiou: Yes, together with Gambroudis[20] and the rest. I don't like this – for no other reason than that they shouldn't think that they can always plant their own men among us, to follow us and impose situations on us. Either they are with us, or they follow the orders of the Junta. I'll be asking for some explanations, both about this and their cooperation with Lalaounis, because I have been tipped off that they have the reserve officers earmarked as praetorians and as the force and fist which will strike here, so as not to use their own men."[21]

Papageorgiou's position was an indication of the chasm between the Junta and pro-*Enosis* factions in the early stages of EOKA B. However, with the passing of time, Greek KYP and the Second Bureau would absorb almost all the *Enosis* faction into their ranks. This success was due to the Junta's efforts in subordinating the pro-*Enosis* press, which it funded.

---

19 They were openly pro-Grivas, founded by the General when he was commander of the Cyprus Supreme Military Defence Command.

20 An active agent of Lalaounis, who, with the help of the National Guard General Staff, was elected president of the Association of Reserve Officers.

21 Telephone conversation between Spyros Papageorgiou and Lefteris Papadopoulos, recorded by Cyprus KYP.

According to a State Department analysis, even before Grivas returned to Cyprus, "Greece got *Mesimvrini* on its payroll, helped *Agon* and probably gained some influence with *Eleftheria*". With Grivas' arrival, *Proini* took off, while *Patris* "suddenly acquired enough money to publish twice a week". Furthermore, after 18 months' suspension of publication due to financial difficulties, the fortnightly journal *O Kosmos Simera* was again in circulation. According to the State Department, "the fact that it [*O Kosmos Simera*] supports Grivas and undermines Makarios in a devious fashion is no surprise at all".[22] The journal's publishers were the mainland Greek photojournalist Babis Avdelopoulos, and Cypriot Themis Ioannides. However, in reality, Vasilis Vintzileos controlled it. His offices were effectively a branch of the local section of Greek KYP, and the publication served as the Service's mouthpiece.[23]

One of the regime's agents also active in the press was Andreas Dimitropoulos, a former Special Forces officer who had served in Cyprus from 1964–67. When he returned to Greece, he was demobbed and worked as a journalist in the newspaper *Estia*. In the frequent telephone conversations he had with *Mesimvrini* in Nicosia, he issued orders to its publisher, George Hadjinicolaou, regarding the cover-up of events connected to Grivas' arrival in Cyprus.

According to information from Cyprus KYP, it was Dimitropoulos who first gave out the information that Grivas had disappeared from Athens. On 2 September 1971, he told Hadjinicolaou that Grivas had vanished from his house and he urged him to publish the information. Hadjinicolaou replied he would first ask Lalaounis. "He'll tell you not to do it, as the Greek government has not issued an announcement. The point is to be law-abiding and for your paper to survive," countered Dimitropoulos.

Subsequently, Hadjinicolaou conveyed the information to Spyros Papageorgiou and asked his opinion as to whether he should publish it:

"Papageorgiou: So what could have happened to Grivas?

Hadjinocalaou: Well, either he got away or they got him.

Papageorgiou: It's hard to verify it, and it will bother them (2nd Bureau and embassy) over here, because Grivas was under police surveillance. How do I know how they'll take it? OK, did this guy tell you this as a fact, or as a rumour?

Hadjinocalaou: I don't know, he says they're his people; he's in thick with Ioannides himself over there. Did they bring him here in view of Makarios' trip to Athens?

Papageorgiou: If it's true, it's big news. There must be something up, though, because I've been informed that Makarios was worried and called S. Eliades for a meeting, but I don't know what for. They are going to meet this morning at 9 o'clock."[24]

Hadjinicolaou subsequently communicated with Lalaounis at the General Staff Headquarters, and briefed him on Grivas' disappearance and on the meeting between Eliades and Makarios. Lalaounis urged him to publish the news of Grivas' disappearance in all its details, without using his name, however. Hadjinicolaou published the news on 2 September, marking it an "international exclusive". After *Mesimvrini*'s revelation, Grivas' disappear-

22 Letter from Crawford to Boyatt, dated 19 November 1971, NARA, RG59, CFPF, 1970-1973, Cyprus.

23 Droushiotis, *Η 'εισβολή' της χούντας*, p. 317.

24 Telephone conversation between Spyros Papageorgiou and Georgios Hadjinicolaou, recorded by Cyprus KYP.

ance became hot news in Cypriot and Greek bulletins, while the international press gave it extensive coverage.

Grivas' arrival in Cyprus and the activities of pro-Grivas Greek officers coincided with the talks being held between Makarios and Papadopoulos in Athens. The pair discussed disagreements over Cyprus, while Makarios took advantage of the opportunity to raise the issue of the Greek embassy's behaviour in undermining him:

"Newspapers supporting the Greek government are publishing articles against me and are stirring up the people. Is it not true, Your Excellency," he said, turning towards Panayiotakos, the Greek ambassador in Cyprus, "that *Mesimvrini* receives £300 every month from the Greek embassy?" "No", retorted Panayiotakos. "I am delighted to hear it denied," Makarios told him, "because I had heard otherwise. Furthermore, is it not true, Your Excellency, that the Association of Reserve Officers, which receives from the embassy the monthly sum of £500, is stirring things up against me?"[25] As Makarios reported, Papadopoulos "didn't appear to be in the know" on everything that was happening in Nicosia, and he expressed the wish for cooperation and understanding with Cyprus. "Your Beatitude, I know you to be a tough negotiator, but I believe it possible for us to work together," he told the Archbishop. Makarios responded: "That is curious, for do you know what they accuse me of in Cyprus? My conciliatoriness…"[26]

At that meeting, Makarios brought up the question of those officers taking action against him, and Papadopoulos told him to request their recall. At the end of September, Makarios did indeed request the recall of certain officers. This was leaked to the press, and a foreign journalist asked Makarios what he would do in the event that all the officers left Cyprus. "If this decision is taken by the Greek government, we can staff the National Guard with other officers," he replied.[27] This put Lalaounis in a rage, and he telephoned the head of recruitment in Greece, Christos Maniopoulos. Lalaounis told him that Makarios' speech had caused reactions among officers, "who were urged to remain calm until relevant orders were received".

"As to the issue at hand, it is advisable for the Armed Forces Headquarters to acquiesce in the submission of questions to Makarios, who will be called upon to give clarifications as to the nationality of the officers that will make up the National Guard." Lalaounis told his interlocutor the following: "Makarios should be asked what nationality they should be, Reds, Yellows, Greens, in other words, in his eyes what shit will they be – will they be Turks?"[28]

Indicative of relations between the Cyprus government and the Greek officers was the following conversation between the head of the Second Bureau of Supreme Tactical Command in Famagusta, Theodoros Frangoyannis and Lalaounis. Frangoyannis had asked Lalaounis to take ensure that the son of police lieutenant Ioannis Vlasiou, Zacharias, would not be transferred from Famagusta. Frangoyannis called the police lieutenant a "good friend and close associate". The following conversation ensued:

Lalaounis: Don't say anything about this, because that faggot Tombazos (Head of Cyprus KYP) is taping everything. Whoever we think is a good man, he thinks is useless. I am telling you this so that that dentist wanker, who came to make us wear glasses, hears it all.

---

25 Nitsa Christodoulou, *op. cit.*, p. 36.
26 *Ibid.*
27 "Οι Έλληνες Αξιωματικοί" [The Greek Officers], *Mesimvrini*, 22 September 1971.
28 Telephone conversation between Pantelis Lalaounis and Theodoros Frangoyannis, recorded by Cyprus KYP.

Frangoyannis: If he's a dentist, that's all he knows.
Lalaounis: He eats shit and he talks shit, but the time of crisis will come and then we'll see about it. Then he'll be looking to change passport. The wanker thinks I don't know he's spying on me. But I'm sorry I can't have him followed, so I could hang out his dirty washing - because he's got some, and I haven't.
Frangoyannis: Let's have him watched, then.
Lalaounis: Nah, I don't need to. I don't deal with shit. Whoever gets mixed up with shit gets eaten by chickens."[29]

At the beginning of November 1971, Lalaounis and sergeant major Grigoris Perdikis approached Panicos Kapsosideris, who had access to the Presidential Palace, and asked him to help them place a microphone in Makarios' office.[30] In the light of that incident, Makarios made representations to Athens and requested Lalaounis' recall. Lalaounis replied through the columns of *Patris*, under the headline, "If Lalaounis goes, we all go!" The article read: "*Patris* is today in a position to reveal that Mr Makarios has indeed asked for the expulsion of Greek officers from Cyprus. This constitutes one of the momentary reappearances of his permanent anti-Greek polemic. He has based himself on the whispers and reports of his stool pigeons, namely that these Greek officers were supposedly involved in machinations against him. Similar attempts of his in the past have been absolutely successful." A stark warning ensued: "If Lalaounis goes, we all abandon Cyprus."[31] Ultimately, Lalaounis was not recalled from Cyprus. He remained in his post in the Second Bureau of the General Staff, and was almost exclusively concerned with EOKA B.

Makarios initially chose not to come into conflict with Grivas, and for about two months after Grivas' secret landing, he did not speak out against him. On the contrary, he sent him messages offering cooperation and promised him political positions – such as Defence Minister – with a view to bringing him out of hiding and undercutting his plans to form armed units. Nevertheless, Grivas remained silent. He neither made any announcement about his plans, nor answered Makarios' offers of cooperation. However, the press that supported him rejected Makarios' overtures as traps: "Leader Dighenis wants neither office, nor ministries, nor greatness, for he rejects with disgust the insidious offer of Mr Makarios and his mouthpieces," wrote *Patris*. "Besides, these offers reflect neither honesty nor good intentions, but are a trap to eliminate Dighenis."[32]

Makarios had information indicating Grivas' aim was to oppose him by force. In schools, student cells had been set up, which, under the guidance of the Second Bureau, organised pro-*Enosis* demonstrations. In charge of the student demonstrations was sergeant major Grigoris Perdikis, who reported directly to Lalaounis.

Makarios' "tolerance period" came to an end on 29 October 1971, when he issued a televised proclamation warning Grivas that his illegal activity would only serve the partitionist plans of the Turks, and pointing out that "it was incredibly naïve to carry out a struggle for *Enosis* with armed units." He added that he would declare *Enosis* without a moment's hesitation if the Greek government would give its consent, but whenever he brought up the issue, the stance from Athens was negative. He also called into question

29 *Ibid.*
30 Nitsa Christodoulou, *op. cit.*, p. 47.
31 "Εάν φύγη ο Λαλαούνης θα φύγωμεν όλοι μας!" [If Lalaounis goes we all go], *Patris*, 6 December 1971.
32 "Εις το κενόν η παγίς του Μακαρίου - Θέσεις δεν θέλει ο Διγενής" [Makarios' Trap Exposed – Dighenis does not want any Offices], *Patris*, 18 October 1971.

Grivas' judgement, and said he had been lured into an adventure that would turn out to be disastrous for him.[33]

At the same time, Makarios began to take the first measures against Grivas. On 6 November, the government announced the first dismissals of civil servants on the grounds of public interest, and on 11 November the Council of Ministers ordered the creation of a special corps in the police aimed at suppressing lawlessness.

In the opposing camp, the Coordinating Committee for the *Enosis* Struggle (*Epitropi Sintonismou Enotikou Agona* - ESEA) was founded, acting as the political wing of EOKA B. ESEA's foundation was announced after a conference at the main office of the Federation of Reserve Officers, which had been thoroughly vetted by the Second Bureau of the General Staff. The executive wing of ESEA was the governing council, whose legal president was George Vasiliades, vice-president Takis Evdokas, and whose general secretary was Photis Papaphotis, who was still in prison serving a four-month sentence for slandering the President of the Republic. He was released on 29 January, a few days after the foundation of ESEA.

In its first proclamation, ESEA described itself as "a purely nationalist movement, above party politics". It sang the praises of the military and leadership qualities of Dighenis, who "will lead the people of Cyprus to new triumphs", and declared that it would fight for *Enosis*, together with all local forces.[34]

Grivas organised EOKA B on the model of EOKA itself. He divided Cyprus into sectors and at the head of each put a sector chief. The most important sector was Limassol, whose chief was Greek Army Major Stavros Stavrou-Syros. Syros had served in Rhodes, and in the autumn of 1971 he voluntarily accepted demobilisation, and arrived in Cyprus to enlist in EOKA B.[35] Other sector heads were Aris Hadjigeorgiou in Nicosia, Kikis Constantinou and Panicos Pamboris in Famagusta and George Raftis in Paphos. Lefteris Papadopoulos was the treasurer of the organisation. Just as in the case of EOKA, there was no administrative staff structure. Grivas kept all powers in his own hands and issued orders to the sector heads, who carried them out.

Apart from the Cypriot sector heads, Grivas asked Cosmas Mastrokolias to get in touch with Major George Carusos, who was in confinement on the island of Samothrace, and ask him to escape and come to Cyprus. According to Carousos, Mastrokolias visited him in December 1971 and gave him Grivas' message. He accepted the invitation, and, with Mastrokolias's help, got ready to escape.

On 1 January 1972, the Greek regime lifted martial law and released all political prisoners. Carousos, now free, got in contact with Mastrokolias, who arranged his immediate departure for Cyprus in a caique. "I landed near Pissouri, on 12 January 1972. I hitchhiked to Limassol and met Marios Christodoulides, who led me to Grivas' hideout, in Diana Mavros' house," Carousos recalled.[36] Subsequently, he established himself in Nicosia and assumed duties as second in command to Grivas.

As far as armaments were concerned, Grivas initially depended on weapons that his sector heads had kept since the time of EOKA. He also ordered raids on National Guard de-

---

33 Makarios III, Archbishop of Cyprus, Άπαντα [Complete Works] (Nicosia: Archbishop Makarios III Foundation), vol. ΙΓ, p. 503.

34 Droushiotis, *Η 'εισβολή' της χούντας*, p. 324.

35 A short while after his arrival, Syros returned to Athens. Lalaounis sent the agent Sotiris Gambroudis after him to follow his movements closely. Greek KYP estimated that Syros was an agent of the Greek Intelligence Service, which was following him in order to confirm his intentions.

36 George Carousos, interview with the author.

pots. A large quantity of weapons was stolen in December 1971 from a warehouse of a reservist battalion at Trikomo. Investigations showed that soldiers involved in EOKA B had taken part in the operation and that it had been carried out with the help of Greek National Guard officers Karahalios, Frangoyannis and Lalaounis.[37] Later, EOKA B was to take possession of a large quantity of Kalashnikov automatics, bought from Lebanese arms smugglers.

Writing about the financing of the organisation, Spyros Papageorgiou says the organisation "needed thousands of pounds a month to cover payments and to support those of its members who had been obliged to become outlaws. Who paid for these sums? The question is not posed for reasons of 'gossip'; it is a matter of substance. Whoever pays wants control. Who paid, and who exercised control in the case of EOKA B? Individuals, however wealthy, could not take on such an economic burden. Naturally, there were those who, out of dedication or calculation, made substantial donations. There were also the 'appeals to honour'. However, the expenses were far greater, and no private purse could possibly have covered them. Grivas took the secret with him to his grave, and it is kept well hidden in the uneasy consciences of two or three people."[38]

These two or three people were the ship owner Andreas Potamianos, Cosmas Mastrokolias and Socrates Eliades, through whom EOKA B was supported financially. In July 1974, Makarios named Potamianos as the main source of EOKA B funding. Also, according to evidence found by Cyprus authorities in the archives of EOKA B, the organisation received annual economic assistance from Athens to the tune of one million pounds.[39]

In an interview he gave to Eric Rouleau of the French newspaper *Le Monde* in September 1974, Makarios also referred to evidence the government had of direct funding of EOKA B by American sources: "For example, we found a cheque of $33,000, which was made out in the United States in the name of Dimitris Haholiades, a leading cadre in EOKA B, who could not give the slightest explanation for this mysterious financial remittance," he said.[40]

In the autumn of 1971, with Grivas preparing for armed action against Makarios, the Cyprus talks were at an impasse as a result of Makarios' refusal to accept exhortations from Athens to reach compromises he felt were unacceptable.

According to the then US ambassador in Nicosia, David Popper, "Greece and Turkey had reached a rough agreement [in Lisbon] over the Cyprus issue," and the Greek government was under pressure to show some results. In Popper's judgement, Greece found herself between hammer and anvil. "She knows that Turkey could either be her best friend and ally or her most fearsome enemy. The Athens government knows full well that they should not let Greece become involved in a war with Turkey. Furthermore, they know that Turkey will not allow the Cyprus problem to remain unsolved ad infinitum. If Greece should find herself in the position where she has to choose between a war with Turkey and a coup in Cyprus, she will definitely choose the second, given that she disposes of the required forces in Cyprus."[41]

---

37 Cyprus KYP report on the theft of arms from the Trikomo National Guard camp, based on intercepted telephone conversations.

38 Papageorgiou, *Μακάριος*, p. 158.

39 *Phileleftheros*, 26 June 1974.

40 Makarios interview with Eric Rouleau, reprinted in *Παγκύπρια Πορεία Αγάπης Αρχιεπισκόπου Μακαρίου Γ* [Pancyprian March of Love of Archbishop Makarios III], annual edition no. 8, p. 148.

41 Clerides, *op. cit.*, vol. 3, p. 142.

Popper's estimation was in line with a note from the Information and Research Bureau of the State Department, according to which Greece at that time received repeated exhortations from Ankara to exert over Makarios and the Greek Cypriots "the kind of control that Ankara has over the Turkish community".[42]

It was under the weight of this pressure that Turkish Foreign Minister Olcay and Greek Deputy Foreign Minister Palamas prepared to meet in New York in October 1971 to discuss the next steps on the Cyprus issue. For this purpose, the Greek ambassador to Nicosia, Constantinos Panayiotakos, also went to New York. Like Palamas, he considered Makarios solely responsible for the lack of progress on the Cyprus issue. Panayiotakos said that during the Palamas-Olcay talks, the Turkish Foreign Minister referred to the possibility of a partition arrangement.[43]

On the margins of the agenda of the General Assembly of the United Nations, Palamas proposed to UN Secretary General, U Thant, a new formula for resumption of the talks, with the participation of two constitutional experts, one from Greece and the other from Turkey. Makarios was opposed to this procedure, because he mistrusted Athens. He maintained that, since the talks were taking place for an independent state and not for *Enosis* or partition, they should be held between the two Cypriot communities, with the good offices of the United Nations. On the other hand, Turkey preferred to deal with Greece rather than with Makarios, and wanted the United Nations excluded from the process.

U Thant adopted a middle way and proposed talks with the participation of representatives from Greece and Turkey, who would have the role of advisors to the Greek Cypriot and Turkish Cypriot negotiators. He further proposed that the talks be held under the aegis of his special representative for Cyprus, Ozorio Tafal. U Thant officially submitted his proposal to the interested parties on 18 October 1971.

Makarios was absent from all these moves because, in light of the Grivas factor, he preferred to remain in Nicosia rather than take part in the general assembly of the United Nations, as he had done in previous years. He was represented by Foreign Minister Spyros Kyprianou, who, in his attempt to undermine Palamas' initiative, came into personal conflict with him. The two men squabbled and Palamas gave instructions to Panayiotakos - who in the meantime had returned to Nicosia - to inform Makarios that the Greek government was cutting off all contact and communication with Kyprianou.[44]

The Greco-Turkish rapprochement over Cyprus, the refusal of Makarios to accept this, and the sudden appearance of Grivas in Cyprus, in combination with a series of other grave events that were taking place on the island, all led to the conclusion that Greece and Turkey had agreed to use Grivas in order to distance Makarios and to proceed to a settlement of the Cyprus problem.

In November 1971, the chargé d'affaires of the US embassy in Nicosia, William Crawford, prepared a report on the situation in Cyprus, concerning the attempt of the Greek government to control the internal Cyprus front, to undermine Makarios and use Grivas to impose the solution of double *Enosis*. This report, which was in the form of a letter, was sent to Tom Boyatt, Director of the Cyprus Desk at the State Department. According to Crawford's report, immediately after the Cypriot parliamentary elections of 1970, the Greek government took the decision to intervene on the island, as a result of the increased pres-

---

42 "Cyprus: 'Ultimatum' thinly veils Athens' real objective". NARA, RG59, CFPF, 1970-1973, Cyprus, State Department, Information and Research Office, Intelligence Note, 17 February 1972.

43 Popper to Secretary of State, "Grivas and partition", NARA, RG59, CFPF, 1970-1973, Cyprus, telegram 2053, Nicosia, 19 November 1971.

44 Panayiotakos, *op. cit.*, p. 119.

ence of AKEL, which had secured 40% of the vote. After Nichat Erim's rise to power in March 1971, and the creation of a climate of cooperation between Greece and Turkey over the solution of the Cyprus problem, the Greek government's attempt to exert control over internal developments in Cyprus was reinforced.

Describing a series of events, with the aim of demonstrating the manner of, and tension over, Greek intervention in Cyprus, Crawford mentioned:

- The substantial economic help given to the right-wing trade union, the Cyprus Workers' Federation (*Synomospondia Ergaton Kyprou* - SEK) for the extension of its activities.
- The bribing of the Cypriot press by the Greek embassy.
- The creation of a branch of the Football Pools organisation (*Prognostika Podosfairou* - PRO-PO) by the general secretary of the Athletics Association, Constantinos Aslanides, through which the funding of anti-communist entities was carried out.
- The visit of Michalakis Savvides to Athens, as head of the Cyprus Chamber of Commerce, during which "energetic programmes of commercial and economic cooperation" were agreed on.
- The visit to Athens of Education Minister Frixos Petrides, and the announcement of new courses designed to promote closer educational cooperation with Greece.
- The visit to Greece of a large group from the Pancyprian Fighters' National Front (*Pankyprio Ethniko Metopo Agoniston* - PEMA), headed by Elias Ipsarides, who were given a reception worthy of distinguished guests.
- The corresponding hospitality extended in Greece to the youth organisation of the Unified Party, (*Pankypria Ethniki Organosi Neolaias* - PEON, during which it received assurances of generous economic assistance.

According to Crawford's report, apart from programmes of cooperation and economic assistance, the Greek government undertook a systematic campaign undermining the prestige of Makarios through the National Guard:

"From many sources we hear about the brainwashing carried out on new Cypriot recruits by the Greek officers. Makarios is presented as the man who has sacrificed the national issue – which could have been brought to a successful conclusion through the Acheson Plan – for the sake of his personal ambitions, and who is ready to undermine the interests of Greece through the encouragement he gives to AKEL and the invitation to the Soviets to get involved in the Cyprus problem. Grivas is depicted as the true national hero, who has returned to lead the island back on the course of *Enosis*. For this aim to succeed, it is accepted that Greeks have to be realists. They must make territorial concessions to Turkey; however, thanks to the past mistakes of Makarios, this involves more than mere recognition of the status quo, where the Turks have their own independent administration in their enclaves on the island."

Crawford linked all these activities to Turkey's plans in Cyprus and the campaign that Grivas had undertaken on the island: "From various reports, you know that Turkey is ready, on short notice, to support the Turkish Cypriots in breaking out from their existing enclaves in North east Cyprus, in order to create a unified zone in which they would exert natural control. This zone would extend from Kyrenia, pass through north Nicosia and reach north Famagusta. The Turkish embassy here, for example advisor Tounapas, recognise that blood will be shed on both sides. However, he stresses that the creation of a separating line will in the end be the only feasible solution and that 'a solution presupposes some sacrifices'".

Crawford goes on to refer to a series of incidents to demonstrate that all this was happening with the complete collusion of Athens and Ankara, not only at government level, but that of military commands:

"We have some vague pictures through private channels of communication between Athens and Ankara. In the course of his visit here, the deputy of Aset [the head of the Greece-Cyprus desk in the Turkish Foreign Ministry] referred to a link functioning between the secretary of Papadopoulos (the name was not given) and ambassador Turkmen. Specifically, he spoke of a message that was received through this channel, from which it appears that Papadopoulos is in favour of double *Enosis* as the only solution. It appears, furthermore, that there exists a military channel, through the Greek military attaché in Ankara. On a higher level, we should like to know the contents of the exchanges that are taking place in Athens now, between the Chief of the Turkish General Staff Tagman, and his Greek counterparts. Concerning Cyprus, we are aware that there is a hot line between 'Bozkurt' [chief of the TMT] and General Charalambopoulos [Commander of the National Guard]. For example, General Lesli tells us that in tense situations he noticed that his (clearly personal) expressions, which he used in a conversation with the leadership of the Turkish fighters [of the TMT] are repeated, one or two hours later, by Charalambopoulos."

With all the above in mind, Crawford comes to the following conclusions:

- Greece is initiating a concerted effort to establish its influence in Cyprus.
- This influence is used to support Grivas and against Makarios.
- Turkey and the Turkish Cypriots are ready militarily to take control of northeastern Cyprus.
- There exists a coordinated mechanism between the Greek and Turkish governments.
- While Greece and Turkey are willing to give negotiations and diplomacy another chance, they state that this is the last, that the deadline is June 1972, and that eventually double *Enosis* is probably the only possible solution of the Cyprus problem, once and for all.

After describing the situation prevailing in Cyprus, William Crawford posed the question to Tom Boyatt concerning what policy America should adopt in Cyprus when the moment would come for it to take up a position. If, in other words, the US should:

- Remain silent and adopt an accommodating stance.
- Say "no".
- Say "no" without meaning it.
- Pronounce a disguised "yes" and accept the plans of her allies.[45]

Tom Boyatt concurred with the observations of Crawford and sent a significant letter to Crawford, pointing out two other factors: the lead-up to the Athens-Ankara rapprochement and to the attempt on the life of Makarios.

Specifically, Tom Boyatt referred to the Evros conference in 1967, during which Papadopoulos offered Turkey a military base in Cyprus, with *Enosis* as the trade-off. According to Boyatt, Papadopoulos at that time underestimated Turkish demands and the conference ended in a fiasco. "At that time, the colonels were prepared to pay whatever the Turks asked in exchange for *Enosis*. It is very probable that this rapprochement on the part of the Greek government has developed by gradual degrees to the point that they are now willing to pay a much higher price for *Enosis*, such as the cession of 15% to 20% of the island to the Turkish government."

---

45 Letter from Crawford to Boyatt, dated 19 November 1971, NARA, RG59, CFPF, 1970-1973, Cyprus.

Referring to the attempts on Makarios' life, Boyatt wrote to Crawford: "As you will no doubt remember, these well-known players, Colonels Aslanides and Papapostolou, whisper far and wide that they were mixed up in the attempt on the life of Makarios in March 1970, and in the assassination of Yorkadjis that followed. It will need a lot of time before the truth of this matter becomes known – if it ever does. In any case, I do not believe there is anyone inside and outside Cyprus who believes that any Cypriot could kill Yorkadjis without Greek back-up."

Concerning Crawford's question as to the policy the United States should follow, Boyatt wrote to him that the State Department had already taken a decision, and its answer was "No" and absolutely "No". That is to say, the US government was opposed to the imposition by force of a 'solution' to the Cyprus problem. This was because "the risks are too high that it will not work and will generate a chaotic disaster providing unique opportunities for Soviet exploitation." Boyatt also pointed out that over and above the danger of the Soviets exploiting the situation, any attempt by Greece and Turkey to dismember Cyprus would be categorically attributed to the United States. For these reasons, Boyatt concluded, America was determined to avoid any situation whatever in which its silence would be linked to the decision of Greece (with or without the collusion of the Turkish government) as to a 'solution' to the Cyprus problem by force.[46]

The policy that the State Department decided to adopt concerning the developments in Cyprus after the arrival of Grivas is described in the telegram numbered 214164 that was sent to the Athens and Nicosia embassies. In the telegram the situation in Cyprus is described, and it points out the fact that various highly placed Greeks "now openly maintain that a partial *Enosis*, let us say 80% of Cyprus, with Greece, is preferable to an unstable state governed by Makarios, who is flirting with the Soviets and the non-aligned." This viewpoint, according to a briefing in the possession of the State Department, was held by the ambassador of Greece in Cyprus Constantinos Panayiotakos, the Commander of the Greek Military Contingent Pavlos Papadakis, Prime Minister George Papadopoulos, as well as George Grivas.

According to the estimation of the State Department, the Greek government inclined towards partition – double *Enosis* – and would impose such a solution at the slightest opportunity; and the appearance of Grivas in Cyprus was presented as just such an opportunity. "The danger lies in the fact that Grivas, who shares the view that double *Enosis* is better than no *Enosis* at all, and who yearns for the defeat of Makarios, will cause such a chaotic situation in Cyprus that it will become incumbent on the Greek government (with the collusion of Turkey) to move in this direction." For this reason, American diplomacy viewed with scepticism the opinion that the appearance of Grivas in Cyprus could be of long-term use as a spur to Makarios accepting some compromise solution.

The State Department was convinced that Makarios would resist any partitionist solution. "Grivas and the Greek government know it, and should carry out a coup in order to bring about a solution of double *Enosis*." In such a scenario, Makarios would take the problem to the United Nations and opportunities would be created for the Soviet Union.

The telegram concludes, "the government of the United States remains opposed to any effort to impose partition and double *Enosis* on Cyprus", because it would not solve the Cyprus problem, but, rather, "place it in more tragic and chaotic context", something that would have the result of bolstering the Soviet position in the eastern Mediterranean.

---

46 Letter from Boyatt to Crawford, dated 2 December 1971, NARA, RG59, CFPF, 1970-1973, Cyprus.

Judging from the past, and from the personality of Grivas, the State Department came to the conclusion that sooner or later he would take up arms. "While we concur with views in diplomatic notes, that the practical steps that the American government can take are limited, the State Department feels that we should leave no stone unturned in an effort to keep the Cyprus problem within a negotiating context."

As a conclusion to this analysis, the State Department gave Athens ambassador Henry Tasca the following instruction, on the assumption that he would agree to it himself: he should meet with Papadopoulos and verbally convey the following:

a. The government of the United States is seriously concerned about the existing situation in Cyprus. The presence of General Grivas has introduced elements of uncertainty, in a situation that always has been inherently explosive. From the time of the arrival of General Grivas in Cyprus, there has been a significant increase in statements relating to *Enosis*, double *Enosis*, partition and other grave deviations from solutions based on negotiations and mutual agreement.
b. In the present climate we wish to have talks with the Greek government, with a view to forestalling a deterioration of the situation in Cyprus. We continue to hold the view that whatever attempt, from whatever quarter, to deviate from the path of talks will lead to violence and crisis, something that would give the Soviet Union the opportunity to infiltrate the region and to the defeat of NATO in the United Nations. The government of the United States continues to maintain that an agreed solution based on independence is in the interest of the Cypriots, as well as of Greece and her allies.
c. The government of the United States has received reports according to which the followers of Grivas in Cyprus proclaim that the Greek government is willing to offer him support. This amounts to Grivas obtaining popular support for dangerous ideas. Naturally, we are aware of the Greek government's attachment to a solution within the framework of the talks... It would be helpful, in our opinion, if the Greek government made clear its anxiety concerning General Grivas' working against our aim of an agreed solution.
d. We request the Greek government to consider the possibility of making a public declaration, pointing out the illegal activities of Grivas, and confirming its conviction that the talks remain the most secure path to peace."

At the same time, instructions were given to ambassador David Popper in Nicosia to come into contact with Makarios, and to convey to him the following:

a. The government of the United States continues to support an agreed solution to the Cyprus problem based on independence, and rejects the so-called military solutions.
b. We have again stressed to the Greek government the position of the United States on this matter.
c. In the present explosive atmosphere, the greatest contribution to an agreed solution would be a resumption of local talks under a new formula. For this reason, the United States proposes to the Archbishop that he rapidly accept the initiative of the general secretary of the United Nations."[47]

The position adopted by the United States against military solutions and in favour of talks for a solution of the Cyprus problem was too important for Makarios to ignore, and after many hesitations he accepted, in December 1971, U Thant's formula for the participa-

---

[47] Sisco to Tasca and Popper, "Grivas situation", NARA, RG59, CFPF, 1970-1973, Cyprus, telegram 214164, State Department, 23 November 1971.

tion of one Turkish and one Greek constitutional expert in the talks, having the status of advisors.

Nevertheless, things had not taken the same turn in Athens and Nicosia, since the US stopped exhorting the Greek government publicly to condemn Grivas' activities. The draft of the above telegram with its instructions to Tasca, clearly mentioned that he should "meet with Papadopoulos and convey to him verbally" the US position on developments in Cyprus. In the final text that was sent to Athens the phrase was added: "unless you have any objection..." It was already known in the State Department that Tasca disagreed with this policy, since in the consultations that had preceded he had expressed different views. In a relevant telegram of his to the State Department, he wrote that he believed "Grivas was not a threat to the United States". And commenting on the intention of the State Department to ask the Greek government to denounce Grivas' activities and to participate in an attempt to have him recalled to Greece, he wrote that he doubted that Papadopoulos had sent Grivas to Cyprus, even if he was trying to use him for his own ends. Tasca also invoked practical difficulties in recalling Grivas to Athens, even if Papadopoulos should want to do so.

Concerning the suggestion of publicly condemning Grivas, Tasca expressed doubt as to whether the Greek government was disposed to make such a proclamation. "Just as Makarios finds it impossible to say that he does not want *Enosis*, despite the fact that this may be true, it is no easy matter for a Greek government to publicly condemn the leading advocate of *Enosis* and the national hero of the Cyprus liberation struggle."[48]

Ultimately, the United States avoided exerting pressure on the Greek government to denounce Grivas' activities and to recall him to Greece. Tasca met Papadopoulos on 20 December 1971. Papadopoulos categorically denied any involvement of the Greek government in the arrival of Grivas in Cyprus. Indeed, he told him that Grivas had twice been involved in a conspiracy against the regime, and against his own person, and that the only reason he had not been arrested was his reputation and his role during the Civil War.

In his telegram concerning his meeting with Papadopoulos, Tasca wrote that the Greek government now had proof that Grivas did indeed support double *Enosis*, and that nothing was worse than either partition or double *Enosis*, because it would lead to grave difficulties. "Grivas was not a man capable of organising the effort he has currently under way, and the real question is who is helping him." Papadopoulos was convinced that hard-core officers Ladas and Aslanides were not involved – even though the British Intelligence Service believed they were concealed behind the activities of Grivas. Papadopoulos expressed to Tasca his speculation that the Americans were mixed up in the Grivas affair.[49]

While the State Department's initiative to neutralise Grivas was weakening, discussion concerning the scenario of a joint Greco-Turkish intervention in Cyprus continued. According to a note of the National Security Council of the United States, there were reports in January 1972 that "high ups on both sides continue to speak of the so-called "forceful" solution, which would result in double *Enosis* (partition), as the best way out".[50]

Partisans of the "forceful solution" policy were the Palamas-Panayiotakis duo, who, on the 14 January 1972, were upgraded to stand-in and Deputy Foreign Minister respectively. In mid-January 1972, as the outgoing ambassador of Greece was preparing to leave the

---

48 Tasca to Secretary of State, "Cyprus: Grivas situation", NARA, RG59, CFPF, 1970-1973, Cyprus, telegram 6177, Athens, 19 November 1971.

49 Tasca to Secretary of State, "Cyprus and Grivas: My meeting with Prime Minister", NARA, RG59, CFPF, 1970-1973, Cyprus, telegram 6644, Athens, 20 December 1971.

50 Harold H. Saunders and Rosemary Neaher to Kissinger, "The Cyprus situation", NARA, NPMS, NSC, Cyprus/Greece, memo of the National Security Council, 10 January 1972.

island to assume his new duties, he told foreign diplomats and Cypriot circles that the most suitable solution in Cyprus was based on "a forcibly imposed partition, giving 20% of the island's territory to the Turkish Cypriots".[51]

These views of Panayiotakos were not new. In November 1971, shortly after the Palamas-Olcay meeting in New York, Panayiotakos told David Popper, American ambassador in Nicosia, that the optimal solution to the Cyprus problem was double *Enosis*, and that was consented to by Grivas, who "changed his ideas since he understood that full *Enosis* was no longer realistically possible. He would be prepared to pay the necessary price to Turkey".[52]

The positions expressed by Panayiotakos were contrary to the official policy of the United States, and on 26 January the head of the Cyprus Desk at the State Department, Tom Boyatt, summoned Georgiades, the Greek chargé d'affaires in Washington, and pointed out the fact to him, on "a personal and informal basis".[53] Boyatt's intervention caused reaction within the State Department. The US ambassador in Nicosia, in an extended analysis of Panayiotakos' proposal concerning partition, the contents of which were accepted by Athens ambassador Henry Tasca, suggested that the United States should not exclude any outcome, all the more so when such an outcome was supported by both Greece and Turkey.

The main points of Popper's analysis were as follows:

- Not only mainland Greeks were mentioning the possibility of a "dynamic solution" to the United States, but Turks, Turkish Cypriots and some of the Greek Cypriot establishment types as well. Their argument is that, since the talks do not make any progress, and since the two sides cannot agree to co-exist, they must live apart.
- Unlike in previous crises in Cyprus, Greece and Turkey will cooperate in the imposition of a military solution. "We are aware that the Greco-Turkish plans in Cyprus continue on a particularly personal basis," he reported. Greco-Turkish cooperation ensures that there will be neither conflict between allies, nor any danger of weakening the southeastern flank of NATO.
- The present course requires the United States "to sit on the lid of a boiling pot without providing a safety valve". The United States are covered by a general exhortation concerning a constitutional solution, while in reality neither of the interested parties is disposed to replace constitutional unity on terms acceptable to the other. At the same time, the alternative path, namely the imposition of a solution by Greece and Turkey, is blocked off.

For these reasons, Popper suggested that Greece and Turkey should be given an alternative choice to the "dangerous games that some of their people seem to be playing" in Cyprus.[54]

In its answer, the State Department mentioned that, despite the fact that it did not agree with some of the judgments contained in the Popper analysis, it nevertheless recognised that the moment was propitious for the study of alternative solutions, in the event of there being a prolonged constitutional deadlock. As to the Panayiotakos' suggestion concerning double *Enosis*, the State Department pronounced the view that it was very dangerous to

---

51 Rogers to Popper, "Views of Panayiotakos", NARA, NPMS, NSC, Cyprus/Greece, telegram 16992, State Department, 29 January 1972.

52 Popper to Secretary of State, "Grivas and partition", NARA, RG59, CFPF, 1970-1973, Cyprus, telegram 2053, Nicosia, 19 November 1971.

53 *Ibid.*

54 Popper to Secretary of State, "Cyprus: How to handle Partition proposals", NARA, NPMS, NSC, Cyprus/Greece, telegram 226, Nicosia, 3 February 1972.

allow Panayiotakos to broadcast his plans without giving him some sort of reply, because "silence might be interpreted as accceptance".[55]

It is therefore clear that, within the State Department itself, there were mutually conflicting views as to American policy on the Cyprus issue. On the one hand, there was the school of thought represented by Tom Boyatt, head of the Cyprus Desk, who believed – dealing with the problem with rationalistic criteria – that the interests of the United States would be better secured by a political solution in Cyprus via the talks process, which would satisfy the claims of the Turks, but would not humiliate the Greeks. This was the official policy of the United States on the Cyprus problem.

On the other hand, there was the policy of encouraging the cooperation between Athens and Ankara to achieve the undermining and final elimination of Makarios, the aim being to arrange a solution of the Cyprus problem within the family, and within the framework of the alliance. This policy was secretly implemented by the secret services, through the branches of the Greek and Turkish Gladio on the island. These two different tendencies would be in mutual conflict until 1974, with the Gladio usually being imposed at every critical turn of the Cyprus problem.

---

55 Rogers to Ankara, Athens and Nicosia, "Cyprus: Partition proposals and peaceful solutions", NARA, NPMS, NSC, Cyprus/Greece, telegram 20730, State Department, 2 December 1972.

The governor of JUSMAPG James Van Fleet (left) and Thrassyvoulos Tsakalotos present the flag of the Democratic Army which fell into their hands during operations by government forces in collaboration with US officers.

A crate with explosives found on the Ayios Georghios and confiscated by the British, being carried to court as evidence.

Plate 2

Extremist Turkish demonstrators holding a poster
of the 'Cyprus is Turkish Association'
during violent attacks against the Greeks of Istanbul.

. Demonstrators attacking properties belonging to Istanbul Greeks.

The British took suppressive measures against the population in order to crush the EOKA struggle.

EOKA murdered 230 Greek Cypriots and only 105 British soldiers.
This murder took place at Kythrea church. The victim was a member of the church choir and the murder took place in front of the congregation and the victim's children.

Plate 4

Following the signing of the Agreements, all Cypriots welcomed Makarios with enthusiasm.

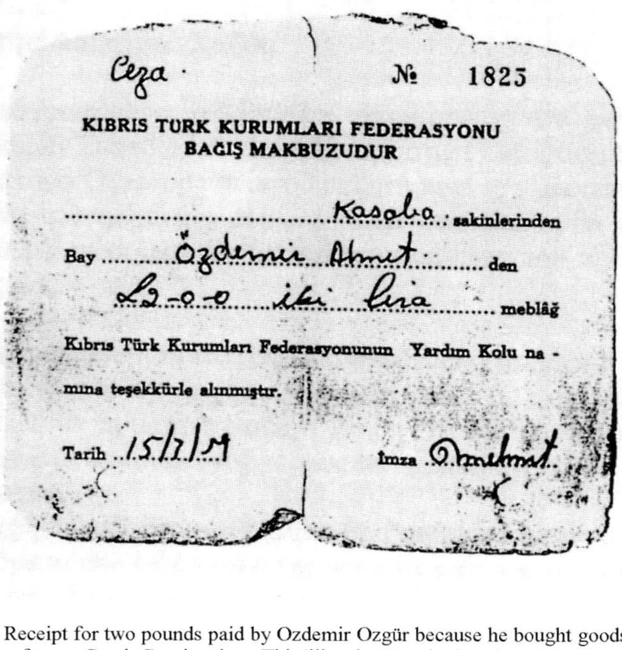

Ceza · № 1825

KIBRIS TÜRK KURUMLARI FEDERASYONU
BAĞIŞ MAKBUZUDUR

......Kasaba...... sakinlerinden

Bay ......Özdemir Ahmet...... den

......£2-0-0 iki lira...... meblâğ

Kıbrıs Türk Kurumları Federasyonunun Yardım Kolu na - mına teşekkürle alınmıştır.

Tarih ..15/7/59.. İmza ..Mehmet..

Receipt for two pounds paid by Ozdemir Ozgür because he bought goods from a Greek Cypriot shop. This 'illegal act' took place in July 1959, five months after the signing of the Agreements.

The three-member crew of the Elmaz outside the court, which sentenced them to one year in prison. The following day they were deported to Turkey.

Polycarpos Georgadjis chats with Denktash during a social gathering.

Plate 6

Nicos Sampson brandishes a pistol as he parades a Turkish flag seized during fighting in Omorphita. Behind him follow women and children taken as hostages.

Nicosia, 1964. Students return to the streets to press their demand for Enosis.

Glafcos Clerides and Rauf Denktash arrive at the latter's home to begin bi-communal negotiations in 1968.

Makarios, Grivas and Colonel Papadopoulos, during a visit to Cyprus by the latter in 1967.

Plate 8

On 8 March 1970 a group of Georgadjis' men and one of Grivas' supporters who had links with the echelon of the Greek KYP in Nicosia and LOK, attempted to assassinate Makarios.

Colonel Papapostolou trapped Georgadjis and murdered him, thereby silencing him.

3. The Coup that Failed

In January 1972, the Cyprus government took receipt of a large quantity of arms it had ordered from Czechoslovakia a year earlier. The arms were destined for the Civil Guard that was being formed, and were to be used in case of conflict with Turkish Cypriot forces in order to avoid the involvement of the National Guard.

Makarios had personally informed Greek Prime Minister George Papadopoulos about the order during his September 1971 visit to Athens, three months before he received the arms. Moreover, the arms were commissioned after deliberation with the Commander of the National Guard, General Charalambopoulos, who worked in tandem with the Director General of the Foreign Ministry, Christodoulos Veniamin, in drawing up the relevant catalogue.[1]

The weapons – 287 tons in all – were unloaded at Xeros port. They were packed in 10,850 crates and were initially transported, for misinformation purposes, to warehouses at the Mitseros Mine to be registered as explosive materials. On 29 January, their transfer began to Nicosia to be stored in the basements of the Archbishopric Palace. The National Guard General Staff, whose agents tracked the unloading and transport of the armaments, gave a full report to Greek ambassador Constantinos Panayiotakos, who was to leave Cyprus in a few days' time to assume his new duties as deputy Foreign Secretary. After consulting Charalambopoulos and cadres in Grivas' organisation, Panayiotakos informed Palamas in Athens about the "clandestine" (as he termed it) delivery of arms. Panayiotakos wrote later in his memoirs that the arms had been destined for the "reinforcement of paramilitary praetorian guards, in the nationalist reserve police corps, well known for their barbarism and use of torture"[2] – a statement that must be treated with some scepticism considering EOKA B had not yet begun its activities, the Reservist Corps had not yet been constituted, and there had been no arrests of *Enosis* activists.

The Greek government decided to take advantage of the opportunity presented by the weapons affair to impose its policy on Makarios. Palamas gave instructions to Panayiotakos to postpone his departure from Cyprus and to approach Makarios, requesting the unconditional handover of the weaponry to the National Guard. Makarios' first reaction was negative. He told Panayiotakos that he hadn't the slightest confidence in the National Guard, implying that the officers that staffed it were assisting the armed units being formed by Grivas.[3]

In the meantime, news of the arrival of the weapons, as well as Greece's reaction, leaked to journalist Spyros Papageorgiou, who prepared an article for the Nicosia newspaper *Mesimvrini*, and for *Estia* of Athens. George Hadjinicolaou, the publisher of *Mesimvrini*, phoned the General Staff Headquarters for Lalaounis' permission to publish the news. Lalaounis suggested that he wait, and so the news was only published in *Estia*.[4] The Cyprus government issued a denial.

---

1 Christodoulos Veniamin conveyed this information with "utmost confidentiality" to William Crawford, the chargé d'affaires at the American embassy in Nicosia. The Americans accepted the version of the Cyprus government, namely that there was an understanding with Athens over the order of arms. (Crawford to Secretary of State, "Makarios rejects GOG ultimate", NARA, RG59, CFPF, 1970-1973, Cyprus, telegram 302, Nicosia, 11 February 1972.)

2 Panayiotakos, *op. cit.*, p. 119.

3 *Ibid.*, p. 103.

4 Telephone conversation between Spyros Papageorgiou and Socratis Eliades, recorded by Cyprus KYP.

At daybreak on 2 February, an EOKA B guerrilla unit attempted to snatch some of the arms, which were still stored in Mitseros Mine, but men from the presidential guard on sentry duty around the warehouses spotted them. The policemen arrested Michalakis Yiasemides, who was armed with an automatic and a revolver. Under interrogation, he confessed to being a member of Grivas' units. Other arrests followed, and the affair grew in importance. Eventually, the government had no choice but to admit that it had imported the weapons.

In Athens, the Greek government was planning its next moves in collusion with Ankara, its ultimate aim being the elimination of Makarios. As emerges from a report by the US National Security Council referring to the crisis over the Czech guns, during consultations between Athens and Ankara, "the Turks indicated to the Greeks that Makarios must go."[5]

Another report by the Research and Information Bureau of the U.S. State Department, referring to the same crisis, says: "There have been several indications that Grivas has come around to realising that he cannot have *Enosis* without paying the price of partition. If Greece and Turkey colluded on the return of Grivas to Cyprus, they may also have agreed on a 'Grivas-type' solution, that they would impose on a Cyprus government that excluded Makarios. The primary actor in this drama would have to be Greece. Turkey would play its part by sitting tight, careful not to provide Makarios with an incident which he could use to rally the Greek Cypriots behind him and to brand Papadopoulos a Turkish 'collaborator'."[6] Thus, throughout the crisis that followed, Turkey refrained from open involvement in the clash between Makarios and the Greek government, allowing her to handle the issue as a domestic problem.[7] The only exception was the recourse to the United Nations, in which Turkey requested that Makarios hand over the arms to UNFICYP. Turkey's recourse occurred after a suggestion by Greek deputy Foreign Minister Palamas himself, with a view to exerting greater pressure on Makarios.[8]

On 8 February, Palamas met US ambassador Henry Tasca and discussed the crisis in relations between Athens and Nicosia. Tasca reported in a telegram that he came away from his talks with Palamas with the impression that the Greek government wanted Makarios replaced. Tasca said Palamas had told him that the Greek government was in contact with Turkey, and that the two countries agreed that "Makarios was an important block to any agreement regarding Cyprus problem". Palamas further told him that the talks on the Cyprus issue would continue, and the arms question would be settled in a "matter of days". Tasca asked him how Athens would impose its policy on Makarios. In reply, Palamas invoked the right of intervention in Cyprus that Greece and Turkey had, based on the London-Zurich Agreements.[9]

On 9 February, Tasca met with George Papadopoulos, to whom he conveyed "our negative attitude toward any 'dynamic' initiative in regard to Cyprus". In his telegram to the State Department, Tasca expressed anxiety over Palamas' reference to the right of intervention, and suggested that further overtures be made to Athens, since both the governments of

---

5 Harold H. Saunders and Rosemary Neaher to Kissinger, "The Cyprus situation", NARA, NPMS, NSC, Cyprus/Greece, memo of the National Security Council, 10 February 1972.

6 "Cyprus: 'Ultimatum' thinly veils Athens' real objective", NARA, NPMS, NSC, Cyprus/Greece, State Department, Information and Research Office, Intelligence Note, 17 February 1972.

7 Handley to Secretary of State, "Cyprus: Turk attitude toward demands of Makarios", NARA, NPMS, NSC, Cyprus/Greece, telegram 975, Ankara, 10 February 1972.

8 Handley to Secretary of State, "Cyprus: Turkish views", NARA, NPMS, NSC, Cyprus/Greece, telegram 1021, Ankara, 12 December 1972.

9 Tasca to Secretary of State, "Cyprus: Strong Greek Government reaction to importation of Czech arms", NARA, NPMS, NSC, Cyprus/Greece, telegram 690, Athens, 8 February 1972.

Turkey and Greece no longer seemed concerned "regarding potential trouble from Grivas and his followers" – a fact that hinted at their encouraging such a possibility.[10] Tasca's suggestion was accepted, and on 11 February he again met with Papadopoulos, to whom he conveyed a message from Secretary of State William Rogers. Tasca repeated to Papadopoulos that "the Greek initiative was potentially highly dangerous", something which surprised Papadopoulos because, as he said, "Greece was one of the forces responsible for guaranteeing peace on the island, which was under threat, and because Greece had an historical obligation towards the Greeks of Cyprus."[11]

On 8 February 1972, the Greek government summoned to Athens its Nicosia ambassador Constantinos Panayiotakos, as well as the Commander of the National Guard General Charalambopoulos, and the Commander of the Greek Contingent to Cyprus, Colonel Pavlos Papadakis, for an extraordinary meeting over the Czech arms affair. At the same time, the Greek embassy mobilised the pro-Grivas press, which passionately supported the Greek government's moves. The full catalogue of the arms received leaked to *Gnomi* newspaper. According to the newspaper, the arms were destined to arming the communists.[12] *Patris*, referring to the Athens meeting, wrote: "Athens reviews developments in Cyprus – Makarios in the dock". And in its leading article, where the abundance of exclamation marks demonstrated the passion with which it was written, it exhorted: "What will Greece do? First and foremost, she should stretch out thumb and forefinger and grab every naughty nationalist by the ear. Greece has historic rights, and must lay claim to them in their entirety. And ourselves? We should stand tall on the ramparts! Determined and ready for everything! Brighter days will dawn. Fellow fighters, we are writing history! And it is our duty to write it brilliantly and radiantly - *Greek* history!..."[13]

The Athens conference took place under the chairmanship of Regent Zoitakis. In attendance were Prime Minister Papadopoulos, vice-presidents of the dictatorship government Patakos and Makarezos, deputy Foreign Minister Palamas, Commander in Chief of the armed forces Angelis, Nicosia ambassador Panayiotakos, Commander of the National Guard Charalambopoulos, and the Commander of the Greek Contingent Papadakis. Charalambopoulos writes that, at the meeting, Papadopoulos pointed out "the 'Makariofication' of state machinery, the expulsion or dissatisfaction of EOKA fighters, the detrimental and dangerous arrival of Grivas in Cyprus, the arrogance of Makarios in the face of Greek national policy, which now he even puts on display internationally with the importation of arms," and came to the conclusion that "Makarios and Grivas are leading us into dangerous complications".[14] According to Charalambopoulos, Panayiotakos introduced a scenario of 'protection' of the Archbishopric by the National Guard in order to prevent "the leakage of weaponry to the irregulars". Charalambopoulos writes that he disagreed, arguing the National Guard was loyal to Makarios. Then Papadopoulos turned to Papadakis:

"What do you say?"

"I do not have such problems," he replied.[15]

---

[10] Tasca to Secretary of State, "Cyprus, Greek reaction to import of Czech arms", NARA, NPMS, NSC, Cyprus/Greece, telegram 704, Athens, 8 February 1972.

[11] Tasca to Secretary of State, "Cyprus, my meeting with prime minister on delivery of note to Makarios", NARA, NPMS, NSC, Cyprus/Greece, telegram 760, Athens, 11 February 1972.

[12] "287 τόννους όπλα έφερεν ο Μακάριος" [Makarios Brings 287 tons of weapons], *Gnomi*, 6 Frebruary 1972.

[13] "Τελειώνει το θέατρον" [The Theatre is Over], *Patris*, 10 February 1972.

[14] Charalambopoulos, *op. cit.*, p. 117.

[15] *Ibid.*, p. 118.

It was finally decided that the Foreign Ministry should prepare a diplomatic note to Makarios, which would request the surrender of the weapons to the UN Peacekeeping Force, as well as a reshuffle of his government. It was further decided that a verbal approach should be made to Makarios, with the demand that he withdraw from the political scene. That same day, Palamas met Turkish ambassador Turkmen, briefed him on the contents of the note, and once more requested that Turkey not involve herself in the crisis and leave the handling of it to Athens, so as not to give ammunition to Makarios.[16]

On 11 February, Panayiotakos visited Makarios in the Presidential Palace, accompanied for the first time by a soldier, who bore a truncheon, and delivered him the diplomatic note.[17] The Greek government:

- Demanded from Makarios that he hand over the arms without delay, to be stored by the UN Peacekeeping Force.
- Pointed out to him that "it should not be forgotten that Athens is, and remains, the ethnic centre.
- Asked him to form a government of national unity.[18]

After delivering the note, Panayiotakos recalls in his memoirs how he took from his pocket a small piece of paper and read to Makarios a verbal message, which said the Greek government considered that, in order to preserve normality and the peaceful existence of Cyprus Hellenism, the "voluntary withdrawal from the political scene of the two protagonists in whom the current tension in Cyprus was concentrated" was imperative. In other words, Greece was demanding the resignation of Makarios and the departure of Grivas.

Panayiotakos told Makarios that he was not empowered to discuss with him the contents of the diplomatic note, but that he would convey to Athens any observations he might make. According to the ambassador's memoirs, Makarios merely complained that Athenss had failed to condemn either the activities of Grivas, or the theft of weapon from the National Guard army camp in Trikomo. Panayiotakos replied he could not condemn Grivas, since he had not yet shown any sign of activity, while he cast doubt on the suggestion that EOKA B was behind the theft of arms. Furious, Makarios told him he was willing to throw the weapons in the sea, in the presence of both Panayiotakos and the Commander of the General Staff, and "launched into unbecoming insults against Grivas, whom he described as 'paranoid' and who he said was aiming at the butchery of Cyprus".[19]

On his departure, Panayiotakos met in the antechamber of Makarios' office the President of the House of Representatives, Glafcos Clerides, and deputies Nicos Sampson and Phidias Paraskevaides. The three of them were waiting to meet Makarios and deliver a note on behalf of all the right-wing deputies, in which they called on him not to reject without discussion the demands of Athens. This attempt at mediation had been undertaken at the initiative of Clerides. On 9 February, all right-wing deputies had met to discuss a proposal to merge Clerides' Unified Party with the Progressive Party, with the aim of increasing his parliamentary strength to 18 deputies, so that he would have an absolute majority. Clerides, however, put to one side the merger issue, and concentrated on discussion of the current crisis. The right-wing deputies met again the following day to discuss how they could intervene. According to a briefing obtained by the American embassy, the first measure they decided upon "was to persuade the Archbishop not to reject out of hand the Greek de-

16 Handley to Secretary of State, "Cyprus: Turk attitude toward GOG demands of Makarios", NARA, NPMS, NSC, Cyprus/Greece, telegram 1019, Ankara, 10 February 1972.

17 Nitsa Christodoulou, *op. cit.*, p. 61.

18 Panayiotakos, *op. cit.*, p. 105.

19 *Ibid.*, p. 106.

mands". The view emerging among the deputies was that Makarios ought to agree to put the arms in quarantine, to reshuffle his government and to restrain the left. The right-wing deputies prepared a memorandum to Makarios, in which they asked him to postpone his answer to the Greek government until he had consulted them, as well as "other nationalist personalities".

The meeting proposed that Clerides hand the memorandum to Makarios. The President of the House accepted, but asked to be accompanied by one Progressive Party deputy and one independent. A delegation was therefore made up of Clerides of the Unified Party, Sampson from the Progressive Party and the independent, Phidias Paraskevaides. The meeting with Makarios was arranged for 11 February, immediately after he was due to see Panayiotakos.[20] According to a briefing Clerides gave to the British High Commissioner, his delegation found Makarios "more agitated than he had ever seen him".[21] They delivered the memorandum and Makarios agreed not to answer the Greek note before consulting them. Subsequently, the delegation on its own initiative undertook to mediate with the Greek side, so they would suspend their demands until efforts had been made to see if there was room for compromise.[22]

Compromise, however, was not an option for the Greek government. Athens had already decided that it would lead its relationship with Makarios into a full rift, with the ultimate aim of removing the Archbishop from power. Panayiotakos' plan would be implemented in four phases:

1. Delivery of the note
2. Publication of its contents
3. The Cypriots would be urged to rise against Makarios
4. The Archbishop would be forced to resign, or be overthrown in a coup.

The success of the plan depended entirely on how public opinion in Cyprus would react. Panayiotakos gave assurances to Athens that in case of open conflict in Cyprus "the Greek Cypriots would choose Greece over Makarios".[23] The Americans disagreed, judging that the Greek government underestimated the popular support enjoyed by Makarios in Cyprus, and they warned Athens it was embarking on a dangerous adventure. Nevertheless, the Greek government believed it had considerable support in Cyprus. Indeed, Palamas saw the Clerides initiative to persuade Makarios to form a government of national unity as proof that the right doubted him.[24]

Makarios' first reaction was to reject the Greek note, while leaving some room for compromise. On 11 February, Christodoulos Veniamin sought out US chargé d'affaires William Crawford (ambassador David Popper was absent from Cyprus) to convey his position. According to Veniamin's briefing of Crawford, Makarios:

- Decided to reject the note and on the evening of that same day to launch an appeal to the Cypriot people.
- Accepted a regular check of the arms by UNFICYP, on condition that Grivas left Cyprus and disbanded his armed units.

---

[20] Memo from Popper to the Department of State, 29 February 1972, "Non-Communist MPs Play an Active Role During the Greek-Cypriot Dispute", NARA, RG59, CFPF, 1970-1973, Cyprus.

[21] *Ibid.*

[22] *Ibid.*

[23] Crawford to State Department, "Czech Arms", NARA, NPMS, NSC, Cyprus/Greece, telegram 288, Nicosia, 1 February 1972.

[24] Tasca to Secretary of State, 11 Fenruary 1972, "Cyprus: Greek appraisal of Makarios first reaction to note", NARA, NPMS, NSC, Cyprus/Greece.

- Said he had for a long time been disposed to make changes in his government, and would probably undertake some form of reshuffle, on the understanding that the impression would not be given that he was acting on the instructions of the Greek government.[25]

In the opposing camp, Panayiotakos met with UN special representative Ozorio Tafal. According to a briefing the UN gave Crawford, Panayiotakos told Tafal that Makarios first had to satisfy the Greek government's demands (surrender weapons, form a government of national unity) and subsequently "step down and absent himself from Cyprus". According to Panayiotakos, if Makarios were to leave Cyprus, so would Grivas. When Tafal told him it was "dangerous to push Makarios into a corner", he replied: "Who is Makarios, anyway? General Grivas is the real hero on this island." Panayiotakos added the note would be made public in a day or two. According to what Tafal understood, the Greeks expected that immediately afterwards, a spontaneous popular uprising against Makarios would break out.[26]

Later the same day, Panayiotakos received the delegation of right-wing deputies headed by Clerides, who discussed with him the proposal for a temporary 'freeze' in the Greek government's demands. In the presence of the three deputies, Panayiotakos telephoned Prime Minister Papadopoulos, who agreed to a 48-hour respite, so that an answer could be given to the note. The delegation asked Panayiotakos for clarifications on the demand for a government of national unity, before negotiating the subject with Makarios. Panayiotakos replied his government did not have a full list of candidates, but had some persons in mind:

- Former Minister of Commerce and Industry Nicos Demetriou, for the Ministry of Foreign Affairs (Athens later excluded him)
- The President of ESEA, George Vasiliades, or the President of DEK Takis Evodokas, for a ministry without portfolio.
- Deputy of the Unified Party Panayiotis Demetriou, with no determined ministry.
- Deputy of the Progressive Party Heracles Hadjierakleous, for the Ministry of Agriculture.
- Nicos Sampson for the Ministry of the Interior.

Panayiotakos told the delegation that after the formation of a government of national unity, Greece would demand the dissolution of the armed pro-*Enosis* units, would call on Grivas to come out of hiding and, if he should wish to go into politics, to do so openly. Subsequently, Athens would issue a declaration in which it supported the independence and sovereignty of Cyprus.[27]

The representatives of the deputies conveyed the Greek proposal to Makarios, who requested that the contents of the note not be made public so as to give time for further consultations, and suggested that Clerides should immediately leave for Athens. Panayiotakos replied Athens would only look favourably on such a development if Clerides was empowered to conform to Athens' demands.[28]

Sticking to a hard line, Panayiotakos continued his contact with foreign diplomats and briefed them on Athens' subsequent moves. On the evening of 11 February, he summoned US chargé d'affaires William Crawford, to whom he complained about the US not giving

---

25 Crawford to Secretary of State, "Makarios rejects GOG ultimate", NARA, RG59, CFPF, 1970-1973, Cyprus, telegram 786, Athens, 11 February 1972.

26 Crawford to Secretary of State, NARA, RG59, CFPF, 1970-1973, Cyprus, telegram 296, Nicosia, 11 February 1972.

27 Memo from Popper to Department of State, 29 February 1972, "Non-Communist MPs Play an Active Role During the Greek-Cypriot Dispute", NARA, RG59, CFPF, 1970-1973, Cyprus.

28 *Ibid.*

full support to his efforts, attributing this stance to a misunderstanding of the real situation in Cyprus. And the real picture, according to Panayiotakos, was that "Makarios was delivering Cyprus to the communists", that "he was destroying democracy" and that "he is a nobody. He has forgotten that Athens is the epicentre of Hellenism, that it is the centre that issues the orders, and the orders must be obeyed".

According to Panayiotakos, Makarios would either accept Greece's suggestions or the Cypriot people would rise up against him. "We know they will kill him," he told Crawford, adding that during his morning meeting with Makarios, he had warned him that he had better resign and leave the country, or he would face the consequences. The Greek ambassador told the US chargé d'affaires that if Makarios were to resign, Grivas would also withdraw. "I have been in contact with Grivas and he has confirmed this," he told him. Panayiotakos maintained there was a strong sentiment in Cyprus in favour of a government of national unity, and expressed his surprise at the fact that in the morning he had met Clerides and Sampson in the antechamber of Makarios' office of Makarios, and they had asked him to form such a government. This move, according to Panayiotakos, "showed the strength of Cypriot sentiment in favour of fundamental reform". Replying to a question from Crawford about the role of Clerides in such a government of national unity, Panayiotakos told him "he would obviously have to have a significant role".

Noting his impressions from his meeting with Panayiotakos, Crawford said he found their conversation "scarcely convincing". He observed that there were no grounds for discussion, because he "was so impassioned" that his behaviour "almost verged on the irrational". Crawford also noted that Panayiotakos' suggestion that, if Makarios did not compromise, Greece would encourage his assassination, was anything but acceptable diplomatic practice.[29]

The crisis in Cyprus had taken such a turn that the intervention of the National Guard appeared certain. On the evening of 11 February, the United Nations reported military movements. According to Crawford's report to the State Department, important formations of the National Guard that were loyal to Greece were on a state of alert for taking up of military positions in Nicosia. On the afternoon of 11 February, the Turkish Cypriot TMT was also in a state of readiness.[30] Indicative of the climate was the telephone despatch given the same day to *Estia* newspaper by journalist Spyros Papageorgiou, who was well informed about the activities of the National Guard. According to Papageorgiou, the General Staff was in a state of high alert. "Orders are being issued continually to military units so as to forestall any eventuality. According to certain information, tanks have been stationed at various vantage points around Nicosia."[31]

Probably so as not to hand the Greek regime an excuse for military intervention, Makarios reversed his decision to issue a proclamation announcing the rejection of the diplomatic note. Crawford, who was informed of this by Veniamin, the Director General of the Foreign Ministry, told the State Department he believed the Cyprus government was waiting for some initiative from the United States, and that it was hoping this might come with the return the following day of US ambassador David Popper.[32]

---

29 Crawford to Secretary of State, "Conversation with Greek undersecretary Panayiotakos", NARA, RG59, CFPF, 1970-1973, Cyprus, telegram 305, Nicosia, 11 February1972.

30 *Ibid.*

31 Telephone conversation between Spyros Papageorgiou and *Estia*, recorded by Cyprus KYP.

32 Crawford to Secretary of State, "Conversation with Veniamin", NARA, NPMS, NSC, Cyprus/Greece, telegram 307, Nicosia, 12 February 1972.

Crawford requested instructions from Secretary of State William Rogers as to whether a meeting should be arranged between Popper and Makarios to have an in-depth discussion of the situation, or whether the United States should keep well away from the crisis.[33] In reply, the State Department sent a telegram to its ambassadors in Nicosia, Athens, and Ankara and at the headquarters of the United Nations, issuing them a clear instruction to remain neutral until the situation became clear. The American approach could be resumed as follows:

- The United States supports the demand made at the United Nations by Greece and Turkey, that the arms from Czechoslovakia come under the control of the UN peacekeeping force.
- A peaceful solution of the problem, in such a way that would satisfy Greece and Turkey, would be an important event in contributing to the cohesiveness of the southern flank of NATO, as well as to the position of the United States in the eastern Mediterranean.
- The extent to which Greece can achieve this goal is difficult to judge, given the different estimates concerning the popular support enjoyed by Makarios, and concerning the evaluation of the Greek government that it could make the population rise up on its side.
- The significance of the action by Clerides urging Makarios in effect to agree to Greek demands to form a government of national unity is difficult to assess.
- Since – unlike in other crises in Cyprus – there was no danger of a war between two NATO members, the United States will not undertake any initiative and will wait.
- If Makarios requests a mediating role from the United States regarding his proposal for the surrender of the arms to UNIFCYP in exchange for Grivas' departure, Popper is to advise the Cyprus government to submit this proposal directly to the Greek government.[34]

The United States stuck to this policy until the end of the crisis. Ambassador David Popper repeatedly asked for approval to meet with Makarios, but the State Department repeatedly refused it. For almost two months there was no meeting between Makarios and Popper.

On 12 February 1972, the Council of Ministers was in session for the entire morning at the Presidential Palace in Nicosia. Makarios feared a coup and gave instructions that all important documents be sealed and transferred from the palace.[35] At the Greek embassy, Panayiotakos was preparing to implement the next, more critical, phase of the Greek government's plan – the publication of the contents of the diplomatic note, on the expectation that the Greek Cypriots would rise up against Makarios. This uprising was to culminate in the intervention of the National Guard and the overthrow of Makarios.

On that day, Cyprus KYP tapped a conversation involving the Director of the Second Bureau of the General Staff, Pantelis Lalaounis, exhorting the volunteers of the 'Mavromatis' association of the Ayios Pavlos area "to act with lightning speed, or else the communists would become masters of the situation and it would be too late".[36] In another conver-

---

33 Crawford to Secretary of State, "U.S. actions upon ambassador Popper's return", NARA, NPMS, NSC, Cyprus/Greece, telegram 306, Nicosia, 12 February 1972.

34 State Department to ambassadors Tasca, Handley, Popper and Philips, NARA, RG59, CFPF, 1970-1973, Cyprus, telegram 25316, State Department, 12 February 1972.

35 Nitsa Christodoulou, *op. cit.*, p. 62.

36 Cyprus KYP report, *op. cit.*, p. 8.

sation with the local section of Greek KYP, Lalaounis appeal to them to untie his hands and "give an order for that which should happen, to happen".[37]

Panayiotakos' attempt to mobilise the Greek Cypriots was launched at a news conference at the Greek embassy, during which the views of the Greek government were made public. Without even keeping up appearances, and behaving like a colonial governor rather than an accredited ambassador in an independent country, Panayiotakos launched a verbal attack on Makarios. He said the note was not an invitation to dialogue and that the Greek government was not waiting for an answer. Asked how Athens would react if Makarios rejected its contents, Panayiotakos said: "Let each person do his duty. As the centre of the Greek nation, we have said what we had to say." Panayiotakos added that the Cyprus government did not represent that part of the population that was of nationalist persuasion, and that there should be a reshuffle to include Grivas supporters in the government. AKEL members, he said, were not essential participants, but they "can play a positive part in the opposition". When journalists reminded him of Makarios' proposal to make Grivas a minister, on condition that he come out of hiding and appear in public, Panayiotakos said: "General Grivas is neither a criminal, nor a conspirator, nor on the run, and it is his right to be in Cyprus and not to want to leave the house where he resides. General Grivas has not expressed a wish to participate in the government. However, he has the absolute right to be involved in the Cyprus national issue. As to the Ministry of Defence that was offered him, without the Ministry of the Interior it has no significance. It is worth nothing."

In his press conference, Panayiotakos publicly expressed for the first time the Greek government's support for the Zurich Agreements, stating that *Enosis* was not the policy of Athens because it was a solution that was desirable but not feasible. He also drew attention to the Treaty of Guarantee, which conferred upon Greece the right of intervention and did not allow Cyprus to import weapons.[38]

Despite the fact that Panayiotakos denounced *Enosis* and supported the Zurich Agreements, which were anathema to Grivas, the pro-Grivas press reported his statements with enthusiasm: "Patriotic statements of the Deputy Foreign Minister – Mr Panayiotakos yesterday lashed out at Makarios", was the headline in *Patris*. The same newspaper, in its first-page article, wrote: "Let the nation be aware that Makarios is already stretching out his hand to give the coup de grace to the Greek Idea. He had better refrain and control himself! He is preparing to pile up new ruins. Nothing slows him down. It is sufficient for him to sit upon his throne, and never mind if Cyprus runs with blood! He cares not if Cyprus is forever cut off from the Greek world. We are going through critical times. Mr Panayiotakos has correctly stated, 'Each person should do his duty'. Of course, we must do ours!..."[39]

During the consultations that Panayiotakos had those days with foreign diplomats, as well as with UN special representative Ozorio Tafal, he told them that he was in contact with Grivas and let it be understood that he was in a position to control his movements. According to evidence gathered by Cyprus KYP, Panayiotakos had secured the assistance of Grivas in the planned coup against Makarios. The coup would be carried out by the Greek Contigent, while EOKA B would also participate, based on the plan under the code name "Sfendoni" (Sling or Catapult). To assist the coup, former Special Forces Commander Dimitrios Papapostolou, who in 1970 had linked up with Polycarpos Georgadjis to organise the attempt on Makarios' life, arrived clandestinely in Cyprus. Papapostolou met

---

37 *Ibid.*, p. 9.

38 Droushiotis, *Η 'εισβολή' της χούντας*, p. 348.

39 "Κατήλθον εις το πεζοδρόμιον" [Coming Down to the Pavement], *Patris*, 17 February 1972.

with two Irish officers of the United Nations, who had known him since 1970 when he had served in Cyprus. Papapostolou, who was wearing civilian clothes, did not explain to them why he had come to Cyprus, but "spoke of the Greek Government's insistence that Makarios give up the Presidency".

This information was conveyed from the United Nations to the American embassy. Briefing Washington, ambassador Popper wrote, "if Makarios is informed about Papapostolou's return to Cyprus, he will lose his sleep".[40] Similar information was also provided by the Turkish embassy in Nicosia. According to Turkish sources, Papapostolou was heading a unit of 25 Greek officers, who had secretly landed in Cyprus.[41]

As for Grivas, his associate George Carusos reports that during those days he had given orders for EOKA B to be ready for participation in an eventual coup.[42] On 10 February, 1972, the wire tapping service of Cyprus KYP recorded a conversation between Colonel Ioannis Zacharias, the Commander of the 1st Supreme Tactical Command in Famagusta, and Vasilios Ragousis, the Chief of Staff of the General Staff, concerning contacts between the National Guard and Grivas:

Zacharias: Is that the Chief of Staff?
Adjutant: No, it's the adjutant. Who's speaking?
Zacharias: Colonel Zacharias from the 1st. Good day, Colonel Zacharias here.
Ragousis: Hi there Ioannis, how are you doing?
Zacharias: Fine Commander; we talked about what we said, and they answered that….
Ragousis: What we said?
Zacharias: Yes, he wants to see you.
Ragousis: Me?
Zacharias: Yes, the General. I am telling you he's here. The Chief of Staff knows about it. Tomorrow, he says that if he's there at 10, I should come.
Ragousis: Yes, Ioannis.
Zacharias: That's what he told me.
Ragousis: OK, Ioannis. Any time, we're right here. Anything else?
Zacharias: Yes, I am going to see the Chief of Staff. Nobody has called him. Nobody has asked him anything, no situation created, nothing.
Ragousis: Tomorrow Di… the General will be here. [Most probably Dighenis]
Zacharias: Yes, but he told me he'll be here at 10, he wants you at 10.
Ragousis: Yes, he'll be here, I tell you, but tonight. He'll arrive tonight [he meant Charalambopoulos, who was absent in Athens, where he had gone for a meeting.]
Zacharias: Yes - no, I'm talking about the other one. [Grivas]
Ragousis: Yes, I mean, does he want to see him? [Charalambopoulos]
Zacharias: No, he wants to see your guy.
Ragousis: A is coming. OK, Yiannis.
Zacharias: Ask me, and I'll think about it, he says, can I go at 10? Yes, go.
Ragousis: OK, fine, Yiannakis.
Zacharias: Regards."[43]

---

[40] Popper to Secretary of State, "Cyprus - Return of Colonel Papapostolou", NARA, RG59, CFPF, 1970-1973, Cyprus, telegram 483, Nicosia, 1 March 1972.

[41] Crawford to American Embassy Athens, "Cyprus - Turk Embassy reports Papapostolou return", NARA, RG59, CFPF, 1970-1973, Cyprus, telegram 691, Nicosia, 2 March 1972.

[42] Carousos, interview with the author.

[43] Telephone conversation between Colonel Zacharias and Chief of Staff Ragousis, recorded by Cyprus KYP.

Analysing the contents of this exchange, Cyprus KYP came to the conclusion that Grivas was in Famagusta, and that on the following day would go to Nicosia to meet Ragousis.[44] The then director of KYP, George Tombazos, confirming the contents of the above conversation, later reported that his service was in a position to track Grivas' movements. "He was brought to Nicosia by Colonel Zacharias, who was to take him to Ragousis. However, Ragousis' sister died and he had had to leave suddenly for Greece, so he brought him to the building of the local section of Greek KYP, next to the Greek embassy, where he had contacts." According to Tombazos, after these contacts, Grivas secretly went to the Greek Contigent camp amid draconian security measures.[45] Also, according to a report by Cyprus KYP, "...on 11.2.72 Grivas was taken by PERDIKIS, on the order of LALAOUNIS to the General Staff Headuarters, where, after the arrival from Athens of CHARALAMBOPOULOS, he had a meeting.[46]

Panayiotakos, who acted as political leader of the coup, had continuous contacts with Athens on 13 February, and pressed for the final order, which, however, was not forthcoming. On 14 February, information was leaked to the press concerning the imminent coup, and an uneasy Panayiotakos made an early morning telephone call to the Foreign Ministry, in order to warn that there was no further room for delay:

"Alexandris, Foreign Ministry: How do you do, Mr Panayiotakos.

Panayiotakos:	Listen, my dear fellow. Since Chorafas is away, whom I urged not to go to Cephallonia for a weekend, but...
Alexandris:	...Who has gone anyway, and is still not back.
Panayiotakos:	He was very optimistic. There has been no decision taken about the matter that... the one of yesterday, because it is urgent.
Alexandris:	I fully appreciate it.
Panayiotakos:	Today everything here is coming out in the open. So, we can't just stay and...
Alexandris:	Yesterday at seven o'clock they came through, the Minister ['Minister' refers to alternate Foreign Minister Palamas] was aware of what you had sent from down there. Also he was aware about... of the fact that from the other side, from beyond the Atlantic, the OK had been given verbally yesterday, via their advisor.
Panayiotakos:	So it's the GREEN LIGHT.
Alexandris:	I can't make it out, because all this has been transmitted and has remained at presidential level.
Panayiotakos:	Well, I don't know, if it doesn't happen today, I'm afraid we'll have missed the boat.
Alexandris:	I get it, sir.
Panayiotakos:	Tell all this to Pesmazoglou [Palamas' diplomatic secretary], please.
Alexandris:	Now it's Mr Xenos. The Minister's office will be run by Mr Xenos.
Panayiotakos:	Because, you understand, they are talking of just about everyone. So there is no secrecy about it.
Alexandris:	So I am to see Mr Xenos and tell him to tell Mr Pesmazoglou.
Panayiotakos:	Can you put me through to Mr Xenos from there?
Alexandris:	No, because this is an outside line.

44 Cyprus KYP report, *op. cit.*, p. 7.
45 Georgios Tombazos, testimony before the Committee on the 'Cyprus File' of the Cyprus House of Representatives.
46 Cyprus KYP report, *op. cit.*, p. 7.

Panayiotakos: Well, anyway, tell him double quick.
Alexandris: Sure. I'll go down there now."

Just as they were trying to get hold of Xenos, to put him through to Nicosia, the Bishop of Kitium entered Panayiotakos' office. However, Xenos was put through immediately.

"Xenos: Good morning, how are you?
Panayiotakos: Good morning. What is happening about what I said yesterday? Is anything going to happen?
Xenos: Right now they have an appointment; they have got to see the Big Boss. [Probably George Papadopoulos]
Panayiotakos: Tell him I'm afraid that if it doesn't happen, we're in for complications.
Xenos: Those opposite [he means Parliament, where Papadopoulos had his 'political' office] are delaying him.
Panayiotakos: There is no reason. None at all.
Xenos: Yesterday we were in touch all day, and the Minister opposite as well, and they told him to wait and see how it will… Now.
Panayiotakos: So you see. Now I have just sent a telegram, look at it and you'll see that almost everything is known around here. So?
Xenos: Exactly. He has asked for an appointment to see him in a few minutes. [Palamas to see Papadopoulos]
Panayiotakos: So will we be in time for the afternoon?
Xenos: We'll see. Give it a couple of minutes to see if they have told him to go.
Panayiotakos: Yes…"

While he was waiting for Xenos to get back to him, Panayiotakos apologised to the Bishop of Kitum, who was sitting in his office waiting for him to finish his phone call.

Panayiotakos (speaking to the Bishop): Forgive me, your Excellency; it's a call from Athens.
Xenos: Still nothing. They are waiting to inform…
Panayiotakos: OK. But any delay… I've told you what I think.
Xenos: It is exactly for that reason he wants to go and see him.
Panayiotakos: I told you, from now on it's not my responsibility. (…) Do what you think best, OK, but what has to be done has to be done quickly.
Xenos: But your guy [Palamas] is backing mine up.
Panayiotakos: Of course. From the moment the GREEN LIGHT has been given from elsewhere.
Xenos: Yeah, yeah.
Panayiotakos: Thanks, bye.
Xenos: And if there is something, I'm to let you know by telex. You understand why it has to be by telex.
Panayiotakos: Agreed."[47]

Panayiotakos urged the Bishop of Kitium to visit Makarios and to indicate he should resign as President. Leaving the Greek embassy, the Bishop passed by the house of Socrates Eliades, where he attended a meeting of members of EOKA B. He then went to the Presidential Palace.

Just as the Bishop was trying to persuade Makarios to accept the diplomatic note, Vaso Loizia, a KYP officer arrived breathlessly, asking to see the President as she had a serious

---

47 Telephone conversation between Panayiotakos and Xenos on line 610481 on 14 February 1972, recorded by Cyprus KYP.

matter to report. She entered Makarios' office, clutching a portable tape recorder and a tape. She had just recorded the Panayiotakos' conversation with the Greek Foreign Ministry. Since Bishop Anthimos was present, she asked that they go upstairs. "We went up," Loizia recalls, "and I told the Archbishop that I had very important information to tell him, but rather than tell him what I knew, it was better if he heard it with his own ears. I took a pair of headphones out of my bag. Being clumsy in their use, the Archbishop had difficulty in wearing them. He listened attentively and calmly to the contents of the tape."[48]

Makarios told Anthimos to leave. He immediately called Clerides and gave him instructions to meet with the American ambassador, David Popper, and to tell him that he had information from Athens that there was to be a coup, that "it would not have the element of surprise" and that "any move by Greece would mean violence". Clerides contacted Popper a little before midday and asked him for an urgent meeting. The American ambassador received Clerides at 3pm. The President of the House briefed him on the information that Makarios had received, and he sent it by priority telegram to Washington. Popper suggested that his counterpart in Athens, Henry Tasca, secure assurances from the Greek government that there would be no outbreak of violence in Cyprus, and that negotiations for a peaceful solution to the crisis would continue.[49]

Late on the afternoon of 14 February, Popper received a telegram from Washington that stated: "Please inform Clerides that we have no information that the Greek Government is moving tonight. You may also inform him that we would be glad to have any information he might have on the subject."[50] The United States had taken Makarios' warnings seriously, and intervened with Athens to abandon its plans.

In the meantime, through the parties and organisations that supported him, Makarios had aroused the Greek Cypriots. On the evening of 14 February, an unprecedented popular mobilisation took place. Crowds of people from all over Cyprus, and mainly from Paphos, gathered in the enclosure of the Archbishopric and outside government offices. When, the following day, it was announced that a coup had been averted, a spontaneous demonstration took place outside the Archbishopric. Addressing the crowds, Makarios said: "Cyprus Hellenism has demonstrated that it forms a wall of granite, on which any machinations aimed at Cyprus will shatter."[51]

This mass popular reaction was the *coup de grace* to Panayiotakos' plans. His judgement that the Greek Cypriots would rise up against Makarios and in favour of the Greek government proved false. Panayiotakos took the blame for the collapse of the Greek government's plan to get rid of Makarios. Panayiotakos was accused of incompetence. Summing up the results of the crisis, Clerides concluded: "Makarios should decorate Panayiotakos for creating national unity." Clerides told Popper that Panayiotakos' greatest mistake was that he "spread the news that the Greek government was demanding Makarios' withdrawal from the Presidency".[52]

The spectacular failure of the Greek government's plan brought disappointment to the Turkish quarter of Nicosia. The Turkish Cypriot leadership had been waiting impatiently

---

48 Vaso Loizia, interview with the author, Nicosia, 2 April 2002.

49 Popper to Secretary of State, "Cyprus: Makarios expects Greeks to move tonight", NARA, NPMS, NSC, Cyprus/Greece, telegram 319, Nicosia, 14 February 1972.

50 Rogers to Popper, NARA, NPMS, NSC, Cyprus/Greece, telegram 25489, Department of State, 14 February 1972.

51 "Ο λαός απρόσβλητος θώραξ του Μακαριωτάτου" [The People are the Unassailable Shield of His Holiness], *Phileleftheros*, 16 February 1972.

52 Popper to Secretary of State, "Cyprus: Clerides on current situation", NARA, RG59, CFPF, 1970-1973, Cyprus, telegram 377, Nicosia, 18 February 1972.

for the coup against Makarios. TMT was on alert, while from the afternoon of 14 February the Interim Turkish Cypriot Administration had confined all Turkish Cypriots to their enclaves.[53] Rauf Denktash was furious with Panayiotakos. According to an Interior Ministry note, prepared on the basis of information received from Denktash's entourage, the hard-line Turkish Cypriot leader considered Panayiotakos' most serious mistake to be the reference in his press conference of 12 February to Greece being faithful to the Zurich Agreements: "Mr Denktash observed that Mr Panayiotakos showed himself to be politically naïve, admitting amongst other things, that Greece recognises the Zurich-London Agreements. From the time of the Papandreou government, and later in 1967, Greece had assured Turkey that she recognised the Zurich-London Agreements, but for understandable reasons she could not make her views public. (…) Although Prime Minister Mr Papadopoulos is considered by Denktash as extremely shrewd, nevertheless he has no politicians at his disposal."[54]

However, Ankara kept itself fully informed concerning developments in Cyprus, and guided the Turkish Cypriots. On 15 February, a top secret message from Ankara to the Turkish Cypriots fell into the hands of the Ministry of the Interior. It described in full all the behind-the-scenes manoeuvres that led to American intervention and the cancellation of the coup.

"After these moves," the message said, "it has been decided that any move on the part of the Greek Military authorities in Cyprus (Greek Contingent – National Guard) be terminated, leaving General Grivas to act and come into direct conflict with the Archbishop."

According to a note signed by the Director General of the Cyprus Ministry of the Interior, Antonakis Anastasiou, "…the Turkish leadership now unshakeably believes that General Grivas will act in the near future with a view to overthrowing the Archbishop, and that General Grivas is living in a room in the Greek embassy. The recent vigilant measures taken by the Turkish Cypriots (stocking up food and refraining from associating with Greek Cypriots in Greek territory) were taken after guidelines from Ankara."[55]

Were Makarios to fall, Athens had fixed on Clerides as his successor. Panayiotakos said in his memoirs that the Greek government "looked with great favour on the person of Glafcos Clerides to fill the office of president: a man of political class, moderate, enjoying general esteem and trust."[56] Greek dictator Papadopoulos also favoured the Clerides solution, as he considered as certain that he would fall into line with the Greek government's aims, especially after his initiative to persuade Makarios not to reject them. On 17 February 1972, Papadopoulos told Britain's ambassador in Athens Hopper that "…Clerides, for one, seemed to be coming over to the Greek side".[57]

Moreover, upset with Panayiotakos, Clerides expressed the view that had the Greek ambassador not handled things so badly "…an agreement could have been reached to remove Makarios from office, and provide for alternative leadership in Cyprus". Speaking on his own initiative to William Crawford on 24 February, he said, "One must admit that there has to be an alternative to continued rule by Makarios."[58] On the same day, Clerides gave an

---

53 Popper to Secretary of State, "Cyprus: Makarios expects Greeks to move tonight", NARA, NPMS, NSC, Cyprus/Greece, telegram 319, Nicosia, 14 February 1972.

54 Cyprus KYP, report based on information gathered in Dentkash's entourage, 18 February 1972.

55 Clerides, *op. cit.*, vol. 3, p. 134.

56 Panayiotakos, *op. cit.*, p. 124.

57 Popper to Secretary of State, "Papadopoulos' Feb 17 meeting with UK amb Hooper on Cyprus", NARA, RG59, CFPF, 1970-1973, Cyprus, telegram 421, Nicosia, 23 February 1972.

58 Popper to Secretary of State, "Cyprus: Clerides as alternative to Makarios", NARA, RG59, CFPF, 1970-1973, Cyprus, telegram 437, Nicosia, 24 February 1972.

interview to Peter Jennings of ABC. "Nobody is irreplaceable," he said of Makarios. Linking this statement to what Clerides had told Crawford, Popper concluded Clerides was keeping open the possibility of "offering himself as an alternative to Makarios" in the eventuality this would be feasible in the next round of conflict with Papadopoulos.[59]

The fact that throughout the crisis Clerides had inclined towards the Greek government inspired negative comments from Makarios' entourage, and on 14 February the Archbishop instructed Clerides to cease his role of mediator, and for several weeks did not summon him to the Presidential Palace. Even Clerides' political friends, such as former Justice Minister Stella Souliotou and the Director of the Hellenic Mining Company Paschalis Paschalides, were critical of the ambivalent stance he had adopted during the crisis with the Junta, and distanced themselves.[60]

Although Clerides had the ambition of succeeding Makarios, he was afraid that if he declared himself, there was a serious risk that he would suffer politically. Thus, throughout the crisis, he chose a middle way between Makarios and the Junta. Only at the beginning of March, when it was clear that Makarios would prevail, did Clerides let it be understood to Tassos Papadopoulos that in the case of Makarios resigning, he would not accept to run for the presidency.[61]

Clerides' stance aroused the displeasure of the pro-Makarios press. According to *Ta Nea*, "within the entourage of Mr Clerides, there has been discussion of his taking power, something considered as inevitable. According to this information, Mr Clerides was negotiating with Athens concerning his assuming the presidency. With this in mind, various people from his entourage made approaches. These persons were making soundings with a view to participating in a Clerides government."[62] *Ta Nea* also published a list of names of those who had been designated by Athens as ministers. They were Loukis Papaphilippou, Panayiotis Dimitriou, Andreas Neocleous and Christodoulos Christodoulou. Two years later, the first three took part in the coupist government of Sampson, Papaphilippou as Cyprus' representative at the United Nations, and the others as ministers. Christodoulou was appointed deputy minister to the President by Clerides in the post-coup government.

From the other side of the political spectrum too, there was open criticism of Clerides from the Grivas faction for his failure to come out openly against Makarios. Pointing at Clerides and the Unified Party, *Patris* wrote: "among the features of the crisis must be noted the revolting stance adopted by some 'nationalists', who refuse to declare themselves or to state publicly why they do not. EOKA organisations, the Unified Party, right wing newspapers, 'nationalist' elements etc., are in consultations day and night, prepare and bring down votes, one after the other, raise their heads, strain their ears to hear if the caterpillar tracks of the tanks are crushing the resistance of Makarios, make 'contacts', urge calm, recall for a while the 'national interest' - but take up a position, they do not. If the officers of ELDYK or of some other corps happen to come out the winners, then these splendid gentlemen would 'declare' themselves, and would put on their evening dress to head for the swearing-in ceremony."[63]

Among those considered to be playing a double game was Nicos Sampson, who appeared to be the champion of consensus politics, probably because he expected to be made a minister. In an article he published in his newspaper *Machi*, he came out in favour of the

---

59 *Ibid.*

60 Nitsa Christodoulou, *op. cit.*, p. 76.

61 *Ibid.*, p. 73.

62 "Ο Κληρίδης ητοίμαζε τους υπουργούς του" [Clerides Preparing his Ministers], *Ta Nea*, 5 March 1972.

63 "Αυτά απαιτούμεν ημείς" [This is what we are Demanding], *Patris*, 9 March 1972.

restoration of relations between Makarios and Athens. The Second Bureau of the General Staff judged that Sampson had either been blackmailed or bribed. The Director of the Second Bureau, Pantelis Lalaounis, tried to ascertain Sampson's inclinations, phoning him on 18 February 1972:

Lalaounis: I read a trashy rag recently over there, where you are writing
Sampson: I'm leaving on Sunday for America. I have a tumour between my lung and heart.
Lalaounis: What? Surely not! Well I wish you the best. And various rumours are going round…
Sampson: What do they say?
Lalaounis: Some say that you were bribed, others that you were afraid – they saw the change in stance (in *Machi*) in the space of two days, and that's the reason you are writing that (an article he wrote) over there.
Sampson: What change?
Lalaounis: The change at *Machi*, which is pretty spineless now.
Sampson: No, no.
Lalaounis: Your situation is serious, is that what you're telling me?
Sampson: Very serious.
Lalaounis: Who's looking after you here – those who come to take your tonsils out and then amputate your leg?
Sampson: No, I have had x-rays done, tests and so forth.
Lalaounis: Why didn't you go to Athens? They've got better doctors over there.
Sampson: My brother-in-law, who came from England, advised me to go to America.
Lalaounis: Are they scaring you on purpose?
Sampson: No, no, I saw it with my own eyes.
Lalaounis: Nicolakis, watch out. Watch out, because some people are after you. Some Intelligence Services, or rather Secret ones, are on to it.
Sampson: I'm not well.
Lalaounis: And you'll leave your newspaper to Fifis [Ioannou]?
Sampson: I'll let you know. Unfortunately I'm not OK. I hope in a month or two, if all goes well.
Lalaounis: And I hope your illness isn't a political one.
Sampson: Oh come on, Pantelis, you're joking surely.
Lalaounis: I see some knives around here - well done, infidels!
Sampson: OK, I've seen it myself today and now they're in a meeting.
Lalaounis: Anyway, take care of it before you leave. I wish you well, and hope everything turns out OK.
Sampson: What will be, will be. Let's hope it's benign.
Lalaounis: You can kill a bull with one punch, mate.
Sampson: In any case, before I leave I'll come to say goodbye. I'm off on Sunday.
Lalaounis: When are you coming up here?
Sampson: I'll call round tomorrow.
Lalaounis: I wish you the best, and keep your chin up.
Sampson: I'm very down.
Lalaounis: OK, I've understood that you were feeling low, but if it was for that reason, I don't know.
Sampson: You never saw me that day I came and sat down. I was hurting. I've been in pain for two months.

Lalaounis: Look, Nicos, I'm telling you this now because some matey types are in and out of your office, let's say Paphians etc. What I'm saying is, let's hope they haven't done you harm.

Sampson: No, I take no notice of that lot. Whoever came to see me, I got rid of them, in fact some were thrown out.

Lalaounis: May God be with you."[64]

On 20 February, Sampson went to the United States and checked in to John Hopkins hospital in Baltimore, where a cyst was removed from his pericardium. Indeed, the American embassy in Nicosia sent a telegram to the State Department requesting that all facilities be made available to him.[65]

The Director of the Cyprus Desk at the State Department, Tom Boyatt, visited Sampson. After his convalescence, Sampson was given a guided tour, and when he returned to Cyprus, he did not hide his gratitude to the United States, while he publicly denounced the very anti-American feelings that had driven him in the early 'sixties. "The Americans," he said in a conversation with a foreign journalist, "are the most hospitable people in the world. All they need is to wise up politically."[66]

---

64 Telephone conversation between Pantelis Lalaounis and Nicos Sampson, 18 February 1972, recorded by Cyprus KYP.

65 Popper to NEA/CYP, NARA, RG59, CFPF, 1970-1973, Cyprus, telegram 398, Nicosia, 19 February 1972.

66 "New Cyprus leader tells of rebel goals", *Washington Star-News*, 18 July 1974.

4. Makarios' Pyrrhic Victory

Immediately after the planned 14 February coup was called off, the Bishops of Kitium, Kyrenia and Paphos, Anthimos, Kyprianos and Gennadios, urged on by the Greek ambassador in Nicosia, Constantinos Panayiotakos, attempted their own ecclesiastical coup: they demanded Makarios' resignation from the civil office of President of the Republic, on the grounds that it ran contrary to the laws of the Church of Cyprus.

During the first years of the Republic, Makarios had had very good relations with Bishops Anthimos and Gennadios. Both of them had been elected Bishops on his suggestion. His relations with the Bishop of Kyrenia, on the other hand, had been bad since 1950, when Makarios was elected Archbishop, an office the Bishop of Kyrenia desperately sought for himself. Around 1968, the three Bishops had formed an anti-Makarios front, and behind the scenes were raising the issue of his resignation from the presidency.

Makarios had information that the three Bishops were cooperating with Grivas after the General arrived in Cyprus. In October 1971, a nun, Evgenia, went to the Bishopric of Kitium, whose seat was in Limassol, to obtain official seals on some icons. By chance, she entered a room in which there was a copier and some printed sheets of paper. "Somewhat sneakily," as Makarios described her action, she took a sheet to the Archbishop. It was a proclamation for the 28th October – the anniversary of Greece's 'no' to Mussolini in 1940 – which was of an anti-Makarios character.[1]

During the same period, the brother of the Bishop of Kyrenia, Renos Kyriakides, submitted a proposal to the local section of Greek KYP, suggesting that the three Bishops demand that Makarios choose between the offices of President and Archbishop. Kyriakides' proposal was brought up by Panayiotakos at a meeting that took place in Athens on 9 February 1972, at which the Czech weapons issue, was under discussion.[2]

It appears that Panayiotakos obtained approval from Athens to use the Bishops for leverage on Makarios to conform to the demands of the 'national centre'. Immediately after his return to Cyprus, Panayiotakos began contacts with Anthimos, who had the leading role among the three. Kyprianos, though fanatically anti-Makarios, had difficulty in his movements due to severe illness, while Gennadios was of advanced age.

Anthimos also had contacts regarding the matter with representatives of Grivas. On 15 February 1972, the day the coup was called off, Socratis Eliades and Marios Christodoulides visited Anthimos at the Limassol Bishopric and met with him in an effort to exert pressure on Makarios to resign from the presidency.[3] On the same day, another meeting took place with other elements from the Grivas faction, at Christodoulides' house. The contacts between Grivas people and the Bishops aroused the interest of the Director of the Second Bureau of the 4th Supreme Tactical Command in Limassol, George Apostolopoulos, whose signal alerted Nicos Dontas of the Second Bureau of the National Guard General Staff. In his reply, Dontas assured Apostolopoulos that the Grivas people "were operating as a link between the embassy, Grivas and the Bishops, and there was no cause for alarm".[4]

On 16 February, Panayiotakos went to Limassol from where he was to sail for Athens, where he was to take up duty as Deputy Foreign Minister. Before his departure, he met Anthimos and Gennadios at the Bishopric, and assured them their attempt to force

---

1 Nitsa Christodoulou, *op. cit.*, p. 50.
2 Panayiotakos, *op. cit.*, p. 124.
3 Cyprus KYP report, *op. cit.*, p. 10.
4 *Ibid.*

Makarios to resign from the presidency would enjoy the support of the 'national centre'. The Bishops agreed to request that Makarios convoke the Holy Synod, in whose presence they would officially present their case concerning the incompatibility between the offices of President and Archbishop. The day after his meeting with Panayiotakos, Anthimos announced via the junta-controlled Athens News Agency that he had asked Makarios to summon the Holy Synod. On 24 February, Anthimos and Gennadios went to Nicosia, met with Kyprianos, who was ill in a clinic, and subsequently went to Makarios and put him their demand. Finally, they agreed that the Holy Synod should meet on 2 March.

The trio's attempt was supported by the Second Bureau of the General Staff and by Greek KYP, which directed the Grivas faction's press campaign in support of the Bishops. On 18 February, Andreas Dimitripoulos of *Estia* in Athens contacted *Mesimvrini* and gave the following instructions: "Stress the intervention of the bishops, because they expose the Church importing communist arms. The Church is suffering in the communist bloc, especially in the Soviet Union. Write that the bishops expressed apprehension over the spread of Communism, which in the long term will directly be to the detriment of Christianity."[5]

At the same time, the cells that the Junta had created in the schools activated student demonstrations. Serious clashes broke out in Limassol and Morphou between student supporters of Makarios and Grivas. Nicos Dontas of the Second Bureau of the General Staff incited the Director of *Mesimvrini*, George Hadjinicolaou, to write in capital letters "Pupils in Limassol were crushed, while a bloodbath is going on in Morphou".[6]

Ironically, while the three bishops claimed Makarios' involvement in politics was an infringement of Church regulations, Panayiotakos had enticed them with promises that they would have a share of power after the Archbishop's fall. In a briefing to the British ambassador in Athens, Palamas explained his plan for the removal of Makarios from power: "Mr. Palamas said [to the ambassador] that, in the opinion of the Greek government, there was no need [in Cyprus] for a President of the Republic, but a government by nationalists, or a National Council. Precedence in the National government or Council would be taken by the Bishops, since in the proposals for the reshuffle of the government would be included suggestions as to the representation of the Bishops in the government that would be so formed."[7]

On 2 March 1972, there was a feverish atmosphere in view of the convocation of the Holy Synod, during which the three Bishops were to call on Makarios to resign. *Patris*, quoting views derived from informed sources, wrote: "Today's convocation of the Holy Synod is of the highest significance to the nation, and forms a milestone in the history of the Cyprus Church and in the *Enosis* struggle of Cypriot Hellenism." At the same time, it warned the Bishops not to make concessions, and to insist on the resignation of Makarios, otherwise even the "Church, with its spiritually nationalistic role, would be considered to be in conflict with the National Centre".[8]

In its editorial in the same edition, *Patris* writes: "Your Graces, tell Makarios with courage that it is imperative that he decide, in the end, what he wants to be: Caesar or Pope? Michael Mouskos [the secular name of Makarios], or Makarios of Cyprus? President

---

5 *Ibid.*

6 *Ibid.*, p. 11.

7 Clerides, *op. cit.*, vol. 3, p. 135.

8 "Παραίτηση του Μακαρίου θα ζητήσουν οι Συνοδικοί" [Synod to Demand Makarios' Resignation], *Patris*, 2 March 1972.

of the 'Republic', or Archbishop of the Orthodox Church? Ethnarch, or real estate go-between? Businessman, or hotelier? Ask him how many people he insists on fooling!

"Your Graces, rise above fears and vested interests, and serve only your people and Greece. Do not give way, do not retreat. At this moment History awaits, with two blank pages. One is sombre, the other pure white! On which would you rather write?"[9]

Confusion also reigned also in the opposing camp. Seventy churchmen from Paphos travelled to Nicosia and stood outside the Archbishopric in an attempt to make Gennadios change his mind. The moment he entered the building, they shouted that he ought to support Makarios. Anthimos was already in the Archbishopric, and when Makarios received him, he tried to sound him out: "I do not think it to be in the national interest, if what information I have is correct," Makarios told him. "Fine, fine, we'll talk about it inside," answered Anthimos.[10] When Kyprianos also arrived – brought from the clinic where he was receiving treatment – the critical session of the Holy Synod began. Makarios started by reporting on Papadopoulos' diplomatic note and his agonising over the Cyprus issue. The Bishops, however, were not interested in that, and turned the discussion towards their demand for Makarios' resignation. The first to speak was Gennadios, who took various papers out his pocket and began to read. One was hand written. Makarios recognised the handwriting and told him it belonged to pro-Grivas priest Papastavros Papagathangelou. The Bishop of Paphos admitted that it was indeed Papagathangelou who had written the note, but insisted the ideas were his own. In another note, Makarios recognised the characters of the typewriter belonging to *Patris* writer Polycarpos Ioannides.[11]

At that critical moment, Makarios withdrew in order to reply to an urgent phone call. On the other end of the line was the Archbishop of Athens, Ieronymos, called on Makarios not to resign from the office of president. Makarios asked him if this message echoed the thoughts of the Greek government. Ieronymos replied that he would get back to him.[12]

When Makarios returned to the convocation, Kyprianos took the floor and told him: "Let us now table that document." The reference was to a written statement by the three Bishops, expressing the opinion that Makarios ought to resign immediately from the office of President of the Republic, since holding worldly rank was incompatible with the regulations of the Church. Then Makarios blazed forth, banging his fists on the table, and the shouts could be heard as far as the offices in the Archbishopric. He said what they were attempting to do was dishonourable, that they had formed an illicit assembly before the Holy Synod convened, and that this was unacceptable.[13]

Makarios was again called to the telephone to talk to Ieronymos, who conveyed the view of the "national centre", that "the national interest demanded reconciliation and not the removal of Makarios from the presidency, even less his defrocking".[14] Ieronymos requested that he convey to the Synod his appeal that the issuing of a statement be postponed for a few hours. Makarios did so, but the Bishops were adamant. Particularly obdurate was Kyprianos, who threatened that "unless the Holy Synod issues an announcement, he would do so personally".[15] Later the same day, the Holy Synod issued the following announcement: "Their Graces, the Bishops of Paphos, Gennadios, of Kitium, Anthimos and of Kyre-

9 "Στρατιά μαρτύρων σας παρακολουθεί" [An Army of Witnesses will Attend], *Patris*, 2 March 1972.
10 Nitsa Christodoulou, *op. cit.*, p. 69.
11 *Ibid.*, p. 70.
12 *Ibid.*
13 *Ibid.*
14 Panayiotakos, *op. cit.*, p. 135.
15 "Η δραματική συνεδρία της Ι. Συνόδου" [Dramatic Meeting of the Holy Synod], *Philelftheros*, 3 March 1972.

nia, Kyprianos, proposed that Makarios resign from presidential office. His Beatitude the Archbishop will give a reply to the suggestion of their Graces the Bishops after having studied it".[16]

The next day in Nicosia there was a huge rally in support of Makarios. In Paphos. 70 priests occupied the Bishopric and hoisted a banner saying: "Gennadios, get out of Paphos". Given the situation prevailing in Paphos, Gennadios was obliged to spend the night of 2 March in the Bishopric of Kitium in Limassol. Even here, however, thousands of people gathered in protest at the actions of the "three". Inside the building were armed EOKA B men, who undertook to guard Anthimos and Gennadios. At daybreak of 3 March, as the armed EOKA B men tried to leave the building, one of them, Polis Argyrides fired his gun and seriously wounded policeman Doros Pontikis, who later died in hospital. The ecclesiastical crisis was stained with blood. In those critical moments when the internal Cyprus front was a boiling cauldron, the Second Bureau of the General Staff urged EOKA B to initiate clashes with police. On March 3, Cyprus KYP recorded a telephone conversation between Lalaounis and the head of the Second Bureau of the 4th Supreme Tactical Command in Limassol, Apostopoulos, in which he said: "Let oil be poured on the fire and if possible let the Bishopric burn."[17]

According to Panayiotakos, who quotes Palamas' testimony, Ieronymos' call to the Holy Synod was made from the prime minister's office and came after intervention by the United States, via its ambassador Henry Tasca.[18] Makarios was seen as an element of stability and the United States government supported his continued presence in power. As the British journalist Charles Foley wrote, Makarios' emergence unscathed from the 1972 crisis "was his finest hour".[19] Naturally, his victory was a Pyrrhic victory, since Papadopoulos' decision to support him found no positive response among Ioannides' hardliners. The officers manning the National Guard and the Greek Military Contingent in Cyprus, most of whom were controlled by Ioannides, continued to back Grivas' subversive activities.

Papadopoulos' about turn in favour of Makarios was immediately felt on the island. On 3 March 1972, the Chargé d'Affaires of the Greek embassy, Alexis Zafeiriou, delivered the following message to Makarios: "The Greek government requests the immediate, written and unconditional acceptance of the contents of the Greek diplomatic note; the speedy implementation of its contents and the purge of the government machinery of any anti-nationalist elements.

"Beyond the above-mentioned, the Greek government has laid down no other conditions, submitted no other demands, and has neither other conditions nor demands."

Zafeiriou told Clerides that his instructions "were to communicate the above-mentioned to the President of the House of Representatives, for it to be conveyed to his Beatitude, and not to discuss it with Mr Clerides."[20]

From the message that Zafeiriou conveyed, it appeared Papadopoulos had withdrawn the demand for Makarios to resign, and had left room for compromise. At that moment, when Papadopoulos appeared too weak to force his resignation, Makarios decided to reply to the note of 11 February – one month after its delivery. His answer was approved by the Council of Ministers on 14 March, and delivered the next day to Papadopoulos.

---

16 Papademetris, Panayiotis, Petrides, *op. cit.*, vol. 14, p. 185.
17 Cyprus KYP report, *op. cit.*, p. 14.
18 Panayiotakos, *op. cit.*, pp. 134-5.
19 "Είδα και συνωμίλησα με τον Γρίβαν" [I saw and talked with Grivas], *Alithia*, 30 October 1972.
20 Clerides, *op. cit.*, vol. 3, p. 139.

In his five-page reply, Makarios described the events that had culminated in the ultimatum of 11 February; he then explained that he refused to hand over the Czech weapons for safe keeping by the National Guard, "because the reasons for the surrender of the arms were the implication by the Greek government regarding their distribution to irresponsible people or the creation of a private army or police force of praetorian guards. I do not believe such a humiliating thought and implication directed at me should exist."

As to Papadopoulos' demand for a government reshuffle, and the inclusion in the Cabinet of a representative from the pro-*Enosis* faction, Makarios stated: "The reshuffle of the Cyprus government, according to the constitution, is the exclusive right of the President of the Republic of Cyprus.

"Mr Papadopoulos should realise that a government appointed from Athens or dependent on the latter would only be to the detriment of the subsequent development of Cyprus.

"Apart from this, I am unable to conceive how a government could function when some of its members would be in favour of a policy of *Enosis*, while others would be in favour of the independence of Cyprus. Such a Council of Ministers does not constitute progress. If your aim is to initiate a struggle for *Enosis*, then both I and the people of Cyprus are ready to enter the struggle, if the Greek government supports it."

Makarios went on to express his views on the theory of the ethnic centre: "We assure you yet again, for the umpteenth time, that we Greek Cypriots are, and feel ourselves to be, a part of the Greek Nation. Nor do we forget that the national centre is Athens, and that it will remain so. The reminder that is conveyed by the note, however, as I understand it, contains the implication that the Greek government has a say in the internal affairs of Cyprus, and even further, has the first and last word concerning the type of solution to the Cyprus issue…

"If the line to follow on the Cyprus issue is that of *Enosis*, Athens has the first word, or, as was stated, precedence. However, the Greek Cypriots are ready to undertake a struggle for *Enosis*, as long as it is not discouraged by Athens. If the policy on Cyprus is a common one, determined jointly by Athens and Nicosia, there is no question of precedence. If, however, Athens accepts a solution to the Cyprus problem that is not accepted by Cyprus Hellenism, the opinion of the Greek Cypriots must have more weight. Because the consequences of any solution whatever are to be borne by them, and they will have to live with the conditions that are created…"

In the rest of the letter, Makarios said the Athens regime did not have the authority to order the resignations of state officials who were not to its liking: "In Cyprus, there are laws, regulations and courts, which take care of the legal provision for the highest positions of State." As to what Panayiotakos had told him concerning the departure from the political scene of both Makarios and Grivas, the Archbishop criticised the Greek ambassador's behaviour, saying: "I cannot help but mention that in Athens foreign diplomats were told that, with Makarios alive, the Cyprus problem would not be solved. I do not think, however, I should expand on this theme. I only note that the statements by Mr Panayiotakos concerning my departure probably inspired the three Bishops to request my resignation from the office of president, it being incompatible with my clerical position." Further on, Makarios mentioned the conspiratorial activities of Greek officers serving in Cyprus: "The A2 Corps of ELDYK supports illegal units and persons who continue to attempt the overthrow of the President of the Republic and of the government.

"… Furthermore, the present activities of Greek officers, especially those at the head of the 2nd Staff Bureau, create scandalous situations, and ones very harmful to harmonious relations between Greece and Cyprus. I am also sad to say that some Greek officers that got involved in the past in paramilitary organisations, such as the '*Ethnikon Metopon*' (National Front), are today mixed up in many illegal activities and demonstrations."[21]

Papadopoulos replied to Makarios within 24 hours in a short letter, in which he evaded the accusations levelled at him, confining himself to stating that Makarios' answer "could in no way be considered satisfactory, nor even constructive. All the more so, as it includes a series of arrogant claims, insinuations and anti-Greek barbs, made in an unacceptable tone; rather let me prefer to push it aside, as I refuse to enter into fruitless opposition during this critical phase of the national issue."

Papadopoulos then referred to the contents of the note, but with discernible signs of retreat from the conditions he had laid down:

1. Concerning the subject of the imported Czech arms, I never intended to depart from what the official agencies of the United Nations consider, or will consider, acceptable.
2. With reference to the subject of the reshuffle of the Cyprus government, I appreciate your confirmation that you will take into consideration the relevant suggestion of the Greek government. A speedy implementation of this will restore harmonious cooperation between Athens and Nicosia.[22]

Both points were accepted by Makarios with relative ease. The arms affair was a lost cause for him from the moment that Turkey got involved, with Ankara demanding that they should be handed over to the United Nations, on pain of putting an end to the Cyprus talks and reinforcing the Turkish Cypriots with an equivalent quantity of weapons.[23] He decided, therefore, to hand them over to the United Nations, and informed the UN Secretary-general accordingly. The arms were moved on 23 April 1972 to an UNFICYP storage depot in the Nicosia airport area, where they remained until April 2002, when they were destroyed on the initiative of the Cyprus government.

Despite the fact that things were beginning to take a favourable turn, Makarios remained in a difficult position due to the ecclesiastical crisis. The actions of the Bishops had hurt his pride: "This matter of the Bishops has hurt me a lot," he told his secretary Nitsa Christodoulidou. "I admit that I admire them for the ways they found to make me pull back. They exploited the question of the arms to the utmost, so much so that I was forced to accept unconditionally. Next, the Bishops…".

He confided to his secretary that if one considered the matter from a strictly legalistic point of view, the "three" had the right to dethrone him, and he would subsequently have to lodge an appeal. "I shall never put up with such humiliation" he said.[24] Thus, the reply he sent to the Bishops on 19 March was not a legal one, but political. First of all, he accused them unequivocally of being urged on by others: "This suggestion to me in the Synod concerning my departure from the presidency was preceded by actions and collusion behind the scenes and by an 'illicit assembly', and the decision given to me was a pre-arranged set-up, since the evidence was clearly inspired from outside clerical circles. Instead of discussion and dialogue during the convocation, you each took out from an envelope a pre-prepared written text, and read it out. It is worthy of note that the Bishop of Paphos expressed his views on the basis of a handwritten paper which, as I observed at the time, was not his because the handwriting was that of another person."

---

21 Makarios III, op. cit, vol. IΓ, p. 537.
22 *Ibid.*, p. 948.
23 Clerides, *op. cit.*, vol. 3, p. 137.
24 Nitsa Christodoulou, *op. cit.*, p. 74.

As to the claim that the office of president, being a worldly one, was in conflict with ecclesiastical regulations, Makarios stated: "The office of president is called worldly. Worldly it would be, in the usual sense of the word, if it were not today bound up with the struggle of Cyprus Hellenism for national survival and its very future. It is also the Greek Cypriots' struggle, not only for their homeland, but also for their faith. It is said that worldly office contains sweetness, as does the wielding of worldly power. I have neither tasted this sweetness, nor have I desired it. To me, the office of president under such peculiar conditions has very often, and in many ways, meant only a cup of bitterness and sorrow."[25]

Encouraged by hard-line officers in the National Guard, the Bishops were determined to proceed with their plan. Wishing to give Makarios a powerful reply, they asked journalist and *Patris* columnist Spyros Papageorgiou to prepare their rebuttal. Papageorgiou recorded his experience as follows: "Bishops Gennadios of Paphos and Anthimos of Kitium called me one night (a little after 20 March 1972) to the Limassol Bishopric. Rifle barrels were pointing from within and without, the stones from the slings were still on the stairs and the Byzantine balconies, while the blood of the dead policeman had still not been washed away. I entered this hornets' nest unseen one night to kiss the Bishops' hands and to ask what they wanted. On the inner staircase of the building and in the corridors were EOKA B men, holding automatic rifles and with hand grenades in their belts. Every now and then they would glance outside through the windows of the darkened rooms, to see whether supporters of Makarios were making suspicious movements in the direction of the building. One of them (they had been together previously in prison), showing me his hand grenades, told me between clenched teeth: 'Can you see them? I'll throw this at them without warning and blow them to bits if they make as if to come over here.'

"It turned out that the Bishops wanted me to compose a letter of indictment against Makarios. Working on the basis of some general guidelines they gave me, I withdrew and wrote quite a few pages, with a cleric for company, who, for security reasons, had a 'Webley' 38 pistol in his belt, under his cassock. I was neither a theologian, nor a canon law expert, not even a mere lawyer. Thus, the text was inevitably a political indictment, which summarised whatever strong stuff had been contained from time to time in journalistic campaigns against Makarios.

"... Therefore, after I had finished the text, I went to the office of Bishop Anthimos for a final approval. This prelate was in state of great frustration. The reason for this frustration was that Grivas' second-in-command, Stavrou, had just arrived, conveying the message that the general did not want any pressure against Makarios at this time. 'There you are, I told you so, the Old Man will land us in a mess,' said Anthimos, who was beginning to suspect what Stavrou knew, namely, that Grivas had already received Makarios' invitation and was ready to meet him secretly."[26]

The reply written by Papageorgiou on behalf of the Bishops was sent by hand to Makarios. The note remained unanswered, with Makarios returning it to the "three" as unacceptable.

Immediately after the outbreak of the ecclesiastical crisis, and while that of the Czech arms was in full swing, Makarios came up with idea of meeting Grivas to smooth over the conflict with him, so he could deal with the confrontation with Athens. The ground was favourable as a result of the doubts sown in Grivas' mind concerning the intentions of the

25 Makarios III, op. cit, vol. ΙΓ, p. 541.
26 Papageorgiou, *Μακάριος*, p. 119.

Greek government, especially after the speeches made by Panayiotakos in favour of the Zurich Agreements.

On 19 February 1972, Makarios called Socrates Eliades to the Presidential Palace and asked him to convey to Grivas his concern over the intentions of Athens regarding the Cyprus issue, and to act as intermediary in arranging a meeting with him. Eliades reaction was positive, but he repeated his demand concerning Snake Island. Makarios promised that it would be fixed, and Eliades undertook to persuade Grivas. As soon as he left the Presidential Palace, he went to the Greek embassy and reported Makarios' desire for reconciliation with Grivas.[27]

Two days later, he brought Makarios a written reply from Grivas: he accepted the proposal in principle, but wanted a written note from Makarios about what was to be discussed. Makarios wrote a note and gave it to Eliades:

"Dear General, Mr S. Eliades read out to me your note, referring to the meeting between us that I had suggested.

"During the meeting, if it should take place, I would like to exchange views on the internal situation, which is showing negative developments, and on the likely prospects for our national cause. Our people are at present divided into 'Makarios supporters' and 'Grivas people'. That is to say, we have become established as symbols of division. We should become symbols of unity for the people. I am of the opinion that it is possible, through understanding and cooperation, for us to create the most powerful of internal fronts, for the benefit of our national cause. The internal situation and the further handling of the Cyprus issue will be the main themes at our meeting. So as to avoid any misunderstanding whatever concerning the purpose of our meeting, it would be advisable that the Greek government be informed accordingly, for the inclusion of a representative."[28] Makarios deliberately included this final reference for reasons of self-defence, in case the note was made public or leaked to the Junta.[29]

When Grivas received the note, he charged a three-member delegation, made up of the President of ESEA George Vasiliades, the Head of the National Democratic Party Takis Evdokas, and Socrates Eliades, to meet with Makarios and request clarifications. The meeting took place at the Presidential Palace on 29 February. The delegation set as a condition that the objective of the meeting would be the declaration of independence as a solution to the Cyprus problem, and the move towards self-determination/*Enosis*. These negotiations came to nothing, and Makarios sought another channel of communication with Grivas through doctor Marios Tritoftides from Limassol, who had a certain sympathy for Grivas, but was considered a moderate. On the other hand, Grivas charged Stavros Stavrou-Syros to make direct contact with Makarios and negotiate the conditions under which the meeting would take place.

The first contact between Makarios and Syros took place at the Archbishopric, on the evening of 21 March; Marios Tritoftides was also present at the meeting. Even though Socrates Eliades was no longer involved in the negotiations, Makarios considered it important to satisfy his demand, and to give him Snake Island. On 23 March 1972, the Council of

27 Droushiotis, *Η 'εισβολή' της χούντας*, p. 379.
28 The correspondence between Makarios and Grivas was published by Grivas in *Ethniki* newspaper during the summer of 1973. Reprinted as an appendix in Papageorgiou, *Μακάριος*.
29 Nitsa Christodoulou, *op. cit.*, p. 67.

Ministers approved a proposal from the Ministry of Commerce and Industry for a long-term lease of the island to Eliades.[30]

After this arrangement, the meeting between Makarios and Grivas was fixed for Saturday 25 March in Nicosia. The meeting place had not been determined in advance. According to the agreement, Syros would go to the Archbishopric and would lead Makarios to where Grivas was, the latter having gone from Limassol to Nicosia the preceding day. On the evening of the 25th , Syros and Tritoftides went to the Archbishopric to accompany Makarios to the meeting place. Makarios held back, however, invoking security reasons, and told Syros that he could not leave the Archbishopric without his bodyguards: "It is impossible to deter my bodyguards from going with me. (….) Perhaps they would initially listen to me, but they would follow us and perhaps cause incidents" Syros asked Makarios not to be afraid, and that he would zig-zag and lose them. Makarios replied that for the good of both of them "this should not happen, and what would people say if they saw me running into a car late at night and going into unknown houses?"[31]

The Archbishop proposed other arrangements and suggested five houses in which the meeting could take place, preference being shown for that of his niece Ersi Constantinidou, near the Hilton. He accepted that the house should be guarded by EOKA B men, but wished to go to the meeting point accompanied by his own men. Syros was eventually persuaded and asked him to write a note to Grivas. Makarios wrote the following note:

"I have good reasons to believe that the implementation of today's meeting, or rather the suggested arrangements for the meeting, present serious dangers for us both.

"I have explained the dangers to Major Stavrou. I warmly urge that other arrangements be made for the meeting, which, I believe, will be very useful and which I desire very much. I greatly regret any inconvenience caused to you. I have made some suggestions to Mr Stavrou."[32] When Makarios cancelled the meeting, probably he was not aware of the fact, later published in the press, that men from the Junta had bugged the house where it was to take place.[33]

Early the next morning, Syros, Tritoftides and the Director General of the Foreign Ministry, Christodoulos Veniamin, met at Veniamin's house in the government compound near the Presidential Palace. They discussed alternative solutions, based on Makarios' suggestions. They ended by agreeing that the meeting should take place at the house of Ersi Constantinidou, daughter of Makarios' brother, Yiakoumis. The meeting was fixed for 8 the same evening.

At five minutes to eight, a BMW of the presidential guard, driven by Dinos Constantinou, with Makarios' adjudant Nicos Thrasyvoulou by his side, and Archbishop Makarios and his nephew Andreas Neophytou at the back, left the Archbishopric and headed up to the Hilton. Following a route that avoided the main roads, the car arrived at eight precisely at the address on 59, Kennedy Avenue.

According to the agreed arrangement, an armed group of EOKA B guerrillas would be at the house at the time of the meeting. On the other hand, a platoon from the Reservist Corps took up positions in an orphanage opposite the house. Ersi Constantinidou described the events as follows: "First Syros arrived and told me to go to the kitchen so that I would

---

30 Socrates Eliades had joined with the British organisation Crown Agents with a view to the tourist development of the region. The area covered 26 donums, and he was to be given permission to build a 400-bed hotel. The agreement would be for 99 years and the rent would be £50 a year.

31 Nitsa Christodoulou, *op. cit.*, p. 81.

32 Makarios-Grivas correspondence in Papageorgiou, *Μακάριος*, appendix.

33 Papademetris, Panayiotis, Petrides, *op. cit.*, vol. 14, p. 204.

not see the faces of the armed EOKA B men. Afterwards I heard them running up the stairs. The same happened when they left. I saw none of them. After the guard settled in, Grivas came to the house. Elli Christodoulidou and Marios Tritoftides accompanied him. Five minutes later, the Archbishop's car could be heard drawing up in the yard."[34]

Makarios later told his secretary of his first impressions: "I was wondering whether I would find Grivas or someone else. As soon as I walked in I saw Ersi in the background and then the Doctor [Tritoftides] and Elli Christodoulides. I wondered if they would let Nicos and Andreas come in with me, but when I saw those I realised there was no problem. On the left I could make out the figure of Grivas. We sat and talked for about an hour and 40 minutes."[35]

What was said between the two emerged from later correspondence between them that was published in the press, as well as from descriptions of Makarios to his secretary, who noted them down in her diary. Makarios briefed Grivas on the attempts of Greece and Turkey to impose a solution to the Cyprus problem that he considered mistaken, and mentioned the Lisbon agreement and the Papadopoulos memorandum. Grivas proposed to Makarios the following plan for a change of course in the Cyprus issue:

"The Archbishop is to resign the office of president, and give up politics.

"Elections are to be announced in advance, with a candidate for president to be one of general acceptance (...).

"I shall not personally involve myself in politics, but will cooperate fully with the Archbishop and take personal responsibility for the implementation of the plan for the solution of the Cyprus problem suggested by me.

"Cooperation will be sought with the Church, being an Ethnarchic entity.

"A Cabinet reshuffle is to take place as speedily as possible, with the assignment of the main ministries, those of Foreign Affairs, of the Interior and Defence, to persons who enjoy general confidence, in order to seek a calming of the present abnormal situation, enlightenment of the people and preparation of the ground for elections, which must take place at the latest within two months.

"The new President-elect of the Republic will table directly the implementation of the principle of self-determination as the solution to the Cyprus issue."[36]

Makarios did not react negatively to Grivas' proposals. Through various questions, he tried to elicit the data on which he had based his plan. He asked to what extent the Junta was prepared to accept the policy of *Enosis*, or whether it would aim for double *Enosis*. Without explaining how, Grivas said that Greece could manoeuvre the Greek Cypriots to a policy of *Enosis*, and completely excluded the possibility of a Turkish invasion. As to the candidate of common acceptance, no mention was made of names. Makarios said only that he would have to be in a position to inspire the people, allowing Grivas to understand that he excluded nothing, without however committing himself to anything.

The meeting ended without any specific conclusion, beyond some confidence-building measures in their relationship. Associates of Grivas, mainly George Carousos, vehemently claim that there was agreement on the basis of the Grivas plan, which was not implemented due to Makarios' backtracking, something that is not supported by other sources. On the contrary, a letter that Grivas sent to Carousos at the beginning of April 1972, said the following: "No definitive agreement was reached with Makarios. I merely laid down condi-

---

34 Droushiotis, *Η 'εισβολή' της χούντας*, p. 385.
35 Nitsa Christodoulou, *op. cit.*, p. 82.
36 Makarios-Grivas correspondence in Papageorgiou, *Μακάριος*, appendix.

tions. (...) Should he accept them, it is a great victory for us. I await an answer from him."[37]

The eventuality of cooperation between Makarios and Grivas provoked displeasure in Junta circles and especially among the hardline officers that were guiding EOKA B, something noted by Grivas in his letter to Carusos: "vigilance and surveillance are required because the Junta is moving against us for fear of a cooperation with Makarios, in which case all its plans collapse. All section leaders will follow us blindly. The only fear is that of an earthquake. However, you'd better get your section leaders together and urge obedience to the decisions of the Chief, and bind them with an oath."[38]

Grivas' note clearly showed his apprehension that, if he were to proceed with his cooperation with Makarios, there were section leaders who might not fall in with his decisions. The strongest reactions came from the Famagusta district, where EOKA B was under the direction of Kikis Constantinou. With a view to soothing reactions, Grivas went on a tour throughout Cyprus at the beginning of April, starting from Famagusta and reaching Morphou, briefing the cadres of his organisations on his intentions.[39]

According to a briefing that Clerides gave American ambassador David Popper, there were two tendencies within Grivas' entourage. On the one hand, there were the politically savvy, who advised Grivas to retain contact with Makarios, but to insist on the demand for his resignation and on his joining Grivas in a higher council that would organise the *Enosis* struggle. These elements adopted the position that Grivas had followed during his meeting with Makarios, concerning the appointment of a president of common acceptance, who would act on the guidance of the higher council. On the other hand, the hardliners favoured military opposition, aiming at breaking off all contact with Makarios, and the implementation of a military action plan as soon as possible. According to Clerides, Grivas' position was becoming daily more untenable. "He had committed himself to seeking a solution to the Cyprus problem through *Enosis* by self-determination. Some of his supporters, especially former associates of Georgadjis and some who had links with Greece, were more interested in the overthrow of Makarios than in what would happen afterwards. But all find it more and more repugnant to go along with the waiting game of Grivas."[40]

The politically aware associates of Grivas began to set up various scenarios for Makarios' succession in the eventuality that he would resign from the presidency. The name of the Director of the Hellenic Mining Company (EME), Paschalis Paschalides, had been leaked to the press as a candidate of common acceptance. Furthermore, according to a confidential report that Clerides made to Popper, men from Grivas' entourage had sounded him out as to whether he would accept the presidency were Makarios to resign, under the following conditions:

- He would limit the influence of the communists in the government.
- He would not exclude *Enosis* from the intercommunal talks.
- He would give the Turkish Cypriots a ministry for Turkish affairs.
- The agreement on the Cyprus problem would be for a specific period of time.
- If the talks failed, the policy of self-determination/*Enosis* was to be implemented.

---

37 Η ζωή και το έργο του Γεωργίου Γρίβα Διγενή, op. cit., p. 140.
38 *Ibid.*
39 Droushiotis, *Η 'εισβολή' της χούντας*, p. 390.
40 Popper to Secretary of State, "Clerides foresees new tension between Grivas and Makarios", NARA, RG59, CFPF, 1970-1973, Cyprus, telegram 947, Nicosia, 29 April 1972.

Clerides told Popper he did not wish to take on the presidency under such conditions.[41]

Of course, these were just scenarios, since the Makarios-Grivas meeting had agreed nothing. On the contrary, only a few days afterwards, Makarios expressed to his secretary his disappointment at the results: "Do you know how much I regret having met Grivas?" He blamed himself for not having reacted to the Grivas' proposals during that meeting, and of having given the impression of being accommodating. "I should have told him, let's say, jokingly: 'but wait a minute, my dear General, have we met just for you to tell me to resign?'" The adventure into which he had plunged himself must have affected him psychologically: "If I were a mirror," he said, "and someone could see inside me, he would see a blackened heart. Do you know what that means? Black as pitch… four fronts. You know, I am inclined to resign."[42]

On 29 March, Makarios and Syros again met at the Archbishopric to discuss the confidence-building measures, of which the main ones were the issuing of a poster marking the anniversary of 1st April – the start of the EOKA struggle in 1955 – with the photographs of Makarios and Grivas and the slogan "Long Live *Enosis*", and the release from confinement of Grivas supporters who were facing charges of conspiracy against the state, or who had been convicted for similar offences.

Syros presented Makarios with a long list of names of EOKA B members whose release Grivas was requesting. Makarios accepted, but excluded those imprisoned for the theft of arms from Trikomo, telling Syros that he did not believe that Grivas would want his name linked with an affair of high treason. Concerning the poster, Makarios said something like that was risky since "some of their own extremists would not look on it favourably". Instead of that, he asked him to convey to Grivas the suggestion that he should appear on the VIP platform during the parade for the anniversary of 1 April.[43]

The first information concerning the Makarios-Grivas meeting soon leaked to the press. On 11 April, the Junta newspaper *Ta Simerina* published in detail the scene of the meeting. And while Turkey had not objected to the presence of Grivas in Cyprus until that moment, suddenly the Turkish press began to suggest that Athens favoured his departure from Cyprus, because the eventual alliance with Makarios would have a negative influence on Greco-Turkish relations.[44]

A few days later and seven months after Grivas' arrival in Cyprus, the Turkish Cypriot leadership protested for the first time about his presence on the island. On 28 April 1972, it issued an announcement in which it recalled the gentleman's agreement of November 1967, according to which "the Greek government promised the government of Turkey that it would confine Grivas to Greece, far from Cyprus."[45]

---

41 Popper to Secretary of State, "Clerides explains state of play in Makarios - Grivas - Athens ball game", NARA, RG59, CFPF, 1970-1973, Cyprus, telegram 805, Nicosia, 6 April 1972.

42 Nitsa Christodoulou, *op. cit.*, p. 83.

43 Droushiotis, *Η 'εισβολή' της χούντας*, p. 388.

44 "Ο κ. Ζαφειρίου ενετάλη να φροντίση όπως ο Γρίβας απομακρυνθή εκ Κύπρου" [Mr Zafeiriou will Ensure that Grivas leaves Cyprus], *Phileleftheros*, 12 April 1972.

45 "Θέμα Γρίβα δημιουργούν οι Τούρκοι" [Turks raise the Grivas Issue], *Phileleftheros*, 29 April 1972.

5. The Makarios-Papadopoulos Alliance

Towards the end of March 1972, a realignment began to emerge within the Junta as a result of Papadopoulos' about-turn towards Makarios. Initially, there was the recall to Athens on 19 March of Pantelis Lalaounis, who, as head of the Second Bureau was landed with the blame for the fiasco of the 14 February coup that never was. Blame was also shared by the leadership of Greek KYP in Nicosia for the assurances it had given that Makarios' removal would be an easy matter. On 22 March, the Regent Zoitakis was sacked from his post, an event linked with the Cyprus developments.[1] George Papadopoulos was sworn in as Regent in his place.

On 29 March, the Head of the command echelon of Greek KYP, Costas Douzinas, summoned the deputy of the Unified Party Michalakis Savvides and briefed him on the change of course by the Greek government, which "is no longer demanding the resignation of Makarios and is pressuring the Bishops into not insisting on the matter any more, or at least not to set a timeframe for his removal. Furthermore, he stressed the need for a solution to be found in order to get through the crisis."[2]

After this development, Makarios called Clerides to the Presidential Palace, "for the first time in many weeks", as Clerides told US ambassador David Popper, to discuss the situation, giving him the task of officially sounding out the Greek Chargé d'Affaires Alexis Zafeirou about Athens' intentions.[3] On 3 April, Clerides sent Makarios the following message:

"Mr Zafeirou said that, if the Cyprus government were to be relieved of three or four ministers who are adversely affecting relations between the two governments since they accuse the Greek government of planning to impose an ethnically unacceptable solution, relations between Athens and Nicosia would substantially improve. In such a case, according to Mr Zafeirou, no importance would be attached any longer to who should take the final decisions, since the two cooperating governments would be adopting the same political approach."[4]

Basically, Athens was abandoning its claim to have the first word on the Cyprus issue, and what it was asking for – probably for reasons of prestige – was a government reshuffle in Nicosia. Clerides continued his contacts with Zafeirou, and on 6 April sent a new report to brief Makarios, in which he mentioned that the Greek government considered imperative the replacement of certain ministers by mutually acceptable figures, but – as Zafeirou had clarified – "there was never any intention of imposing any individual persons."[5]

Those ministers the Greek government wished to replace were Foreign Minister Spyros Kyprianou, "because he is to blame for actions offensive to the Greek government", Education Minister Frixos Petrides, because "he is known for his many actions that were at the expense of Greek education", Interior Minister Epaminondas Komodromos, who "is not charged with anti-Greek activities, but lacks initiative, decisiveness and the ability to take responsibility, especially in times of crisis, and clearly lacks essential qualities, attempting

---

1 According to British journalist Charles Foley, the only foreign journalist to meet Grivas throughout the activity of EOKA B, in October 1972, Zoitakis had been the person who had encouraged Grivas to return to Cyprus. ("Είδα και συνωμίλησα με τον Γρίβαν" [I saw and talked with Grivas], *Alithia*, 30 October 1972).

2 Clerides, *op. cit.*, vol. 3, p. 155.

3 Popper to Secretary of State, "Clerides sees hope for reconciliation with Greece", NARA, NPMS, NSC, Cyprus/Greece, Nicosia , 31 March 1972.

4 Clerides, *op. cit.*, vol. 3, p. 156.

5 *Ibid.*, p. 155.

to cover up his inadequacy through untimely and harmful statements". In his public appearances, Komodromos would constantly speak of *Enosis*, a fact that upset Ankara as much as Athens. Furthermore, Greece wanted the replacement of Government Spokesman Miltiades Christodoulou – "known for his past, and for his recent behaviour" – of the head of Cyprus KYP George Tombazos, "known for his anti-Greek tendencies, and for his association with Mr Lyssarides". On the list was also Mayor of Nicosia, Lellos Demetriades, "as he has clearly anti-Greek tendencies and an unacceptable stance vis-à-vis Greek officers".[6]

An initiative aiming at the normalisation of relations between Athens and Nicosia was undertaken by the Greek regime through Savvas Constantopoulos, publisher of the newspaper *Eleftheros Kosmos*. Constantopoulos was the theoretician of the dictatorship, a close associate of Papadopoulos, and was at the head of the American anti-communist campaign in the Greek press.

At the end of March, on his return from the USA, where he had undergone surgery, Nicos Sampson stopped over in Athens and was received by George Papadopoulos, with whom he discussed the situation in Cyprus. As soon as he got back to Nicosia, he met US embassy official Joseph Lawrence and briefed him on his talks with Papadopoulos. According to Sampson, Papadopoulos had told him that the Greek government no longer demanded the resignation of Makarios, and that its wish was that the Archbishop should see out his term, which ended in February 1973. Nevertheless, Papadopoulos insisted on a government reshuffle, and told Sampson that he had him earmarked for the Ministry of the Interior.

Sampson also met Makarios and informed him of Papadopoulos' intention to send Constantopoulos to Cyprus as his personal envoy to negotiate the government reshuffle with him. According to Sampson, Makarios told him that if the Greek government had not decided to send Constantopoulos to Cyprus, he would have invited him himself.[7]

Commissioner for Cooperative Development, Andreas Azinas, who had a close personal relationship with Constantopoulos and, through him, with Papadopoulos[8], also informed the American embassy about the Greek government's initiative. Azinas went to Athens at the beginning of April 1972, made contact with Papadopoulos and discussed with him the demand for a Cabinet reshuffle in Cyprus. According to the briefing that Azinas gave to the American embassy, Constantopoulos arranged for a visit by Makarios to Athens and for a meeting with Papadopoulos.[9]

On 17 April, Makarios received a neatly tied up and sealed envelope bearing many signatures of Constantopoulos. Inside, there was a note and a list of names of possible ministers, which had been drawn up by Constantopoulos "after serious consultations with the regime", as he wrote in his explanatory note. Pavlos Pavlakis, a former deputy was earmarked for the Ministry of Foreign Affairs; for that of the Interior, the regime wanted Cy-

---

6 *Ibid.*, p. 158.

7 Popper to Secretary of State, "Cyprus: Conversation with Nicos Sampson", NARA, RG59, CFPF, 1970-1973, Cyprus, telegram 799, Nicosia, 5 April 1972.

8 On 21 April 1967, Azinas was in Athens and, through Constantopoulos, made contact with Papadopoulos. Azinas says he had frequent contacts with Papadopoulos, which took place with Makarios' knowledge. "It was the only way to make certain things known to Athens and at the same time to learn exactly what was going on there," he says. ("Εγώ είχα με τη χούντα ντόμπρες σχέσεις" [I had Frank Relations with the Junta], *Philelftheros*, 15 July 1999.) However, according to the diary of Makarios' secretary, Nitsa Christodoulou, Makarios mistrusted the accuracy of the information that Azinas ferried back and forth to Athens, and he trusted neither him nor Constantopoulos. (Nitsa Christodoulou, *op. cit.*, p. 88.)

9 Memo from Popper to Department of State, 25 May 1972, "Discussion with Greek Cypriot Cooperatives Commissioner Azinas", NARA, RG59, CFPF, 1970-1973, Cyprus.

prus' ambassador to Athens, Nicos Kranidiotis; for the Education Ministry Costis Hadjicostis, whom Makarios had placed in the Press Office of the High Commission in London, or Constantinos Spyridakis; for the position of Director of the Public Information Office Charalambos Hassapis; and as Head of KYP, Nicos Sampson.

Addressing his secretary, Makarios commented the proposal to appoint Sampson as Head of KYP: "If I put Sampson in KYP, it would be as if I was paying the head of their secret services. He comes to me and tells me various things and wants – from what I can understand – to be a minister. I listen to him and feel like saying to him: 'my friend, you're not right for the position of minister', but I can't."[10] Makarios also told his private secretary that the Junta had Sampson eating out of their hand, because of an appeal that his newspaper *Machi* had made for Greece to buy Mirage aeroplanes, the money from which it appeared he had appropriated for himself.[11]

On 3 May, Makarios asked Clerides to inform Zafeirou that he would be proceeding to a Cabinet reshuffle in the middle of June, and that on the next day he would brief the members of the Council of Ministers. The dismissal of Spyros Kyprianou was considered certain, after Palamas' refusal ever to work with him again. Kyprianou resigned on 5 May and on 16 June Makarios announced the reshuffle. As new Foreign Minister he appointed Yannis Christofides. He also replaced Interior Minister Komodromos with George Ioannides and Education Minister Frixos Petrides with Andreas Kouros. Makarios did not consult the Athens regime over the composition of the new government, the only exception being in the case of the Ministry of Education.[12]

After Makarios had come through the danger he had been facing from the Junta, he decided to close the account he had opened with Grivas. On 3 April 1972, he conveyed to Grivas through Marios Tritoftides that he agreed with whatever had been discussed at their meeting of 26 March concerning the Cyprus issue and the adoption of an *Enosis* policy, but he believed that this had to be implemented by gradual stages. Makarios invoked the disagreement of the Greek government, the probable reactions of Briatian and the United States and the danger of a Turkish intervention.[13]

Reacting, Grivas sent a letter to Marios Tritoftides on 17 April, which was chiefly addressed to Makarios. In the letter, he repeated what had been said at their meeting concerning Makarios' resignation and the support for a jointly agreed candidate, whose slogan in the elections would be 'Self-determination/*Enosis*'. Commenting on the reservations expressed by Makarios invoking the Greek government's disagreement, Grivas wrote: "The correct alignment of this issue should be a different one. You should directly table what we and the Greek Cypriot people of the island desire, and call on the Greek government to adopt a position on this matter, and make this known to the interested parties in the Cyprus question."

Referring to London and Washington's disagreement with the policy of *Enosis*, Grivas wrote: "If the British and the Americans, who are responsible for the present situation in Cyprus, wish to appease the Turks, they can do so at their own expense, not ours." As to the possible reaction of Turkey, he wrote: "She is not capable of carrying out an invasion of Cyprus and especially under the present conditions."[14]

---

10 Nitsa Christodoulou, *op. cit.*, p. 88.
11 *Ibid.*
12 *Ibid.*, p. 100.
13 Makarios-Grivas correspondence in Papageorgiou, *Μακάριος*, appendix.
14 *Ibid.*

Makarios made a point-by-point response directly to Grivas on 4 May. "I had reservations about the successful outcome of your plan and fears that it would probably unwittingly lead to the establishment of conditions facilitating partition and double *Enosis*. (...) I sincerely believe that under the present conditions, the cause of *Enosis* will not be promoted based on your suggestions. The steady and unwavering devotion to *Enosis* naturally constitutes the first and main factor. But not that alone. There are other objective factors that do not depend upon us, to ignore which would be harmful to the national interest.

"The struggle of Cyprus Hellenism, in today's circumstances and conditions, is rather one of a defensive nature. That is, I have been fighting a rearguard action to avoid the imposition of an unacceptable solution to the Cyprus problem. And to date our defence has proved successful. I have defended us against – and refused to accept – a solution that would commit the future of our nation. *Enosis* is a compass to our national orientation as well as a living, intense aspiration. However, *Enosis* cannot be realised if first the danger of another undesirable solution is not removed and avoided. I would not hesitate immediately to change my political line, according to your suggestion, if the Greek government was in agreement with this. (...) If the Greek government, weighing up the capabilities of other factors present, takes a negative stance, then the consequences for *Enosis* would be counterproductive. Furthermore, I do not exclude the possibility that the danger of double *Enosis* is unavoidable, even if I have been determined to face up to it. (...) The change of political course today – and especially in the face of Greek disagreement – will lead to our international isolation. And Cyprus will be easy prey for Turkey, which, taking advantage of most existing conditions, is continually hardening her position."[15]

Grivas replied to Makarios on 16 May. In his reply, he evaded Makarios' assertions, retorting that his views were "vague and stereotyped" and were an attempt at "evasion when confronted by issues clearly stated by me". Grivas wondered at the invitation to work together, since his views on the Cyprus problem "were known to us through repeated speeches of mine, which were characterised by my unshakeable devotion to a speedy and immediate solution of *Enosis*".

Concerning Makarios' reservations about the position adopted by Athens on *Enosis*, Grivas said: "If you believe the policy of self-determination/*Enosis* is correct, you should be bound in all frankness and sincerity to first suggest this to the Greek government. I believe that no Greek government will refuse to help the Greek Cypriot people, or to share the necessary sacrifices, if we first declare ourselves determined to fight..."

Concluding his letter, in answer to a proposal by Marios Tritoftides for another meeting with Makarios, Grivas laid down an ultimatum: "A second meeting between us, as suggested by the intermediary on his own initiative, should it be accepted by you, would be completely pointless, unless you were to decide to accept my basic suggestions and to inform me of this in writing as soon as possible."[16] This letter put an end to the cycle of negotiations between Makarios and Grivas.

The timing of Makarios' decision to disengage from the dialogue with Grivas – immediately after the crisis in his relations with Papadopoulos had blown over – aroused bitterness in the Grivas camp. In his letter to Tritoftides, Grivas had referred to the disagreements expressed by some of his supporters as to whether he should meet Makarios, and to the efforts he had made to convince them. "These people were, and perhaps still are, of the

---

15 *Ibid.*
16 *Ibid.*

opinion that the gesture of the Archbishop concerning us meeting together was a bluff, which he used as a 'bogey' to alarm the Greek government."[17]

Makarios's decision to meet Grivas was certainly a tactical move, at a time when he was facing pressure to resign on a number of fronts. Grivas had every reason to be furious with the flirtation between Makarios and Papadopoulos. He felt especially betrayed by the Greek government, which had abandoned him and attempted to build bridges with Makarios. He expressed his fury in a written order that he issued, in which he distanced himself as much from Makarios as from Papadopoulos. "I have no links with, nor am I attached to, any political faction whatsoever, nor to any government, whether of Greece or of Cyprus... I shall cooperate with the Devil himself if this cooperation were indeed to secure *Enosis* for us..."[18]

Grivas distanced himself from the government of Greece, but not from the Greek officers serving in Cyprus. The officers loyal to Ioannides in the National Guard and the Greek Contingent appeared as "healthy forces of the Revolution". They distanced themselves from the nascent alliance between Papadopoulos and Makarios, and instigated military action in EOKA B, while exhorting the Bishops to proceed with the dethroning of Makarios.

On the afternoon of 14 May 1972, Bishop Anthimos called the Commander of the Academy of Reservist Officers, Evangelos Tsapoyias, to the Limassol Bishopric, and asked him to facilitate a meeting with Grivas within the army camp. The meeting took place the next day, in the chapel at the Academy. According to Nicos Dontas of the 2nd Bureau of the General Staff, the reason for choosing such a location was to make the army aware of the meeting and of what was being discussed.[19]

Grivas and Anthimos decided that the effort to force Makarios to resign should continue. That day, Anthimos gave Grivas £10,000 "as financial support for the organisation and for the purchase of weaponry".[20]

After the meeting between Anthimos and Grivas, the three Bishops once again initiated the procedure to dethrone Makarios, charging him with involvement in politics. In their letter dated 1 June 1972, the three Bishops gave Makarios ten days' notice to resign from the office of president: "We address His Beatitude on this final occasion and demand from Him that He immediately and without delay give up the office of President of the Cyprus Republic, it being incompatible with the position of Archbishop, and that He confine himself to clearly ecclesiastical and Ethnarchic duties.

"We make it known to His Beatitude that we expect His answer at the beginning of 10 June. In the event that His Beatitude should wish to continue to hold this position in clear opposition to Sacred Canonical regulations, we inform Him, with great regret, that we will be obliged to impose the provided sanctions, according to the Holy Regulations and the Constitution of the Most Holy Church of Cyprus."[21]

Makarios replied to the ultimatum at the very last moment: "My Greek and Archiepiscopal conscience concerning my mission as Ethnarch does not permit me, at this time of the present greatest peril, to abandon the people, who are looking to us. This flight and desertion of the people on my part would be considered a betrayal. In the face of the oncoming wolves the pastor does not abandon his sheep and run away."[22]

---

17 *Ibid.*
18 *Ibid.*
19 Cyprus KYP report, *op. cit.*, p. 16.
20 *Ibid.*, p. 17.
21 Makarios III, op. cit, vol. IΓ, p. 937.
22 *Ibid.*, p. 589.

Despite Makarios' refusal to fall in with their request, the three gave way and did not implement their threat to dethrone him. This time, Makarios had the support of the Greek government and, through the latter, that of the Church of Greece, which put pressure on the Bishops not to take things to extremes.

In spite of the Greek government's about-turn in its relations with Makarios, the Deputy Foreign Minister, Panayiotakos, maintained a policy of confrontation. In contacts with an American diplomat at the beginning of June 1972, he said: "the Greek government will not forget that the government of the United States did not help in its attempt to remove Makarios." In the same conversation, Panayiotakos laid full blame for the stagnation in the Cyprus talks on Makarios, and maintained that only his removal could bring about a solution. In fact, he warned that as long as Makarios remained President of Cyprus, the island was in danger of becoming the Cuba of the Mediterranean.

Panayiotakos' approach provoked a reaction from Tom Boyatt, Head of the Cyprus Desk at the State Department. Boyatt sent a telegram to the embassy in Athens, making his position clear on the three points raised by Panayiotakos:

1. Concerning the lack of progress in the talks, Boyatt wrote that the stagnation observed since 1968 could not be laid exclusively at the door of Makarios. "The Archbishop has been the major factor in the lack of progress, since he has been satisfied to live with the status quo, which is favourable to him. However, it must also be said that the Turkish Cypriots, with the support of Turkey, have shown very little inclination to make significant compromises on key issues. The record demonstrates that the government of Cyprus has made some concessions in the area of local autonomy. Obviously, the government of Cyprus has not gone as far as the Turkish Cypriots would want, nor as far as will be necessary to reach an agreement. More flexibility on both sides is required."
2. Referring to Panayiotakos' claim that Makarios' removal would open the path to a solution, Boyatt remarked: "Makarios enjoys broad political support precisely because the majority of Cypriots have adopted his views on the Cyprus problem. If Makarios were to be sidelined, it not certain to what extent any eventual succeeding government would either be stable enough internally, or powerful enough, to make more compromises on the Cyprus issue than Makarios."
3. Finally, concerning the communist threat, Boyatt noted, "Makarios, the conservative cleric and capitalist, is certainly not a communist. The Archbishop accepts the support of the communists, but he uses them more than they use him." In the same telegram, Boyatt pointed out the contradictory nature of Greek policy on Cyprus. "On the one hand, we have the serious accusations of Panayiotakos, and on the other, the assurances from Palamas that the Greek government is not behind the recent pressure from the Bishops, as well as strong indications that Papadopoulos is in contact with Makarios through unofficial channels, and that he believes that the Archbishop should remain in place."[23]

Indeed, Greek policy on Cyprus continued to show divisions. On the one hand there was Papadopoulos, who, after the failure of the attempt to remove Makarios, revised his policy; and, on the other, the hard-line section of the Junta, which persisted in a policy of confrontation with Makarios. As a politician, Papadopoulos made his policy match that of the US

---

23 Note from Boyatt, 16 June 1972, "Panayotakos' comments", NARA, RG59, CFPF, 1970-1973, Cyprus.

State Department, while Ioannides, as Head of the Greek Gladio, followed that of the US secret services.

The dividing lines between the two tendencies were becoming more and more discernible, while they were reflected in the behaviour of Greek representatives in Nicosia. The embassy, following the directives of the Foreign Ministry, began to keep its distance from the Bishops and from EOKA B, while Greek KYP, the National Guard and the Greek Contingent's officers fomented conflict with Makarios.

As Adonis Kyros – who at that time was a warm supporter of Grivas' action in Cyprus and was in the know regarding the behind the scenes intrigues – maintains: "...the exercise of secret diplomacy by the United States in foreign countries is always implemented through alternative scenarios, which are set in motion by different services. Thus, while the official American diplomacy of the State Department follows at first sight a certain, specific line, in the background, agents of the secret services (C.I.A. and D.I.A) are drawing up other plans, which will probably be preferred during the course of developments. A game with two or even three different 'frames'."[24]

The intercommunal talks, which resumed on 8 June 1972, were a cause for friction between these two tendencies. The intensified Cyprus talks, as they were called, were conducted between Clerides and Denktash, under the aegis of the representative of the UN Secretary-general in Cyprus, Vivian Ozorio Tafal, and with the participation of the Greek Michalis Dekleris and the Turk Orhan Aldikasti with the status of advisors. The State Department encouraged the talks, and the Greek government supported them. Grivas opposed them, since they were taking place on the basis of independence and not of *Enosis*.

On 9 August, six months after Panayiotakos' departure, Efstathios Lagakos was accredited as the new Greek ambassador to Cyprus. With his accreditation, relations between Athens and Nicosia were fully normalised. The instructions that Lagakos had received from Athens were to put a curb on the three Bishops, and to make it clear to them that the Greek government supported Makarios. Lagakos met with the three in Limassol. Kyprianos was ill in bed, and Lagakos first spoke with Anthimos and Gennadios, in the former's office at the Limassol Bishopric. As Lagakos wrote later, he tried to explain to the Bishops that their effort was doomed: "'If you were to proceed, Your Graces, you will be on your own. And then you face the inevitable reactions and condemnation of the Cypriot people.' The answer I received from the Bishop of Kitium was utterly unexpected, coming from a man of the cloth and one whom I knew to be serene and deliberate. In a wrathful, acid tone of voice, he told me: 'Mr. Ambassador, we shall proceed, and let them hang me in Metaxas Square in Nicosia'.

"Naturally, I remained speechless. I understood that the discussion was over and I asked to see the Bishop of Kyrenia. The indisposed cleric, always known for his virulent anti-Makarios sentiments, received me lying on a bed, with his face half covered by the sheets. The chilly reception I got did not prevent me from repeating in every detail what I had said a little while previously to the two other Bishops. Kyprianos heard me out, making no comment or interruption.

"Finally, I asked him: 'What do you say, Your Grace?' After a few moments of disquieting silence, I received another unforeseeable and incomprehensible reply: 'I, Mr. Ambassador, say: Long live Pavlos Melas. Long live Grivas'."[25]

---

24 "Το σκοτεινό παρασκήνιο χούντας και Ε.Ο.Κ.Α. Β" [The Sinister Background of the Junta and EOKA B], *Eleftherotypia*, 4 December 2001.

25 Menelaos Alexandrakis, Byron Theodorakopoulos, Efstathios Lagakos, *Το Κυπριακό 1950-1974, Μια ενδοσκόπηση* [The Cyprus Problem 1950-1974, an Examination] (Athens: Elliniki Evroedotiki, 1987), p. 58.

The support Makarios received from Athens caused confusion in the Grivas camp. The president of the political wing of EOKA B, ESEA, George Vasiliades, asked for a meeting with Lagakos and an explanation of the positions taken up by his government. Lagakos said of the meeting that he had pointed out the dangers inherent in the turn towards *Enosis*, due to the possibility of Turkish intervention. After a heated discussion, "my interlocutor completely lost his cool and, out of his mind, shouted out passionately these terrible and incoherent words: 'He (Makarios) has got to go, even if, from behind bars, I see Nicosia in flames'. This phrase, full of hatred and malevolence, that has etched itself in my memory, was the sudden end to a meaningless discussion. And at the moment that the former Supreme Court judge of Cyprus left my office, I was thinking with sorrow and melancholy, 'So that's it! Makarios out. And what about *Enosis*?'"[26]

ESEA continued to pressure Greece to adopt the policy of Grivas. In November 1972, Grivas decided to send an ESEA delegation to Athens to brief the Greek government on his position. Acting on instructions from Athens, Lagakos tried to discourage them. The delegation, however, ignored his hints. The Greek government refused to receive Grivas' envoys and gave orders that "all doors were to be closed to them". According to Vasiliades, "on behalf of the military regime, we were received with complete formality and coldness by Stylianos Pattakos, who emphasised that there is a common Athens-Nicosia policy in force and that all were obliged to follow it. He added that the Commander-in-chief of the struggle was G. Papadopoulos, and the Colonel in charge on the battlefield was Archbishop Makarios…" [27]

The Greek embassy in Nicosia, in line with its government's policy of support for Makarios, issued guidelines to the pro- Grivas publisher of *Mesimvrini* and *Proini* newspapers to support the Greek positions and to tone down the criticism of Makarios. Hadjinicolaou did not fully comply with the guidelines and the Head of the Press Office at the embassy, Christodoulides, and the First Secretary, Nezerittis, continually remonstrated with him. When Hadjinicolaou did not conform, they cut off his funding.[28] On 6 November, Hadjinicolaou made an urgent appeal to the embassy to provide financial help to pay off accumulated debts, but he received a negative response. Hadjinicolaou had the support of Nicos Dontas of the 2nd Bureau of the General Staff, who described the embassy's decision as ill considered, and urged him to turn to Socrates Eliades. Under pressure from his debtors, Hadjinicolaou also approached Andreas Azinas and discussed with him the financing of his newspapers through the funds of the Cooperative Movement. Azinas laid down as a condition his support for Makarios. In the end, Hadjinicolaou failed to find finance and the publication of the two newspapers, which had accumulated debts of £12,000, was ceased.[29]

Triggered by the vacuum created by the closure of the newspapers, a conflict broke out among the ranks of the Grivas camp. The cause of the clash was the rivalry between ESEA and the National Democratic Party (*Dimokratikon Ethnikon Komma* – DEK) over the control of the pro-*Enosis* press. The ESEA, with the approval of Grivas, was preparing to publish the daily *Ethniki*, which had ceased publication in 1960. On the other hand, DEK was planning to publish as a daily the weekly newspaper *Gnomi*, which was its mouthpiece. The rivalry between ESEA and DEK reflected their different political approach. ESEA was in favour of armed opposition to Makarios, while DEK supported the action of a political opposition within the framework of the existing political establishment. Its view was that the

---

26 *Ibid.*, p. 64.
27 Athanasiou, *op. cit.*, p. 204.
28 Cyprus KYP, report on the financial problems of the pro-EOKA B press.
29 *Ibid.*

Enosis faction should take part in the presidential elections of 1973, with its president Takis Evdokas as a candidate, while ESEA, considered participation in the elections to be a waste of time.

Grivas attempted to thwart DEK's plans, and on 8 October a general order circulated to all the members of EOKA B, making clear that he was the voice of the opposition and that all organised bodies should put themselves under his command:

"The times do not permit party political squabbling, ambitions or goals. All have the obligation to rise to the occasion and answer the call of the Homeland. Let all call to mind how the EOKA struggle was waged, where there was one Leader and all, without petty party demands, served the Freedom Struggle.

"Our slogan and our credo is:

UNITY FOR *ENOSIS* UNDER A WORTHY LEADERSHIP."[30]

Despite Grivas' warnings, it appears there was support for the political orientation of DEK, upon which a new order came back, more severe, stating that:

"I command the following:

I ABSOLUTELY FORBID

a. Any cooperation with any Party whatsoever, and the involvement in any party political activity whatever by Members of the Organisation. Whoever believes that they will better serve the Struggle through activities in Party politics should declare it from now and leave any active units of EOKA. We do not allow anyone to receive orders from others outside the Organisation to achieve our National Objective.
b. The writing of slogans or sticking of posters, apart from those approved by EOKA.
c. The use of students or other young people in the Youth Organisation of EOKA, either for demonstrations or for the distribution of announcements, or for any other reason whatsoever, without an accompanying Order.

All must realise that EOKA neither is, nor will become, an unfenced field where anyone may enter and reap what they want. The Struggle demands iron obedience to the ONE, and not spasmodic moves of various people. This ONE is the LEADER, and nobody else."[31]

The conflict between ESEA and DEK was reaching its peak, as the deadline for the submission of nominations for the presidential elections of 1973 approached. Grivas tried to find a middle way in the rivalry over the control of the *Enosis* press, proposing the immediate resumption of publication of *Mesimvrini*, the deferment of the publication of *Ethniki*, and the brief deferment of the publication of *Gnomi* as a daily. The political bureau of DEK rejected Grivas' formula, and on 21 November 1972, announced that daily publication of *Gnomi* would begin in December. This declaration aggravated the situation, and Grivas called a meeting in Limassol to discuss the issue. Socrates Eliades, Costakis Ioannides, Gabriel Minas, Stavros Zakos, Lefteris Papadopoulos and others attended the meeting. The discussion was heated, and matters were heading towards an impasse, when there was a last attempt at consensus on the basis of some general principles laid down by Grivas:

a. There is a basis for cooperation, all are welcome in the struggle and nobody is to be excluded.
b. There is no intention on the part of Grivas to eliminate or neutralise anyone.[32]

---

30 Andros Pavlides, *Φάκελος Κύπρος* [The Cyprus File] (Nicosia, 1982), p. 513.
31 *Ibid.*, p. 514.
32 Cyprus KYP, report on the financial problems of the pro-EOKA B press.

It was agreed that a committee should be formed that would discuss the issue on the basis of these principles. Eventually, the committee reached deadlock, and *Gnomi* circulated as a daily on 22 December 1972. The same day *Mesimvrini* resumed publication, while preparations were made for the publication of *Ethniki*.

During those days another meeting of the cadres of ESEA and DEK took place, in which an attempt was made to bridge their differences. Socrates Eliades and Takis Evdokas disagreed bitterly and almost came to blows. Indicative of the climate that prevailed is the following telephone conversation between Socrates Eliades and Photis Papaphotis, on 27 December:

"Eliades: Good day, Photis, best wishes.
Papaphotis: Same to you, how are you doing?
Eliades: How am I? I feel like hell.
Papaphotis: Why?
Eliades: Why, because of that thing that happened to me; is there anything in its right place, now?
Papaphotis: Oh, forget it now.
Eliades: I can't forget it.
Papaphotis: Holidays, Christmas.
Eliades: I'm going to dump the lot of you.
Papaphotis: Are you on about that again?
Eliades: So, we let the idiots sling mud at us, right?
Papaphotis: Still going on about that?
Eliades: You called me over there to go to ESEA to put up with that stream of insults and attacks?
Papaphotis: No change of tune, Mr Socrates?
Eliades: No, it's no good, Photis, it doesn't bother me, I've got other things in my life to interest me, apart from the papers and Evdokas; why does Evdokas exist, because a nutter threw a stone in the cesspit, one who gobbled up Freud and the son of Freud [Evdokas is a psychiatrist], and we have to put up with all this, OK? Go and have a good time with Evdokas and leave me alone, all of you.
Papaphotis: So you called me just to tell me all this, right?
Eliades: No, mate, I want you for some other things too.
Papaphotis: Well, give up all this then.
Eliades: I've got nothing to do with stupid, screwed-up guys, I've got enough experience, and brains to go with it, to stand up for myself, morally, and from any other point of view, to have to stand for attacks by these pygmies, without warning – me! I don't want anything to do with anyone, mate, let them all forget me, all of you, because I'm fed up with pettiness. If Evdokas wants to form a party, or to create a theory, let him do it, what the hell do I care, what do I care, I've got other principles, got another creed of my own, I'm in a different class. If Evdokas is party leader let him become president, fine, what have I got to do with *Gnomi*, what do I care about *Gnomi* anyway?
Papaphotis: Well, anyway, tonight we've got a meeting, if you want to bring this up…
Eliades: What time?
Papaphotis: Half past six.
Eliades: I'll come to say it all for the last time, so it's written down, because Mr Minas doesn't write down what I say, I'll ask you to write down what I say.

Papaphotis: OK.
Eliades: What, mate, do you mean we've ended up being the laughing-stock for idiots, for clowns to laugh at us?"[33]

The clash between DEK and ESEA triggered by the presidential elections got more intense as the date for the submission of nominations approached. Grivas' opinion, which ESEA was told was irrevocable, was that "there is to be no participation and, by any possible means and ways, there should be abstention from the presidential elections". As a result of Grivas' insistence, disagreements came to the surface even in DEK itself, culminating in the resignation of Takis Evdokas from the leadership of the party, on 12 January 1973. The duties of president were undertaken temporarily by the general secretary of DEK, Polycarpos Petrides.

33 Telephone conversation between Socratis Eliades and Photis Papaphotis on 27 December 1972, recorded by Cyprus KYP.

6. The armed violence of EOKA B

Throughout 1972, EOKA B undertook almost no action at all, as Grivas devoted himself to drawing up his plans. According to information that Clerides gave American Chargé d'Affaires William Crawford, Grivas in September 1972 took delivery of a large quantity of arms and distributed them to his men. Again according to Clerides, the weapons had been bought through an arms dealer from Lebanon and arrived in Cyprus in three caiques. Their value was estimated at CY£180,000 ($486,000 dollars), an enormous sum for the period.[1]

The arrival of weapons for Grivas' units came to the attention of the Turkish Foreign Ministry, which made a diplomatic demarche to the UN representative in Cyprus, Ozorio Tafal. Nevertheless, compared to Ankara's reaction to Makarios' import of Czech arms, this one was muted to indifferent: the Turkish government conveyed to the UN, through its ambassador in Nicosia, a message whose tone was low key. According to British diplomats in Ankara, the Turkish protest was probably more of a formality and would not lead to any other action.[2]

The import of weapons was a key element of the organisation that Grivas was carrying out in preparation for armed action to eliminate Makarios. According to his plans, EOKA B would carry out armed operations including assassinations, bombings and the ransacking of police stations. This activity would culminate in the takeover of the state through a coup, which was planned to take place before 20 July 1973.

From September 1972, Grivas had fixed on 'Apollo' as a codename for the coup, which would be heralded by action by EOKA B. Subsequently, sections of the National Guard would proceed, "on the outbreak of this, to the Revolution with all the war material at their disposal, all their artillery and armoured vehicles". In order to prevent the reinforcement of government forces from rural areas, the plan made provision for EOKA B to cut off routes. "When the objective has been achieved, a Central Revolutionary Command will be established, which will proceed to a purge of hostile elements in the essential services, such as the police, CyTA (the Cyprus Telecommunications Authority) and CyBC (the Cyprus Broadcasting Corporation)." Again, according to the plan, the "Revolutionary Command" would then move to "arrest leaders and significant elements in the government ranks, who would be shut into concentration camps, created for the purpose". The 'Apollo' plan made detailed provision for its targets, as it did for precise number of fighters and the type and quantity of weaponry that would be employed in achieving them. The plan provided also for the use of armoured vehicles.[3]

While Grivas was preparing his armed action against Makarios, the intercommunal talks taking place in Nicosia between Clerides and Denktash with the participation of constitutional experts Dekleris and Aldikasti were making very good progress, to the point where Makarios expressed optimism for a positive outcome. Indeed, Makarios told US ambassador David Popper on 13 November 1972 that he was convinced the prospects for an agreement with the Turkish Cypriots were the best since the talks had begun in 1968.

---

1 Popper to Secretary of State, "Arms delivery to Grivas", NARA, RG59, CFPF, 1970-1973, Cyprus, telegram 1717, Nicosia, 19 September 1973.

2 "GOT complaint re Grivas's arms importation", NARA, RG59, CFPF, 1970-1973, Cyprus, telegram 7874, Ankara, 3 November 1973.

3 Cyprus KYP, 'Apollo' coup plan.

Makarios told Popper "he was in a position to control any action initiated by the supporters of Grivas" and that "the Cypriot people had tired of the continually repeated crises, that they wanted a solution, and they wanted it soon". Makarios in fact gave the American ambassador reliable information on the movements of Grivas: "He is living undisturbed in the house of one Christodoulides in Limassol, travels frequently to pre-arranged houses in Nicosia and Paphos, and proceeds with his work of organisation."[4]

In contrast, Clerides expressed his fears that Grivas would declare himself before the conclusion of the talks, seeking to wreck any agreement that would definitively exclude *Enosis*. He estimated that Grivas would very soon go into action, attacking government targets and police stations, and he considered the presidential elections of February 1973 as a critical time. According to Clerides, who spoke with Popper on 16 November 1972, Grivas' aim would be to pressure Makarios not to stand as a candidate, or, in the event that he did, to reduce his vote considerably, to the point where it would be evident that he had only been elected with the 40 per cent represented by the votes of the Communists and their fellow travellers. Clerides in fact revealed to Popper that some from the Grivas camp had sounded him out to see if he might stand against Makarios. They promised him that, if he accepted the proposal, they would stop speaking out against the talks. According to Popper, Clerides was of the persuasion "that if he accepted the support of Grivas, they would cast him off at the first opportunity unless he adopted their views, something he could not do".[5]

Clerides felt the 1973 presidential elections should be postponed so as not to affect the intercommunal talks. Makarios, however, wanted elections to confirm the broad acceptance he enjoyed among the Cypriot people, and not - as the Grivas faction accused him - only among the communists. Eventually, the elections were announced for 8 February.

On 1 February, Greek dictator George Papadopoulos made a statement that was broadcast by the Greek National Radio and Television Corporation (*Ethnikon Idrima Radiofonias kai Tileorasis* - EIRT), dropping clear hints against the action being taken by Grivas: "Greeks are taking up weapons against each other, with mutual slaughter and anarchy, and our national issue is going down the drain." The statement was interpreted as an intervention in favour of Makarios ahead of the impending presidential elections. It was even splashed in headlines in *Phileleftheros*, Makarios' mouthpiece.[6]

Grivas responded with a spectacular operation by EOKA B. On the evening of 7 February, 17 police stations across Cyprus were blown up. The next day, Makarios was declared President of the Republic without election, since there was no opposing candidate. Papadopoulos congratulated Makarios on his re-election, and *Phileleftheros* again made headline news out of his cordial telegram, interpreting the action of the "Regent of the Mother Country" as a moral defeat for the outlaws, that is, for EOKA B.[7]

The Greek officers serving in Cyprus felt differently about it, however, as they felt no sympathy for Papadopoulos' overtures towards Makarios. Indicative of their attitude was the following incident: on the day of Makarios' proclamation as president, a massive rally was organised in Nicosia. Makarios' aim was to prove that, despite the fact that there had been no elections, he enjoyed the support of the great majority of the population. The Head of the Second Bureau of the National Guard General Staff, Costas Papayiannis, and Nicos

---

4 Popper to Secretary of State, "Cyprus: Makarios unruffled of Greek Cypriot unrest", NARA, RG59, CFPF, 1970-1973, Cyprus, telegram 2077, Nicosia, 13 November 1972.

5 Popper to Secretary of State, "Cyprus - Clerides on Grivas forces and future political development", NARA, RG59, CFPF, 1970-1973, Cyprus, telegram 2096, Nicosia, 16 November 1972.

6 "Κατά της αναρχίας η Ελλάς" [Greece against Anarchy], *Philelftheros*, 2 February 1973.

7 "Η Ελλάς συγχαίρει τον Μακάριον" [Greece Congratulates Makarios], *Philelftheros*, 10 February 1973.

Dontas, sent reports to the General Staff in Athens, to the effect that "only red-shirted communists with red carnations took part in the rally". They also wrote that the prevailing slogan in the rally was "*Ohi Enosis*" ["No to *Enosis*"]. As a result of representations by the local section of Greek KYP, Athens asked its ambassador Lagakos to protest to the Cyprus government about the 'anti-*Enosis*' behaviour of the crowd. The Commander of the National Guard handed over a tape to Greek KYP to confirm that the specific slogan could be heard. On 26 February, the tape was presented to Makarios by ambassador Lagakos, who found himself in a difficult position when obliged to admit that the slogan that could be heard was not "*Ohi Enosis*" but "*Ohi Anohi*" ["No tolerance"]![8]

In his speech at the 8 February rally, bolstered by the renewed popular mandate as well as by the support from Papadopoulos, Makarios unleashed an attack on Grivas, whom he directly accused of drawing up plans for the imposition of partition: "What aims do they serve, what plans are they promoting, those armed units and bombers and those instigators of disorder, who have been active for months? They are promoting *Enosis*, is the answer from the authors of these acts. Those who undertake or encourage this action are the gravediggers of *Enosis*. Instead of *Enosis*, they are promoting the partition of Cyprus, and its Turkification. And they are committing a crime against Cyprus, a crime against the Nation. If they do not come to their senses, History will judge them mercilessly."

In his speech, Makarios extended an olive branch to those who renounced illegal action, and called on the opposition to work with him in an attempt to solve the Cyprus issue. "The national struggle's stadium is very spacious, and there is room in the arena for all who wish to participate,"[9] he said.

In reply, ESEA unconditionally rejected any cooperation whatsoever with Makarios: "Since he wields power, there is no arena, nor does a national struggle exist, because the latter has been replaced by concessions, by a national fatalism, by lust for power, by office-seekers and gold-diggers."[10] Despite the negative response from the *Enosis* faction, Makarios formally invited ESEA, as well as the National Democratic Party (DEK) and its president, Takis Evdokas, who had just resigned, to a meeting at the Presidential Palace, "for a discussion of the internal situation and to bridge the chasms on the internal front".[11]

Grivas, piqued at having being sidelined, reacted angrily. An announcement by ESEA, which expressed Grivas' views, reported: "The Leader of the *Enosis* faction is Grivas, and no other may act in the name of the *Enosis* supporters without the approval and consent of Dighenis."[12]

In the meantime, the mechanisms of both Greek KYP and the Second Bureau were set in motion with a view to discouraging the DEK from accepting the invitation.[13] On 19 February, ESEA officially declined the invitation and reminded Makarios of the suggestions put to him by Grivas at their meeting in 1972.

On 28 February 1973, Makarios addressed the House of Representatives as he took the oath of office as President of the Republic. In his speech, he called on all those who disagreed with his handling of the Cyprus issue to express their difference of opinion through democratic means, and not to resort to violence. Referring to the rejection of his invitation, he said: "I shall nevertheless always keep open the window to dialogue. And my invitation

---

8 Cyprus KYP, report, *op. cit.*, pp. 35-36.
9 Makarios III, op. cit, vol. IΓ, p. 393.
10 Papademetris, Panayiotis , Petrides, *op. cit.*, vol. 14, p. 259.
11 *Ibid.*
12 *Ibid.*, p. 260.
13 Cyprus KYP, report, *op. cit.*, p. 31.

shall always stand. Illegal actions and the use of violence can only lead to catastrophe."[14] Grivas, however, insisted on direct action, while ceasing to recognise Makarios as the legitimately elected President. In his note to ESEA dated 27 February 1973, he clarified his position: "Makarios has today been elected President unlawfully since he did not follow democratic regulations, depriving us from claiming the office through honest elections." In the same note, he asked that the pro-*Enosis* press be given instructions to call him merely Archbishop and "to take down his photograph from any place that lies within my control".[15]

During that fluid period in 1973, with the Greek Cypriot community on the brink of civil war, Ankara decided to upgrade the role of Rauf Denktash. Fazil Kutchuk, the Vice President of the Republic of Cyprus, was considered too much of a moderate to handle the crisis that was brewing.

In contrast to Greece, which was facing difficulties in imposing its policy on Cyprus, Turkey had absolute control over the Turkish Cypriots through the all-powerful TMT organisation. As Arif Hasan Tahsin writes, "for someone to be part of the Turkish Cypriot leadership, he must have a certificate of approval from Turkey, bearing the 'seal' of Ankara".[16] Ankara felt Kutchuk was no longer of any use, and it was decided to replace him with Denktash in the 1973 elections.[17] Fazil Kutchuk, however, was not willing to withdraw in favour of Denktash and was preparing to stand against him in an electoral shoot-out.

In September 1972, *Halkin Sesi* newspaper, which belonged to Kutchuk, undertook a campaign against the Turkish Interim Administration that was controlled by Denktash, using as a pretext certain decisions that had been taken concerning the cooperative movement. The *Halkin Sesi* campaign was the fuse that sparked open conflict between Kutchuk and Denktash over the impending elections for vice-president.

According to US ambassador David Popper, after *Halkin Sesi* had published an article critical of Denktash, the Turkish commander of TMT, known only by the pseudonym 'Bayraktar', flew into a rage and phoned Kutchuk's son Mehmet – the editor of the paper – calling on him to present himself at the secret headquarters of TMT in the Turkish enclave of Nicosia. The young Mehmet Kutchuk refused and took refuge in the palace of the vice-president of the Republic. Bayraktar ordered a TMT squad to seize him, but the TMT men were unwilling to violate the palace of the vice-president and, after intense negotiations, in which the Turkish embassy in Nicosia took part, Mehmet Kutchuk was delivered to Bayraktar, with the condition that he was to be accompanied by his father.

According to Popper, the interrogation of Kutchuk was conducted in a tense atmosphere, with insults and threats. Fazil Kutchuk intervened, protesting at the treatment that his son was receiving. "The vice-president told Bayraktar that the community was not under martial law, and that he had no legal right to censor the press." He also told him that his main mission was to train the TMT, and that he would protest to the Turkish government about his interference in the internal affairs of the community. In reply, Bayraktar told

14 Papademetris, Panayiotis, Petrides, *op. cit.*, vol. 14, p. 261.

15 *Ibid.*

16 Arif Tahsin, *Η άνοδος του Ντενκτάς στην κορυφή* [Denktash's Rise to Power] (Nicosia: Archeio/4, Diafaneia, 2001), p. 184.

17 Despite their attempt to secede from the Cyprus Republic, the Turkish Cypriots implemented the clauses of the constitution allowing them to hold separate elections for the positions of vice-president and deputies to the House of Representatives. Thus, the Turkish Cypriot Interim Administration, as the breakaway government that they had established was termed at the time, announced elections for the selection of a vice-president.

Kutchuk "he no longer had the support of the Turkish government" and that "Ankara would demand a change in the leadership in the 1973 elections".[18]

Kutchuk was so angry, according to Popper, that he submitted his resignation to the Turkish government. Eventually, however, he was persuaded to withdraw it. Arif Tahsin writes: "As the 1973 elections for vice-president approached, the seal was held by Kutchuk and he made his way to Ankara to find out if he was to continue or not. It seems to me that everyone in the country apart from him knew long before that this affair was over and finished.

"...Everyone expected that on his return he would announce that he would not stand for election. But he returned with great brio, and, to the large crowd that was waiting for him outside the palace, he spoke grand words: 'They want to eat me alive! My meat cannot be cooked even in a pressure cooker!'...

"Denktash had thought of everything. He had closed all doors to Kutchuk. Dr Kutchuk had not realised what was happening, or it was not in his interest to show that he understood. After his 'pressure cooker' speech, he got his rarely driven Chevrolet out of the garage and drove around the streets..."[19]

Eventually, however, when it became clear that Ankara's preference was for Denktash, Kutchuk withdrew his candidature on 1 January 1973. However, according to Tahsin, the words of praise from Turkish officials that came when he announced his withdrawal aroused suspicions that some bargaining had occurred behind the scenes. "In other words, something similar to the Rommel case. As is known, Hitler had told Rommel: 'you can choose between suicide, in which case you will be buried with full military honours, and execution', and obliged him to commit suicide. From what it appears, the resignation of Dr Kutchuk was something similar."[20]

Apart from Kutchuk, the President of the Turkish Republican Party, Midhat Berberoglu, was also seeking the vice-presidency, and had even begun his electoral campaign. According to a report by the American ambassador, Berberoglu declared during his electoral campaign that he was against the involvement of the Turkish military in politics, and committed himself to abolishing the "police state" that prevailed in the Turkish enclaves. He also vowed to solve the Cyprus problem in three months. Berberoglu was accused by the Turkish Cypriot military leadership of accepting financial aid from the Cyprus left wing and of having links with AKEL. According to Popper, in a speech he made in Nicosia on 11 February 1973, Denktash accused Berberoglu of betraying his community to secure financial aid from the communists. After this, the regime's police informed Berberoglu that they were no longer in a position to ensure his personal safety.

As Popper points out, the police tore up Berberoglu's posters and cut the phone lines at his party office, while his employees received threats from TMT. Denktash informed the American embassy in Nicosia "he had received direct instructions from [Turkish] Prime Minister Melen and President Sunay to eliminate Berberoglu from the electoral race". Berberoglu asked for, and got, a meeting with the Turkish envoy Inhan and with Bayraktar, who demanded that he withdraw from the elections. Berberoglu emerged terrified from the meeting. An official from the American embassy who met Berberoglu on 15 February 1973 "found him hiding in his office, utterly terrified, with the window blinds lowered and the telephone disconnected". Berberoglu withdrew the next day without giving any explana-

[18] Memo from Popper to Department of State, Nicosia 30 September 1972, "Cyprus: Denktash vs. Kuchuk vs. Bayraktar: A New Equation", NARA, RG59, CFPF, 1970-1973, Cyprus.

[19] Tahsin, *op. cit.*, p. 184.

[20] *Ibid.*, p. 190.

tion, only 12 hours after he had assured the Turkish Cypriot community that he would proceed with his electoral campaign. After Berberoglu's removal, Denktash, unopposed, was proclaimed Vice-President of the Cyprus Republic.[21]

Shortly after Makarios' re-election as President, the three Bishops repeated their demand for his resignation. On 22 February, they sent him an indictment and a 'warrant of appearance', summoning him to appear before them on 7 March to be tried on the charge of exercising temporal power in violation of ecclesiastical regulations. They also warned him that, should he refuse to make his appearance, "the Holy Synod would proceed with the hearing and the case would be decided in absentia".[22]

Once again the Greek government disagreed with the move. The Foreign Ministry gave instructions to ambassador Lagakos to try to dissuade them. Lagakos visited the Bishops and warned them that the Greek government would not back them up. He assured them that this would be Makarios' last term of office, and promised to take the initiative to persuade him over the unification of the nationalists and a reduction in the influence of the communists. However, no sooner had Lagakos left the Bishopric, than two colonels visited the Bishops and told them to proceed and not to pay attention to anyone else. In a telephone conversation with Spyros Papageorgiou, Socratis Eliades said: "Lagakos went to the Bishops to scare them, and two colonels arrived after him, urging the Bishops to go ahead, in the name of God, and to brush aside any advice and recommendations to the contrary that have been made merely for show."[23]

Once again, the co-ordinating role in the attempt to remove Makarios was played by the Second Bureau and by the local section of Greek KYP. The leader among the Bishops, Bishop Anthimos of Limassol, was under the constant surveillance of the Second Bureau, which was behind his every move. At the same time, Greek KYP gathered information from his entourage, confirming his final intentions.[24]

The three Bishops were also in contact with Grivas. In a document addressed to ESEA dated 27 February 1973, Grivas gave instructions concerning the moves that would follow Makarios' removal: "After his removal by the Bishops, there must be a consensus among them as to what common measures to adopt. For this purpose, you must come into contact with the Bishops from now, and determine the topics that will need studying as far as their feasibility and implementation are concerned."[25]

Makarios replied to the warrant of appearance one day before the date set for his "trial". Rejecting the indictment, he wrote to the Bishops that they were motivated "by a spirit that was unknown to him", and that the Holy Synod that they had convened was unconstitutional, and any decision it took would therefore automatically be null and void.[26]

The Bishops met on 7 March and sentenced him to be dethroned. Their decision, announced the following day, read: "The Holy Synod, being the guardian of the authority of the Church, which to a great extent has fallen into anarchy and discord owing to the ecclesiastical infraction of the Archbishop, and having, as the Sacred Regulations dictate, treated him for a long time with tolerance, now proceeds with great regret to the removal of

---

21 Memo from Popper to Department of State, Nicosia, 2 March 1973, "Cyprus: Vice Presidential Election, An Exercise in Futility", NARA, RG59, CFPF, 1970-1973, Cyprus.
22 Papademetris, Panayiotis, Petrides, *op. cit.*, vol. 14, p. 223.
23 Cyprus KYP, report, *op. cit.*, p. 37.
24 *Ibid.*, p. 36.
25 Papageorgiou, *Μακάριος*, p. 226.
26 Makarios III, op. cit, vol. ΙΔ, p. 474.

Makarios III Archbishop of Cyprus from Episcopal and any other ecclesiastical office, and returns him to the rank of a layman."[27]

Commenting on the decision of the Bishops, Makarios stated that the "Sentence of Removal" issued by the three Bishops in an "illicit conciliabule" in Limassol, was by definition null, and void of any value whatsoever. "I do not conceal, however, my deepest sorrow because the three Bishops, instigated by others and ignoring the trying circumstances through which Cyprus is now passing, have demonstrated that they lack the conscience befitting their high priestly station, as well as a sense of national responsibility, in dishonourably carrying out today my spiritual assassination. I ask God for their absolution, since 'they know not what they do'."[28] Subsequently, Makarios mentioned the measures he would take against the three, in essence proclaiming the initiation of the process leading to their removal: "Under the burden of my responsibilities as the Leader of the Church of Cyprus, and of my obligations as Leader of the Nation, it is incumbent upon me to take all those measures dictated by the present circumstances for the protection of the people from corruption within, as well as for the safeguarding of the authority of the Church, which the priests and pastors have shown to be acceptable to, and respected by, the flock, and not considered as scapegoats."[29]

The decision of the Bishops was condemned by the Greek government. On 17 March, deputy Foreign Minister Phaedon Anninos Cavalieratos said: "We consider the situation concerning His Beatitude the Archbishop of Cyprus to remain as it was before this decision was taken."[30] Following the government's lead, the Church of Greece announced on 20 March that "it will continue normal relations with Archbishop Makarios".[31]

The Greek government's stance caused indignation in EOKA B. The cadres of the organisation felt betrayed and began to express their discontent to Greek officers serving in Cyprus. The pro-Ioannides officers Papayiannis and Kondilis discussed the policy of Athens, and expressed the following views:

> "a) The statements by Cavalieratos were a blow for EOKA B, and are creating difficulties and problems in the area of relations, and more generally, in that of cooperation with the members of EOKA B.
>
> b) The National Guard is in a state of continual perplexity as to the stance it should soon adopt in the eventuality of a military confrontation between EOKA B and the government."[32]

The Greek government's stance on the ecclesiastical crisis made itself felt in relations between officers and EOKA B. On 22 March, the Head of the Second Bureau of the General Staff Costas Papayiannis received information from Lefteris Delipasis of the Second Bureau in Larnaca that "the invitations sent on the occasion of the commemoration of 25th March (the Greek national holiday), to associations and organisations loyal to Grivas were returned, after orders from EOKA B".[33] The officers gave assurances to EOKA B that the

---

27 Papademetris, Panayiotis, Petrides, *op. cit.*, vol. 14, p. 224.

28 *Ibid.*

29 *Ibid.*

30 "Ράπισμα εξ Αθηνών κατά των '3'" [Athens blow against the '3'], *Phileleftheros*, 18 March 1973.

31 "Ολοκληρούται η καταδίκη των '3'" [Full Condemnation of the '3'], *Phileleftheros*, 21 March 1973.

32 Cyprus KYP, report, *op. cit.*, p. 30.

33 *Ibid.*, p. 39.

stance adopted by the Greek government was one of expedience, and that in fact it supported the Bishops. In spite of this, the EOKA B supporters continued to express their displeasure in various ways. The Larnaca Commander, Thomopoulos, in his report to the Head of Greek KYP in Nicosia Costas Douzinas, stated that "EOKA B men were making life hard for them", while Captain Andreas Avgoustis, also a member of EOKA B, addressing Costas Rados, said "en masse they accused both Makarios and the Greek government and enquired to what extent there could be grounds for cooperation after the well known statements concerning a change of policy. Rados noted that there was no cause for concern and apprehension, because everything will be OK."[34]

The Bishops had allowed Makarios until 9 April to lodge an appeal against their decision. As the deadline came and went, The Bishops of Kitium and Paphos, Anthimos and Gennadios, went to Athens and requested meetings with the Greek government, with a view to clarifying the real intentions of the regime. Papadopoulos, however, did not allow any contact with them to take place. The two Bishops returned to Cyprus empty-handed and disappointed with the stance adopted by the motherland, which had encouraged them one year earlier to proceed with the removal of Makarios.

On 13 April, the Bishops met again and finalised their decision. In a statement, they said their decision "was already final and definitive, and the dethroned person would henceforth be known as Michael Christodoulou Mouskos" – Makarios' name prior to his ordination. In the same decision they named as the *locum tenens* of the 'vacant' archiepiscopal throne the first Bishop by seniority, Gennadios of Paphos.[35] Makarios again rejected the decision of the three as null and void. "Nothing always comes out of nothing. In any case, the way the Bishops have ended up is sad. Blind in soul and intellect, they have followed a very slippery path and have shown themselves unworthy of the militant Church of Cyprus and of embattled Cyprus itself. May God have mercy on them."[36]

After the "dethronement" of Makarios, EOKA B swung into action and, as Papageorgiou writes, ordered its supporters to attend Church on Easter Sunday 29 April. They should flood the churches of the island with their families and all those whom they could influence – "not in order to hear the message of the Resurrection, but to make every effort, even to quarrel if necessary, so that the 'encyclical of dethronement' of Makarios be read out". It was a secret operation, with the special orders giving the following emphasis: "Immediately after the end of the service, the sub-section commanders should submit reports in detail on the results for various villages in their territories".[37]

During this time, Grivas had stepped up his armed straggle against Makarios. After the simultaneous assault on 17 police stations, on the eve of Makarios' proclamation as President on 7 February 1973, many other attacks on police stations and other government targets followed. One element of Grivas' plans for the takeover of the state was reprisals against the police forces that had opposed EOKA B, or that had taken part in operations aimed at the break-up of the organisation. On 4 March 1973, he sent to Stavros Stavrou Syros the following confidential personal order:

"Draw up a plan for a series of reprisals in the event of supporters being beaten up by Praetorians among the presidential guard, or by the paramilitaries of Makarios.

---

34 *Ibid.*
35 Papademetris, Panayiotis, Petrides, *op. cit.*, vol. 14, p. 227.
36 *Ibid.*
37 Papageorgiou, *Μακάριος*, p. 173.

"This will provide for:

- The execution of torturers.
- Assaults on police stations, or more likely those to which the torturers belong, or those in whose territory the beatings up of supporters occurred.

"In any case the police stations must be easy prey for occupation. These will be blown up and those officers in charge of these, as long as they are not supporters of ours, are to be beaten up."[38]

In response to this order, Syros drew up a plan called 'Gronthos' (Clenched Fist), whose goal was the beating up and execution of Makarios supporters. On 5 March, Syros circulated an order among 10 EOKA B section leaders, asking them to prepare lists of possible targets. "In the lists should be included all the police stations in your section (for occupation, looting-destruction-elimination) and the most important cadres of the opposition in each village (for beating-up or execution)."[39] The section leaders sent Syros detailed lists with all the proposed targets in Cyprus, and the plan was put into action.

Within the framework of 'Gronthos', an armed group attacked the police station at Xylotymbou on 25 March. After a half-hour battle they occupied the station, beat up the policemen and blew up the building. On the same day, another unit of armed men attacked Lefkara police station, but withdrew after failing to occupy it. On 3 April, Kokkinotrimithia police station was blown up; on 5 April, Angastina police station was destroyed, and on 13 April Kalavassos police station suffered the same fate.

On 5 April 1973, Grivas ordered the first assassination. The victim was Georgios Photiou, a cadre of Lyssarides' party, EDEK. In an announcement circulated the following day, EOKA B claimed responsibility: "Our policy is to avoid bloodshed. But the murdering state irregulars had better understand that they will suffer the same fate as Photiou if they do not come to their senses."[40]

A few days after Photiou's murder, EOKA B had its own first casualty, Georgios Kountouresis from Kato Zodia, who was killed on the night of 8 April during an attack against Koutraphas police station. The EOKA B section leader in the Morphou area, Ioannis Kasinis, had organised the operation. His men had brought explosives and petrol cans to blow up the police station and then set fire to it. However, they were detected by the policemen manning the station, who put up resistance. During the exchange of fire that followed, Kountouresis was killed. The EOKA B group fled, abandoning Kountouresis on the scene. The dead man was found at dawn, when the police began to search the area.

Kountouresis left a widow and three children, but Nicos Dontas at the Second Bureau of the General Staff expressed his satisfaction at developments, since the death would serve further to harden attitudes on the internal front. When Dontas was informed by Georgios Hadjisavvas that the EOKA B attack on the Koutraphas police station had left one of its men dead, he said: "That's good. When you go to an ambush, don't you expect casualties? If that's not what I want, I stay at home…"[41]

In the wake of the Koutraphas incident, Makarios launched a fresh attack on Grivas. Referring to the "criminal acts in Cyprus, which General Grivas initiated and is actively pursuing", he described Koutraphas police station as a "national sentry post" because it was adjacent to the Turkish Cypriot sentry post of the area. Referring to the victims (apart from the dead EOKA B man, there were three wounded policemen), he said: "National ruins, eco-

[38] Papademetris, Panayiotis, Petrides, *op. cit.*, vol. 14, p. 271.
[39] *Ibid.*
[40] Papageorgiou, *Μακάριος*, p. 171.
[41] Cyprus KYP, report, *op. cit.*, p. 48.

nomic ruins, mourning and grief of widows and orphans - such are the sad sum to date of the heroic foolishness of General Grivas."[42]

Kountouresis' death provoked reactions within the ranks of EOKA B. Various sources say George Carousos opposed Grivas' decision to engage in violent confrontation between EOKA B and government forces, on the grounds that this tactic would lead to civil war. Carousos appears to have sent a letter to Grivas telling him he should cease taking unilateral decisions, and that a council should be formed. Among other things, he told him "he was friendless and surrounded by bad advisors". Grivas, who could not tolerate criticism, replied that he was relieved of his duties and offered to send him with safe conduct to Greece. Carousos did not accept the offer and was marginalised.[43]

As a result of Grivas' armed action, as well as the attempted ecclesiastical coup against him, Makarios sought greater rapprochement with Athens. One of the issues that worried the regime was the increase in the electoral power of AKEL in the parliamentary elections of 1970, and the support the communist party offered Makarios. To distance himself from AKEL, Makarios undertook the initiative of unifying the two parties of the centre right, the *Eniaion Komma* (Unified Party) of Clerides and the *Proodeftiki Parataxi* (Progressive Party) controlled by Andreas Azinas.[44] From 9 February 1973, Makarios had given the green light to Azinas to proceed with negotiations with Clerides,[45] and on 20 February, a meeting took place between Clerides and the leaders of the Progressive Party.

As Clerides told David Popper, there was no difficulty in unifying the two parties. He told him also that there was the possibility of absorbing some of the cadres of the National Democratic Party into the new set up.[46] On 27 February, the leadership of the two parties reached agreement to merge. The name of the new party was to be *Ethniki Proodeftiki Parataxi Ethnikofronon* - EPPE (Unified Nationalist Progressive Party). Its president would be Clerides and vice-president Tassos Papadopoulos. An announcement was even prepared, to be made public the following day, when, suddenly, the deal collapsed. According to information given to the American embassy by Tassos Papadopoulos, Andreas Azinas and the deputy of the Unified Party Andreas Neocleous, the collapse was due to reactions by conservative elements of the Unified Party, who feared that the unification would result in an increase in Makarios' influence in the party. Similar objections, according to Foreign Minister Ioannis Christofides, also came from the Progressive Party.[47]

American diplomacy in Cyprus encouraged the unification of the parties of the Right, looking favourably on the prospects of Makarios becoming independent of AKEL. The Americans linked the unification of the two parties with the future of the talks for the solution of the Cyprus problem, and considered the unified right wing as an antidote to the increasing armed action of EOKA B.

In March 1973, the US Military Attaché at the Nicosia embassy, Colonel Whitely, had contacts with right wing elements that were on friendly terms with EOKA B, among whom were Renos Kyriakides, Costas Ioannides and Andreas Neocleous, whom he tried to con-

---

42 Papademetris, Panayiotis, Petrides, *op. cit.*, vol. 14, p. 280.

43 *Ibid.*, p. 276.

44 Popper to Secretary of State, "Christophides visit to Athens", NARA, NPMS, NSC, Cyprus/Greece, telegram 198, Nicosia, 31 January 1973.

45 Popper to Secretary of State, "Makarios moves to unite centrist parties", NARA, RG59, CFPF, 1970-1973, Cyprus, telegram 367, Nicosia, 20 February 1973.

46 *Ibid.*

47 Memo from Popper to Department of State, 16 March 1973, "Efforts to Merge Unified Party and Progressive Front Collapse", NARA, RG59, CFPF, 1970-1973, Cyprus.

vince of the necessity of right wing unity. He said the United States supported a solution including independence, that the pro-*Enosis* struggle of EOKA B was doomed to failure, and that a coup against Makarios would precipitate a Turkish invasion.[48]

Neocleous briefed Nicos Dontas of the Second Bureau of the General Staff concerning these contacts, while Renos Kyriakides did the same with the Greek military contingent. According to a memorandum from the Greek contingent to Armed Forces Headquarters in Athens, Whitely told Kyriakides the following:

- America supports only a solution that includes independence.
- Cypriot *Enosis* supporters will have to abandon their ideology, or else they will suffer.
- The Greek government is not helping the US because it does not denounce Grivas and his supporters, as it had been asked to do.
- Glafcos Clerides is under the influence of the Americans, and it is for this reason that he has adopted a pro-Makarios stance.
- The solution of the Cyprus issue through military means is not in the Greek interest because Turkey can occupy Greece in one day.[49]

The American Military Attaché also had a meeting with the Head of the Second Bureau of the National Guard General Staff Costas Papayiannis, and gave him the following information:

1. As things stand today, Turkey is not likely to accept an independent and unified state, but will aim at a separate Community and Administration, something which he himself sees as the only feasible solution, given the present conditions.
2. Turkey today has powerful armed forces, something that should be taken into serious consideration by the Greek side.
3. He provided information about the armed capability of the Turkish Cypriots.[50]

At the same time the British Military Attaché Colonel Stoker undertook a similar initiative. On 19 March 1973, Stoker gave a reception in Nicosia in honour of incoming British High Commissioner Stephen Olver. Stoker sought out Costas Papayiannis, whom he told of the existence of a plan for a Turkish invasion of Cyprus. In the discussion that followed, Stoker referred to the following topics:

1. To the increasing capability of the Turkish Army.
2. To the likely build up to the invasion.
3. To details of the implementation of the invasion plan.
4. To the layout of Turkish units facing the island
5. To airborne forces.
6. To the possibility of transportation of sections by air.
7. To the possibility of transportation of support weapons and logistics units.

On 27 March, Stoker visited National Guard Headquarters and gave the following information:

a) The threat to the island is increasing steadily.
b) The Turkish Staff Officers entertain no other solution other than that of partition (dismemberment).[51]

---

48 Cyprus KYP, report, *op. cit.*, p. 41.
49 Athanasiou, *op. cit.*, p. 216.
50 *Ibid.*, p. 225.
51 *Ibid.*, p. 216.

Colonel Stoker referred to the capability of the Turkish army, probable moves in an invasion, and the basic Turkish weaponry that has its sights trained on Cyprus. He also referred to the internal situation in Cyprus, and expressed his judgement that Grivas was not likely to confine himself to sporadic assaults on police stations, but aimed at more decisive and spectacular actions. He stated that he himself had information about a plan to assassinate Makarios or Lyssarides, and asked to learn what the National Guard knew of all this.

In another meeting he had with the Chief of Staff of the National Guard on 13 April, Stoker handed him a photocopy of a map showing all Turkish airborne forces, and analysed for him all the possibilities for transportation of Turkish forces to Cyprus by air. The British Military Attaché also analysed the scenarios for a Turkish invasion, referred to the intercommunal talks, and expressed his concern about Grivas' activities.[52]

Basing itself on the information given by the military attachés of Britain and the United States, the leadership of the Greek KYP in Nicosia drew up a report briefing the Greek Armed Forces leadership and making appraisals as to why the information had been given:

"The United States, being interested in stability in Cyprus, desires nothing more than the preservation of Greco-Turkish relations, and is set on an immediate and definitive solution to the Cyprus problem through the intercommunal talks. To this end, in the light of the general situation in the eastern Mediterranean, they by no means desire the creation of any kind of crisis in the Cyprus issue."[53] For this reason "the appearance of Grivas in Cyprus and the activities of the Grivas camp have caused concern to the Americans, which consider this to be creating an abnormal situation on the island, and to be a factor that is causing a slowdown in the progress of the talks."[54]

As to Great Britain, the report said:

"Britain is adopting a neutral stance. It appears to desire the preservation of stability on the island, but not a definitive solution to the problem, as her interests in the island (Bases, etc.) would not be secured."[55] The report also notes that probably "the highlighting of the Turkish threat by both of the military attachés was aimed at averting such a possibility (coup by Grivas)" and that "the Great Powers, with or without the cooperation of the Cyprus government, are presenting the Turkish threat as being of the greatest gravity in order to calm down the situation in the internal Greek Cypriot front, so as to avert any possible complication of the Cyprus problem."[56]

The information that the British and the Americans quoted concerning an imminent coup against Makarios appeared to be well founded. On 30 March, an ESEA delegation headed by its president, George Vasiliades, paid a visit to Greek ambassador Efstathios Lagakos. According to a briefing by the Armed Forces Headquarters, "during the conversation clear hints were repeatedly made as to the need for the overthrow of Makarios by force, and threats were levelled concerning bloody reprisals".

Grivas undertook similar soundings within the National Guard. The same report states: "Recently, a greater - and now concerted - attempt on the part of elements of the pro-*Enosis* faction has shown itself, to sound out the General Staff and some provincial military commands in order to find out the real intentions of the National Guard in the event of the outbreak of a more serious military enterprise by Grivas (a coup). This is basically what the leadership of the Coordinating Committee for the Enosis Struggle (ESEA) and the Bishops

---

52 *Ibid.*, p. 219.
53 *Ibid.*, pp. 226-7.
54 *Ibid.*, p. 218.
55 *Ibid.*, p. 227.
56 *Ibid.*, p. 228.

(mainly the Bishop of Kitium) are seeking, and they are letting it be clearly understood that this is the aim of Grivas.

"It is the estimation of the General Staff that Grivas – partly due to organisational weakness, but also motivated by the recent official position of the Greek government on the ecclesiastical issue – feels isolated and seeks to come into contact with an official Greek element so as to be informed about:

1. The true and innermost disposition of the Greek government with regard to Makarios, and not that imposed by circumstances and political expediency.
2. The position of the Greek government regarding himself and his action in Cyprus to date.
3. The position of the Greek government concerning more serious action on his part, aiming at the overthrow of Makarios.
4. The attitude of the National Guard in the eventuality of a final military confrontation with Makarios."[57]

Therefore, in the spring of 1973, western diplomats were discouraging any coup against Makarios and were pressing Athens to denounce EOKA B, which was stepping up its armed action against the Cyprus government. Glafcos Clerides was also pressing in this same direction, and, using as a pretext the ecclesiastical crisis and EOKA B's increased military activity, he expressed his intention to resign as interlocutor in the Cyprus talks.

The Greek government, which aligned itself with the policy of the West on the Cyprus problem, appealed to Clerides not to resign, and invited him to Athens for talks to discuss the future course of the Cyprus issue. Subsequently, Athens stated publicly that it considered the appropriate procedure for the solution of the Cyprus problem to be "the intensification of the internal Cyprus talks, which, as was well known, it supported and continued to support unconditionally". It expressed its appreciation for the work carried out by Clerides, and its conviction that "he would wish to continue until the favourable outcome of the talks, the speedy continuation and promotion of which was essential to the benefit of all the interested parties".

In the same announcement, the Greek government condemned, albeit indirectly, the actions of EOKA B: "The government addresses an appeal to the patriotism of all those who, directly or indirectly, through words or deeds (that the national centre absolutely and categorically condemns), undermine the talks and dangerously disturb the climate necessary to their successful outcome"[58]

Grivas reacted to this announcement, and, in a pamphlet circulated on 25 April, he stated: "I warn everyone that I am not one of those who submits to threats, however powerful the opponent may be. The EOKA struggle has proved this. Those who deny their country will realise, as well the Americans, the British and the Turks, that our spirit cannot be broken.

"We shall fight and, if we have to, we shall fall.

"This is our REPLY.

"'Heroic foolishness' Mr Mouskos no doubt would say. Better, however, a 'heroic foolishness', such as that of EOKA, which has vindicated claims and made its presence felt, rather than treason."[59]

---

57 *Ibid.*, p. 210-212.
58 Papademetris, Panayiotis, Petrides, *op. cit.*, vol. 14, p. 290.
59 *Ibid.*, p. 290.

Bolstered by the support from Athens, Makarios decided to clear up his row with the three Bishops and to fight Grivas. First he called a convocation of the Supreme Holy Synod in order to dethrone the three rebel Bishops. Invitations were handed personally to all the patriarchates by the then Bishop of Constantia, later Archbishop Chrysostomos. They all sent back a positive response, with the exception of the Ecumenical Patriarch and the leader of the Church of Greece. At the beginning of July, their delegates arrived in Cyprus. The Bishops considered the Synod to be unconstitutional since "it had been summoned by a dethroned Bishop", and in their letter they called upon the hierarchs to avoid "any irregular involvement in the sphere of the Most Holy Church of Cyprus", and asked them to exert their influence to achieve "the universal, unreserved acceptance of the Sacred Canons".[60]

The Supreme Synod met at the Archbishopric on 5 and 6 July. It decided on the annulment of the dethronement of Makarios, and urged the three to repent: "Therefore, in a spirit of love and basing ourselves on justice, we call the Bishops to repentance for, and renunciation of, that which was initiated by them, in order to restore peace and unity in the Church."[61] The members of the Synod attempted to pay a visit on the Bishops so as to communicate their decision, but the latter refused to receive them. "Let a thousand Patriarchs and a thousand Popes come; as far as we are concerned, Makarios is dethroned. Let the Patriarchs quote us regulations that permit clerics to take part in politics."[62] Ultimately, the decision of the Supreme Synod was conveyed to the three via envoys, with an invitation to appear before them so that they could present their views. The Bishops refused to respond, and Anthimos declared: "We are not obliged to obey an illegal conciliabule. Its invitation is rejected."[63]

When all attempts at mediation failed, the Supreme Synod met again on 14 July, this time with the participation of Makarios, and decided on the dethronement of the three Bishops. All the Churches, with the exception of that of Greece, accepted the decision. The Greek officers mourned the dethronement of the three. Douzinas of Greek KYP and Tsangayiannis of the Second Bureau gave instructions that there was to be no music by the orchestra of the Officers Club of the Greek Contingent on the day of the dethronement.[64]

At the same time Makarios took tough measures against EOKA B. Since April 1973, he had proceeded to the setting up of the Reservist Police Force, which came to be known by the single word 'Reservists'. The Reservists Corps was reinforced by hundreds of auxiliary police officers and its exclusive raison d'être was the suppression of EOKA B. The operations it carried out resulted in mass arrests of members and supporters of the illegal organisation.

As a result of the virtual civil war conditions created by EOKA B's increased activity and of the political impasse following the dethronement of the three Bishops, Grivas came under pressure to abandon his campaign of violence. On 17 July 1973, ESEA sent him a written suggestion concerning politicisation of the struggle for *Enosis*, and proposed the creation of a political entity, which would represent the pro-*Enosis* camp.

Interpreting ESEA's move as one of censure, Grivas rejected the proposal out of hand. "For me there is neither hesitation, nor reason for not continuing the struggle on the mili-

---

60 Papademetris, Panayiotis, Petrides, *op. cit.*, vol. 14, p. 228.
61 *Ibid.*, p. 231.
62 *Ibid.*, p. 228.
63 *Ibid.*, p. 229.
64 Cyprus KYP, report, *op. cit.*, p. 59.

tary level… In fact, I feel that this question should not even have been put to me." And he repeated his long-standing position that only through the violent removal of Makarios could *Enosis* be achieved: "I believe that a mere political struggle against Mouskos in order to put the Cyprus issue back on the correct track of self-determination, or only to remove him from power, will not be crowned with success, due to the well known special conditions that prevail."

Similarly absolute were Grivas' views on the form of the struggle: "The military struggle, however, will be waged by me in the way I see fit, and with methods of my choosing," he wrote, and citing as an example the Bishops' failed attempt to unseat Makarios, he said: "They did not realise that where Mouskos is concerned, and in the face of his abundant wealth, the sacred regulations are worth nothing (…) and only the law of the mighty prevails - in Cypriot dialect, the '*toppouza*' (truncheon)."

In his note, Grivas repeated the views he had expressed at the end of 1972, when he raised the question of the participation of the pro-*Enosis* faction in the elections, stating that he considered political action unnecessary and that in the event that Makarios was overthrown he would not call on politicians to govern: "It would be foolish to believe that we shall call on Clerides or [secretary general of AKEL Ezekias] Papaioannou, or whoever else, to govern. We bear responsibility for the creation of the new State," he wrote, implying that he would personally undertake to govern after the overthrow of Makarios.[65]

To ESEA's suggestion for the creation of a political movement that would act as the mouthpiece of the *Enosis* faction, Grivas replied that the ESEA should be staffed by new, capable cadres, and maintained "there was a need for the creation of a new party based on principles. This could be achieved within the ranks of the ESEA, where it would be nurtured and would make its appearance at the appropriate moment."[66] Using this as a pretext, Grivas proceeded to a re-structuring of ESEA. Stelios Christides assumed the position of General Secretary, replacing Photis Papaphotis, who was in continuous conflict with Socrates Eliades.

In fact, as ESEA was suggesting to abandon armed activity, Grivas was preparing the decisive blow against Makarios. According to Spyros Papageorgiou, around June 1973, Grivas said in a general order to members of EOKA B: "We have shown that we have the power and ability to decide, plan and carry out operations wherever and whenever we wish, and not where or when the adversary wishes." The adversary, Papageorgiou added, was always Makarios and the Cypriot state, which had to be crushed. "Without mercy, without pity or hesitation we shall turn on the miserable bastards," the order stated, before ending on a pompous note: "VICTORY has begun to glow red, with its brilliant, shining ray. Brave soldiers of Hellas, man the ramparts, stand tall, unshakeable and implacable. [67]

On 18 July, EOKA B carried out a big operation, in which 50 armed men occupied Vatylis police station in broad daylight. The operation was considered to be a dress rehearsal for the implementation of the 'Apollo' coup plot. The aim was to take over and blow up the police station, and to cut off the old Nicosia-Famagusta road as well as a secondary road that led to the Turkish village of Strongilos.

As Spyros Papageorgiou wrote, during those days, "Grivas had made up his mind, or rather had decided to implement certain decisions: the elimination of Makarios, and the seizure of power through a coup". According to Papageorgiou, on 23 July 1973, EOKA B

---

65 Papademetris, Panayiotis, Petrides, *op. cit.*, vol. 14, p. 283.
66 *Ibid.*
67 Papageorgiou, *Μακάριος*, p. 161.

ordered the execution of exercise 'Express One', "which aimed at testing alarm and communication systems, from headquarters level down to that of unit leaders. A secret order from EOKA B headquarters stressed that: 'conclusions drawn from the exercise will be valuable. The Exercise must remain secret'."[68]

As for the elimination of Makarios, Grivas was working on various parallel schemes. One of these, action plan 7)S.E.)2)791, which was found in Syros' archive, provided for the assassination of Makarios in an ambush at a spot along his daily route from the Archbishopric to the Presidential Palace. The plan described the best points along the route, those where guards were positioned, and the places that could be used by the would-be assassins.

The police found in Syros' archives 40 numbered photographs, which showed the junctions on the route followed by Makarios. Furthermore, 17 other numbered photographs were found of the new route taken once works began on a new sewage system. In the photographs, arrows showed the positions of the security guards. There was also a full series of photographs of the Archbishopric, which had been taken from all angles of the building. The plan envisaged a simultaneous attack on Makarios' car and against the police in his escort. The attempt was to be made during the evening ride and the plan was to be carried out by an armed group, referred to by the coded numbers "13-13".[69]

A second plan drawn up by Grivas provided for Makarios' car to be blown up. A parked vehicle would be used, booby-trapped with large quantities of explosives that would be detonated electronically. Papageorgiou writes: "From the summer of 1973 up to the autumn of the same year, three EOKA B units were working, completely independently of each other, on plans for a remote electronic blast against Makarios." He also writes: "Grivas knew of the activities of two of the groups and guided them personally," while the third probably "was working without approval, on its own initiative or that of others".[70]

In July 1973, EOKA B tested a remote controlled electronically detonated explosive device. The test showed the receiver to be over sensitive, obtaining signals from irrelevant sources. Naturally, the test was conducted without explosives. In August, the whole system was perfected through the purchase from Britain of crystals with dedicated frequencies. The name of the plan was "*Floga*"[flame], but after the arrest of a leading EOKA B member, Grivas gave orders for it to be changed to "*Lampsis*"[glow].[71] According to Papageorgiou, the plan "was for a powerful explosion at the bastion of the walls, at the point where Makarios' car turned in towards the Archbishopric, to be activated by observers with detonators from the Lartides apartment block opposite the walls, with explosive materials that would be set off using the system with a transmitter and receiver."[72]

At the beginning of August, Grivas had ready another plan to assassinate Makarios. It consisted of an ambush in the Platania area, on the Nicosia-Troodos road. An EOKA B unit had been ordered to hit Makarios and his escort with machine-gun fire, when he would be going, as was his custom, to stay the weekend on Troodos on Friday 3 August. Information concerning the ambush leaked to Cyprus KYP, and its head, Georgios Tombazos, warned Makarios not to go to Troodos.[73] Eventually, Makarios left for Troodos on Thursday rather

---

68 *Ibid.*, p. 179.
69 akarios III, op. cit, vol. IΔ, p. 626.
70 Papageorgiou, *Μακάριος*, p. 180.
71 *Ibid.*, pp. 181-182.
72 "Πώς οι ενωτικοί χρησιμοποιηθήκαμε για την καταστροφή" [How we *Enosis* Supporters were used for Catastrophe], *Simerini*, 14 July 1996.
73 Georgios Tombazos, testimony before the Committee on the 'Cyprus File' of the Cyprus House of Representatives.

than Friday. A little before his departure, the presidential guard and the police combed the area from Kakopetria to Troodos, and discovered a large machine gun near a bend in the road, ready for use.

The affair was revealed to the press, and on 11 August Grivas circulated an announcement with the title "We Accuse", in which he stated the following: "The facts about a so-called ambush are false. They go contrary to the military code, as well as to the tactics, technique and plans of EOKA."[74] Nevertheless, when on 13 October Ioannis Kasinis' unit was neutralised, those arrested were found to have in their possession documents relating to the ambush, while in statements to police they admitted the existence of the specific plan to assassinate Makarios using automatic weapons.

During the same period, Grivas also drew up a plan for the occupation of the entire area surrounding the Troodos range, in which *Enosis* with Greece would be declared. This plan had been prepared by Michael Kalogeropoulos-Diakos.[75] In the summer of 1973, Grivas gave him the order for the plan to be implemented, but according to the director of Cyprus KYP, Tombazos, he could not carry it out because the EOKA B man in charge in Kakopetria did not have the men at his disposal that he had claimed he had.[76]

By the summer of 1973, Grivas' plans to overthrow Makarios had all but collapsed following a string of successes by Makarios' security forces, which almost broke Grivas' organisation. On 25 July, the Reservists eliminated one of the extreme hard-line units of EOKA B, which had its refuge in the Mazokambos area, in Parekklesia. Grivas was furious and gave the order for the execution of the unit's head, Aristophanes Pouris "to make an example of him", because he was considered responsible for the arrests. Grivas gave the order through Syros, but the execution was cancelled after the intervention of Carousos, who had once again had become active in the organisation.[77]

Carousos' intervention saved Pouris' life, but Grivas in the meanwhile had taken revenge against the Reservists, ordering the blowing up of the central police station in Limassol. On the night of 26 July, 24 hours after the Parekklesia operation, there was an anonymous telephone call to the station. "EOKA here; the station is full of bombs ready to go off. If there are any prisoners, take care of their safety," it said, and rang off. Half an hour later there was a massive explosion and the whole of the west wing of the station was blown up. A further explosion was sparked in the ammunition warehouse and hellfire followed from the detonations of bullets. Ricochets wounded 10 policemen and two National Guardsmen. The explosion was in the wing that housed a department of the Limassol Military Command, and collaboration between police members of EOKA B and military personnel would almost certainly have been necessary for the operation.

On 9 August, police arrested Stavros Stavrou-Syros, the Limassol section leader and Grivas' close associate. The arrest took place in the house of teacher Andreas Pavlou in Limassol, where Syros lived, together with the wanted National Guard officer and secretary of the pro-Grivas Limassol Fighters' Association (SAPEL), Dimitris Spourgitis. When Reservists surrounded the house where Syros was hiding, he began to burn documents from his personal archive. A police officer knocked on the door and, when the occupants refused to open, ordered his men to force it. A group of police officers burst in to the hall and the

---

74 Papageorgiou, *Μακάριος*, p. 185.

75 Michail Kalyeropoulos-Diakos, interview with the author, Limassol, 15 March 2001.

76 Georgios Tombazos, testimony before the Committee on the 'Cyprus File' of the Cyprus House of Representatives.

77 "Διετάχθη εκτέλεσις στελέχους του Γρίβα" [Execution Order against one of Grivas' Cadres], *Phileleftheros*, 15 September 1973.

one at their head gave the order to get ready to fire. At that moment, Syros appeared from the back, and told them: "Don't fire. I am Syros and I surrender". Addressing the officer in charge, he said: "You've caught a big fish."[78]

The Reservists hurried to the room where documents were burning and put out the flames, preserving the greater part of Syros' files. Among the documents found was the plan for a coup, 'Apollo', as well as the plan for the assassination of Makarios. The police obtained evidence from the documents that led them to Famagusta, to the house of Kikis Constantinou, which they searched. Constantinou escaped arrest, but the entire section of the 'Apollo' plan concerning the Famagusta area was found in his house.

The government immediately published some of the files, laying stress on the 'Apollo' Plan. The Government Spokesman pointed out that Kyrenia was exempt from the operations, and interpreted the fact as proof of Grivas' intention to leave Kyrenia in the hands of the Turks. Grivas was aggrieved at the government's attempt to paint him as a traitor and, on 22 August, circulated an announcement which, for the first time, bore the signature G. Grivas-Dighenis. In the announcement, headed "Look who is the partitionist", he referred to "dishonest methods" used by Makarios in order to associate him with partition.

"By means of a forged document, which he presents as supposedly composed by me, he deliberately lets out that we are more or less ready to hand over the Kyrenia district to the Turks," Grivas stated, and after making various assertions claiming it was Makarios who was responsible for the risk of partition, he again set out his position regarding *Enosis*: "We have repeatedly declared, and do declare today also, that we desire *Enosis* without the cession of territory, whether Cypriot or Greek, to the Turks, because if by any chance the Turks demand in return for *Enosis* only economic compensation, then it should not be the Cyprus people who should pay, but those presently responsible for the situation in Cyprus, the *British* and *Americans*."[79]

Despite Grivas' categorical denials of the authenticity of the 'Apollo' plan, it was eventually proved to be genuine, and, until today, none of his close associates have repeated the claim that it was a forged document. Moreover, at the moment when the 'Apollo' Plan had begun to be implemented in February 1973, Socrates Eliades had met with the First Secretary of the US embassy, Joseph Lawrence, and told him that Grivas had admitted that for *Enosis* to be successful there had to be concessions to Turkey that would satisfy her demands on national security. To a question by Lawrence as to how Grivas interpreted these demands, Eliades reminded him that during the negotiations over the Acheson Plan, a long-term lease to Turkey of a military base in Cyprus had been accepted. "Although the General objected to the cession of the whole Karpass peninsula to Turkey, he has realised that some area of the island has doubtless to be ceded."[80]

As a result of Syros' arrest and the seizure of his archives, there followed mass arrests of EOKA B members in Limassol. The success of the security forces badly affected morale among the organisation's members. In an attempt to revive spirits, Grivas gave an order to the section leaders: "When one struggles to overcome the adversary, and gives him punches, it is natural to receive some in return. The winner will be he who can endure the blows of the enemy so as to deliver the decisive and fatal blow." He called on his men to hold their ranks, "like a wall confronting the murderous and anti-national plans of Mous-

---

78 "Καίριον πλήγμα", [Decisive Blow], *Phileleftheros*, 10 August 1973.

79 Papademetris, Panayiotis, Petrides, *op. cit.*, vol. 14, p. 268.

80 Memo from Popper to Department of State, 23 February 1973, "Grivas Associate Socratis Eliades Discusses General's Objectives", NARA, RG59, CFPF, 1970-1973, Cyprus.

kos, so that when the moment comes, that same wall will fall on Mouskos and his supporters and will crush them."[81]

Syros' rival Lefteris Papadopoulos took over as section leader in Limassol after the arrest. Papadopoulos considered Syros an agent of Makarios since the attempted reconciliation between Makarios and Grivas in 1972. As soon as he took up his duties, Papadopoulos sent a letter to Spyros Papageorgiou in Nicosia telling him that Syros' arrest was a set up:

"I have taken over the Section of that wretched Stavrou. Keep it quiet. Few are aware of it.

"Whether I live or die, remember what I am writing to you. Stavrou was a traitor, consciously and willingly. Keep this letter in a safe place. If something bad happens to me, throw it in his face. Only I know what harm he did. If only I could see you and tell you: he is a shameless wretch, one of the worst. If I were in Mouskos' place, I would do one of two things: either I would set him free, thanking him in a public speech for what he offered to him and did against the organisation, or I would make him Minister of the Interior so he could arrest his fellow fighters. I spit on him! Disgusting! No bigger bastard has ever lived.

"But I hope to survive so as to speak my piece to everybody. Because only I know every member."[82]

Papadopoulos accused Syros of giving up without a fight, and stated: "Are we going to let them beat the hell out of us without paying for it? I know, you can't write it down, or else I'd write to the bastard, that if they don't get me between the eyes, there'll be many a mother crying. I'll shout it in the streets. And, do you know, my fingers are itching. I'll f*** them in the a***."[83]

EOKA B suffered serious blows in the psychological domain as well, as a result of the violence that began to appear as an obstacle to Grivas. In all the towns of Cyprus, armed pro-Makarios groups were formed, which were under the control of Vassos Lyssarides. Makarios encouraged the formation of these groups following the end of the Czech weapons affair, with a view to reinforcing the security forces in the event of an all-out assault by the National Guard and EOKA B. According to evidence from the United Nations, on the day the coup of 14 February was planned, the balance of forces was overwhelmingly in favour of anti-Makarios elements. Makarios could depend only on an elite police force of 300-400 men, which was later absorbed into the Reservists. In the opponents' camp there were 300-400 armed men loyal to Grivas, the National Guard and the majority of the members of the police force. According to an UNFICYP report, "Makarios could expect little or no help from the 3,000 men of the Cyprus police. Its leadership was loyal to Makarios, but from there on down there are persons who had been appointed by Georgadjis." UNFICYP estimated that "if it happens that the far more powerful National Guard takes action against Makarios, the majority of the Cyprus police would either remain inactive or would go over to the other side." It added that of the 9,500 men of the National Guard, 3,000 were in or near Nicosia. These forces were loyal to the Commander of the National Guard, Charalambopoulos, and among them could be included the special Commando units. UNFICYP also estimated that, "in the event that the supporters of Grivas provoke an outbreak of violent actions in specific areas of Cyprus, Charalambopoulos would take over all the most important points of Nicosia and in a few hours would declare martial law."[84]

---

81 Papademetris, Panayiotis, Petrides, *op. cit.*, vol. 14, p. 315.

82 Papageorgiou, *Μακάριος*, p. 200.

83 *Ibid.*

84 Popper to Secretary of State, "UNFICYP estimate of force alignment pro and anti Makarios", NARA, RG59, CFPF, 1970-1973, Cyprus, telegram 328, Nicosia 14 February 1972.

Aware of this imbalance, Makarios moved to reinforce the Reservists, who were loyal to him, with an illegal force of civil guards, which came under the orders of Vassos Lyssarides. In order to arm this force, weapons were imported illegally from neighbouring Arab countries, mainly from Syria. The cost of purchasing and transporting the weapons to Cyprus was covered by funds and means that Andreas Azinas had at his disposal in the coffers of the Cooperatives.

These paramilitary groups did not undertake organised armed action against Grivas supporters. Nevertheless, there were violent clashes, manifesting themselves mainly through bomb attacks against members and supporters of Grivas' organisation. Furthermore, there is evidence that some of the bombers belonged to the ranks of Makarios supporters, but also had links with Greek KYP.

The first bomb attacks against Grivas supporters occurred in Larnaca, on New Year's Eve 1973, when in one night there were 15 explosions. The next wave of mass bombings happened on the night of 15 to 16 March. In all, 30 bombs exploded (20 in Limassol, five in Nicosia and five in Paphos). According to the leader of these units in the Limassol area, Menelaos Kanakis, the aim of the bomb attacks was to step up the psychological pressure against supporters of EOKA B.[85]

However, this logic favoured the plans of Greek KYP and of the Second Bureau of the General Staff. The officers in charge looked favourably on the onset of violence with victims among the Grivas-*Enosis* supporters. After a series of incidents in Larnaca, Nicos Dontas urged EOKA B not to respond with reprisals and to issue an announcement "through which they would tell the people that at this time only Lyssarides supporters were setting off bombs".[86]

Often, Makarios supporters set off bombs in reprisal for bomb attacks by EOKA B, and vice-versa. In one incident, on the night of 27 to 28 July 1973, Makarios supporters responded immediately to each bomb set off by Grivas men. By daylight, 60 explosions had occurred in Limassol.

The bomb attacks by Makarios supporters bestowed 'legitimacy' on EOKA B, and Grivas' action began to take on the character of civil strife. Makarios attempted to distance himself from the actions of pro-government groups, but he was not convincing. In a speech on 9 September, he admitted the existence of pro-government groups and requested their dissolution: "I have condemned not only violence but counter-violence. Today I repeat that armed groups that support the government through violent methods only do harm to the state. Clearly and unequivocally I state that I consider their dissolution to be a service rendered."[87] Naturally, he took no substantial measures for the dissolution of these groups, which had been formed with his approval. Moreover, relatives of his were involved in operations to import arms for these groups.

Apart from blaming the government for the actions of pro-Makarios paramilitary groups, the Grivas faction made accusations concerning the continually increasing frequency of incidents involving the beating of prisoners. Often, those suspected of being involved in EOKA B's terrorist activities appeared in court with clear signs of maltreatment. One serious incident occurred at daybreak of 20 October 1973 at the Central Prisons in Nicosia. The previous day, 14 prison guards had been dismissed for "reasons of public in-

---

85 Menelaos Kanakis, interview with the author, Nicosia, 21 December 2000.
86 Cyprus KYP, report, *op. cit.*, p. 44.
87 Papademetris, Panayiotis, Petrides, *op. cit.*, vol. 14, p. 290.

terest", after the government accused them of helping prisoners escape, acting as links between imprisoned EOKA B members and their organisation.

The vacuum was filled by the secondment of a section from the Reservist Corps to the Central Prisons, which were overflowing as a result of mass arrests. The prison authorities decided to transfer a number of convicts from one wing to another. During the move, which occurred at daybreak, the prisoners were attacked by the platoon of Reservists, who were waiting for them in the courtyard. After medical examination, it was determined that at least 20 prisoners had been beaten up.

This episode came to the attention of the House committees for Internal and Legal affairs, which arrived at a unanimous conclusion, confirming that the Reservists had assaulted the convicts, assaults which were termed "unjustifiable and inadmissible".[88]

The complaints concerning maltreatment were also investigated by the International Legal Committee. The envoy of the Committee, George Garret, visited Cyprus and determined that:

> "Prisoners had received blows and had been hit with weapons, kicked and suffered burns.
>
> Prisoners were threatened with execution.
>
> Those arrested in a good state of health appeared before the court twenty-four hours later with signs of ill treatment and violence."[89]

When Makarios was asked about the beatings on 29 October 1973, he answered: "There have been accusations of ill-treatment of prisoners and relevant enquiries have been instigated. The conclusions of the investigation, however, and the available testimony as to the incidents charged do not provide evidence sufficient to warrant taking them to court. But of course the complainants may themselves have recourse to justice."[90]

As Garret states in his report, the Attorney General of the Republic undertook to investigate the complaints of ill treatment, "but in practice the complaints were referred to the police for investigation, against whom the complaints had been made in the first place".[91]

Makarios' apparent tacit approval of state violence fed a climate of sympathy for EOKA B. Grivas presented his organisation as a continuation of the anti-colonial EOKA struggle for *Enosis*, and equated the "anti-national" Makarios with British Governor Harding. The ideal of *Enosis* was still very much present in the awareness of the Greek Cypriots, and the revolutionary character of the action of EOKA B began to create positive impressions, especially among the young, fed by the spirit infused into the proclamations and directives of Grivas.

---

88 *Ibid.*, p. 319.
89 *Ibid.*, p. 320.
90 *Ibid.*
91 *Ibid.*

7. The second junta in power

While Grivas was drawing up plans to overthrow Makarios in Cyprus in the summer of 1973, he was also in contact with Dimitrios Ioannides in Athens. Grivas saw Ioannides as representing the 'healthy' forces within the Greek army, and EOKA B looked forward to his support for the decisive blow against Makarios. Ioannides was seen as an *Enosis* man, while Papadopoulos was considered a supporter of independence.

Grivas was in contact with Ioannides in June 1973. In a note to Carousos regarding the 'Apollo' plan, he wrote he had also taken into consideration "current conditions prevailing in Greece". What, however, *were* the conditions in Greece to which Grivas was referring? "It is now a certainty," writes Spyros Papageorgiou, "that Grivas, through a man of his in Athens, was in contact with the Second Junta," whose leader was Ioannides.[1]

The question of cooperation between Ioannides and Grivas was discussed in two telephone conversations between Socrates Eliades and Andreas Potamianos – the link man between EOKA B and Ioannides – on 28 and 30 June 1973. From the decoding of these conversations, which were conducted using code words, Cyprus KYP gleaned that Eliades had sent a letter to Potamianos on behalf of Grivas via the head of the Second Bureau of the National Guard General Staff, Costas Papayiannis, asking for clarifications and commitments concerning the support that Ioannides would give Grivas in the event of any attempt to overthrow Makarios.[2]

Potamianos replied to Grivas through Eliades that he agreed totally with his views and he assured him that "he solemnly undertook personally to persuade Ioannides concerning this". Eliades told Potamianos: "Ioannides had better ask himself some serious questions, because if the operation is crowned with success they will be the big gainers, and they should stop telling us: go on, go on, and then, when we need their help, hang back."[3]3

At the same time, Ioannides was planning to overthrow Papadopoulos and establish a new regime. Unlike Papadopoulos, who adjusted to official American policy on Cyprus, supported Makarios and the continuation of intercommunal talks, Ioannides, as the leader of Greek Gladio, was a hardliner. He supported *Enosis* and Grivas' armed struggle to achieve it, and hated Makarios.

By July 1973, Cyprus policy had divided the Greek junta into two wings. On the one side, was the pro-Makarios policy supported by Prime Minister George Papadopoulos, and on the other side the pro-Grivas policy supported by Ioannides.

Savvas Constantopoulos, the theoretician of Greece's 21st April coup, undertook to give his public support to Papadopoulos' policy on Cyprus. In an article published on 8 August 1973, he analysed the unfeasibility of *Enosis* without territorial concessions to Turkey, and expressed his support for independence as an honourable solution. Constantopoulos proposed that Papadopoulos should invite Makarios and Grivas to Athens to discuss jointly a way out for the Cyprus problem. He suggested they should dissolve all armed groups, that their weapons be surrendered to the Greek Contingent, and that a referendum should be held for the people to choose between a 'sacrificial solution', that is, *Enosis*, and a 'solution of necessity', i.e. independence.[4]

---

1 Papageorgiou, *Μακάριος*, p. 165.

2 Cyprus KYP report, *op. cit.*, p. 56.

3 *Ibid.*

4 "Δεν απορρίπτεται η πρότασις διά δημοψήφισμα εις Κύπρον" [Suggestion for a Cyprus Referendum not Rejected], *Phileleftheros*, 9 August 1973.

Constantopoulos' proposal was immediately accepted by Makarios, who found it constructive. "It is with pleasure that I would accept an invitation of President George Papadopoulos to travel to Athens to discuss the Cyprus problem and the internal Cyprus situation, in a meeting in which Grivas will participate."[5]

Grivas gave written instructions to Spyros Papageorgiou to reply to Constantopoulos' article.[6] On 9 August, *Ethniki* newspaper called Constantopoulos "a self-appointed intermediary" and rejected his proposals.[7]

The Cyprus issue was discussed at a meeting of the Supreme National Security Council in Athens on 13 August. According to information that Adonis Kyros conveyed by telephone to Nicosia, "the view was raised in the Council by Papadopoulos that, since there is no possibility of *Enosis* but rather a danger of partition, it was better to go for independence and wait and see after five years".[8] Ioannides opposed this position, supporting the *Enosis* line of Grivas. Papadopoulos disagreed, and a rift appeared between the two leaders of the Junta. According to a briefing that Costas Papayiannis made to Costas Rados, the two men quarrelled and "Ioannides got up and left, after submitting a request for a one-month leave of absence". Pavlos Papadakis attempted, according to Papayiannis, to communicate with Ioannides, but could not find him anywhere.[9]

Back in Cyprus, Grivas had ordered the kidnapping of Justice Minister Christos Vakis. On the night of 27 July 1973, EOKA B men in police uniform went to the house, knocked on the door and told him that the Leader wanted to see him. His wife panicked and the armed men calmed her down, giving their military word of honour that Vakis would return in two hours. The minister acquiesced, and followed his kidnappers. His wife waited until some hours had passed and when Vakis did not return, reported the kidnapping to the police. Carousos organised the operation, and its execution was entrusted to one of the battle-hardened units of EOKA B, which had its headquarters in Larnaca village near Lapithos, in the Pentadactylos range.

The kidnapping of the Justice Minister was seen by the government as an enormous provocation, and instructions were issued to the police to carry out mass arrests of members of the pro-*Enosis* movement. In 48 hours, the jails filled with prisoners. All the elements that supported Grivas, including members of the ESEA and journalists, were suspected of the kidnapping and were interrogated. In this climate of bitterness, a platoon of Reservists on the night of 28 July raided the premises of *Gnomi* and *Ethniki* newspapers, destroyed the pages that were ready for publication, beating and arresting journalists and workers.[10]

On a political level, Makarios aimed harsh words at Grivas, describing his actions as "the crude and abominable manifestation of violence on the part of the criminal gangs of General Grivas". Grivas' aim, Makarios said, was "the creation of a climate of fear and terror so as to impose undemocratic views, which, I steadfastly believe, will lead to the ruin of our national issue and the ruin of Cyprus Hellenism".[11]

---

5 Papademetris, Panayiotis, Petrides, *op. cit.*, vol. 14, p. 307.

6 Spyros Papageorgiou, *Από την Ζυρίχην εις τον Αττίλαν* [From Zurich to Attila] (Athens: G. Ladia Publications, 1980), vol. 3, pp. 161-165.

7 Papademetris, Panayiotis, Petrides, *op. cit.*, vol. 14, p. 307.

8 Cyprus KYP report, *op. cit.*, p. 66.

9 *Ibid.*, p. 64.

10 Papademetris, Panayiotis, Petrides, *op. cit.*, vol. 14, p. 320.

11 *Ibid.*, p. 294.

Grivas claimed responsibility for the kidnapping of the Minister of Justice in a proclamation circulated on 2 August, and laid down the following conditions for his release:

1. Political freedoms are to be granted to the Greek Cypriot people so it may express freely and voluntarily its will concerning the national issue (…)
2. Genuine elections are to be held to choose the President of the Republic.
3. The current President of the Republic is to choose between Church and State.
4. A general amnesty is to be declared for political convicts, and all political prisoners are to be released.
5. Dismissed policemen are to be reinstated, as are other civil servants.

The announcement carried an ultimatum, namely, that if the conditions were not met, "we are determined to proceed at any cost".[12]

Makarios replied on 3 August, rejecting the ultimatum and saying Grivas was out of tune: "What will the future hold, if, taking one's example from Grivas, one were to express another insane view, using similar criminal methods to subsequently put conditions for the imposition of one's point of view?"

To Grivas' demand for his resignation, Makarios replied: "I am the organ and mouthpiece of the will of the people, and on the will of people do I depend. On the contrary, Grivas plots in secret and secretly directs criminal activities. He has not the courage to show himself before the people." Makarios concluded with yet another dig at Grivas: "It would appear that Grivas aims at making the end of his life coincide with the ruin of Cyprus."[13]

Grivas answered Makarios with a lengthy manifesto, in which he blamed him for all the evils that had befallen Cyprus, the most important being that he had repeatedly torpedoed plans for *Enosis*, and concluded as follows: "If Cyprus remains an independent state and does not become part of Greece, and is governed in the way it is governed today, its fate is sealed. *Turkification* or *Sovietisation*." He felt he could not remain inactive: "My decision is taken. *Fight to the finish* for the salvation of Cyprus. (…) He wants war; *he shall have it.* (….) We shall wage the struggle with tenacity and self-sacrifice. If we should fall in the course of it, our 'heroic band' will offer something to Cyprus and to our descendants, while I shall cover the murderers in eternal shame, I and the National Idea that we represent."[14]

The kidnapping of Vakis sparked Papadopoulos' direct intervention in the Cyprus developments as he openly requested that Grivas dissolve his units. In a message broadcast by the CyBC on 24 August, Papadopoulos called on Grivas immediately to bring his action to an end:

"The National Centre has publicly criticised the actions of the illegal organisation of General Grivas, which undermine the coordinated policy of the National Centre for the solution of the Cyprus issue through intensified talks within Cyprus, aiming at securing an independent, sovereign and unified state…

"Already, the National Centre finds itself in the position of appealing to the patriotic sentiments of General Grivas-Dighenis and calling upon him to put an immediate end to armed action and to disband his organisation."[15]

Makarios accepted Papadopoulos' speech with obvious satisfaction: "The illegal elements should listen and conform to the exhortation of the Motherland. Violence and violent

---

12 Papademetris, Panayiotis, Petrides, *op. cit.*, vol. 14, p. 290.
13 *Ibid.*, p. 296.
14 *Ibid.*, p. 302.
15 "Ο Γρίβας να καταθέση τα όπλα" [Grivas Should Lay down his Arms], *Phileleftheros*, 25 August 1973.

reprisals can only cause hardships to Cyprus, and they greatly harm our national issue," he stated in one of his speeches.[16]

Grivas' reaction was utterly negative. In a proclamation circulated on 27 August, he said Papadopoulos' speech "made a very distressing impression on him". He appeared all the more upset because although he was lower in rank, he had addressed his message to him via CyBC: "Unethical also was the manner through which your message was conveyed, via the broadcasting corporation of my opponent. You do not, however, address yourself to yours truly… When you were a simple lieutenant, I as adjutant in the Operations Department of the General Staff was participating in the preparations for the war against Italy."

As for Papadopoulos' exhortation to disband EOKA B, Grivas replied by reminding him that within the Makarios faction were also the communists: "Do you not wish to accept (….) that in their ranks the majority is made up of legitimised 'illegals', the communists? And how can the fact be reconciled that in Greece the communists are dangerous and hostile to us, while in Cyprus they should be our allies?"

Grivas came to the conclusion that Papadopoulos was indirectly supporting the communists in Cyprus, and called upon his co-revolutionaries to take a stand: "Thus, you may divide the Cyprus people into two groups: on the one side are *we*, genuine Greece and free Greek Cyprus. On the other, are the anti-Hellenes and those who betray the national idea. You have preferred to support the second. A truly strange decision. This, however, is of concern to us. It concerns also the Greek government and the Greek people. Furthermore, it concerns the OFFICERS, THE FELLOW REVOLUTIONARIES OF THE 21ST OF APRIL."[17] This reference of Grivas, written in capital letters, was a clear message to the Ioannides faction, with which he was already in contact, and who he was asking for assistance so that EOKA B could break out of the impasse.

Finally, Grivas released the Minister of Justice on the night of 26 August. In a proclamation circulated on 27 August, he declared his release as a gesture of good will "for a democratic normalisation of the situation".[18]

Grivas was convinced Papadopoulos had turned against him after advice from the British ambassador in Athens. A leaflet found on EOKA B fighters arrested in Korfi in Limassol read: "It has been ascertained that the British ambassador in Athens requested from the Greek Prime Minister to condemn our action in Cyprus. A Greek leader has appeared who bows before the will of the British representative in Athens. Let everyone in Athens see the terrible state they are in. The Greek leaders of today bow their heads at the mere whim of Britain. For this reason, all true Greeks must condemn the statement of Papadopoulos."[19]

In Nicosia, Grivas ordered a war of attrition against Papadopoulos, accusing him of forming an alliance with Makarios to the benefit of "the communists and anti-Greek elements".[20] The Athens newspaper *Estia* also joined the game, publishing on 30 August "corroborated information" that Makarios was due to meet Papadopoulos in Athens on 10 September, on a stop-over to Malta, and that foreign elements were "implacably applying pressure for a joint statement renouncing *Enosis* and accepting the process of a referendum in

16 Papademetris, Panayiotis, Petrides, *op. cit.*, vol. 14, p. 308.
17 *Ibid.*, p. 309.
18 "Ο πρόεδρος ηύχετο εκτέλεσιν του κ. Βάκη" [The President Wishes Vakis had been Executed], *Ethniki*, 28 August 1973.
19 "Γρίβας: εχθροί μας είναι οι Μακάριος και Παπαδόπουλος" [Grivas: Makarios and Papadopoulos are our Enemies], *Phileleftheros*, 10 October 1973.
20 "Μόνον τους ανθέλληνας ικανοποιεί ο κ. Γ. Παπαδόπουλος" [Only the Anti-Greeks are Satisfied with Papadopoulos], *Ethniki*, 25 August 1973.

Cyprus based on the question 'Partition or Independence?'." The article also claimed Papadopoulos was to put the National Guard at Makarios' disposal for him to use against the pro-*Enosis* faction. It also warned Athens that Makarios was using the Greek government to further his policies and that, after achieving a solution contrary to national interests, he would land Greece with the responsibility.[21]

While the Papadopoulos-Ioannides confrontation was under way over Cyprus, within the ranks of the regime in Greece, certain important changes were taking place. A 'referendum' organised by Papadopoulos abolished the monarchy and on 18 August 1973, he was sworn in as President of the 'Republic'. Immediately afterwards, he proposed that Spyros Markezinis take on the premiership and form a civilian government. Grivas looked favourably on Markezinis, because in the past they had been political allies, with Markezinis taking a public stand against the Zurich agreements and in favour of *Enosis* when he had been in opposition to Karamanlis.

At the beginning of September, on the pretext of Markezinis' assumption of office as prime minister, Grivas instructed Spyros Papageorgiou to write an article in *Ethniki* reminding Markezinis of the positions he had adopted over the years in favour of *Enosis*. He also instructed him to write another article calling on Papadopoulos to resign, citing the revelations in *Estia* concerning the renunciation of *Enosis* at the behest of the Anglo-Americans. Grivas further gave the order for the following slogan to be inserted as a front-page headline in *Ethniki*: "YES to Democracy, NO to dictatorship".

Papageorgiou briefed the secretary of ESEA, Stelios Christides, by telephone on 3 September concerning the line that Grivas had ordered:

"Papageorgiou:	I'm preparing a tune for Markezinis, one whole page from top to bottom.
Christides:	Are you getting at him about Papadopoulos?
Papageorgiou:	As from tomorrow. I told you, three days ago I was given the line to follow.
Christides:	Keep on at the bastard, so we get rid of Papadopoulos.
Papageorgiou:	Whatever the other guy [Grivas] told me, I'll let him have it without any reservation, and you know it.
Christides:	Great, right on."[22]

Papageorgiou published his article against Papadopoulos the following day. It was the newspaper's lead story under the headline "Papadopoulos Must Go". Quoting reliable political circles in Nicosia and Athens, the article said Papadopoulos' statement asking Grivas to leave Cyprus, "not only had no effect at all on the supporters of the *Enosis* struggle of General Grivas, but provoked intense reactions among them".

Papageorgiou referred to *Estia*'s revelations concerning the 'Anglo-American plan' for the renunciation of *Enosis* and for a partitionist solution to the Cyprus problem, arguing these "justified the views of General Grivas-Dighenis and his struggle to overturn any possible anti-national solution to the Cyprus issue, but also aroused among the Greek nation such a negative reaction to the policy of appeasement followed by the President of Greece Mr G. Papadopoulos in the face of pressures from the Anglo-Americans, that today his resignation from presidential office is being seen as a panhellenic demand".[23]

---

21 "Θα αποκηρύξη την Ένωσιν ο πρόεδρος της Κύπρου!" [Cyprus President to renounce *Enosis*!], *Ethniki*, 1 September 1973.

22 Cyprus KYP report, *op. cit.*, p. 64.

23 "Να φύγει ο Παπαδόπουλος" [Papadopoulos Must Go], *Ethniki*, 4 September 1973.

Papageorgiou's article left Greek officers bewildered. Costas Papayiannis of the Second Bureau of the General Staff visited Socrates Eliades and the teacher Gavriel Minas, whom he tried to persuade to moderate the attacks against Papadopoulos. Eliades and Minas quarrelled with Stelios Christides, who contacted Papageorgiou and informed him accordingly:

"Christides: The Minas-Socrates duo confronted me with the article against Papadopoulos.

Papageorgiou: Well, at least one of them got a written order to start things off, but he's doing the opposite.

Christides: The other guy Papayiannis was present, and told him something in connection with it.

Papageorg: Now I understand his cunning.

Christides: From what Kyros told me, Papadopoulos has made the Revolutionary Council face a dilemma with the Constantopoulos article – Independence or Partition."[24]

Despite Papayiannis' intervention, *Ethniki* intensified its campaign, describing Papadopoulos in its columns as a danger to the nation. However, it made a clear attempt to get the rest of the members of the Junta on its side: "No other member of the Revolution or of the Greek government of today has taken a public stand on this question. According to us, this intensifies Mr Papadopoulos' isolation. Moreover, the impression has been created lately that all the associates of the President have been overshadowed by him."

Going a step further, *Ethniki* warned Papadopoulos of the price of his isolation: "The Greek officers associates of Mr Papadopoulos would do well to pay attention to historical developments. (…) Let Mr Papadopoulos himself beware, because loneliness is a bad thing. And there is no worse loneliness than that of the man who finds himself at the top."[25]

At the same time, Grivas newspapers began to be flooded by telegrams from nationalist organisations protesting about Papadopoulos' "foreign-instigated statement". The fact that Grivas' aim was the fall of Papadopoulos, not that of the regime, is clear from the exhortation by Adonis Kyrou, the well-informed editor of *Estia* newspaper, to Christides concerning the line taken by *Ethniki*, which should "stick to the strictly personal framework against Papadopoulos and not more generally against the Revolutionary Council, which, in contrast, would help concerning his patriotic sentiments". According to Kyrou, "the polemic against Papadopoulos must proceed in such a way that all is concentrated on his person, and not against the remaining members of the Revolutionary Council, leaving, however, a way out in the hope that he will come round".[26]

On 25 September 1973, Grivas, in an interview published in the Athens newspaper *To Vima*, charged that Makarios was plotting his assassination, and that the Athens regime "had sent to Cyprus four majors, whose names I am aware of, with a view to arresting or assassinating me".[27]

Makarios reacted immediately. "I am under the impression that Grivas is possessed by a fear that his life is in danger. (…) He criticises others for what he himself does," he said, seizing the opportunity to expose him before the regime: "Grivas' claim… constitutes a

---

24 Cyprus KYP report, *op. cit.*, p. 66.

25 "Κίνδυνοι διά το Έθνος" [The Nation in Danger], *Ethniki*, 7 September 1973.

26 Cyprus KYP report, *op. cit.*, p. 65.

27 Grivas replied in writing to a questionnaire from *Vima*. The answers were given on 17 September. Papademetris, Panayiotis, Petrides, *op. cit.*, vol. 14, p. 312.

terrible accusation against Greece. And the accuser should demonstrate what truth there is to his claim. Otherwise, he is himself open to the charge of slander."[28]

Grivas linked his accusation to Papadopoulos' condemnation of EOKA B's activities. He insisted that the intervention had been at the instigation of the British ambassador in Athens, and that the conspiracy was an extension of what Savvas Constantopoulos had written against him. "I am ashamed for the Greek officer corps, since such members exist in their ranks. For that reason I am keeping silent over their names and will reveal them only to their authorities in Cyprus, should they ask me for them. I too have my eye on them, and it would be better if they were recalled to where they came from."[29]

The Greek Ministry of National Security called Grivas' speech an insult to the Greek officer corps. "It is extremely sad that passions have reached the point where such slanders are concocted," an announcement declared, concluding with the order that the Commander of the National Guard, General Denisis, who had succeeded Charalambopoulos, should request the names of the officers in question.[30]

On 27 September, the names of Grivas' alleged would-be assassins, in fact not four but three, were handed by Socrates Eliades to the Chief of Staff, Pavlos Papadakis, who went to Athens for this reason. The same names were given also by the Greek embassy to Costas Bourlos of the Second Bureau of the General Staff. They were Majors Napoleon Damaskinos, commander of the 31st Commando Battalion, Constantinos Raftopoulos, Commander of the 32nd Commando Battalion, and one Liapis, who was serving in the Communications Regiment.[31]

On 5 October, the Greek Ministry of National Defence announced that two persons attached to Grivas' entourage had given to the Commander of the National Guard the names of three officers "without the slightest proof that could support the charges against them". The announcement stated that Grivas "had relied on malicious people and spurious information, and consequently the Ministry of National Defence is not disposed to take any further action".[32]

At least two of the Majors, who were commanders of commando battalions, Damaskinos and Raftopoulos, belonged to the Dimitris Ioannides group. During the 15 July coup, both of them participated in the offensive against the Presidential Palace. Later, during the days of the coup, they were accused of stealing a safe from there.

Socrates Eliades considered Grivas' assassination claim to be a faux pas, and blamed Cosmas Mastrokolias for the turn that events had taken. In a telephone conversation with the Secretary of ESEA, Stelios Christides, on 26 September 1973, Eliades protested that they had "handled the affair very superficially and hurried to make it public before checking the relevant information". Furious, Eliades expressed his view that it would be "difficult for Grivas to prove his claim, which he certainly bases on incorrect information, if he takes into consideration that the information from Athens to date has been false".[33]

As the Grivas-Papadopoulos clash grew, funding for EOKA B from Athens was cut off. Squabbles then broke out among Grivas cadres over the manner in which the whole matter had been handled. Some blamed Potamianos, while others, among them Eliades, blamed

---

28 *Ibid.*, p. 311.
29 *Ibid.*, p. 312.
30 "Το πάθος του Γρίβα έφθασε μέχρι σημείου τυφλώσεως" [Grivas' Passion has Reached the Point of Blindness], *Phileleftheros*, 27 September 1973.
31 Cyprus KYP report, *op. cit.*, p. 69.
32 Papademetris, Panayiotis, Petrides, *op. cit.*, vol. 14, p. 313.
33 Cyprus KYP report, *op. cit.*, p. 69.

Mastrokolias, making insinuations that "rashly and very hastily he had conveyed the information to Grivas".[34]

On 30 October, Eliades complained bitterly to Potamianos about not receiving funding from Athens. Among other things, he told Potamianos: "I thought, Andreas, you were better than the others; unfortunately, you are just like the other mainland Greeks. I have lost my self-respect and my identity as a human being." Potamianos observed that Mastrokolias considered him responsible for the turn that matters had taken, and Eliades, white with fury, said that "Antonis [Mastrokolias' pseudonym] and the others can go to hell, they are all idiots, for having announced an assassination conspiracy against Grivas by four Greek officers. It is unheard of. I forbid you to mention my name."[35]

The discussion continued the next day. A furious Eliades urged Potamianos to tell Mastrokolias "to stop writing what he does to Grivas, because he is doing great harm. He is writing rubbish, he is a scoundrel because he is living in fantasy land. He is equally guilty for the organisation ending up where it has and I am not about to become his accomplice in the ruination of this country." Finally, Potamianos gave assurances "that the matter of money will be worked out and it will be sent via Marios Christofides, who is in Athens".[36]

Ironically, according to information in the possession of Cyprus KYP, the three Majors probably were preparing something during those days, but the target was not Grivas but Makarios. The three of them "were detected by men from the secret services making suspicious contacts with (...) elements from the *Enosis* ranks, among whom was Papastavros [Papagathangelou]."[37]

A telephone conversation between Leandros Hadjimarkou and Papagathangelou aroused suspicions that the three Majors were planning something in collusion with Grivas men. Specifically, Hadjimarkou told Papagathangelou that the three officers "should be very careful about the operation" that they would carry out, because according to a message he had got that very minute "it was a big trap".[38] The following day, 7 October, there was an assassination attempt against Makarios at Ayios Sergios in the Famagusta area. The attempt was organised by the Famagusta EOKA B section leader Kikis Constantinou, without the knowledge of Grivas.

The attackers booby-trapped the tarmac with a large quantity of powerful explosives, which were to be detonated at the moment Makarios' car passed over it. The explosives were placed some kilometres outside the village. Later, the Piyi to Ayios Sergios road – an alternative route to and from Nicosia – was found booby-trapped in the same way.

The detonation of the explosives was entrusted to Kyriacos Tsekouras, who, in a detailed statement given after his arrest, described exactly how he had executed the operation. Tsekouras had been driven to the spot where the road was booby-trapped two days earlier in order to survey the area. Some way from the road there was a ditch, in which went a cable ending in an electric switch, wrapped in sticky tape for safety purposes.

Tsekouras' escort told him: "It's all ready. Count nine cypress trees just as Makarios' car is coming, and as soon as he arrives, press the button. Got it?" He explained that under the tarmac there were four hidden bombs. They were joined in such a way as to go off simultaneously. "The plan is perfect. All you've got to do is to keep cool," he told him.

---

34 Cyprus KYP report, *op. cit.*, p. 73.
35 *Ibid.*
36 *Ibid.*
37 *Ibid.*, p. 71.
38 *Ibid.*

Tsekouras was then driven to Trikomo, to the house of Andreas Nicolaou Kamilos, the leader of the operation. Kamilos took Tsekouras apart and told him: "Are you familiar with this sort of job? Have you seen the layout? What do you think about it?" "It's OK," answered Tsekouras, and Kamilos continued: "All four are linked together. One press, and they all go off at the same time. It makes a great blast and if you do it OK, it will blow him up to the bell tower. It all depends on you. You've only got to keep cool, nothing else." Tsekouras was worried about his escape route, and Kamilos said there would be a man there with a car or motorcycle to get him out. Kamilos told him: "If the plan succeeds we can hang up our pistols and you wanted guys will walk free."[39]

Tsekouras stayed in hiding until the evening before the attempt, when he was driven to the point where the attack was to take place. They left him there alone and he waited for daybreak so as to blow up the motorcade with Makarios in it. At 6.45am a deafening explosion was heard, and the tarmac was blown into the air. The presidential motorcade, however, was kilometres away. Tsekouras, confused as he was, was arrested a little later near the point of the explosion. He immediately confessed that he had caused the explosion, and claimed he had intentionally set off the explosive device because he had changed his mind: "My nerves were continually on edge and I was thinking of finding a way out of this criminal act. Finally, I came to the conclusion that it wasn't right for me to kill the Archbishop and I set off the bombs before the Archbishop's car arrived and after checking that at that moment there was no vehicle passing by the cypress trees, so as to avoid any possible casualties."[40]

This version, however, does not ring true. From the moment the bombs were in position, the electric switch was wrapped with sticky tape for safety reasons and for protection against damp. The time drew near, Tsekouras tried to remove the tape so as to be ready to press the button. Doing this, he set off the device prematurely. When police investigators found the sticky tape at the scene of the incident, they suspected what had really happened. Under interrogation, Tsekouras confessed that in trying to remove the tape he had set off the device prematurely. The information was conveyed to Makarios, who, for ulterior motives, gave instructions that Tsekouras' first version be adopted. He considered it in his favour that it should be put around that a hard-line member of EOKA B could not bring himself to kill him.[41]

Makarios' motorcade arrived at the scene of the ambush a few minutes after the explosion. Makarios got out of his car and walked to the point where the tarmac had blown up. He then went to Ayios Sergios and conducted the service as usual. After the end of the liturgy, he spoke to the crowd that had gathered. Next, he rested at the house of the mother of Dionysis Malas, a relative and associate of his. As Malas later testified, men from his close entourage who were playing a double game, tried to persuade him to leave by a different route, and return to Nicosia via Piyi village.[42] Ultimately, Makarios decided to return by the same route. Two days later it was found that the road through Piyi was also booby-trapped.

News of the attempt to kill Makarios fell like a thunderbolt on Grivas' entourage, who had no idea about Kikis Constantinou's plans. Grivas believed the whole matter was an artifice devised by Makarios to gain public sympathy. The day following the attempt, the newspaper *Patris* wrote on the subject: "An unprecedented bluff, satanic in its conception

---

39 Tsekouras statement to police, Cyprus KYP.

40 *Ibid.*

41 Police investigating officer, interview with the author, on condition of anonymity. The information was confirmed by a second police source.

42 Dionysis Malas, interview with the author, Paphos, 21 October 2000.

and monstrous in its execution. These words only can convey the harsh reality of yesterday's so-called 'assassination attempt' against the Governor in Ayios Sergios of Famagusta district. (...)

"*Patris* is in a position to reveal and protest to the Cyprus people that the Legendary Leader of the Enosis Struggle, General Georgios Grivas-Dighenis, and EOKA, have not the slightest connection with yesterday's explosion in Ayios Sergios, which black government propaganda has hastened to present as an assassination attempt against the Governor. (...)

"The satanic plot in Ayios Sergios – as stated categorically by these pro-*Enosis* elements – was conceived by sick minds, who naively believe that it is possible through these crude means, to halt the torrent of the *Enosis* Struggle, being no longer able to face up to them honourably, like men."[43]

In the meanwhile, EOKA B wheels had been set in motion to get information as to what had actually happened. Lawyer Kyriakos Saveriades contacted Costas Adamides, also a lawyer, and gave him the following instructions: "You'd better go and see Tsekouras, who has been arrested for the attempt in Ayios Sergios, because we need information on this matter. At all costs, we have to make contact so as to get information out of him."[44]

Furthermore, Carousos entrusted his trusty Panicos Pambouris with investigating the matter. As Antonakis Genakritis, who was a member of Kikis Constantinou's unit, mentioned in a later deposition, Pambouris visited him after the attempt and asked him for information about Tsekouras. "I told him that relevant orders had been given by Carousos and Grivas for the carrying out of investigations, and he spoke out in ugly terms against Kikis Constantinou."[45]

Very soon, Grivas was informed that the attempt was the work of Constantinou, and did not pursue his claims that it was a set-up by Makarios. Makarios, however, returned to the charge and reminded Grivas of the attempt "about which he maintains a guilty silence".[46]

Grivas had no rebuttal to Makarios. However, he could not admit that he had lost control of EOKA B and that his cadres had channels of communication with other centres, from which they received instructions.

On 1 October 1973, in Athens, the new government of Spyros Markezinis was sworn in. Grivas said he would observe a truce until he had an indication of the new prime minister's intentions. The period was difficult for EOKA B. During the preceding months the organisation had suffered serious blows from the Reservists, having at the same time to face the consequences of the public clash between Grivas and George Papadopoulos. To these problems had been added that of centrifugal tendencies, as was shown by the attempt in Ayios Sergios. In the light of these problems, calls began to re-emerge within the organisation – and mainly in ESEA ranks – for a renunciation of armed action and towards politicisation of the EOKA B struggle.

A few days after Markezinis' swearing-in ceremony, the publisher Adonis Kyrou came to Cyprus to attend a libel case against the newspaper *Estia*. With Markezinis' consent, Kyrou sounded out Socrates Eliades as to what extent a conference was possible that would involve the leadership of ESEA and other cadres from the Grivas faction, in order to discuss the future of the *Enosis* struggle. The conference took place in the middle of October at the house of Socrates Eliades in Nicosia. It gathered together Kyriacos Saveriades, Glaf-

---

43 "Μπλόφα η 'απόπειρα'" ['Attempt' was a Bluff], *Patris*, 8 October 1973.
44 Cyprus KYP report, *op. cit.*, p. 72.
45 Cyprus KYP, Antonis Genakritis report on the activities of EOKA B.
46 Papademetris, Panayiotis, Petrides, *op. cit.*, vol. 14, p. 322.

cos Cassoulides, Gabriel Minas, Costas Tselos, Christakis Charalambous, Socrates Eliades, Polycarpos Ioannides, Costas Ioannides, Georgios Kaiser and Takis Evdokas. They were subsequently joined by businessman Pantelis Dimitriou from Larnaca, a bosom friend of Dimitrios Ioannides.

When Kyrou returned to Greece, he sent a note to Markezinis informing him of what had been said at the conference. Markezinis published in his memoirs extensive extracts from the note: "The conference began with an exposé by Mr Adonis Kyros concerning the futile 'further armed civil strife, and the necessity for politicisation of the *Enosis* struggle, so that the Athens government is not hampered in its international diplomatic demarches'. Those participating in the conference appeared in principle – at least those who were among the 'moderates' – to be well disposed towards the proposal. Suddenly, however, Socrates Eliades interrupted the discussion, gave the floor to Mr P. Dimitriou, who began speaking of 'the Greek Army, which will soon provide the solution and will hoist the Greek flag over all Cyprus', and anticipated that 'soon *Enosis* will become a reality, and it is sufficient to have faith in the army and to comply with the orders from the Leadership'."[47]

After Pantelis Dimitriou, Eliades took the floor, "urging blind faith in Dighenis, with a tone of undiluted optimism". Following these interventions, "Mr Adonis Kyros thought it superfluous to prolong the conference, which was interrupted, coming to no conclusion. After the conference, Mr Eliades gave a dinner, which was unexpectedly attended by the most senior officer of the National Guard, Brigadier Pavlos Papadakis, accompanied by a colonel from ELDYK 'probably – according to those participating – in order to emphasise the concern of the Greek Army'. Both of them belonged to the entourage of Brigadier D. Ioannides."[48]

When Grivas was informed on 20 October of what had been discussed at the conference, he sent Kyrou a densely written letter of four and a half pages, the contents of which were addressed more to Markezinis. Grivas utterly excluded the possibility of reaching an understanding with Makarios and considered a political struggle unrealistic. "As for Mouskos, he will never voluntarily resign from the presidency. He shows contempt for all, sacred regulations, governments, etc. – Through political means he cannot easily be eliminated, because as long as he holds power he will never accept a confrontation on the political level on equal terms. (…)

"I have come to the view that he has respect for nobody, not even the Greek government, only for the illegal units 'of Grivas' – and this because he has successful past experience in 'seeing off' all Greek governments without exception, and for this reason he enjoys observing that he has outlived 14 Greek governments." And he ended with the conclusion that "if his groups were dissolved, Makarios would remain, on both the internal and external fronts, perfectly in control".

In what followed, Grivas sought to persuade Markezinis that the only prospect was the continuation of the armed struggle, and he complained about the lack of financial support: "We have a great capability for armed action, if only I were to receive a relatively small increase in certain funds, which I have repeatedly asked for". And again he stressed, complainingly: "The lack of even rudimentary economic means has adversely affected the military domain. A starving bear cannot dance."[49]

---

47 Spyridon V. Markezinis, *Αναμνήσεις 1972-1974* [Recollections, 1972-1974] (Athens: Sp. V. Markezinis editions, 1979), p. 317.

48 *Ibid.*, p. 318.

49 *Ibid.*, p. 321.

Later, as Markezinis writes, Grivas returned to the theme of a political struggle, which he thought "would never be successful under the conditions in which the internal situation finds itself today in Cyprus". He believed that politicisation satisfied only the politicians, observing that "no outlawed national struggle was ever conducted through political parties", and stressed that politicisation could only be considered when the situation in Cyprus had achieved democratic standards. (...)

"I shall never do anything in violation of my conscience and of what I believe in. I see with crystal clarity what our struggle needs in order to bear fruit, and it can do so. Unfortunately, I do not find understanding, nor do I dispose of the means to achieve it alone."[50]

That which Grivas saw with 'crystal clarity' was the overthrow of Makarios through a coup, and the means that he did not have at his disposal towards this end were money and arms. For this reason, the day after he wrote the letter to Kyros, he addressed Markezinis directly, and directly requested help in overthrowing Makarios:

"Dear Sir,

With the opportunity afforded by the arrival of our man [Kyros], I would like to stress the following:

I am chiefly asking for two things.

1. Sufficient economic support so as to respond to our great needs vis-à-vis the imprisoned fighters and their families.
2. Reinforcements of between 500 and 600 men.

The key to the Cyprus problem lies in the above two elements. If we secure them, we shall solve it by ourselves. Let no other solution be sought.

There is a way to eliminate him completely. A success rate of 80-90%. Is it agreed?

This will occur on the precondition that we shall have acquired the above, so that we prevail in this, absolutely.

The matter must be faced with realism and determination, and not patchily.

I shall personally take responsibility for the execution of my plan."[51]

Nevertheless, Markezinis, following Papadopoulos' line, still sought common ground with Makarios, whom he met in Athens on 6 November as the Archbishop was on his way to Malta. The two men had an initial exchange of views on how to lower tensions in Cyprus. Makarios promised to cooperate and, as a sign of good will, on his return to Cyprus, he ordered the release of some prisoners and gave instructions for the activities of the Reservists to be halted. This initiative, however, was destined to remain half-finished. In Athens, the regime entered a period of crisis, on account of the student uprising.

In November 1973, students in Greece began to mobilise for the democratisation of the universities. The first student gatherings took place on 14 November in the faculties of Law and Medicine of the Athens University, as well in the Polytechnic, where they were demanding that elections to student bodies be held in December, as had been arranged, and not in February 1974 as the Junta wanted.

Later that same day, students from all the faculties began to pour into the Polytechnic. This mobilisation developed into the most powerful and massive anti-Junta demonstration since the imposition of the dictatorship. With slogans such as "Bread – Education – Freedom", "Democracy", "Down with the Junta", the students demanded an end to the dictatorship. In three days, the students' demonstration took on the character of a general uprising against the regime. In the Polytechnic, which had been occupied by students, the first free

50 *Ibid.*, p. 319.
51 *Ibid.*, p. 323.

radio station began to broadcast, calling on the population to revolt. At three o'clock in the morning of 17 November, the tanks that were lined up outside the Polytechnic were ordered to move against the students. In the assault that followed, six students were killed, while in total 23 people lost their lives. The same day in Cyprus, Colonel Athanasios Liaskonis of the Seventh Bureau of the General Staff gave an order by telephone to Stathis Soulis of the Second Bureau of the Third Supreme Tactical Command to inform officers and soldiers in all units about the events at the Polytechnic:

1. Communism in Greece today is leading the students astray and is attempting to disturb the peace and serenity of the Greek people, and to impose a communist dictatorship on Greece.
2. In this, its anti-national attempt, it finds itself up against all nationalist-minded people, who form the Greek population as a whole.
3. The nationalist population is determined to face up decisively to these few organisers and instigators, so that Greece, which has been considered until today to be an oasis of calm and serenity, can continue on its progressive course in all domains of economic and cultural activity.
4. Faithful to its oath and to the revolution, the Greek army constitutes the guarantor of calm, prosperity and of the integrity of the homeland.

After Liaskonis had finished his briefing, Soulis asked him: "Is there a march on Athens yet?" And Liaskonis replied: "Not yet."[52]

Ultimately, the march anticipated by the officers loyal to Ioannides materialised on 25 November 1973, when Ioannides overthrew Papadopoulos in a military coup. The Grivas faction welcomed the change in Greece with enthusiasm. Cosmas Mastrokolias from now openly appeared as the link between the new regime and EOKA B, and had frequent contact with the Secretary of ESEA, Stelios Christides, to whom he gave instructions on the stance that EOKA B should adopt towards the new regime. Christides, briefing Spyros Papageorgiou by telephone, told him:

"Things will go great with the coup in Greece. The situation is in Cyprus' favour; it is clearly an anti-Makarios movement, dissatisfied for a very long time, and rightly or wrongly linked with the Cyprus problem."[53]

On the same day, Papageorgiou discussed the new situation in Greece with George Hadjinicolaou, editor of *Mesimvrini*:

"Hadjinicolaou: Just wait, the greatest thing for us is that Lalaounis has been posted to Army Headquarters.

Papageorgiou:Just *you* hold on. Ioannides from the ESA is at the head of the movement, and in fact has given the order that Moustakias [the man with the moustache – Grivas] be informed that everything is OK."[54]

Pantelis Lalaounis had in 1972 been the head of the Second Bureau of the General Staff, but had been recalled to Greece after the 14 February coup fiasco. In a conversation he had with Costas Bourlos at the Second Bureau, Lalaounis immediately linked the Ioannides coup with Cyprus.[55]

On 26 November, *Patris* gave a triumphant dimension to the overthrow of Papadopoulos, writing: "The healthy armed forces of the nation, in a bloodless revolution, yesterday overthrew Mr G. Papadopoulos and took into its powerful hands the fate of the nation, so as

52 Cyprus KYP report, *op. cit.*, p. 75.
53 *Ibid.*, p. 76.
54 *Ibid.*, p. 77.
55 *Ibid.*

to lead it on the course of its national destiny."[56] In its leading article, the paper wrote: "A development has occurred in Greece which, one way or the other, will prove historic. There has been a military coup that has overthrown Mr. G. Papadopoulos."[57]

Equally positive was the stance adopted by Grivas' undisputed mouthpiece, *Ethniki*, which described the change in Greece as, "a very promising development". It reminded everyone that it had been the only newspaper in the Greek world that had written, "right up on its first page in its biggest letters 'Papadopoulos Must Go'."[58]

Mastrokolias was taking note from Athens of the coverage given by the Cyprus press to the developments in Greece. In a conversation he had on 28 November with Stelios Christides, he expressed his satisfaction with the support from the pro-*Enosis* press: "*Ethniki* was very good. I am optimistic about the change because things are definitely developing in our favour. There must be no hanging back." Christides asked Mastrokolias if he had seen *Machi*, and the latter replied: "It is favourable, and I know why. *Machi* belongs to Sampson, and he has received instructions directly from Ioannides."[59]

Mastrokolias then laid down the following policy:

(a) Open and full support to Ioannides assures complete success for the aims of the organisation. One can expect everything from him. No unnecessary carelessness must occur, so that others do not take the initiative into their own hands.

(b) It is expected that telegrams expressing solidarity will be immediately sent by all member organisations and bodies to the Military Command of Ioannides.

(c) Ioannides must perceive no sign of relaxation, and you must convey down there to the authorities that we have not stopped for an instant following closely the situation here from the very first moment. The support of Ioannides for Grivas is clear and open. Evidence of this is the broadcasting by EIRT [The Greek National Broadcasting Corporation] of telegrams from ESEA, reservists, etc. Ultimately, it must be emphasised that there must be mass support in favour of Ioannides, heartfelt, and from all sides.[60]

Even if Grivas had pinned all his hopes for Makarios' overthrow in his personal relationship with Markezinis, he saw the fall of Papadopoulos with a favourable eye, considering the new Junta would be more decisive than the previous one: "We shall judge the change in Greece on the basis of the new government's handling of the Cyprus issue," he wrote in a note to ESEA, on the day of the Ioannides coup. "Although I believe that those entering government will be more bold and realistic than their predecessors, nevertheless, we should initially remain guarded until their intentions are made manifest."[61]

The seizure of power by the second Junta coincided with the lifting of the suspension of EOKA B action that Grivas had ordered to give Markezinis time to form a Cyprus policy. The day Ioannides toppled Papadopoulos in Athens, the Limassol EOKA B section leader Lefteris Papadopoulos organised the theft of a great quantity of dynamite from the Kalavassos mine. After the operation, he wrote his news to Spyros Papageorgiou:

"The section has recovered from the blows it received and has begun its warm-up. It carried out its first serious action tonight. A small force carried out an operation with mathematical precision, based on a prepared plan, in which it made off with about two tons

---

56 "Ανετράπη χθες ο Γ. Παπαδόπουλος" [Papadopoulos Overthrown yesterday], *Patris*, 26 November 1973.

57 "Με εμπιστοσύνην" [With Trust], *Patris*, 26 November 1973.

58 "Χαιρετίζομεν και αναμένομεν" [We Welcome and We Expect], *Ethniki*, 26 November 1973.

59 Cyprus KYP report, *op. cit.*, p. 77.

60 *Ibid.*, p. 78.

61 Papademetris, Panayiotis, Petrides, *op. cit.*, vol. 14, p. 325.

of dynamite."[62] Papadopoulos then referred to the fall of Markezinis, which he initially saw as a development favouring Makarios: "Mouskos will foam at the mouth and his smile of satisfaction at Markezinis' sidelining will freeze when he hears that two tons of dynamite have been seized."[63]

The theft of the dynamite from Kalavassos marked the onset of a new cycle of violence by EOKA B. A few days later, on 31 October, Grivas gave instructions to Lefteris Papadopoulos to form a hit squad at the soonest: "Mission: to reinforce guerrilla units against the enemy operating against them."[64] This platoon, according to Grivas' instructions, could be used for the formation of an urban squad.

Grivas, who intended to intensify his struggle against Makarios with attacks against government targets, was in contact with Ioannides. As Papageorgiou writes, "it is now certain that EOKA B began to make contact with the Ioannides regime from December 1973. This cooperation was handled exclusively by Grivas, who did not allow any of his associates in Cyprus to be informed as to what were the conditions of this cooperation, and its ultimate aims."[65]

When later the central archives of EOKA B were discovered in Nicosia, it emerged that Grivas had discussed an action plan with this staff, which envisaged "lightning executions of important government cadres, as well as of members of the security forces, especially indiscriminate strikes against the police, against supporters of President Makarios and the government, as well as some against public and private property".[66] An order was also found in the EOKA B archives that said: "Kill Makarios supporters wherever you find them."[67]

Grivas' plan was put into action on 10 December 1973. Two men dressed as policemen on the Parekklesia to Mazokambos road flagged down a car driven by Antonis Andronikou, carrying his 15-year-old daughter Eleni and his father-in-law Chrysanthos, and asked for his driving licence. Next, they asked him to leave the others behind and take them to Parekklesia. Andronikou was never seen alive again. Two days later, a shepherd found his body in a deserted place, riddled with bullets and almost unrecognisable.[68] Andronikou was murdered because EOKA B suspected him of having given information to police that had led to the arrest of a guerrilla unit in the Mazokambos area the preceding July.

Makarios condemned the crime and called Grivas a common murderer lacking a conscience and recognising no ethical bounds. "There are probably people who may believe that Grivas came to Cyprus to struggle for *Enosis*. Grivas is shown to be a common criminal and a bloodthirsty murderer, and he has caused many hardships to Cyprus through all his actions."[69]

Andronikou's murder happened at the worst time for EOKA B. The next day, the Committee for Internal and Legal Affairs had been due to submit to the House of Representatives a report blaming the government for the inadmissible use of violence by members of the security forces against prisoners, members and sympathisers of EOKA B. In the discussion that followed, the President of the House, Glafcos Clerides, announced that he had

---

62 *Ibid.*, p. 326.

63 *Ibid.*

64 Papageorgiou, *Μακάριος*, p. 225.

65 *Ibid.*

66 "Σχέδιον Δολοφονιών – Δολιοφθορών" [Assassination – Sabotage Plan]. *Phileleftheros*, 23 June 1974.

67 *Ibid.*

68 Papademetris, Panayiotis, Petrides, *op. cit.*, vol. 14, p. 327.

69 *Ibid.*

registered the following topic for debate: "The clear violation of human rights by groups belonging to General Grivas through the murder of Cypriot citizens."

Makarios' statements and Clerides' action infuriated Grivas. On 19 December, a leaflet circulated launching a bitter attack on Makarios. The many words written in capital letters reveal its emotional charge:

"When he who holds the HIGHEST OFFICE in the state is led astray into uttering vulgar insults heard only in bordellos and such against his adversary, who for 58 years has selflessly devoted himself to serving the nation, he is not merely a slanderer but unworthy of holding such office…

"We could call the Governor [Makarios], with evidence that brooks no contradiction: A PERJURER, the INSTIGATOR of the murders of national fighters; the DESTROYER of Cyprus (the one he took charge of, and the one he reduced to such a state), a RENOUNCER of national ideals and the creator of a personal regime; a squanderer of public funds and of the fortune of the monasteries, his aim being to corrupt the national conscience of the people; a PROMOTER of civil strife; a VIOLATOR of the Sacred Canons of the Church and RESPONSIBLE for the division existing within the Church of Cyprus - to confine ourselves merely to this."

In the same leaflet, Grivas also attacked Clerides, who he said had been "egged on by others". "A man renounced by his father and mother. The latter, when I came to Cyprus in 1964 paid me a visit, begging me to bring her son back on the correct path… is it not decadence for Cyprus to have such a leader?"[70]

Grivas accused Clerides of condemning the activities of EOKA B, which – in his words – had taken up a defensive posture, and of turning a blind eye to state violence against arrested *Enosis* supporters. Clerides replied to Grivas during the discussion of the subject in the House, condemning the violence committed by EOKA B together with violence by the state: "There is strong evidence that state officials have proceeded to violate human rights, without any measures being taken against them," he said. Clerides accused the government of "not lacking in responsibility for the unacceptable situation prevailing in Cyprus, the chief characteristics of which are the breach of law and infringement of human rights". He defended, however, the legitimacy of the government, which had given Grivas the option of elections, which he had refused to accept. "The government had the duty and obligation, within the framework of the law, to defend itself, not to give way to violence, and to strengthen the instruments of authority in order to impose law and order. However, in no instance had it tolerated the creation of armed paramilitary units, or the committing of crimes by the latter against other citizens, nor the refusal to attempt their arrest, punishment and disarming."[71]

Eventually, the House passed a motion in which it called on Grivas to renounce violence and dissolve his illegal units, and on the government to take the necessary measures to disarm pro-government paramilitaries. On the political level, it suggested the calling of a conference to be presided over by the Greek government, with the participation of all sides, to examine the policy to be followed on the national issue.[72]

On the day that the House called on Grivas to give up violence, an armed EOKA B unit was in action in Omodhos village, murdering Evriviades Charalambous. The next day,

---

70 *Ibid.*, pp. 328-330.

71 *Ibid.*, pp. 332-334.

72 *Ibid.*, p. 334.

EOKA B murdered Stelios Mavros from Platres, as he was returning home by car from neighbouring Phini village.

On 26 January, in a statement in *Phileftheros* newspaper, Clerides called on Grivas to take an open stand on the murders. "If he does not denounce the murders, in the very next sitting of the House I shall call on the House to condemn General Grivas as a common murderer."[73] Grivas reacted with fury, and in a handwritten note gave instructions to the Secretary of the ESEA Stelios Christides to criticise Clerides harshly.[74] Christides never managed to carry out the order. The next day, Grivas died in Limassol, in the house of Elli Christodoulidou.

73 *Ibid.*, p. 335.
74 Andreas Athanasiou, *Ο άγνωστος πόλεμος Αθηνών – Λευκωσίας* [The Unknown War between Athens and Nicosia] (Athens: Tzionis Publications, 1989), p. 258.

Grivas at the time when he was preparing his return to Cyprus;
behind him is a bust of himself that he kept at his home in Athens.

January 1972. Turkish Cypriots march through the Turkish quarter of Nicosia to protest against Enosis and in favour of partition. Grivas' plans completely ignored the Turkish threat.

Plate 10

Pupils clash with police during a pro-Grivas demonstration.
The National Guard command and the Greek intelligence services
used the pupils to mould public opinion in favour of Enosis.

While Greek officers helped EOKA B, their Turkish counterparts were arming
and training even the female population inside the enclaves.

Marios and Elli Christodoulidou sit on either side of Grivas. Grivas moved between his hideout in Diana Mavrou's house and the Christodoulides family home in Limassol.

Grivas, at the house of Elli Christodoulidou in Limassol where he was hiding, dictates to Diana Mavrou, who acted as his secretary.

Plate 12

Panayiotakos at the Presidential Palace for the presentation of his credentials.
On 11 February he visited Makarios and, on behalf of the Greek government, urged him to resign.

The three bishops and their advisors meet at the Bishopric of Kitium in Limassol.

In 1973, Denktash obtained Ankara's seal of approval and was elected vice-president of the Republic of Cyprus after the more moderate Fazil Kutchuk had been forced to withdraw from the running.

The Supreme Holy Synod, which dethroned the three bishops. Standing is the Bishop of Constantia (later Archbishop) Chrysostomos, who played a leading role in the procedure.

Plate 14

The aftermath of an EOKA B raid on a police station.

The Reservists make their presence felt on the roads of Cyprus immediately after their formation.

Stavros Stavrou-Syros is led out of a police van to court for a remand hearing.

Members of EOKA B arrested in Limassol in August 1973 were, for security reasons, transferred to Nicosia for their trials.

Plate 16

A Greek flag with an Enosis inscription hangs outside a shop belonging to a Grivas supporter in Nicosia. The shop was wrecked by a bomb placed by Makarios supporters.

The point of the explosion on the booby-trapped Nicosia to Famagusta road, where Makarios escaped yet another assassination attempt. Reaching out to help Makarios is Patroclos Stavrou.

Makarios addresses his supporters, immediately after the assassination attempt against him in the Famagusta district.

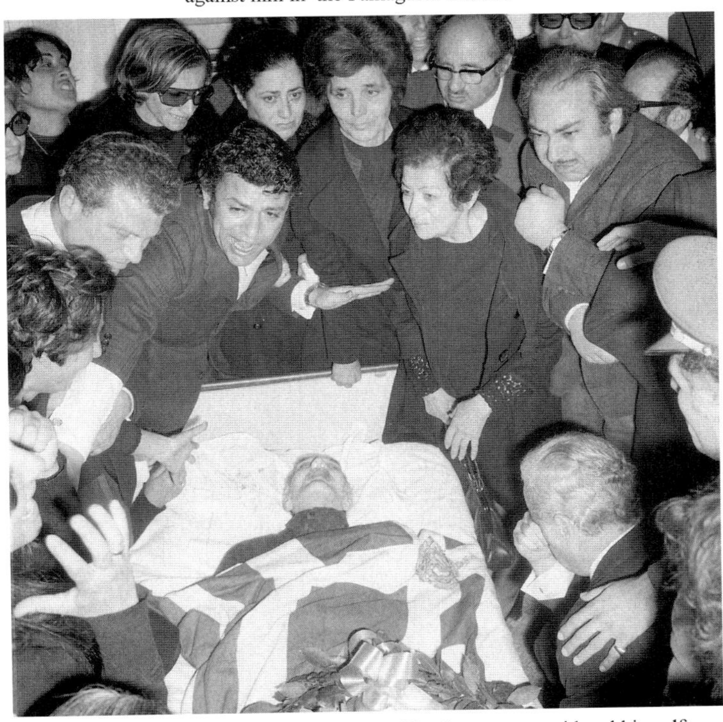

Nicos Sampson mourns over Grivas' coffin. Sampson considered himself to be Grivas' natural successor at the head of EOKA B because of his ties with Ioannides.

Plate 18

The leadership of the National Guard and the Greek ambassador Efstathios Lagakos attended the funeral of Georgios Grivas.

8. EOKA B after Grivas

From June 1973, information began to leak out that Grivas was suffering from a serious illness and that he had undergone surgery. When journalists questioned Makarios about this, he said that the government, if requested, would offer Grivas medical care. Grivas referred to the matter of his health in his statement to the people of Cyprus following the kidnapping of Justice Minister Christos Vakis. He called the press statements and the words of Makarios "a dance of cannibals, with him as the conductor of the orchestra", and the offer of medical care by Makarios "an artifice" and "an impertinence". He denied that he had any health problems: "I state that I am as much sound in body as, above all, I am in mind, unlike many other men younger in years, whose actions are irresponsible. To the sorrow of Mr President and his type of smelly cannibalism, I shall live enough years to see my dream, to which I have devoted so much, fulfilled. As for the President, may God be merciful."[1]

Despite the denials, the reality was that Grivas was suffering seriously from heart problems. The pathologist-cardiologist Doros Papapetrou, who was also his nephew, said in a written statement after Grivas' death, that he had first examined him in March 1972 and determined that he was suffering from a narrowing of the aorta. He kept him under observation and the state of his health was unchanged until the beginning of October 1973, when it worsened, and during most hours of the day he was confined to his bed. In the following months he visited him once a week, until January 1974 when the state of his health worsened even further. After radiological examination, the "diastasis of the left ventricle of the heart and the almost complete disappearance of its systole" was observed. From this moment onwards, according to Dr Papapetrou, events moved rapidly. "The last time I visited him was on the evening of 26 January 1974, the eve of his death. It was clear that the end was imminent."[2]

On the morning of Sunday, 27 January 1974, Grivas was moved from the house of Diana Mavrou to that of Elli Christodoulidou in Limassol. At about 1.30pm he was in a room writing, when Elli Christodoulidou interrupted him to tell him it was time to have lunch. Her account is as follows:

"That day he asked me for steak and boiled vegetables, which I made for him. In a few minutes I went to the kitchen to get the food ready, while the Leader went to the toilet. CyBC radio was broadcasting the news at that time and I heard that while some deputies in Greece were making a speech, the podium had collapsed and they fell. Hearing this, I called out to Dighenis, 'Leader, Leader, did you hear what happened in Greece?' 'What happened?' he replied, whereupon I repeated the news item to him, at the same time hearing the toilet flush and immediately afterwards the sound of the door knob of the toilet door. But that was accompanied by the noise of someone falling, whereupon I ran, opened the toilet door and saw the Leader lying on the ground."

Her daughter called doctor Gaston Schizas, who soon arrived at her home. "On hearing that Dighenis had fainted, Schizas hurriedly went into the house, at the time I was trying to give Dighenis the kiss of life. The doctor took the hand of Dighenis to feel his pulse, while at the same time opening one eye with a finger, and told me 'he died and fell, and even if I had been here I could not have saved him'. I asked the doctor as he was leaving not to say anything until I could inform the Leader's associates. This I did immediately and in a few minutes Andreas Angelopoulos, Lefteris Papadopoulos and Panicos [Soteriou] arrived. The

---

1 Papademetris, Panayiotis, Petrides, *op. cit.*, vol. 14, p. 300.

2 *Ibid.*, p. 338.

decision was made not to announce anything until we could work out what to do. Thus, we hid the dead Leader in a part of the house, as if nothing had happened."[3]

When Grivas died, Makarios was at the Presidential Palace in Nicosia talking with his associate, Dionysis Malas. It was about 2.30 in the afternoon when his personal telephone rang. At the other end of the line was Dr Schizas, who informed him of Grivas' death. He told him he had personally seen and touched the dead body of the leader of EOKA B. Makarios telephoned the Greek embassy and informed ambassador Lagakos.[4] The information was passed around by word of mouth and in Limassol the close associates of Grivas began to gather.

The newspapers announced Grivas' death the next morning. In Limassol, thousands of his supporters gathered around Elli Christodoulidou's house. Grivas' body was displayed for the public to pay their respects and people from across Cyprus passed by his hideout to say their last farewell. In a gesture of goodwill, Makarios declared three days of national mourning and announced a general amnesty. The prisons opened and the wanted guerrillas of EOKA B came down from the hills and proceeded to the place where the body of their leader lay.

In the meanwhile, behind the scenes, negotiations over the funeral arrangements began. ESEA issued an announcement stating that Grivas' desire was to be buried in Greece and thanked the Greek embassy for the "understanding and assistance shown as to the carrying out of this last wish".[5] Ioannides' wish, however, was that Grivas be buried in Cyprus, and he sent Mastrokolias to the island to arrange it. The next day Mastrokolias sent a message to Ioannides through Andreas Potamianos, informing him that all "had gone according to his wish and would take place as per instructions. The funeral will take place in Cyprus, everyone from ELDYK will be present, and Gennadios will preside". Speaking to Mastrokolias, Potamianos complained about ESEA's announcement that Grivas' remains would be taken for burial in Greece: "They shouldn't think over there that just anyone can issue announcements and say what they like."[6]

Despite all this, ESEA insisted the burial should take place in Athens. Ioannides, however, gave instructions to Papadakis "for action to be taken so that Grivas be buried in Cyprus and not in Athens".[7] Eventually, ESEA accepted that the funeral should take place in Cyprus, presided over by dethroned Bishop Gennadios. Due to Makarios' refusal to provide a church to a dethroned bishop, it was decided the funeral would take place in an open area, outside the house of Elli Christodoulidou. Potamianos suggested to Athens that a Minister be sent to make a formal attendance. Ultimately, the Greek government was represented by ambassador Lagakos, and the Greek Army by Othonas Kyriakopoulos. Present also were many Greek officers serving in Cyprus, while, following guidelines from Athens, the leader of National Guard General Denisis, the commander of Greek Contingent colonel Kondilis and the ambassador of Greece in Nicosia Lagakos laid wreaths.

As soon as Grivas' death became known, the battle to succeed him began. Among the pretenders was Nicos Sampson, who, drawing on his acquaintance with Ioannides, hoped to be anointed leader of the Grivas faction. Sampson had never had any connection with EOKA B as an organisation. His links were with the Second Bureau and with Greek KYP,

---

3 "Πώς πέθανε ο Γεώργιος Γρίβας Διγενής" [How George Grivas Dighenis Died], *Simerini*, 26 January 1997.

4 Dionysis Malas, interview with the author.

5 Cyprus KYP report, *op. cit.*, p. 80.

6 *Ibid.*, p. 81.

7 *Ibid.*, p. 82.

while he also maintained a channel of communication with Makarios. Sampson moved within both factions, that of Makarios and Grivas, as he depended financially on both of them. He had received large loans from Kykkos Monastery and from the Junta-controlled National Bank of Greece in order to found the newspaper *Machi*, which he could not pay off. In fact, towards the end of 1972, the National Bank of Greece set procedures in motion to force a sale of his property. It was then that Sampson turned to Nicos Dontas of the Second Bureau for help:

"Sampson: The day before yesterday I was going to come and see you, but I had some work and couldn't. I received a letter from the Bank, and I wanted to show it to you. From the National Bank.

Dontas: Call by here, but not today. What do you want from me now?

Sampson: I got a letter from the National Bank, about a loan I got a long time ago for the printing press for £25,000, and with interest it has now become £44,135 and they are telling me that if I don't pay up within 15 days they are going to close the account etc., close the place down and go to court. They're nuts, my friend.

Dontas: They're all pro-Greek over there. You can pay that off little by little.

Sampson: Now I'm going to put some money in, because for many years, as you know, things weren't going well. From today it's 9% on the £44,000 etc, etc. (...)

Dontas: All these guys do is to put their foot in it. They put people off instead of attracting them. Get hold of Douzinas. He's got connections. Don't say I told you. You tell him that I know them. Tell him that if I get hold of a machine gun and get going, I'll fire like a madman.

Sampson: They're idiots. At this moment in time, who would come and bother you?

Dontas: That is, if these guys had any national feelings about such things. They only look at their finances. They don't look at motives, nothing. Anyway, go round and call on Douzinas."[8]

Sampson's move must have brought results, since the National Bank of Greece did not go to court. However, *Machi* began to lean heavily in the Junta's favour.

In late 1973, Sampson came out openly in favour of EOKA B. In the discussions that took place in the House in January 1974 concerning the activity of EOKA B, Sampson harshly criticised the government and accused the police of mistreating prisoners. When, therefore, Grivas died a few days later, Sampson considered himself the natural leader of the pro-*Enosis* faction. On 30 January, he invited the leadership of ESEA to a conference at the offices of *Machi*. In that meeting, as Stelios Christides reports, Sampson banged his fist on the table, said that he had to be the leader of the *Enosis* faction, since Ioannides trusted him, and demanded to be the principal speaker at the funeral. According to Christides, there were reactions from within ESEA. Ultimately, it was decided that its president, Georgios Vasiliades, would be the speaker.[9] Nevertheless, at the funeral, Sampson impulsively took the microphone and uttered his own speech, proclaiming the continuation of the struggle for *Enosis*:

"Dighenis did not die! Dighenis lives, and will always live, in our souls. Our Dighenis guides us on the road of duty and honour. We, his children, who lived and fought at his side, swear a sacred oath that we shall continue his struggle." According to *Machi*, when Sampson finished his speech, "he made the victory sign towards the crowds that were

---

8 Telephone conversation between Dontas and Sampson, recorded by Cyprus KYP.

9 Stelios Christides, interview with the author, Athens.

brimming with enthusiasm, and called on the people to shout long live Dighenis and *Enosis*".[10] Subsequently, he bent down and placed beside the body a copy of the newspaper. "Thus, the Great Field Marshal got to know in writing of his posthumous triumph."[11]

Sampson, in the guise of being Grivas' successor, published statements by Elli Christodoulidou in his newspaper, according to which the leader of EOKA B had a special esteem for him, on account of the position he had adopted during the discussion that had taken place in the House: "I so much want, dear Elli," the legendary Dighenis had apparently said, "to meet him, embrace him, kiss him and hold him tightly in my arms." Then Dighenis said, "Today I have read *Machi*. Again Nicos has made me very happy."[12]

Not being an official member of EOKA B, Sampson could not ultimately become the leader of the organisation. However, he continued to appear as the political leader of the pro-*Enosis* faction, and would tour the countryside making speeches to nationalist organisations. He was particularly active in his electoral district in Famagusta. Antonis Karras and Christos Solomis accompanied him in his sorties.

Within the EOKA B leadership, Colonel Georgios Carousos was seen as Grivas' natural successor. On Monday 28 January, with Grivas still not buried, Carousos called journalist Spyros Papageorgiou to his hideout in Nicosia to discuss the future of EOKA B. According to Papageorgiou, Carousos was interested in learning from him "what the feeling was among the public… what were those of the fighters, what the probable reactions of Athens would be, what was best for EOKA and for the *Enosis* struggle".[13]

As Papageorgiou writes, Carousos had taken the decision to break off the armed struggle so as to take advantage of the amnesty offered by Makarios. He had a proclamation ready, which he sent to ESEA for them to circulate. The next day, ESEA published an announcement signed by the "Commander of EOKA B", which stated:

"EOKA B has ordered the cessation of its action, with a view to providing time for the tranquility essential for a responsible, positive and patriotic handling of the national issue. This presupposes that this will meet with a broad response from the security services, but also from those who guide the paramilitaries, for the good of our people.

"Any action against some our people who happen to be imprisoned, wanted or free agents, as well as any loss of *Enosis* supporters' property, will provoke serious reaction from the organisation, since the responsibility will lie at the door of careless people or those who wrongly suppose that the dead leader left behind rudderless orphans. The present announcement does not mean imposing conditions, but is an offer prompted by duty to the whole, in the certainty that it will be appreciated. Let men of all persuasions and tendencies give examples of their patriotism and discretion."[14]

However, the most important part of Carousos' announcement was censored, that which referred to the organisation's willingness to cease armed action and for EOKA B guerrillas to give themselves up under certain conditions. It said the organisation would not surrender its weapons, but would keep them in storage, so that they could be used in the future when it would make its appearance "under a common national leadership aspiring solely to *Eno-*

---

10 "Σαμψών: Θα συνεχίσωμεν τον αγώνα του Διγενή" [Sampson: we shall continue the Struggle of Dighenis], *Machi*, 31 January 1974.

11 "Η *Μάχη* συνώδευσε τον Εθνάρχην" [*Machi* Accompanied the Leader of the Nation], *Machi*, 31 January 1974.

12 "Πόσην χαρά μου έδωσεν ο Ν. Σαμψών" [Nicos Sampson Made me so Happy], *Machi*, 30 January 1974.

13 Kardianos, *op. cit.*, p. 18.

14 *Ibid.*, p. 20.

sis, or when those in government might repeat what in our opinion has been to this day their harsh tactics".

Also censored was the extract stating that the guerrillas would appear without their weapons and warning the authorities "not to create for them significant problems because this would be a diversion".[15]

The censorship of Carousos' announcement was a clear indication of the dissent within the ranks of EOKA B as to the future of the organisation. On the one hand, there were the moderates that Carousos represented and who sought the politicisation of the *Enosis* struggle. On the other, were the hard-liners, the Ioannides supporters urging the continuation of armed action. The hard line was expressed by Famagusta section leader Kikis Constantinou and Limassol section leader Lefteris Papadopoulos, who were jostling for the leadership.

The day after Grivas died, Kikis Constantinou called a meeting at the house of Antonis Petevis, in the Famagusta area, which was attended by his associates Stavros Zakos, Panicos Pamboris, Dimitrakis Avgoustis and Antonis Genakritis. At that meeting they discussed the subject of the amnesty announced by Makarios. "Kikis Constantinou maintained that this should be ignored, and, to show how determined he was in his views, he threw down a revolver saying he would continue the struggle alone if necessary, and would execute anyone who stood in his way."[16]

The other pretender to the succession, Lefteris Papadopoulos, also made his intentions clear just hours after Grivas' death. In an order that he circulated on 28 January, in his capacity of Limassol section leader, he stated: "Fighters of EOKA! Let us do our duty! Our great Leader, laden with glory and fame, has fallen on the ramparts of our National obligations, a faithful warrior of our Great Homeland, bequeathing to us his sacred and unbreakable will: 'remain faithful unto death to the national aspiration to *Enosis*, always certain that victory will crown our struggle with success'. These were the last words of our declining leader, who has passed away in the certainty that none among us are heedless violators of His will.

"Fighters of EOKA! Severe and relentless observer of the laws of our homeland, as you recall, he bound us by a sacred oath to our much beloved and suffering country."[17]

On 2 February, Carousos issued a new proclamation, in which he extolled Dighenis' struggle, thanked the Greek government and the National Guard who had honoured him, and called on the members of EOKA B to continue the struggle for *Enosis*, without clarifying if this struggle would be armed or political. At the end of the proclamation, he addressed Makarios personally and commented on the amnesty that he had declared on condition the wanted men returned home and abandoned armed action: "These you call 'wanted' hold their heads high. Enemies of the Greeks, they are not; they are, however, fighters for *Enosis*. And if they are to return to their villages and towns, to their jobs and families, then it is with heads held high that they will return. We shall continue our fight for *Enosis*."[18]

Even if the proclamation was not entirely clear on the aims of the new commander of EOKA B, the government interpreted it as accepting the politicisation of the *Enosis* struggle. Makarios hastened to allow the new EOKA B leadership time. The Government Spokesman, commenting on Carousos' proclamation, announced that Makarios had given

---

15 *Ibid.*, p. 21.

16 Cyprus KYP, Antonis Genakritis report on the activities of EOKA B.

17 Kardianos, *op. cit.*, p. 21.

18 "Πολιτικοποιείται ο αγών της 'ΕΟΚΑ Β'" [The EOKA B Struggle Turns Political], *Phileleftheros*, 2 February 1974.

instructions that wanted men were not to be pursued "until the situation had been clarified".[19]

Carousos' ambivalent stance did not meet with the approval of the Ioannides-leaning hard-liners. Andreas Potamianos, commenting on the contents of Carousos' leaflet, told Socrates Eliades in a telephone conversation: "it's nauseating, and they should be careful as to what consequences may come of this rubbish". In reply, Eliades said: "the situation is UNDER CONTROL, don't worry about it."[20]

The future of EOKA B was discussed in a big meeting that took place in the penthouse of an apartment block in Nicosia, on Sunday 3 February 1974. George Karousos participated, as did the section leaders and members of ESEA. According to Papageorgiou, there was a heated discussion, and strong arguments were put forward both for and against continuing the struggle. The future of EOKA B, however, was not to be determined in Cyprus. Athens had already come to its decisions and what remained was for these to be imposed on the dissenters.

Lefteris Papadopoulos, who was already behaving like the new leader, was one of those who supported the continuation of the armed struggle at the February 3 meeting. And while the discussion had not finished and no decision had been taken, Papadopoulos, according to Papageorgiou, "left the rest to discuss policy and withdrew to draw up his own!" He shut himself in a room to write the leading article for the next day's edition of *Patris*, in which there would be a reference to the future of EOKA B.[21]

The policy outlined by Papadopoulos was crystal clear from the title of his article: "Come and get them!" And in the text that followed he dispelled any contrary impression there might be:

"No! EOKA does not surrender. It will not give up so much as a single bullet. Whoever wants any, we have them in the muzzles of our guns and let them come for them if they dare. NOT A SINGLE ONE of the wanted men will give himself up. Nobody should harbour the slightest illusion about this. Dighenis has defined our mission, and in this mission we must in no way be wanting, unless we are to be considered deserters and traitors. *Enosis* supporters! ... FREEDOM or DEATH, and *Enosis* with our Mother Greece."[22]

This was the policy of the Ioannides regime, which Cosmas Mastrokolias brought in writing from Athens a few days later. Mastrokolias came to Cyprus immediately after Grivas' death and attended his funeral. Subsequently, he returned to Athens for consultations regarding the future of EOKA B. He came back to Nicosia on 7 February to attend the first memorial service for Grivas, and stayed on the island until 6 March when the Cyprus government deported him. During this period, in collusion with Andreas Potamianos and Socrates Eliades, care was taken to arrange the matter of Grivas' succession, and to ensure that Ioannides maintained control of the organisation. Mastrokolias had brought with him from Athens a protocol of cooperation that defined the relations between EOKA B and the Ioannides regime, in which the positions it set out are summarised as follows:

(a) "The military rulers in Athens consider that EOKA must be preserved at all costs, and should not surrender its weapons; nor should its guerrillas return to legitimacy and a quiet life.
(b) The National Centre has taken on the maintenance and protection of the *Enosis* fighters
(c) A military man will be sent from Greece to take over the command.

---

19 "Δεν θα διωχθούν οι καταζητούμενοι" [Wanted Men Will not be Pursued], *Phileleftheros*, 3 February 1974.
20 Telephone conversation between Eliades and Potamianos, recorded by Cyprus KYP.
21 Kardianos, *op. cit.*, p. 23.
22 "Μολών Λαβέ" [Come and get them!], *Patris*, 14 February 1974.

(d) The Commander of EOKA, Georgios Carousos, should relinquish the leadership and immediately return to Greece."[23]

After Athens adopted this position, all reaction subsided. The organisation complied with the Junta's suggestions and on 11 February the section leaders "in an atmosphere of jubilation", signed the protocol "since, as it was believed, the National Centre had assumed its historic responsibilities in the struggle for the *Enosis* of Cyprus..."[24]

The way matters were developing, Carousos had no further part to play in EOKA B. Immediately after Grivas' death, the decision had been taken to remove him; he therefore had to leave Cyprus at the soonest, and the implementation of the decision was assigned to ship owner Andreas Potamianos, who arrived on the island on 30 January to attend Grivas' funeral. Accompanying him were Colonel Nasos Sklavenitis and Captain Vasilis Mouyios who would take Carousos away by sea.

While Potamianos, Sklavenitis and Mastrokolias left Cyprus after the funeral, Mouyios ended up at the El Greco hotel in Kyrenia, waiting for instructions. On 15 February, Mastrokolias – who had already returned to Cyprus – and Socrates Eliades visited Mouyios in Kyrenia and arranged with him for Carousos' departure. Mouyios undertook to take Carousos to Rhodes in a small schooner called *Iason II* that belonged to an Englishman, and which was rented for £500 and $150.[25]

Carousos accepted the arrangements and, in his message to EOKA B guerrillas, he stated: "This is my duty and I do it in complete awareness of my debt to the Homeland, to you and to our struggle. Accept the new Command with confidence and honour and in its wake proceed along the straight, clear road, the wide, Greek one."[26]

Mouyios left from Larnaca marina on board the *Jason II* at 5.30pm on 19 February. When it reached the open sea, it made a turn and approached a bay in the Xylophagou area, from where it took Carousos on board. Kikis Constantinou conducted the departing EOKA B Commander to the shore.[27]

Cyprus KYP was aware of Carousos' departure and had the information that colonel Ioannis Davos would be in the same boat, coming to Cyprus as the new leader of the organisation. They devised a plan to follow the *Jason II* from sea and air, with the aim of arresting the new leader. A small plane from the aeroclub, piloted by Andreas Kallias as pilot with Reservist lieutenant Takis Tsangaris on board, would follow from the coaster that was carrying Carousos. Its destination was Rhodes, but because of a stormy sea it approached Castellorizo. The Reservist's collaborator Andreas Leontiades reached Castellorizo via Turkey, and he followed Carousos' movements. As Leontiades reported, Carousos was received by the harbour master of Castellorizo, and did not act as if was a hunted man.[28]

As the crew of *Jason II* later declared in their statement to police, the Castellorizo port authorities provided Carousos with every facility. After making many phone calls, he left for Rhodes. On 23 February, "Potamianos informed Socrates Eliades about Carousos' arrival at his destination, and that it was expected he would visit Athens the following day".[29] On its return to Cyprus, the *Jason II* was stopped by the police coastguard and escorted to

---

23 Kardianos, *op. cit.*, p. 24.
24 *Ibid.*, p. 26.
25 Cyprus KYP, Mouyios' deposition to police.
26 Kardianos, *op. cit.*, p. 25.
27 *Ibid.*
28 Georgios Tombazos, testimony before the Committee on the 'Cyprus File' of the Cyprus House of Representatives.
29 Cyprus KYP report, *op. cit.*, p. 89.

Paphos port. The crew were arrested and in their statements to the police, confessed everything.

The removal of Georgios Carousos left Lefteris Papadopoulos and Kikis Constantinou to wrangle between themselves over the leadership of EOKA B.

The former was supported by Cosmas Mastrokolias, and the latter by Andreas Potamianos. Constantinou wanted to show his determination to claim the EOKA B leadership through the theft of weapons - with the help of National Guard officers - from the storage depot of the 201 Infantry Battalion. The theft was soon discovered and the Head of the General Staff, General Denisis, was informed, going to Famagusta on 5 February to investigate the incident.

On the same day, the Head of the First Supreme Tactical Command, Colonel Tsortsakis, reported to the General Staff Headquarters: "Everything indicates that, from investigations to date and from information given by local military authorities, the stolen weaponry is in Famagusta and behind the operation is Kikis Constantinou".[30]

Once it was conformed that Constantinou had organised the theft, an initiative was undertaken "on behalf of the National Guard and Grivas elements towards Kikis Constantinou so the matter could be settled in some way to avoid commotion and the consequences likely to ensue from an eventual leak to the press".[31] Socratis Eliades informed the Chief of Staff Pavlos Papadakis on 6 February that he would take care of persuading Constantinou to return the stolen arms, putting an end to the matter without the finger being pointed at anyone.[32]

Colonel Tsortsakis had a meeting with Constantinou, and discussed the matter with him. Informing the General Staff about it on 8 February, he said that Constantinou, "for reasons of self-respect and honour, is adamant about not returning the weapons unless he is given weapons of the same quality from other areas".[33] Papamichael, who was in charge of the storage depot, also met with Constantinou to try and persuade him to return the guns, invoking the consequences that he himself would suffer as the one responsible for their safe keeping. Papamichael informed Costas Bourlos at the Second Bureau about this meeting on 9 February: "According to Kikis, the stolen arms are absolutely necessary to him and there is no need for worry and so much anguish about such trivial matters."[34] Papamichael told him that if he did not surrender the arms, the result would be the breaking off of relations with the National Guard. Reacting, Constantinou "stated categorically that he was fully aware of the consequences and he was ready to hand them over only if he was given others from other sources within the National Guard".[35]

Constantinou's action caused a split within EOKA B. His close associate Stavros Zakos, who had no idea of Constantinou's plans, was furious with him. As was Lefteris Papadopoulos, who saw his action as an opportunity to eliminate him as a candidate for the leadership of the organisation. Zakos discussed the matter of the arms with the Head of the First Supreme Tactical Command Tsortsakis on 12 February. He told him he had made enormous efforts to have them returned, and that he had met with Socratis Eliades and other

---

[30] *Ibid.*, p. 91.
[31] *Ibid.*, p. 93.
[32] *Ibid.*
[33] *Ibid.*
[34] *Ibid.*
[35] *Ibid.*

Nicosia members, but that nothing had come out of it because of the negative stance adopted by Kikis Constantinou, whom he called "paranoid".[36]

Tsortsakis told General Denisis on 13 February that "Kikis Constantinou had dug his heels in and in fact tonight at ten o'clock he is leaving and going to another district, where he will be for six to seven days". Tsortsakis told Denisis that he was expecting a meeting with Socratis Eliades, and that a similar one with other people "had ended in failure, with squabbling and bitter discussion".[37]

Eliades and Mastrokolias hurried to Famagusta to make one last attempt to persuade Kikis Constantinou. On 14 February, Eliades informed Zakos about his visit to the area and told him, "initially Kikis Constantinou appeared to be persuaded to hand over the weapons, and in fact gave undertakings to arrange the matter". A little later, however, Tsortsakis informed Costas Bourlos of the Second Bureau that Constantinou had conveyed to him "that the arms would not be surrendered because he had received instructions from Athens". Tsortsakis told Bourlos to inform the Commander of the National Guard accordingly, "with the conclusion that there is collusion coming from high up".[38] Actually, at that stage, Kikis Constantinou had been appointed by Athens as the new leader of EOKA B.

On 14 February, Socratis Eliades discussed in a telephone conversation with Potamianos in Athens the subject of the leadership of the organisation. The candidates were Colonel Nasos Sklavenitis, adjutant to Grivas when he was Military Commander of Cyprus in 1964 , Kikis Constantinou and Lefteris Papadopoulos. Sklavenitis' dispatch to Cyprus was finally vetoed, and it was decided the appointment of Commander, and not Leader, would be between Constantinou and Papadopoulos. Potamianos, who was in favour of Constantinou, sounded out Cosmas Mastrokolias, who was still in Cyprus and was pushing Lefteris Papadopoulos for the leadership:

"Potamianos:	I wrote to you about a plot of land in Famagusta, what do you think? Is it a good deal? [He is referring to Kikis Constantinou]
Mastrokolias:	The information is that it is OK, it's advantageous.
Potamianos:	Do you think we should buy it?
Mastrokolias:	Why not, let's see about it.
Potamianos:	I also called Yiannis [Sklavenitis], and the plot of his brother [Nasos Sklavenitis] is a bit problematic, so I was saying it might be better if we went for the Famagusta plot.
Mastrokolias:	hat can I say? It's good, let's have a look at that too these days. But since one is excluded, what do you want me to say? Better we talk it over when you come down for the memorial service."[39]

Because the rivalry between Constantinou and Papadopoulos was intense, Athens eventually arrived at the following solution: Nasos Sklavenitis, who was based in Greece, was designated as the new leader of EOKA B, and in Cyprus a local administration was set up with Kikis Constantinou as military commander, and Lefteris Papadopoulos as political leader.

Spyros Papageorgiou writes that the leadership was entrusted to Kikis Constantinou on 2 March 1974, in a meeting he had with a Greek army major in a house opposite the Melkonian Armenian school in Nicosia.

---

36 *Ibid.*, p. 94.
37 *Ibid.*, p. 95.
38 *Ibid.*
39 *Ibid.*, p. 89.

According to Papageorgiou, the following exchange took place between them:

"Major: I am instructed to entrust you with the leadership of the organisation.

Constantinou: OK, but won't a superior officer come from Greece to take command, as was agreed?

Major: I don't know when he's coming. He may come on the eve of the day when something is going to happen.

Constantinou: Also, the problem concerning arms is huge. We have 5,000 members and have only 1,000 weapons.

Major: That will be taken care of, too. Together with Lefteris [Papadopoulos] prepare a detailed report tomorrow on all the needs of the organisation. I shall deliver it to Athens."[40]

According to Petros Petrides, the Major who talked to Constantinou was Nasos Sklavenitis.[41]

On 8 March 1974, the two local leaders settled into the same hideout, and set up a joint general staff. But relations between the two were never harmonious. Each undertook initiatives behind the other's back, with Lefteris Papadopoulos gaining control of the organisation through the favour he enjoyed with Cosmas Mastrokolias. The impossibility of the two co-existing forced Constantinou to withdraw from the General Staff they had established, and Papadopoulos considered himself de facto to be the sole leader of EOKA B.

The infighting permeated the lower levels of EOKA B, and breakaway tendencies began to appear. Petrides says the two leaders met on 20 April to resolve their differences, but the discussion developed into a Homeric tussle. After that, Constantinou turned to Athens. On 23 April, through a personal envoy, he sent a report to Mastrokolias in which he accused his fellow leader of rash and harmful actions. He stated that he was in a position to restore discipline in the organisation, but asked for clarifications as to his position, and to what extent he continued to enjoy the trust of Athens.

The envoy returned to Nicosia with a message, in which Athens asked him to be patient for a few days until Sklavenitis returned from Kozani where he was posted, and took charge of the 'K Desk', the department of the Army Headquarters in Athens that was responsible for Cyprus. Sklavenitis would take over as leader of EOKA B, and would direct its activities from Greece.[42]

On 24 April, masked EOKA B men raided Pano Anglisides village, entering a café and beating up some of its patrons, entering houses, ill-treating Makarios supporters in front of their children. Among those beaten up was the village priest, who was hit with chains that the masked intruders left at the scene of the crime. Before leaving the village, they gathered in the village square and fired shots in the air. The next day, the police collected about 1,000 cartridge cases.[43]

In reaction to this move, the government declared EOKA B to be an illegal organisation. Until then, all prosecutions of EOKA B members had been carried out based on clauses of the penal code. Once the organisation was outlawed, any relations with the organisation, such as those of sympathetic newspapers or political organisations, such as ESEA, were deemed criminal in themselves. The press, however, declared from the outset its refusal to

40 Kardianos, *op. cit.*, p. 26.

41 Papademetris, Panayiotis, Petrides, *op. cit.*, vol. 14, p. 355.

42 *Ibid.*

43 "Νυχτερινή επιδρομή παρανόμων εις Π. Αγγλισίδες" [Night Raid by Banned Group in Pano Anglisides], *Philelftheros*, 23 April 1974.

comply. The newspaper *Ethniki*, the prominent EOKA B mouthpiece, hit the newsstands the following day under the headline: "Long Live EOKA B!"[44]

The government had set a 48-hour deadline for all wanted men to return to their homes by midday Saturday, 27 April. Those who complied would suffer no consequences. Kikis Constantinou requested guidelines from Athens as to what the wanted men should do. The written reply that arrived through Mastrokolias stated: "The reply to M. must be a massive NO."[45] With this reply, the Ioannides Junta was sending the message that EOKA B still had a role to play. Thus, the two estranged joint leaders decided to put their differences aside for a while, and issued a joint order to the wanted men to ignore Makarios' proposal. Despite this, 16 of the 70 wanted men turned up. Among these was a large group from the Famagusta area, who opposed Kikis Constantinou and had leanings towards Carousos.

Meanwhile in Athens, Nasos Sklavenitis (*nom de guerre* Navaronis) assumed his duties as leader of EOKA B at the beginning of May. The joint leaders in Cyprus were informed by a special message, which mentioned that in the future they would receive instructions directly from Andreas Potamianos, whose code name was Aeneas. Mastrokolias' role had been restricted.

While significant changes were under way in Athens in the administrative structure of EOKA B, in Cyprus, the organisation continued to show centrifugal tendencies. Paphos section leader Georgios Raftis, who was after a leading role in EOKA B, ordered the theft of a large quantity of weapons from the National Guard's Conscript Training Centre (*Kentro Ekpaidevsis Neosillekton* – KEN) in Yeroskipou outside Paphos in an attempt to strengthen his position. The General Staff was informed about the theft, as well as about the involvement of EOKA B. On 11 May, the head of Greek KYP in Nicosia informed KYP headquarters in Athens, stating that "120 heavy guns from the training centre in Yeroskipou had vanished, and the manager of the weapons store, whose membership of EOKA B had been confirmed, had disappeared".[46]4

In the course of the investigations, the military authorities acquired a full picture of the circumstances surrounding the theft. They knew the names of the men who took the weapons, the registration numbers of the cars used in their transportation, as well as evidence concerning the soldiers who had helped in the operation, among whom were Major Karoubalis, acting on instructions from Raftis.

On 13 May, the Head of the Yeroskipoutraining centre, Katerinakis, informed Costas Bourlos, Head of the Second Bureau of the National Guard General Staff, about the theft. Referring to the course of the investigations, Bourlos told Katerinakis to take care "nothing important that came out of the investigations should come to the attention of the police". Major Karoubalis was asked for a written report, but Bourlos advised him to avoid referring to some of the evidence that he had revealed to him in the guise of information, so to as "limit the consequences to the minimum where he was concerned".[47]

As a result of police investigations, almost the whole of Raftis' unit was arrested. Lefteris Papadopoulos, who was in contact with Raftis, asked for a large part of the arms to be handed over to him. Raftis, however, wanted to keep the greatest part for himself. Papadopoulos insisted, and a quarrel broke out.[48] In the correspondence between them, a furious Papadopoulos called Raftis incompetent, irresponsible, even a government informer. Raftis (whose pseudonym was 'Galinos') admitted that the theft of the arms had

44 "Ζήτω η ΕΟΚΑ Β!" [Long Live Eoka B!], *Ethniki*, 26 April 1974.

45 Papademetris, Panayiotis, Petrides, *op. cit.*, vol. 14, p. 359.

46 *Ibid.*

47 *Ibid.*, p. 102.

48 Papademetris, Panayiotis, Petrides, *op. cit.*, vol. 14, p. 364.

(whose pseudonym was 'Galinos') admitted that the theft of the arms had been on his initiative, but denied that he was responsible for the turn of events and the arrests, stating that "police interrogators go in for sadistic torture" against prisoners to make them talk. "Here we are all responsible, because we didn't terrorise the interrogators." he said.[49]

The conflict between Papadopoulos and Raftis plumbed new depths, after a request by Raftis for the execution of members of the Tselepos family in Paphos, whom he termed traitors and considered to be the cause of the police beginning to discover the weapons that he had hidden in different spots: "They must be executed. They are pernicious cowards and spendthrifts," 'Galinos' wrote to Papadopoulos. 'Theseus' (another pseudonym of Papadopoulos') replied: "You are a bastard, incompetent and insane. You have ruined us with this affair and now have the cheek to slander your opponents. I am sorry, but the organisation is not run by carnivores that eat its very own flesh."

In reply, Raftis demanded a higher position in the Paphos organisation, as well as £500 in assistance for the families of those who had been arrested for the arms theft. Papadopoulos answered angrily: "Galinos, I do not wish to hear such demands from you again. Since all the men in your section have been arrested, why are you asking to remain in Paphos? As for the money you are demanding, the request is denied because they all confessed."

Raftis insisted on his demands for more money and a place on the General Staff of EOKA B, threatening that if this was not accepted, he would resign from the organisation. Papadopoulos replied: "I am afraid you are not handling your section's financial affairs successfully. You are getting the lion's share and leaving your fellow fighters deprived. You a man of shaky conscience and dubious patriotic feelings, you use the resignation bogey. I wonder as to your motives in offering to resign. Will you perhaps join the government, and fight against us; if not, what do you intend to do?"[50]

Lefteris Papadopoulos was chafing with impatience at the apparent stagnation in the implementation of the Junta's plans to overthrow Makarios. He felt Athens had abandoned Cyprus, and was fretting over their failure to send weapons, while he had bitter complaints against the regime because they were threatening to cut off funding over his refusal to recognise Kikis Constantinou as military commander of the organisation.

Thus, Papadopoulos decided to address Ioannides in writing and to lay before him all the matters that concerned him. He wrote on 14 May, only a few days after the theft of the weapons by Raftis:

"As you will see, I am addressing you today as a matter of extreme urgency, despite the fact that at this time you must be preoccupied with so many problems. Convinced, however, that the Cyprus national issue has a high place in your concerns and worries, I have summoned up the courage to address you, even if this is contrary to the hierarchy's regulations."

Papadopoulos reminded Ioannides of the instructions he had sent via Sklavenitis to Cyprus after Grivas' death, concerning the preservation of the organisation and the removal of Carousos, as well as the obligation he had undertaken to cover the needs of EOKA B in weapons and finances.

"Doubtless, you will accept that up to now the organisation has fulfilled in an exemplary fashion all those obligations that it had undertaken. Nobody could seriously maintain anything to the contrary."

---

49 "Από τα έγγραφα που κατέστρεψαν" [From the Documents they Destroyed], *Phileleftheros*, 11 July 1974.

50 "Αποκαλύψεις από αλληλογραφίαν μεταξύ Λ. Παπαδοπούλου - Γ. Ράφτη" [Revelations from Correspondence between L. Papadopoulos and G. Raftis], *Phileleftheros*, 20 June 1974.

Subsequently, he writes flattering words about Ioannides, as well as expressing his own bitterness at the lack of response concerning what had been promised:

"First, we have had no specific reply to the question of arms.

"Secondly, we have had no responsible and specific reply concerning the sending or not of someone to undertake command.

"Thirdly, we have not been indicated a direction to move towards concerning the Organisation's mission after the death of Dighenis. Perhaps it is because the plans and the course of action differ."

Further on, Papadopoulos refers to the joint military leader, who he more or less describes as incapable and unstable:

"Threats are being made through messages that any upright man would reject, all the more by freedom fighters that are suffering great misfortunes for Greece's sake, about the sending of money, the reason being that all the members do not obey the instruction – which is one that would wipe out the Organisation – to recognise a certain person from Cyprus [Kikis Constantinou] as Head of the Organisation.

"In fact, not only does the person in question not surpass in ability the other members, but also he has shown conduct that is such as to raise many doubts, both as to his mental condition as well as to his disposition to obey the instructions from the National Centre.

Furthermore Papadopoulos referred to the threat to cut off the financial support he received from Athens. "Is this given in the name of the *Enosis* struggle, or on behalf of specific individuals? If the latter, then let it be cut off. If, however, the former is true, I regret to observe that the way in which the offer is made, and the threat to withhold it, is not proper."

Papadopoulos went on to call Ioannides to face up to his "historic obligations", and to lend an attentive ear so that he might finally come to a decision concerning Cyprus' "complete national integration":

"I only point out, with much pain and with a bleeding heart, that we are the last fighting generation left in that great Greek island of Cyprus. If the goal is not achieved now, then Cyprus will be lost forever to the Nation. And probably we shall not survive the catastrophe. Nor should we, in any case! You, however, will live on and perhaps remember us. But then it will be too late!!

"Two things can arise as a result of this letter. First, you listen to us for the good of suffering Cyprus. Secondly, you ignore it. It is just that time is running out fast. And I fear that in our time another beloved Greek territory will be added to the list of those that have been lost."[51]

After receiving Papadopoulos' letter, Athens decided to let both of the joint leaders go, and to appoint a third person as Commander of EOKA B. This was Croesus Christodoulides, who was invited to Athens at the end of May 1974. Andreas Potamianos, who met him at the airport, took him to the Cyprus Desk at the Army Headquarters, where he met Nasos Sklavenitis.[52]

---

[51] Cyprus KYP, letter from Papadopoulos to Ioannides.

[52] Papademetris, Panayiotis, Petrides, *op. cit.*, vol. 14, p. 364.

9. The 15 July Coup

When Dimitrios Ioannides came to power in Greece, the breach in relations between Athens and Nicosia came as little surprise. According to the US Congress' Pike Report[1], after the Ioannides coup of 25 November, "the [State Department and CIA] commentators concluded that relations between Greece and Makarios were destined to deteriorate". They said that Ioannides' hatred of Makarios, "whom he considered to be pro-communist or worse, 'verged on the pathological'. More to the point, Makarios was thought to be the stumbling block in connection with Ioannides' hopes for *Enosis*. Observers concurred that a serious confrontation was only a matter of time."

According to Tom Boyatt, Head of the Cyprus Desk at the State Department, there was information from the end of 1973 that a coup was imminent. Boyatt recalled how he began to receive increasing evidence that the government of Greece, the Greek CIA, and the Greek military, "were backing the radical rejectionist front on Cyprus which wanted to overthrow Makarios and declare Cyprus part of Greece". Boyatt said he knew that a possible Greek coup in Cyprus would provoke a Turkish invasion in a scenario that would see two NATO armies, both American trained, fighting each other, illegally, with American supplied weapons. "That would damage our position in the eastern Mediterranean for a generation and provided – who knew at the time – what opportunities for the Soviets."[2]

Boyatt prepared a telegram with instructions to the American ambassador in Athens, Henry Tasca, requesting that he meet with Ioannides and make it clear to him that "the United States were opposed to any attempt to overthrow Makarios and install a pro-Junta government". As Boyatt states, he wrote the telegram in February 1974, but the moment he showed it to his superiors, they immediately rejected it because at that time nobody from the establishment wanted to upset Athens.[3]

Ioannides, who had taken the decision to overthrow Makarios, began to discuss his plans with the President and the Prime Minister of the regime, Phaedon Gizikis and Adamantios Androutsopoulos, as well as with the head of the Armed Forces, Grigorios Bonanos. The discussions took place at Androutsopoulos' residence, between February and March 1974. In the depositions made by the organisers of the coup to the Investigative Committee of the Greek Parliament on the Cyprus File, the dates differed as to when the final decision was taken. Bonanos puts the decision in February, while Gizikis mentions April.[4] What is certain is that by April, the decision to overthrow Makarios had already been taken. The first thought had been to stage the coup in May, during Makarios' absence in China, where he was due for an official visit.

According to the depositions of Gizikis and Bonanos, the decision was taken "at the insistent suggestion of Dimitrios Ioannides".[5] As the leading protagonists state, everyone except Ioannides expressed fears that the coup would provoke a military intervention by

---

1 The Pike Committee – which derived its name from its chairman, Otis Pike – was established in 1975 and investigated the activities of US intelligence services overseas, including in Cyprus. Pike Report, published in *The Village Voice*, 16 February 1976, special supplement, "The CIA Report the President Doesn't Want you to Read. Cyprus: Failure of Intelligence Policy".

2 Tom Boyatt, "Advocacy and Dissent within the System", presentation at FSI September 30, 1992, Association for Diplomatic Studies and Training (ADST), Oral History Collection.

3 Ibid.

4 Greek Parliament, *Πόρισμα της Εξεταστικής Επιτροπής για τον «Φάκελο της Κύπρου»* [Findings of the Investigative Committee on the 'Cyprus File'] (Athens: Eleftheri Skepsi, 1989), p. 70.

5 *Ibid.*, p. 71.

Turkey. However, their hesitations subsided when Ioannides assured them that he had "firm and continual promises and guarantees from all the parties involved and above all from the United States, that she [Turkey] would not intervene".[6]

Ioannides' plans came to the attention of Makarios, who gave instructions to Cyprus' ambassador in Washington, Nicos Dimitriou, to inform the State Department accordingly. Dimitriou requested a meeting with the then deputy Foreign Minister in charge of Middle East Affairs, Roger Davies, and the director of the Cyprus Desk at the State Department, Tom Boyatt. "I have reliable intelligence estimates," the usually calm ambassador told Davies "that a serious effort will be made to assassinate Archbishop Makarios before Greek Easter."[7] Dimitriou warned of the consequences of a Greco-Turkish war and asked the United States to take action. Davies told him that the Americans also had such information, but were not in a position to confirm anything. Tom Boyatt later told Dimitriou: "I am as worried as you are."[8]

After his meeting with Dimitriou, Boyatt prepared another telegram, milder than the one that had been rejected. This telegram fell into the hands of the assistant Secretary of State in charge of political affairs in the State Department, Joseph Sisco, in April 1974. According to Boyatt, as soon as Sisco got the memorandum in his hands, he replied: "Look, this is very difficult. Nobody in Washington wants to do anything like that, and they in the White House especially don't want to hear anything against the Greeks. Don't ask me why. I don't know why, but I do know that is how they feel."[9]

Boyatt was among those American diplomats that considered Makarios to be a stabilising element and should be supported. Ambassador Henry Tasca was dismissive. According to Laurence Stern, Tasca shared the view that prevailed in higher precincts of the department that Boyatt "was a mother hen who needlessly worried his colleagues in Washington and Athens with dire predictions of coups against Makarios".[10]

Tasca's stance stimulated Boyatt to prepare a draft telegram in which he analysed Ioannides' policy against Makarios. Laurence Stern revealed this text in his book *The Wrong Horse*. The views of Athens were appreciated, stated a draft of Boyatt's document. Yet, for a number of years, the Greek military had clung to the notion that "Makarios was a red priest and that Cyprus was a Mediterranean Cuba". The Greek military still expressed a strong emotional commitment to *Enosis*. Turkey was also regarded as the sworn, hereditary enemy. This position, the document continued, was fraught with danger and impelled the Junta toward actions that were dangerous to all parties to the dispute.

Boyatt pointed out that the Junta had a consistent record for years of supporting anti-Makarios and pro-*Enosis* elements on the island. There was no evidence, the draft insisted, that the Greek government was trying to control its troops in Cyprus. In fact, the evidence was just to the contrary: the government was encouraging anti-Makarios activity by its troops.

Boyatt went on to warn that if Cyprus became embroiled in war, it was not an internal affair but rather a full-scale international debacle that would bring two NATO allies to a

---

6 *Ibid.*

7 Stern, *op. cit.*, p. 120.

8 "Σταίητ Ντηπάρτμεντ, 'Φάκελος Κύπρου'" [State Department, the 'Cyprus File'], *I Kathimerini*, 5-6 June 1983.

9 Boyatt, presentation at FSI, *op. cit.*

10 Stern, *op. cit.*, p. 121.

serious military confrontation. Once again, Boyatt urged that Tasca make these points directly to the leaders of the Junta government.[11]

Meanwhile, in contrast to the Papadopoulos dictatorship, which had seen communication and understanding between Athens and Ankara over the Cyprus issue, relations between the two countries under Ioannides entered into a period of cold war. On 26 January 1974, Bulent Ecevit was elected Prime Minister of Turkey. The rise of Ecevit to power coincided with the hardening of Turkey's position over the Cyprus issue. While the intensified intercommunal talks between Clerides and Denktash had made significant progress to the point where an agreement was considered just a matter of time, Ecevit made speeches on 28 March, in which Turkey demanded a federal solution. These speeches caused furious reactions from the Greek Cypriot side and the talks were suspended for two months, from 9 April until 4 June 1974. In the same period, there was a further souring of relations between Greece and Turkey over the vast oil reserves believed to exist under the Aegean. In Greece and in Cyprus, the pro-Junta newspapers beat their war drums and, in an eventual military conflict, took it for granted that the Turks would be crushed. Ioannides believed that the oil gave him the power to settle his accounts with both Makarios and Turkey. This question was discussed on 7 March 1974 with his man in Nicosia, Pavlos Papadakis:

"Ioannides: I've read something in the newspapers, can't you keep quiet over there, for goodness sake?

Papadakis: Tomorrow I'll send you a signal so you can see, I hope, that we'll quieten down.

Ioannides: Look, at this time we have much worse problems elsewhere, as you can see. You'd better realise, Pavlos, that the oil is much more important than we thought. There's a lot of it, enough in any case to buy out Cyprus eight times over.

Papadakis: That's what I say, and thanks for telling me about it.

Ioannides: Tell Makarios we'll buy him a gold throne like the Queen of Sheba's (they both laugh), solid gold.

Papadakis: Of course, we're all with you on this.

Ioannides: Up to now we were a Cinderella state, now we'll be Americans, things are getting better, and for that reason we'd better all be patient. Just be aware that there will be better prospects for everyone. Whichever Turkish Cypriot gets away over there, we'll give him his weight in gold and make an Aga Khan out of him.

Papadakis: If he does leave… quite right."[12]

Turkey meanwhile had put herself on a war footing, ready for an invasion of Cyprus. As Lieutenant Alexandros Simeoforides, in charge of the Kyrenia Greek KYP echelon, testified to a Greek Parliamentary Investigating Committee, the Turkish 39th Division – which was not attached to NATO, and formed a part of the Turkish national army – had from the time of its formation been facing Cyprus. According to Simeoforides, from April to June 1974 warplanes suddenly began to fly with high-ranking officers as pilots, while usually lower-ranking pilots had flown them for training purposes. The division every summer used to carry out landing exercises from Mersin towards the Antioch area. "When the exercises of the 39th Division had been completed – 15th June I think it was – everyone from simple

---

11 *Ibid.*, p. 126.

12 Cyprus KYP report, *op. cit.*, p. 97.

soldier to general was denied leave (...). In July (....) not only the 39th Division, but also the whole army was put on alert."[13]

In the spring of 1974, the Junta had taken the final decision to overthrow Makarios, a crisis had developed in the Aegean over oil, Ecevit had torpedoed the talks and Turkey was making military preparations for an invasion of Cyprus. Ioannides was by now looking for a pretext to proceed with his plans. In March 1974, his man in Cyprus, the chief of Staff of the National Guard Pavlos Papadakis, provoked a clash with the Cyprus government over the selection procedure concerning candidate reserve officers (YEA in its Greek acronym), or cadets as they were called. According to a law regulating the National Guard, the leadership of the force made the selection of the reserve officers, but the final list had to be submitted for approval by the Council of Ministers. From 1964, when the National Guard had been established, until 1973, the approval of the list of candidates for reserve officers by the Council of Ministers had been a mere formality.

In March 1974, a committee chaired by Chief of Staff Papadakis drew up the list of the National Guard intake from the preceding January. When it was submitted to the Council of Ministers, 57 out of total of 160 candidates were rejected as supporters of EOKA B. The Commander of the National Guard, Georgios Denisis, tried to persuade Makarios to accept the list as it was. Makarios was adamant, and replied that it was not advisable "to promote to the rank of officer persons who were not law-abiding", invoking the participation of cadet officers in actions against the government and making particular reference to the arms thefts from National Guard camps that had been carried out with the assistance of cadets. In a letter to General Denisis, he said that cadet reserve officers, both within and without the Guard, systematically made anti-government propaganda, and were organisers and protagonists at anti-government demonstrations. "They often take the leading role in incidents of an anti-government character, and through all their actions they make the National Guard a breeding ground for anti-government elements that feeds the terrorist organisation EOKA B."[14]

The National Guard leadership turned to Athens for instructions as to how to handle the matter. The deputy commander of the Armed Forces, Othon Kyriakopoulos, who directed National Guard affairs on behalf of Ioannides, gave instructions by telephone to Denisis on 27 March 1974: "The same tactics and procedure should be followed as in 1973."[15] That is, the objections of the Council of Ministers were to be disregarded.

Makarios proposed an alternative solution: he gave the leadership of the National Guard a list of 800 names and suggested they choose whoever they wanted from among these. The National Guard refused to accept this arrangement, and arbitrarily proceeded to register all those cadets who had been selected in the Reservist Officers' Academy. Subsequently, it turned to the government and asked for funds to pay their wages. A letter from the General Staff to the Ministry of Defence and Internal Affairs justified the registration of the non-approved cadets in the Officers' Academy, stating there was no specifically negative evidence, and that "the General Staff has strong doubts as to the correctness of the lack of approval by the Council of Ministers".[16]

In reply, Makarios told General Denisis that the Council of Ministers had "no obligation whatsoever in this case to place before the National Guard General Staff any evidence at all

[13] Greek Parliament, *op. cit.*, p. 90.
[14] Papademetris, Panayiotis, Petrides, *op. cit.*, vol. 14, p. 367.
[15] Cyprus KYP report, *op. cit.*, p. 97.
[16] *Ibid.*, p. 98.

for its consideration as to how it forms its opinion. Nor has the General Staff any right in any way to doubt, never mind to disregard, the decisions of the government and to act contrary to the law." Makarios concluded his letter to Denisis by stating that for this and other reasons, which "have shaken its trust in the National Guard", the government was examining ways "to restore the situation to a healthy state".[17]

The conclusion of the letter, which was simultaneously distributed to the press as an announcement, made crystal clear Makarios' intention - using the issue of the candidate reserve officers as a pretext – of breaking the dependency of the National Guard on officers from Greece that supported EOKA B. The conflict was becoming extremely serious, and General Denisis visited Athens on 6 June to discuss the situation with the Greek government.

Spurred on by the crisis over the reserve officers, Greek Foreign Minister Spyridon Tetenes, in cooperation with Armed Forces Headquarters, prepared an announcement that was issued from the Athens News Agency and was attributed "to a reliable Athens source", saying that in the Greek capital it was recognised that certain National Guard officers - especially cadets – had taken part in demonstrations against the government of Cyprus, something which went contrary to existing military regulations. Further on, the statement mentioned that the suspects had suffered legal sanctions and that these incidents should not be generalised and that the Greek officers as a whole should not suffer the consequences. It concluded by urging that a solution to the differences be found through dialogue between the Cyprus government and the National Guard.[18] Subsequently, Tetenes sent a letter to the General Staff – which was also drawn up with the Armed Forces Headquarters – proposing that the matter of the cadets be discussed with Makarios until a mutually acceptable solution could be found.

This move from Athens caused confusion within the General Staff. The Head of the Second Bureau, Costas Bourlos, contacted Sklavenitis by telephone on 13 June, and, commenting on Tetenes' letter, said that General Denisis was completely in the dark and was waiting for instructions as to what was to be done. The following exchange took place between them:

"Bourlos: If Makarios sets out his views and demands, what do we do? Do we bargain?
Sklavenitis: I'm telling you from now, go along up to a point, when the guys finish the question, and we'll see afterwards.
Bourlos: It's a different matter, if the bargaining fails tomorrow.
Sklavenitis: I am sending a signal on the basis of what we said."

Because the intentions of the armed forces headquarters were unclear, Bourlos repeatedly asked Sklavenitis to clarify whether bargaining should take place with Makarios, but he got "no responsible reply, either from Sklavenitis or from the armed forces headquarters".

Bourlos insisted, and told Sklavenitis, "since, according to Lagakos, the contents of the Tetenes letter was drawn up with the Armed Forces HQ and bargaining had been set up, there have to be clear instructions".[19] Sklavenitis urged Bourlos to send a message directly to the Armed Forces HQ, with all information related to the Tetenes letter, together with his own views and proposals. Bourlos sent the message, but 48 hours passed without any response. Sklavenitis avoided giving instructions concerning the negotiations with Makarios,

17 Papademetris, Panayiotis, Petrides, *op. cit.*, vol. 14, p. 369.
18 *Ibid.*
19 Cyprus KYP report, *op. cit.*, p. 106.

and Bourlos returned to the subject on 15 June, informing him that Makarios "within the next two-three days will put an end to the cadets affair, and a ruling from headquarters is imperative".[20]

The next day, Bourlos called Sklavenitis again and told him: "Makarios insists on his initial views, namely, the exclusion of all the chosen cadets who do not abide by the laws of the state, within the next five days". Sklavenitis replied in the following ironic manner: "The poor, unfortunate fellow may change his mind."[21] Sklavenitis' words revealed the regime's intentions. The Armed Forces headquarters were not interested in dialogue. What Tetenes referred to in the announcement was probably a tactical manoeuvre on the regime's part, while, behind the scenes, the final arrangements had been set in motion for the overthrow of Makarios.

According to evidence gathered by Cyprus KYP through telephone tapping, the coup plan initially provided for the concentration of forces (active ones and reservists) in the five large towns, and mainly in Nicosia, where the greatest blow would be struck. Cooperation with EOKA B consisted "in the provocation of a series of incidents", working together with units of soldiers, in clashes with the security forces loyal to Makarios, and in the "assassination of government figures". These actions would aim at creating disorder on a wider scale and would facilitate the takeover of "nerves centres" such as the Cyprus Telecommunications Authority, the radio station and the Presidential Palace. The action would reach its climax during the first days of July, so as to prepare the ground for the "decisive blow" before 20 July 1974.[22]

Basing itself on this plan, EOKA B would initiate a final cycle of violence in Cyprus, with murders and attacks against government targets. The EOKA B operations would create internal disorder, increasing by stages and culminating in the coup. The existence of this plan is confirmed more or less by Spyros Papageorgiou, who writes that Ioannides entrusted the job of starting the fresh cycle of violence to Lefteris Papadopoulos, since Kikis Constantinou "had fallen into disgrace" and was hiding in villages of the Famagusta District, together with 18 guerrillas loyal to him, out of fear of being eliminated. As Papageorgiou writes: "executions had to begin instantly and, as far as possible, on the widest possible scale." Thus, "the laconic order" was issued from Athens in June 1974: "Go for the jugular! In case of resistance, you will not be alone!"[23] Lefteris Papadopoulos was in a state of anxiety and asked for the opinion of Papageorgiou, who states that his exhortation "was persistently dissuasive, emphasising that '*Enosis* fighters cannot become murderers". But even the recipient of the "frightful order" showed apprehension as to the consequences of the bloody operation, which "Cypriot fighters were being urged to carry out".[24]

Despite his initial hesitation, Papadopoulos appears finally to have complied with the order he received from Athens, since EOKA B in early June initiated a new cycle of violence, its main feature being executions. On 13 June, nine bomb blasts destroyed property belonging to Makarios supporters in Famagusta. On 16 June, Andreas Armeftis, a Makarios supporter and District Secretary of the Cyprus Agriculture Union, was murdered in Limassol. The next day a police patrol was ambushed on the Nicosia-Limassol road. There was resistance and one of the ambushers, Andreas Stokkos, was killed, while a policeman was

---

20 *Ibid.*, p. 107.
21 *Ibid.*
22 *Ibid.*, p. 116.
23 Kardianos, *op. cit.*, p. 28.
24 *Ibid.*

wounded. The same day, EOKA B murdered Andreas Ellinas in Limassol and wounded two other persons accompanying him. The violent incidents continued day after day. On 18 June in Engomi, Famagusta, Andreas Marangos was murdered. When Papadopoulos was arrested on 11 July 1974, police testified in court that papers found in his possession made him a suspect in the murders of Andreas Ellinas, Andreas Armeftis, Georgios Photiou and Antonis Andronikou. The first two had been murdered just days before his arrest.

In the same period, according to Papageorgiou, the following letter arrived from Athens to EOKA B: "A select team of 50 daring men are to be in an immediate state of readiness, equipped with the appropriate weapons, who will undertake a commando operation whose nature will become clear through a well-known person that will arrive by sea."[25]

This order is similar to that which Grivas had given Lefteris Papadopoulos in December 1973, so he could form a company for action inside built-up areas. Furthermore, the action started by EOKA B with the murder of Makarios supporters had many aspects in common with the December 1973-January 1974 period, when Ioannides had given the order to create internal chaos to facilitate his plan for a coup. Probably these plans were cancelled because of the sudden death of Grivas and were again set in motion in the middle of 1974.

Ioannides' plan for internal destabilisation was thwarted yet again through a chance incident. On 18 June, the day of Marangos' murder, police discovered the headquarters of EOKA B and a large part of the archives of Lefteris Papadopoulos. Papadopoulos had his headquarters in a flat in an apartment block near the Nicosia Ecclesiastical College. In the basement of the same apartment block, the daughter of Papastavros Papagathangelou, Maro, lived with her husband Christakis Panayides. Papagathangelou, a priest and one of the instigators of the ecclesiastical coup and prominent cadre of EOKA B, had initiated his children into the organisation. His son Lakis was one of the closest associates of Lefteris Papadopoulos. His other son Costas was Papadopoulos' messenger in his contacts with Sklavenitis in Athens. And his daughter Maro put the apartment at the disposal of the organisation, which used it as a communications link between Lefteris Papadopoulos and EOKA B.

On 18 June 1973, KYP intercepted a phone conversation between Maro Papastavrou and her father; on the basis of the information gathered, KYP told the Reservists that Maro's brother Costas, on his way from Athens, had visited a wanted person in the apartment block in which she was living.[26] On the afternoon of the same day, the Reservists burst into Maro Papastavrou's flat in the basement of the building, but found nothing significant.

However, Lefteris Papadopoulos, who was in the flat on the floor above, caught sight of the Reservists, took fright, set fire to his archives and fled the block. A woman who lived in the area saw him leave, armed, while noticing the smoke coming from the window of the flat. She alerted the police, who rushed to the area. They managed to put out the fire, preserving a large part of the archives.[27]

In those archives, the police found important and considerable evidence concerning the activities of EOKA B, its connection with the Junta, the plans for the overthrow of Makarios through a coup, the funding of the organisation, as well as Papadopoulos' correspondence with Ioannides. The government exploited this material and, allowing information to leak to the press, caused panic within the ranks of EOKA B. Commenting on the

---

25 Kardianos, *op. cit.*, p. 28.
26 Cyprus KYP report, *op. cit.*, p. 108.
27 Eftichios Salatas, interview with the author.

discovery of Papadopoulos' archives, Georgios Raftis wrote to Papageorgiou: "God always punishes arrogance. This has happened to 'Myron'. He abandoned his weapons in his hide-out and – his final, fatal mistake – all the archives of the organisation. Let's see the scale of the catastrophe that we are going to suffer."[28]

Lefteris Papadopoulos, in an attempt to maintain morale, sent a document to EOKA B sections, stating that whatever the pro-government newspapers were writing was the result of a "government forgery". Commenting, Raftis wrote to Papageorgiou: "He must have lost his mind! Part of the documents consisted of correspondence between the two of us. He is taking us for idiots."[29] Indeed, when Papadopoulos' message accusing the government of forgery was published in *Mesimvrini*, the police leaked to *Phileleftheros* copies of Papadopoulos' handwritten correspondence with Raftis.[30]

After the discovery of the EOKA B archives, many of the organisation's cadres began to believe the cause was lost and one by one withdrew. Some, such as Spyros Papageorgiou, Stelios Christides, Spyros Arotis and others, fled to Athens. The disintegration of the organisation forced the revision of those elements of the plans to overthrow Makarios that involved substantial input from EOKA B. The decision to stage a coup, however, was not cancelled. The National Guard and the Greek Military Contingent would carry it out, and EOKA B would come onto the scene after it had prevailed.

On 3 June, Ioannides approached his CIA link, deputy station head Ronald Eastes, and informed him that he would overthrow Makarios with the use of force. The CIA sent a report to Washington, which also notified the State Department, according to which Ioannides had stated that, "Greece is capable of removing Makarios and his main supporters right from the start, within 24 hours, with little or no bloodshed, without the assistance of EOKA B. The Turks will readily agree to the removal of Makarios, an old enemy. (…) Ioannides was praying for some unforeseen favour, 'manna from heaven'. Ioannides pointed out that if Makarios decided upon some form of extreme provocation to Greece in order to gain a tactical advantage, he (Ioannides) was not certain whether he should pull Greek forces out of Cyprus and leave Makarios to defend himself alone, or expel Makarios once and for all and take Greece into direct negotiations with Turkey over the future of Cyprus."[31]

This CIA report was included on 7 June 1974 in the top-secret briefing bulletin that circulated each morning in the White House, the *National Intelligence Daily*. On 20 June, Ioannides again told a link of his with the CIA that, "if Makarios continued with his provocations, the Greeks would have only two choices left: to write Cyprus off, with is substantial Greek population, or to eliminate the Archbishop from the equation".[32] Based on this new information from Athens, a new report was drawn up by the CIA, concerning Ioannides' intention to overthrow Makarios.

In the wake of these developments, the Head of the Cyprus Desk, Tom Boyatt, reintroduced his proposal to send a message directly to Ioannides that the United States was opposed to upsetting the status quo in Cyprus. According to the Pike Report, Secretary of State Henry Kissinger, responding to the danger signals sent by officials of the State Department, on 29 June approved a telegram addressed to the American ambassador in Ath-

28 Papageorgiou, *Μακάριος*, p. 233.
29 *Ibid.*
30 "Από τα έγγραφα που κατέστρεψαν" [From the Documents they Destroyed], *Phileleftheros*, 11 July 1974
31 Pike report, *op. cit.*
32 *Ibid.*

ens, Henry Tasca, giving him instructions "personally to convey to Ioannides the opposition of the United States to any adventure in Cyprus".[33]

The telegram, which was prepared by John Day of the Bureau for Greek Affairs, and was signed by Sisco, read as follows:

"We share the anxieties expressed by Athens and Nicosia concerning the seriousness of the relations between the Greek and Cyprus governments. From several reports, it is clear that Ioannides is seriously seeking a way to remove Makarios from power.

"In our view, an attempt to remove Makarios through force entails unacceptable risks of creating chaos, a possible cause of a Greco-Turkish confrontation, the involvement of the Soviets in the Cyprus situation, and complications in the course of US-USSR détente.

"We are aware that Ioannides suffers from a psychosis as regards Communism, both in Greece as well as in Cyprus, and his antipathy for Makarios verges on the pathological. Until recently, our impression has been that he preferred to gain time on the Cyprus issue until he stabilised his position on the internal front. Now, however, it appears that he considers Makarios is trying to take advantage of Greco-Turkish tensions and the difficulties of the Greek regime, so as to limit Greek influence on the island, and that this attempt is a personal provocation that he cannot ignore."

The telegram continued with instructions to ambassador Tasca personally to inform Ioannides that "the United States was opposed to any adventure in Cyprus".[34]

Tasca, who disagreed with the State Department's concerns, refused to comply, considering such an action would bring about the opposite results. According to Boyatt, Tasca reacted describing his instructions as "terrible". Tasca said that he could not do something like it, because the Greek government would be alienated and the U.S. would have no influence over it. "I reject these instructions. You'd better change them!" So, according to Boyatt he had to start all over again, "this time being up against not only the US ambassador to Athens, but also the establishment of the Defence Ministry and the CIA, which in the meanwhile had heard about my instructions".[35]

Boyatt sent a new message to Tasca and told him to proceed on the basis of the instructions that had been given to him initially. He recommended that Tasca find Ioannides and indicate to him that he should not proceed with a coup against Makarios. On 1 July, Tasca sent a telegram to the State Department, stating he continued to believe that the moment was not appropriate for direct contact with Ioannides. Instead of Ioannides, Tasca met Gizikis on 2 July and conveyed to him Washington's message that the crisis in Cyprus had to be dealt with through peaceful means. Boyatt noted that the American embassy in Athens had carried out his instructions faint-heartedly.[36]

According to the Pike Report, the embassy was not careful to stress to Ioannides the scale of American anxiety as to the probability of a coup attempt in Cyprus. This led to the view "that, either the US authorities were not paying attention to information about the developing crisis, or, simply, they allowed it to happen by not warning Ioannides against it, severely, directly and clearly".[37] When Tasca was called before the Pike Committee to give explanations about his behaviour, he said he did not consider Boyatt's reports to be ones of warning, because they did not contain the element "frequent warning" and were not based

---

33 *Ibid.*
34 *Ibid.*
35 Boyatt, presentation at FSI, *op. cit.*
36 *Ibid.*
37 Henry Tasca, interview with Jack Bush, U.S. intelligence agencies and activities: Committee proceedings. Select Committee on Intelligence, U.S. House of Representatives, part 4, p. 1534.

on any specific information.[38] The Pike Committee finally absolved Tasca of any responsibility, accepting his claim that he had no access to CIA messages. Nevertheless, another member of the Bureau for Southeastern Europe at the State Department, John Day, later stated it would have been impossible for Tasca not to have seen the CIA report that referred to Ioannides' intention to stage a coup: "It was of such importance that it must have passed through his hands." Commenting on Tasca's claims to ignorance, he said: "I cannot believe that Tasca could say what he said. Either he is not telling the truth or he has lost his memory."[39]

At the end of June, Makarios decided to settle accounts with Ioannides, taking the initiative himself. Making use of incontrovertible evidence of EOKA B's collusion with the Athens regime found in the Papadopoulos archive – among which was the letter from Papadopoulos to Ioannides – he would expose the Junta for its undermining interference in Cyprus. His aim was to purge the National Guard by using this crisis, expelling all the Greek officers serving in the force. Cypriot officers would fill the vacuum left by the departure of the Greek officers, while the period of compulsory service of the National Guardsmen would be reduced from 26 to 14 months. The Cyprus government was preparing the ground for a settling of scores with the Junta. The Government Spokesman stated on 24 June that the leadership of EOKA B was in Athens and in Cyprus there were a coordinator and local leaders. "Instructions from Athens are conveyed by the coordinator to the local leadership." Two days later he went a step further, stating that "those in Athens who lead EOKA B are members of the Revolutionary Military Regime".[40]

On 1 July 1974, the Council of Ministers decided to reduce the period of service in the National Guard. Already, Makarios had prepared a letter to the Greek President, Phaidon Gizikis, in which he formally requested the recall of the Greek officers serving in the National Guard. Makarios began his letter by stating that Grivas had come to Cyprus at the instigation of Athens, and that from the first day of his arrival on the island he had had contacts with Greek officers: "The National Guard, staffed and controlled by Greek officers, was from the beginning the main supply material – whether animate or inanimate – of 'EOKA B', the members and supporters of which assumed the honourable and self-styled title of the '*Enosis* faction'."

He continued that despite the fact that it was inconceivable to him that the Greek government should support civil strife, the support of EOKA B by Greek officers was an incontrovertible fact: "Within National Guard camps there is frequently outspoken propaganda by Greek officers in favour of 'EOKA B'. It is also a well known and indisputable fact that the Cyprus opposition press that supports the criminal activities of 'EOKA B' gets its funding from Athens, gets guidance and policy from those in charge of the 2nd Bureau of the General Staff and the Cyprus echelon of the Greek Central Information Agency."

Subsequently, he referred to the Greek government's suggestion that he ask for the recall of those officers involved in criminal activities, saying such actions would not cure the ill: "I am sad to say, Mr President, that the root of the evil is very deep and goes as far as Athens. It is from there that the tree of evil is nourished and maintained and spreads, and its bitter fruit is now being tasted by Cyprus Hellenism. And to be absolutely clear, I state that

---

38 *Ibid.*

39 "Σταίητ Ντηπάρτμεντ, 'Φάκελος Κύπρου'" [State Department, the 'Cyprus File'], *I Kathimerini*, 5-6 June 1983.

40 "Η Εθνική Φρουρά οριστικώς θα γίνη όργανον του Κράτους" [The National Guard will become a Full Organ of the State], *Phileleftheros*, 26 June 1974.

members of the military regime in Greece support and direct the activity of the terrorist organisation 'EOKA B'."

After mentioning the guidance, funding and control of EOKA B by Athens, he alluded to the correspondence that Lefteris Papadopoulos had had with Ioannides (without naming the latter) and attached a copy of the letter that was found in his archive. Next, Makarios expressed his antipathy for the military regime, especially in Greece, "the country that gave birth to democracy and nursed it in its bosom". Nevertheless, he mentioned that despite this, he remained constant to the principle of cooperation with the Greek government, which was, however, plotting against him: "Up to now, I have felt more than once, and on some occasions almost brushed against the invisible hand from Athens that was seeking my physical elimination. However, with the national interest in mind, I have remained silent."

Makarios then referred to the recent crisis in his relations with Athens and, after briefly describing the background of his differences with the National Guard over the question of the cadet officers, he said the Guard should be the instrument of the state and not be controlled from Athens: "The National Guard, in its present form and staffed as it is, has deflected from its aims and become a breeding ground of outlaws, a centre of conspiracies against the state and a source of nourishment for 'EOKA B'". After mentioning the transfer of stolen weapons from the Paphos reservists' training centre in National Guard vehicles, he wrote that for this aberration "full responsibility must be borne by Greek officers, some of whom are involved from head to toe in 'EOKA B' activities and are participants in it". Makarios directly charged Athens with the blame, stating: "The Greek government, through a simple nod, could put an end to this sad situation. The National Centre could order the cessation of violence and terrorism by 'EOKA B', since it is from Athens that the organisation derives its strength and means of existence, as is testified by written evidence and proof."

After listing all these charges, Makarios informed the Greek government of his decision to reshape the National Guard because the Cyprus people had lost confidence in it: "I have reduced the military service so as to lessen the numbers at the head of the National Guard and the scale of the evil. (...) And it will be requested that the National Guard officers from Greece be recalled. Their remaining in the National Guard under the present administration will be detrimental to the relations between Athens and Nicosia." Makarios told Gizikis he would be happy if he should wish to send to Cyprus about 100 officers as trainers and military advisors to help in the reorganisation and reshaping of the Cyprus armed forces. "I hope, in the meanwhile, that orders have been issued from Athens to 'EOKA B' to cease its activities, though unless it is definitively disbanded, it is not excluded that a new cycle of violence and murder will recur."

After expressing his sorrow at having said "many unpleasant things" so that he could describe "in a language of crude sincerity" the situation in Cyprus, Makarios concluded his letter by stating that he did not wish an interruption to his collaboration with the Greek government. "It is necessary, however, to bear in mind that I am not an appointed prefect or governor of the Greek government in Cyprus, but an elected leader of a large part of the Greek nation, and demand an appropriate treatment by the National Centre."[41]

In speeches he made on 5 July, after the delivery of the letter but before it was made public, Makarios said the decision of the Cyprus government to seek the recall of the officers was irrevocable, and that any refusal to implement it would lead to a crisis in relations between Athens and Nicosia, for which responsibility would lie on the shoulders of those

41 Makarios, letter to Gizkis.

breaking the law. "If the Greek government does not accept the decisions of the Cyprus government, this means it is fomenting rebellion by the National Guard against the government," he stated.[42]

It is clear, both from the contents of the letter, as well as from his statements that followed, that Makarios was provoking a crisis. He was even accused of being the cause of the coup through his "rash" action in sending and making public his letter to Gizikis. However, the decision to stage the coup of 15 July had been taken before the delivery of the letter. From the end of June, Ioannides had informed Bonanos of his decision to overthrow Makarios, and he asked him to call Pavlos Papadakis, Head of the 12th Division on the Evros River and former Chief of Staff of the National Guard, to Athens to take part in the planning of the coup. Ioannides himself called Brigadier Michalis Georgitsis, Head of the Third Supreme Tactical Command of the National Guard stationed in Nicosia, to Athens from Cyprus, as well as Colonel Constantinos Kombokis, Head of the National Guard Commando forces. He had chosen these two officers as leaders of the coup.[43]

At 7.30pm on 2 July, one day before the delivery of the letter, there was a secret meeting at Bonanos' office at Armed Forces Headquarters between Ioannides, Bonanos, Papadakis, Georgitsis and Kombokis. Bonanos briefed the three officers on the decision to oust Makarios through a military coup, which was to be carried out on 15 July 1974. Bonanos said the government and the military leadership had taken the decision. He appointed Brigadier Georgitsis as leader of the coup, and Colonel Constantinos Kombokis as his deputy. Papadakis, who was very familiar with the situation in Cyprus, would assist from Athens. Bonanos told Georgitsis and Kombokis that, for any communication they might wish to have with the Armed Forces headquarters, they were not permitted to use any means other than a messenger. Major Constantinos Kontosis was chosen for this role. After Bonanos' briefing, Georgitsis expressed certain concerns as to the possible consequences of the coup and especially his fears of Turkish military intervention. Bonanos and Ioannides, "interrupting Georgitsis, said there was no cause for worry because there are assurances that nobody will intervene since 'there was cover'. They did not define exactly who was providing the 'cover', but it appeared to be from America."[44]

Finally, it was agreed that another meeting should take place the following morning with the participation of staff officers to discuss details and draw up an action plan. The operation – as its organisers termed the coup – was planned in general terms in the meeting that occurred on 3 July at 10.30am, in the presence of Papadakis, Ioannides, Georgitsis, Kombokis as well as Ioannides' confidants, Lieutenant Colonel Michael Pilichos and Major Palaenis Charalambos. The details of the coup would be determined in Cyprus by Georgitsis and Kombokis, who would make an on-the-spot study of the situation. The appointed liaison officer, Major Constantinos Kontosis of the Second Bureau of the General Staff, would go to Athens to take the plans to Ioannides and Bonanos, and would bring back their final evaluation. Pilichos and Palaenis undertook to compose the "proclamation to the Cyprus people", which Kontosis would commit to memory, together with the names of those who would be offered ministries in the new Cyprus government.[45]

While in Nicosia and Athens preparations for the coup were entering their final phase, in Washington on 3 July a CIA report was circulating that stated that "a person, that was

---

[42] Papademetris, Panayiotis, Petrides, *op. cit.*, vol. 14, p. 372.
[43] Greek Parliament, *op. cit.*, p. 74.
[44] *Ibid.*, p. 74.
[45] Bitos, *op. cit.*, p. 185.

later characterised as an 'indeterminate source', supplied the information that despite Makarios' aggressiveness, Ioannides had changed his mind: in the end, the coup would not take place".[46]

Makarios, who was seriously concerned about a coup, secretly sent George Tombazos, the head of Cyprus KYP, to Czechoslovakia to buy guns. On 4 July, a cargo of 1,000 automatic weapons and some machine guns arrived in Cyprus by air for the arming of yet another battalion of the Reservist Corps.[47] On 5 July, the Nicosia newspaper *Apogevmatini*, which usually published information issuing from the Presidential Palace, forecast with almost absolute accuracy the coup plan of 15 July. The newspaper reported that the coup plan, which was a variation of the well-known 'Apollo' plan, provided for Makarios' assassination. In the event of success, a certain person will assume power, who has already been chosen and who in "substance will be but a puppet during a period of transition". Naturally, the newspaper assumed that via the coup the partition of Cyprus would be achieved, "given that the Turks on their part have their own plans, just waiting for this golden opportunity."[48]

Commenting on the article, Makarios stated that in his opinion, there was no possibility of a coup. However, he stated that in the event of a coup, "there is no chance of success" because it was not possible for the Cyprus people to tolerate being slaves to coupists. "Its active resistance will be evident in a variety of ways."[49]

While Makarios was warning of the resistance he would put up, the National Guard was preparing for the coup in the utmost secrecy. Its Commander, Lieutenant General Denisis, did not take part in this process, as he was opposed to the overthrow of Makarios by a coup. Denisis had committed all National Guard units to not making a move without his personal order. Papadakis, Georgitsis and Kombokis requested his removal from Cyprus so they could make use of the National Guard.[50]

According to the findings of the Greek Parliament's Investigative Committee, Denisis had asked Georgitsis to convey to Ioannides and Bonanos his opposition to a coup. He also told him to express his fears concerning the risks he felt such an action would entail, as well as his fears of Turkish military intervention.[51] When Georgitsis returned to Cyprus on 6 July, Denisis asked him to brief him about why Bonanos had invited him to Athens, and he asked him if he had conveyed his reservations. Georgitsis concealed the truth from him, and said that the subject of his discussion with military headquarters was the problems created in the structure of the National Guard by Makarios' decision to shorten military service.[52]

Nevertheless, Denisis was aware of where things were leading. He attempted, in fact, to prevent his wife Elli, who was in Athens, from returning to Cyprus. In a telephone conversation he had with her on 4 July 1974, the following exchange took place:

"Denisis: Did you see the papers today? Get *Eleftheros Laos.*
Elli: I got *Eleftheria* and *Ethniki.*
Denisis: *Eleftheria* doesn't say anything.
Elli: We saw it in the others. Look, Giorgos, I've talked it over with your daughter and she's asking why you are creating such difficulties.

46 Pike report, *op. cit.*
47 Georgios Tombazos, testimony before the Committee on the 'Cyprus File' of the Cyprus House of Representatives.
48 "Πραξικόπημα" [Coup], *Apogevmatini*, 5 July 1974.
49 Papademetris, Panayiotis, Petrides, *op. cit.*, vol. 14, p. 377.
50 Grigorios Bonanos, *Η αλήθεια* [The Truth] (Athens, 1986), p. 218.
51 Greek Parliament, *op. cit.*, p. 75.
52 *Ibid.*

Denisis: She's still very young, but I expected *you* to understand, after so many years involved with military life.
Elli: Fine, OK, what happened?
Denisis: I'll tell you on Saturday.
Elli: I say I should come. Your daughter is shouting why this, why that?
Denisis: I'm not going to go on about it, just you listen to what Vassilis says (their son).
Elli: He's away in Spetses.
Denisis: Listen (in a severe tone), do you remember what happened in Larissa? (Larissa saw the outbreak of the King's counter-coup in December 1967)
Elli: So, what happened, Giorgos? OK, I remember.
Denisis: Don't you care about that?
Elli: No, it's none of our concern.
Denisis: None at all? You don't care, OK, but tell me, you don't understand the reason at all?
Elli: Of course, we get it, but I'm telling you this thing is none of our concern.
Denisis: Do you remember that time when Kalokerinos used to be in Larissa? Well, the same will happen to you now.
Elli: And you, will you stay there?
Denisis: Who, me… well, OK.
Elli: So, none of us then.
Denisis: OK, we'll discuss it on Saturday. What I've told you is more important than anything else."[53]

On 9 July 1974, Georgitsis and Kombokis called those officers that would lead the units participating in the coup to a meeting in Nicosia, and briefed them. After the discussion, it was unanimously agreed that the coup should not take place, because the units were very spread out, preparation was inadequate, and – the main thing – there was a risk that Turkey would intervene. Next, the deputy Head of the Greek Military Contingent, Constantinos Papayiannis, proposed that his unit should not participate in the coup for reasons of convenience, since it was a purely Greek military force. Also, due to the prevailing tension between the government and the National Guard, the police, Reservists and the Presidential Guard were on continuous alert in the evenings, while they had under surveillance all the National Guard camps and officers' houses, something which ruled out any chance of surprise.[54]

On 10 July, Major Kontosis went to Athens and conveyed to Ioannides and Bonanos the concerns expressed at the Nicosia meeting. After consulting with Bonanos, Ioannides gave an order to Kontosis to convey to Georgitsis and Kombokis that their concerns had been rejected, and that it was the order of the Head of the Armed Forces and of the government that they should proceed to implement the decision to oust Makarios. The only modifications to the initial plan that Ioannides approved were the limiting of the Greek Contingent's role to covering Nicosia airport and the change of the time of the coup from the evening to 8.30am. The change of time occurred because of the information that in the evenings the camps and officers' houses were under surveillance.[55]

---

53 Cyprus KYP archive, conversation between Denisis and his wife Elli monitored by the intelligence service on 4 July 1974.
54 Georgios P. Sergis, *Η μάχη της Κύπρου* [Cyprus' Struggle] (Athens, 1996), p. 187.
55 Greek Parliament, *op. cit.*, pp. 75-76.

Major Kontosis, after committing to memory the proclamation that would be broadcast from the Cyprus Broadcasting Corporation's radio after the coup had prevailed, as well as the names of the persons who would be proposed to lead the coupist government, returned to Nicosia. Kontosis stated in his deposition to the Greek Parliament's Investigating Committee that he did not remember these names accurately, but various sources mention the names of the President of the Supreme Court Michalakis Triantafillides, of former minister Zenon Severis, as well as those of judges Loizos Hadjiloizou and Tasos Hadjianastasiou.[56]

On the morning of 13 July, there was a meeting at the Greek Contingent camp, which was attended by officers Michael Georgitsis, Panayiotis Yiannakodimos, Constantinos Kombokis, Constantinos Papayiannis and Constantinos Kontosis. At the meeting, the final decisions of Armed Forces Headquarters were announced, as brought from Athens by Kontosis:

- The operation will definitely be carried out, due to reasons of the highest national importance.
- The action will be implemented on 15 July.
- The code words for the beginning of the operation are "Alexander has gone to hospital".
- None of the Guards other than that of Nicosia will be notified.
- The Paphos Guard will be reinforced only by the 'Leventis' patrol.
- The whole of the Greek Contingent may be used in the operation.
- The proclamation concerning the names of the president and members of the new Cyprus government will be issued by Major Kontosis only on the morning of 15 July.[57]

The plans for the coup provided no role whatever for EOKA B, probably because the organisation was on the verge of dissolution as a result of the successive triumphs of the Reservists and the police. Also, the organisation was being racked by continuous squabbles and rivalries between Lefteris Papdopoulos and Kikis Constantinou. Papadopoulos had regained some important role in the organisation after taking over the leadership from Croesos Christodoulides, while Kikis Constantinou was acting independently in the Famagusta area. He refused to work with the leadership of EOKA B and was locked in opposition to Christodoulides, the latter deciding at the beginning of July 1974 to withdraw, invoking personal reasons. Papadopoulos was told of Christodoulides' intended resignation, and wrote to him on 9 July to ask him to charge Kikis with being a breakaway, while appealing to him not to resign before 15 July. "You cannot write that your resignation is due to family reasons. You'll be sneered at by everyone. Be careful not to include such reasons. If you listen to me you won't be the loser. And as I stressed, not before the 15th of the month – I'm asking you seriously, and insist on this."[58]

From the insistence of Papadopoulos, it is clear that he knew that 15 July had been set as the date for the coup. Papadopoulos finally convinced Christodoulides not to resign. The latter, in his note to EOKA B section leaders, accused Constantinou of causing a split and called them to a meeting to decide on what should follow.[59]

A few days later, on 11 July, the Reservists arrested Papadopoulos at the house of Andreas Mitsingas in Nicosia. The house had come under surveillance after information that it was where the EOKA B leadership used to hold meetings. Papadopoulos, despite the fact that he had harshly criticised Syros for surrendering without resistance, followed his exam-

---

56 *Ibid.*
57 Bitos, *op. cit.*, p. 188.
58 Papageorgiou, *Μακάριος*, pp. 240-241.
59 Pavlides, *op. cit.*, p. 710.

ple and came out with his hands in the air. With him were arrested the lawyer Kyriacos Saveriades, Lieutenant Andreas Papapetrou and Nicosia section leader Aris Hadjigeorgiou.

After Papadopoulos' arrest, panic spread throughout the EOKA B leadership. Lieutenants Croesos Christodoulides and Andreas Avgoustis, who were on the wanted list, turned up voluntarily and gave themselves up to police. Although there remained about 125 wanted men in the mountains, EOKA B was rudderless, and in reality had fallen apart.

Since it was so obvious that a coup was imminent, especially to Makarios – who had even hastily imported weapons from Czechoslovakia – why did he not take measures to prevent it? When he was asked about this after the coup, he gave the answer that he credited the Greek officers with more patriotism. Makarios' answer is far too simplistic to explain his stance. In reality, the Junta had contrived an entire misinformation campaign at his expense, a fact that Makarios probably did not wish to admit. While Ioannides was preparing the coup set for 15 July, the Greek government on 6 July conveyed through its ambassador Efstathios Lagakos an invitation to Makarios to go to Athens for talks. Informing Cypriot Foreign Minister Yiannis Christofides by phone, Lagakos told him that he had proposed Makarios' visit to Athens to discuss the whole matter; while accepting the invitation, Makarios set as a precondition that the Greek government accept his decision to purge the National Guard.[60]

In the meanwhile, the Prime Minister of the regime, Androutsopoulos, sent Savvas Constantopoulos, publisher of the newspaper *Eleftheros Kosmos*, to Cyprus on 7 July. As his personal envoy, he had instructions to act as an intermediary with Makarios to defuse the crisis. Androutsopoulos was in reality a puppet, having neither the power nor the influence to undertake any initiative that would conflict Ioannides' plans. US ambassador Henry Tasca said of Androutsopoulos that he doubted very much "if he ever took any serious decision related to Greece's security, in connection with either Cyprus or with Turkey, without this going through Ioannides first."[61]

Androutsopoulos writes in his memoirs that his instructions to Constantopoulos were to stress to Makarios that in view of the "great dangers to the nation" he ought to hold talks with Greece "as a Greek should with the Motherland", and to accept to this end the Greek government's invitation to visit Athens.[62] Makarios immediately received Constantopoulos, and in the evening held a dinner in his honour at the Presidential Palace. After dinner, Makarios discussed with him the problem of his relations with Athens. He analysed for Constantopoulos the background to the crisis, placing emphasis on the involvement of Greek officers with EOKA B. He declared his readiness for reconciliation, but set as a basic precondition the dissolution of EOKA B and the purging of the National Guard.

Behind the scenes, Constantopoulos' personal friend Andreas Azinas - who as he himself admitted maintained links both with Papadopoulos and Ioannides – was also involved.[63] Azinas mentions that Constantopoulos made a compromise proposal to Makarios, according to which he would withdraw his demand for an immediate recall of all the Greek officers. Instead, certain officers would be recalled in a first phase, while gradually they

60 Cyprus KYP report, *op. cit.*, p. 121.

61 Tasca, interview with Jack Bush, U.S. intelligence agencies and activities: Committee proceedings. Select Committee on Intelligence, U.S. House of Representatives, part 4, p. 1534.

62 Androutsopoulos, *op. cit.*, p. 256.

63 "Εγώ είχα με τη χούντα ντόμπρες σχέσεις" [I had Frank Relations with the Junta], *Philelftheros*, 15 July 1999.

would all be replaced with officers approved by Makarios. Azinas maintains that Makarios accepted the proposal and was waiting for an answer from Athens.[64]

On 8 July, Azinas accompanied Constantopoulos to Nicosia airport, from where he left for Athens. Constantopoulos went directly from the airport to Androutsopoulos' office and briefed him on his conversation with Makarios. Androutsopoulos writes in his memoirs that Constantopoulos was very disappointed on his return from Cyprus, and that in a reply to his question concerning Makarios' thoughts, told him: "Makarios is finished. He has stopped thinking of anything other than his role as the Panhellenic leader after the fall of the Athens government. (…) Makarios has closed his mind and thrown away the keys."[65]

Makarios, however, considered the cooperation he had with Constantopoulos to be positive. Foreign Minister Yiannis Christofides discussed by telephone what had been said with ambassador Efstathios Lagakos. Christofides was not present at the meeting, but had been briefed by Makarios:

"Lagakos: Did Constantopoulos just listen? Didn't he convey anything?

Christofides: Well, Makarios didn't tell me much but it seems that Androutsopoulos sent Constantopoulos.

Lagakos: Ah, personally.

Christofides: It seems it has something to do with Androutsopoulos. Of course, it was about what you also conveyed, nothing more than what the Archbishop already knew, and he told him his position. He explained to him that during the last four to five years he has gone through the hardships that he has gone – from what I can make out because I wasn't there – but it seems that it was a long conversation and from what I have been told lasted until half past midnight.

Lagakos: All the better, because he will have understood better and will convey it even more efficiently.

Christofides: According to what Makarios understood, Constantopoulos finally agreed with him, and this is a good sign because, together with my views that he will convey, perhaps the situation will calm down.

Lagakos: I shall have a word tomorrow in Athens about having asked you to exert your influence, and say that you did, but found yourself faced with the same attitude and that you were in difficulties. I shall add, however, that you always believed that the clearing up of misunderstandings would be a very helpful thing if they were to achieve it.

Christofides: Yes, it is my personal view and I do strongly believe it."[66]

In parallel to that of Constantopoulos, Christofides undertook an initiative of his own for the normalisation of relations between Athens and Nicosia. The question was discussed at a meeting of the Council of Ministers on 11 July, to which the President of the House Glafcos Clerides was also summoned. The Council of Ministers approved a compromise formula from Christofides, which would be submitted to the Greek government. Christofides visited Lagakos at his residence and announced to him the following:

"In my attempt to avert a clash with the National Centre and at the same time to avoid a qualitative weakening of the National Guard, it was today suggested at the Council of Ministers, in the presence of the Archbishop and President of the House Glafcos Clerides, that,

---

64 Andreas Azinas, interview with the author, Nicosia, 28 March 2001.

65 Androutsopoulos, *op. cit.*, p. 256.

66 Cyprus KYP report, *op. cit.*, p. 122.

if Athens makes urgent and effective endeavours to break up EOKA B, the Cyprus government will accept a review of:

a) The staffing of the National Guard by Greek officers,
b) Their required numbers,
c) The authority of these from now on, under the guise of 'trainers and advisors'
d) To whom the Greek officers will owe allegiance
e) Announced measures for the reduction of military service and consequently reduction of the numbers of National Guard forces are not to be modified, at least as regards the immediate future, without this excluding a possible revision by the Cyprus government of the numbers of the National Guard forces according to the island's defence needs."

Finally, Christofides underlined that the Council of Ministers had "absolutely no doubt" that Athens could proceed to the dissolution of EOKA B, as long as they took effective practical measures in this direction, "including the cutting off of any financial assistance from Athens", something which the Cyprus government "is in a position to ascertain".[67]

Christofides' message was conveyed to Athens and the first reactions were positive, as Constantopoulos told Makarios by telephone. As Azinas relates, Constantopoulos called him and conveyed that the easing of the crisis was a question of time. "Thus, on 11 July, I left free of cares and went to London, accompanying my father-in-law, who was to have a heart operation."[68] Recently, Andreas Azinas has revised his version of events. In another exchange, he claimed that his father-in-law went to London for medical tests, because it was suspected that he had cancer of the bowel.[69] The contradictory accounts that Azinas gives as to the reason for his visit to London, as well as the fact that he took all his family with him, give rise to the reasonable suspicion that he had been warned about the imminent coup. In contrast, Makarios put his faith in Constantopoulos' assurances that something positive was in the pipeline.

On Saturday, 13 July, the Junta called a meeting in Athens to discuss its relations with Nicosia. The meeting was attended by the Head of the Armed Forces General Bonanos, Army Chief Galatsanos, the chiefs of the Air Force Papanicolaou and of the Navy Arapakis, Lieutenant-General Denisis, the Head of the Greek Contingent Colonel Nicolaides, the Head of the Second Bureau of the National Guard Colonel Bourlos, the Head of the echelon of Greek KYP in Nicosia Lieutenant Colonel Ziotopoulos, the former head of the Greek Contingent Major Kondilis, other officers, ambassador Lagakos, the Foreign Minister Constantinos Kypraios (Tetenes had just resigned), and others. The meeting concluded without completing its discussion and it was announced that it would resume on Monday, 15 July.

On Sunday, 14 July, while Makarios was in his country residence in Troodos, he received a telephone call from businessman Costas Manglis, who had returned hurriedly from Athens to Cyprus to convey to him information that he had got through Evangelos Averof that there was going to be a coup. Makarios did not hurry to meet him and fixed an appointment for Monday in the morning, when he would have returned to Nicosia. "Even if Manglis had told me that a coup was going to take place, I still would have seen him on Monday," he later said.[70]

---

[67] Clerides, *op. cit.*, vol. 3, pp. 326-327.

[68] "Πώς και γιατί φτάσαμε στο 1974" [How and Why we Came to 1974], *Simerini*, 16 July 2000.

[69] Azinas, interview with the author.

[70] "Ο πρόεδρος Μακάριος ιστορεί: "Πώς γλύτωσα απ' τον θάνατο" [President Makarios Reveals: 'How I Escaped Death], *To Vima*, 24 July 1977.

Makarios had fallen into the trap set by the Junta and was under the impression that the meeting that took place in Athens was a continuation of the negotiations to ease the crisis, and that no other development was to be expected before Monday's meeting. "I did not expect a coup on that day precisely," Makarios acknowledged in a private interview. "I was informed by the Greek ambassador that there was to be a meeting in Athens on Monday [July 15]. I thought that after the Monday meeting had been held, I could take whatever precautions were necessary," Makarios told American journalist Lawrence Stern.[71] Makarios had, in fact, been invited by the Greek government to attend the session in Athens, which was described to him as a proceeding to discuss both his letter and the future of Cyprus. "I told the ambassador that I didn't see any reason to go to Athens to discuss those things. I wonder," he mused, a quizzical smile on his face, "what might have happened if I had accepted that kind invitation."[72] That question was answered many years later by the deputy Head of the Armed Forces, Othonas Kyriakopoulos, who played an active role behind the scenes during the period of the second Junta. According to Kyriakopoulos, if Makarios had gone to Athens, he would have been arrested and sent to Mount Athos.

Apart from the soothing assurances given to him by Constantopoulos, Makarios received information that Soviet Foreign Minister Gromyko had made representations to Washington, Ankara and Athens, warning them the Soviet Union would react. Also, the information reached him that the USA had approached Ioannides and recommended that he should not topple Makarios.[73]

Although Tasca claimed he did not consider Boyatt's worries concerning a coup to be serious and refused to intervene with Ioannides, he proceeded to an action that was unusual in diplomatic practice: on at least two occasions, he showed to third parties the telegrams that he had received from Washington, indicating that he should meet with Ioannides. According to the deposition made before the Greek Parliament's Investigating Committee by the General Secretary of the Foreign Ministry, Angelos Vlachos, about the end of June Tasca showed him two telegrams that Kissinger had addressed him, in which he was ordering him to find Ioannides and prevent him from proceeding to any action against Makarios. Tasca also showed a similar telegram to Evangelos Averof, a few days before the coup of 15 July.[74] Tasca's behaviour can be interpreted as a deliberate leak, so Makarios would be convinced Washington was intervening in Athens and that the precedent of the aborted coup of February 1972 was being repeated.

While in Athens Tasca was leaking the information of American intervention, in Nicosia the US embassy was more than certain that a coup was about to take place. The deputy head of the US diplomatic mission, Lindsay Grant, sent a telegram concerning the situation in Cyprus, in which he wrote: "We believe that they will attempt to kill Makarios." Grant, who had been posted elsewhere and was preparing to leave Cyprus, hastened the departure of his wife. "I knew what was going to happen. I was sure of it," he states. In fact, Grant even took care to get his cat out of Cyprus on 15 July. "My cat took the last flight to leave from Nicosia Airport," he says.[75]

---

71 Stern, *op. cit.*, p. 135.

72 *Ibid.*

73 Georgios Tombazos, testimony before the Committee on the 'Cyprus File' of the Cyprus House of Representatives.

74 Greek Parliament, *op. cit.*, p. 80.

75 Lindsay Grant, interview with Charles Stewart Kennedy, 31 January 1990, Association for Diplomatic Studies and Training (ADST), Oral History Collection.

Despite all this, on 12 July a reassuring telegram arrived at the State Department from the Athens CIA station, which, according to Boyatt, reported the following: "We have come into contact with Brigadier Ioannides, who has assured us that the Greek government is not involved and will not be involved in any clandestine activity designed to overthrow Archbishop Makarios, and to damage the situation in the eastern Mediterranean."[76]

On 14 July, the CIA circulated a report that there was no danger of a coup. According to the conclusions of the Pike Committee, "at almost the same moment that Ioannides was unleashing his forces, a CIA bulletin reassured its readers with the heading: 'Ioannides is beginning to follow a conservative policy, wishing to gain time in his dispute with Archbishop Makarios'."[77]

In Washington, at 3am on 15 July (in Cyprus it was 10am) a call from the State Department's centre of operations woke Tom Boyatt and called him urgently to his office, because there was fighting in Nicosia. "I went to the State Department, up to the operations centre, and they told me: 'Here's what we've got'. And he placed two pieces of paper in front of me. On the left was the daily Intelligence Summary drawn up by the entire intelligence community for the President, the vice-President, the Secretary of State and the highest officials. And it said, in its lead item: 'we have been assured by Brigadier Ioannides that Greece will not move its forces on Cyprus against Makarios'. On the right was a cable from the embassy in Nicosia, describing the fighting between Cypriots loyal to Makarios and those Cypriots and Greeks trying to overthrow him."[78]

"The CIA reporting at this stage was so bad it was hard to believe," said Lawrence Stern, quoting a diplomat intimately involved in this sequence of events (probably Boyatt). "The intelligence service had been totally blind."[79] It is naïve to believe the CIA was blind. On the contrary, it was in a position to see, not only the coup unfolding, but also the Turkish invasion that followed: in the period 14-28 July 1974, the Americans changed the orbit of their spy satellite, model Keyhole-9 (KH-9) known as 'Big Bird', so that it would fly over Cyprus twice every 24 hours, night and day.[80]

It is absurd for anyone to accept that the Junta fooled the CIA, given the access the latter had to the Greek military. On the contrary, as is revealed in a telegram from the US embassy in Athens, Ioannides had informed Washington on 14 July that it would topple Makarios within 24 hours. On 15 July 1974, the head of the Europe Desk at the State Department, Arthur Hartman, submitted a memorandum to Secretary of State Henry Kissinger concerning what had preceded the coup, which was already under way in Cyprus. To this memo was attached a report of a conversation that Ioannides' liaison had had with the CIA the day following the coup, during which the latter admitted that the United States had been told about the coup 24 hours before it began.[81] This briefing was done through the CIA, which was the only channel of communication that Ioannides had with Washington. At the same time, therefore, the CIA was assuring the American State Department that there was no danger, while it encouraged Ioannides to proceed. As Phaedon Gizikis revealed to Averof, "Ioannides, who had contacts with the CIA, had told him that the CIA had repeatedly

---

76 Boyatt, presentation at FSI, *op. cit.*
77 Pike report, *op. cit.*
78 Boyatt, presentation at FSI, *op. cit.*
79 Stern, *op. cit.*, p. 131.
80 "Οι Άγγλοι αφήνουν τη διχοτόμηση στους Αμερικανούς" [The British Leave Partition to the Americans], *Eleftherotypia*, 18 July 1994.
81 Tasca to Secretary of State, "Cyprus coup: Meeting with general Ioannides", NARA, Records of the Executive Secretariat - Briefing Books, 1958-76, Lot 75D146, Cyprus, 17 July 1974, telegram 4528, Athens, 16 July 1974.

told him the USA would not look unfavourably on the removal of Makarios". He also told him that he had in his possession an intercepted message, according to which "Turkey would look with favour on the replacement of Makarios, in whom they did not have the slightest trust".[82]

Furthermore, as the then Head of the Armed Forces, Grigorios Bonanos testified, during those days the Head of KYP, Stathopoulos, who had a channel of communication with the CIA, had given him the following information:

a) "The Athens CIA station head, whose identity I am ignorant of, told Stathopoulos that now is the suitable opportunity to intervene in Cyprus, that the Americans do not want Makarios in power and 'are on our side'.
b) That the Greek American businessman Tom Papas, who was visiting Stathopoulos, told him that the Makarios situation had to be cleared up and that now was the appropriate chance. He also told him that 'America is with us'."[83]

Early on Monday morning, 15 July, Makarios set out from Troodos to return to Nicosia. All along the route, the Reservists and the Presidential Guard maintained draconian security measures. At about 7.30am, the motorcade that escorted him passed by the Greek Military Contingent camp to the west of Nicosia, without noticing any suspicious activity. When they entered the Presidential Palace, the guard withdrew for a rest, except for 10 men that stayed to ensure Makarios' personal safety. In town, everyone was already at work. The streets were empty of morning traffic and nothing presaged what was to follow.

At 7.15am, Brigadier Georgitsis, taking with him all the staff officers of the Third Supreme Tactical Command on the pretext that he was going for reconnaissance, entered the Greek Contingent camp. At 8am, together with the deputy commander of the Greek Contingent, Lieutenant Colonel Constantinos Papayiannis, they entered the operations room, where everything was ready for the coup to begin. Georgitsis signed the relevant order, with the code words "Alexander has entered hospital".[84]

The coup was to take place based on the plan 'Aphrodite 3', which provided for the takeover of the Presidential Palace, police headquarters, Cyprus Broadcasting Corporation (CyBC), Cyprus Telecommunications Authority (CyTA) and other vital installations. The most important operation was the occupation of the Presidential Palace and the elimination of Makarios. The order of Ioannides to Georgitsis was to deliver Makarios dead or alive.[85] The leader of the operation against the Presidential Palace was the head of the Mountain Commando Regiments, Constantinos Kombokis. According to the plan, the building would be taken over by commandos from the 31st and 32nd Commando Battalions, who had gathered in the camp of the 21st Motorised Reconnaissance unit, in the BMH area west of Nicosia. The Commando forces would be supported by 10 Marmon Harrington armoured cars (two platoons) and 10 Russian T-34 tanks (another two platoons) from the 23rd Motorised Armoured Vehicles unit. The two Marmon Harrington platoons and one of the T-34 platoons would start out from the BMH camp. Following two different routes, they would reach the Presidential Palace and would carry out the assault through two gates, to the east. The west side would be sealed by the second platoon of T34s, which would come from the camp of the 23rd Motorised Armoured Vehicles unit, west of Nicosia. The 9th Tactical

---

82 Greek Parliament, *op. cit.*, p. 193.
83 Bonanos, *op. cit.*, p. 218.
84 Bitos, *op. cit.*, p. 185.
85 Greek Parliament, *op. cit.*, p. 86.

Group, which was exactly opposite the rear of the building, would also play its part in surrounding the Presidential Palace, together with one platoon of Commandos.[86]

A company of 31st Commando Battalion was the first to enter the Presidential Palace. The armoured cars and tanks followed, firing their machine guns at the building. At that moment, Makarios was receiving 30 Egyptian Sunday School children, whom he had invited to Cyprus. "After I greeted each child separately and shook each hand, the one at the head of the group, a boy of about 17, began to read out a handwritten address to me," Makarios describes. Hardly had he begun to address him, when the first shots were heard. The child was terrified and stopped his address. "Even though I did not realise what had caused the firing, I told the child that it was nothing, and to continue his address." The child continued, but so did the firing. In the meanwhile, an officer of the presidential guard entered the living room to tell Makarios that National Guard tanks and armoured cars had arrived in front of the building's entrance. "I could not believe that a coup was taking place. Together with the children, I left the living room that had many doors and windows and was exposed, and we went to the palace's corridor." With his associates and the children, Makarios remained in the corridor for about 15 minutes, while heavy guns were firing at the palace. "The girls from Cairo began to cry and I was trying to reassure them, saying they shouldn't be afraid because the palace was protected by brave men, the presidential guard."[87]

The building began to catch fire on its east wing and Makarios decided to leave it from the west, as it was not surrounded. Escorted by his aide-de-camp Nicos Thrasyvoulou, his nephew Andreas Neophytou and his guard officer Andreas Potamaris, he left from the west door of his office. They followed a path that led down to the riverbed. On its bank, they met Reservist Captain Takis Tsangaris, whose company had just occupied the camp of the 9th Tactical Group, thus creating an escape corridor for Makarios.

When the first shots began to be fired at the Presidential Palace, the third company of Reservists, whose commander was Takis Tsangaris, had just returned from the surveillance points along the route from Troodos to Nicosia taken by Makarios. Tsangaris took three platoons from his company and made for the west side of the palace, while the fourth platoon remained to guard the Metochi of Kykkos Monastery. Ten minutes after his departure, Tsangaris' company attacked and occupied the 9th Tactical Group's army camp without resistance. Some officers were wearing battle dress instead of office uniform, probably because they had been alerted about the coup.[88] Tsangaris and a platoon went down to the bed of the Pediaios River, and then up to the Presidential Palace on the opposite bank. At this point, he spotted the commando platoon that was moving towards the rear of the palace. The Reservists fired at them and the platoon broke up.[89]

At that time, shots could be heard from the direction of the Kykkos Metochi. A group of three tanks from the 23rd Armoured Brigade, whose task was to clear the Metochi building had come up against anti-tank fire from the platoon of the third company of the Reservists. In the meantime, the tank platoon that was supposed to encircle the palace from the west was delayed by half an hour. The tanks had left their camp at Kokkinotrimithia village at 8.15, the same time as the start of the assault on the Presidential Palace. But as they left the

---

86 Sergis, *op. cit.*, pp. 190-191.
87 *To Vima, art. cit.*
88 Sergis, *op. cit.*, p. 194.
89 *Ibid.*

army camp, the leading tank ground to halt through mechanical failure. All this had combined to make the platoon late in arriving at the palace.[90]

Not knowing what was happening in the area, Makarios and his escort had planned to take refuge in the Kykkos Metochi. They commandeered an oncoming car, but within a few metres it ran out of fuel. Soon they found another car and set off for Metochi, but they nearly bumped into the tanks that were heading for the west wing of the palace. When they realised the danger, they turned and escaped from Nicosia in the direction of Klirou village. From there, through the Pitsillia region, they took the road towards the Troodos Mountains, heading for Kykkos Monastery. Makarios ascribes his escape to a miracle. If he had left the palace a few minutes sooner, he would have reached Metochi and certainly been captured because it was immediately hit by tanks and occupied. If he had left the palace a few minutes later, the noose would have tightened and there would have been no way out. "Even on the road to Troodos, the coupists had set up roadblocks at certain points. And the roadblocks were put in place only minutes after I had passed through," he later explained to journalist Stavros Psycharis.[91]

The manner of Makarios' escape fed the rumour that he knew about the coup, and that his escape was part of the plan. This rumour has its roots in the claim by the leader of the operation against the Presidential Palace, Constantinos Kombokis, made before the Greek Parliament Committee on the Cyprus File, that he intentionally left the west wing unguarded on the orders of Ioannides, so that Makarios could escape.[92] Kombokis' allegations are absolutely unfounded.

In Nicosia, at 8.30am, a section of Naval administration occupied the Cyprus Telecommunications Authority. Subsequently, sections of the 33rd Commando Battalion, backed up by tanks from the 23rd Armoured Brigade, took over the Paphos Gate police station. Almost at the same time, police headquarters was taken over from the inside – it was in the same building as the National Guard HQ – by officers from the General Staff and men from Naval Command, with Vice-Admiral Papayiannis at their head. At 9.30am the Greek Contingent took Nicosia airport, while the Presidential Palace fell at 10am, gutted by fire. Around midday, the Reservists' camp in the CyBC area was taken over, and next the Central Prisons.[93]

After the Presidential Palace, the coupists' most important target was the Cyprus Broadcasting Corporation (CyBC), which was totally unguarded and was occupied at 8.30am. After going off the air for 10 minutes, it began broadcasting marshal music and at frequent intervals it would announce that "in a short while there will be announcements by the National Guard to the Cyprus people". The delivery of the announcements was under the supervision of a Greek officer. At one point, instead of saying 'Cyprus people', the female announcer, who was confused, said 'Cyprus army'. Then a voice with a Greek accent could be heard correcting her: 'Not army, people.'[94]

The first National Guard message was broadcast at 9.45am, stating that it had intervened to stop the internecine strife among Greeks, and concluded as follows: "The National Guard is master of the situation. Makarios is dead." The announcement of Makarios' death before determining that he was really dead was part of the plan. This had been decided at

90 Pavlides, *op. cit.*, p. 754.
91 *To Vima, art. cit.*
92 Greek Parliament, *op. cit.*, pp. 85-86.
93 Bitos, *op. cit.*, p. 196.
94 *Eikones* magazine, supplement devoted to the 1974 coup, 8-11 July 1977.

the Athens meeting of 2 July, when the final decision to stage the coup had been taken. It was intended as a part of a psychological war, and aimed at minimising his supporters' resistance.[95]

Around midday, Makarios reached Troodos. From there, escorted by the presidential guard that was at his summer residence, he headed for Kykkos Monastery. Half way along the route, they stopped for a rest. There, for the first time, Makarios attempted to communicate with his guard in Nicosia. There was a wireless there and Makarios asked his escort what code he should use. They told him that he should call 'Akropolis from One'. Akropolis was the code name for the Archbishopric and 'One' was his. "Therefore, as soon as I called on the wireless 'Akropolis from One', I heard the reply: 'Akropolis here'. 'This is the Archbishop speaking,' I said. I immediately heard shouts and tears that I could not explain. The explanation was that they had thought I was dead, and now heard my voice. I was alive (…). I hadn't heard a radio and consequently was not aware that they had killed me off."[96] As the Junta had foreseen, the broadcasting of the false report of Makarios' death facilitated the coup in Nicosia. But the coupists, who had tuned into police wavelengths, also heard Makarios' conversation with the Archbishopric. They then started to search the palace for some secret escape tunnel.

It appears Nicos Sampson had no involvement in the organisation of the coup, but expected it to happen and offer his help from the very beginning. On 5 July ten days before the coup, he appeared before the Chief of Staff of the National Guard, Panayiotis Yiannakodimos, and told him "he had the forces to purge the island of the anti-Greeks and that he was willing to take on the government of the island after Greece had toppled Makarios".[97]

On the morning of 15 July, when the coup broke out, he was at his home. He went by car to his office at *Machi* newspaper. At 8.45, when the tanks were passing by the *Machi* premises on their way to the Presidential Palace, the newspaper staff, with Sampson at their head, went out into the street and greeted the tank crews with enthusiasm.[98]

Sampson then left his office and headed for his house in Lakatamia. On the way, he met a military vehicle with four unarmed National Guardsmen. He asked them to follow him, led them to his house and armed them with Sterling guns that he had hidden there. Together with the policemen he had as guards, the soldiers escorted him to the air force camp in Lakatamia. At the entrance to the camp he came across two Greek officers and all together moved into the camp. When he returned, he told his escort: "I have received an order from the General Staff of the National Guard to go over there." When Sampson reached the General Staff HQ, he went to the office of Chief of Staff Yiannakodimos, to whom he had proposed 10 days earlier that he should undertake the presidency. After embraces and expressions of enthusiasm, Sampson undertook initiatives as though he was a leading member of the coup.[99]

The leader of the coup, Michael Georgitsis, entrusted Sampson with going, one by one, to the houses of those selected in advance for the presidency, to ask them to go to the General Staff HQ to undertake their duties. But the highest Counsel of the Republic Michalakis Triantafillides was abroad, while the former minister, Zenon Severis, refused, citing health

---

95 Greek Parliament, *op. cit.*, p. 78.

96 *To Vima, art. cit.*

97 Bitos, *op. cit.*, p. 183.

98 *Eikones* magazine, *art. cit.*

99 "Το πραξικόπημα και η ενοχή του Σαμψών" [The Coup and Sampson's Guilt], *Phileleftheros*, 24 August 1976.

problems. Those in charge of the coup blamed Sampson for not finding a president, believing he either had not gone to find them, or did not inform them that they would be sworn in as president,[100] probably because he was interested in the job himself.

Around midday, Sampson sent a military vehicle that took his friend and associate Andreas Parisinos to the General Staff. Also on his instructions, the dethroned Bishop of Paphos, Gennadios, was taken there, as 'locum for the Archiepiscopal throne', in order to swear in the coupist government. The initial decision of the leaders of the coup was to appoint Sampson as Minister of the Interior and Defence, an office he had been interested in since the days of Georgadjis. Therefore they sent his police guard to his house to fetch him a jacket and tie for the swearing in. With time passing and no president in sight, Kombokis, who saw Sampson pacing an office, told him: "go and put a tie on, and come to be sworn in as President."[101]

Gennadios swore in Sampson at 3pm at the General Staff HQ. After the swearing-in, he addressed a recorded announcement to the Cyprus people on CyBC. "In the name of God and men, and after being honourably elected by the armed forces of our people, I have today assumed the Presidency of the Republic of Cyprus," he stated, and pledged the immediate restoration of law and order, peace, and the continuation of the Cyprus talks and the same foreign policy.[102]

Sampson formed a government under the strict supervision of the Junta. Dimis Dimitriou, who had excellent relations with the US embassy, was made Foreign Minister. Minister of the Interior was businessman Pantelis Dimitriou from Larnaca, a personal friend of Dimitrios Ioannides. Two deputies from the Unified Party participated in the coupist government: Panayiotis Dimitriou as Minister of Education, and Andreas Neocleous at the Agriculture Ministry. Both were from Clerides' party, and both loyal to Vasilis Vintzileos of Greek KYP. Ministerial portfolios were also given to two active members of EOKA B, who had been arrested two days earlier together with Lefteris Papadopoulos, namely lawyer Aris Hadjigeorgiou, EOKA B section leader, who was given the Ministry of Commerce and Industry, and Kyriakos Saveriades, vice-president of ESEA, who got the Ministry of Communications and Works. Sampson chose only two members of the government: his personal friend, Andreas Parisinos, who was appointed undersecretary to the President, and Yiannakis Drousiotis from Paphos, who went to the Ministry of Labour and Social Services. One of Makarios' ministers, Odysseas Ioannides, President of the Progressive Faction, accepted to stay on at the Ministry of Health under the coupist government.[103]

Paphos was the only town in Cyprus not to fall into the hands of the coupists. On the contrary, armed Makarios supporters occupied National Guard camps, locked officers up in the detention centres and distributed weapons among the citizens. At Paphos harbour was the Naval Station of the National Guard. From daybreak on 15 July, the patrol boat *Leventis* had sailed there, its mission to blockade the little harbour. In the afternoon, when the town was under the full control of the resistance, the *Leventis* received an order to take the Station staff on board and sail for Famagusta.[104]

---

100 Bitos, *op. cit.*, p. 204.
101 Greek Parliament, *op. cit.*, p. 79.
102 Papageorgiou, *Μακάριος*, p. 282.
103 This party was founded by Andreas Azinas in 1969. During the same period Sampson founded the Progressive Party; subsequently, the two parties merged.
104 Bitos, *op. cit.*, p. 202.

Nicos Nicolaides, who had an electronic workshop in Paphos, put a short-range radio transmitter into operation and called on the people to resist the coup. Later, Free Paphos Radio Station, as it was called, connected with a large CyBC relay station at Coral Bay. Its broadcast covered much of Cyprus, and could be heard in neighbouring countries. Makarios heard the station, and decided to go to Paphos to address a proclamation from there to the Cyprus people and to urge them to resist. "I immediately left the monastery and reached Paphos Bishopric at 7 in the evening." On his way to Paphos he also passed through his village, Panayia. He did not stop at all in the village; however, some villagers saw him in his car and immediately, through the ringing of bells, transmitted the message that he was not dead, as the state radio was saying, but alive and on his way to Paphos.[105]

The radio station announced that Makarios was arriving in Paphos, and thousands gathered outside the Bishopric. Makarios addressed the crowd. Later a message to the people of Cyprus was recorded and broadcast by Free Paphos Radio:

"Greek Cypriots.

You know the voice you hear. You know who is speaking. I am Makarios... The coup of the Junta has failed. I was the Junta's target. And as long as I am alive, the Junta will not succeed... The Junta has decided to destroy Cyprus. To partition it. But it will not succeed. Put up resistance in every way to the Junta. Do not be afraid... Join all the legitimate state forces. The Junta must not, and will not, succeed. From now onwards, the fight, above all else!"[106]

When the leaders of the coup realised that Makarios had escaped to Paphos alive, on the evening of 15 July, they ordered that three columns should be formed from parts of the National Guard to put down the resistance there and arrest Makarios. The *Leventis* was ordered to return and bombard targets in the town.[107] The first column left Nicosia on the afternoon of 16 July and, following the main road, arrived in Paphos by sunset. The other two columns took the Troodos forest route and arrived in Paphos at 10 in the evening.[108]

On the morning of 16 July, Weckman-Munoz the special representative of the UN Secretary-General, and the Head of UNFICYP General Chad, went to Paphos by helicopter and visited Makarios. The two UN officials asked him if he wanted them to take any measures for his protection. Makarios replied in the negative and asked them to convey his appeal to Secretary-General Kurt Waldheim to call a session of the Security Council and to condemn the coup.[109] Makarios' intention was to move to Limassol. However, when information came that the town had fallen to the coupists, who were moving on Paphos, he changed his mind. "My thought was to go to my village, which is high up and dominates almost all the Paphos district." He believed that the coupist tanks could never reach as far as there. But the Bishop, deputies and Mayor of Paphos were of a different opinion. They advised him to flee Cyprus. "When I heard this suggestion for the first time, my reaction was very sharp. I couldn't come to terms with such a thought. The people, who I had urged to resist, would think I had abandoned them and had left to save my own skin".

Finally, Makarios decided to leave and the only way was by air, through the British bases. In Paphos there was a detachment of the International Peacekeeping Force. Makarios conveyed to its commander the request to communicate with his headquarters in Nicosia and to convey to them on his behalf his wish – after coming to an understanding with the

---

105 *To Vima, art. cit.*
106 Papademetris, Panayiotis, Petrides, *op. cit.*, vol. 15, p. 40.
107 Bitos, *op. cit.*, p. 202.
108 *Ibid.*, p. 203.
109 *To Vima, art. cit.*

British bases – to have a helicopter sent to Paphos to take him to Akrotiri Base, and from there to leave Cyprus. [110]

While these consultations were taking place, the patrol boat *Leventis* began its bombardment of the Bishopric. Makarios left the building and went to the UN camp. He remained there for three hours until negotiations had finished and the helicopter came to take him. After Makarios' departure, Free Paphos Radio Station was hit from the sea, and fell silent. In the afternoon, powerful military forces entered the town and took control. By the evening of 16 July the whole of Cyprus was under the control of the coupists.

At Akrotiri, Makarios embarked on a British plane, which would take him to London. The aeroplane landed in Malta for refuelling. There the Prime Minister of Malta, Dom Mintoff, with whom Makarios enjoyed good personal relations, received him. On Mintoff's insistence, he stayed overnight, and the next morning left for London, his ultimate destination being the Security Council of the United Nations.

From 15 July, the General Staff called up all National Guard Reservist Officers. Most of these had been selected as officers because they were Junta sympathisers. On top of these, EOKA B supporters gathered in Nicosia. About 800 supporters of the organisation registered as policemen and were armed.[111] Weapons taken from those imported by Makarios from Czechoslovakia on 4 July, which were found in the basements of the Archbishopric, were also handed out to citizens. The Reservist Officers and the others formed armed groups and began to carry out searches, make arrests and interrogate people. Similar duties were undertaken throughout Cyprus by EOKA B units that came down from the mountains, together with supporters of the organisation.[112] Within a few days, several thousand prisoners were piled up in Nicosia Central Prisons, and in police detention cells in all the towns.

One of the first decisions of the new regime was to appoint EOKA B section leaders as military administrators in all towns. At the same time, EOKA B supporters replaced all the police chiefs. The military administrators bore the title of advisor to the police chief. In reality, they had the power and the police chiefs carried out their orders. Initially, the General Staff appointed Petros Andreou as Chief of Police. As soon as Sampson was sworn in as President, he demoted Andreou to Deputy Chief and appointed as Chief his friend Michalakis Pantelides.[113] The friendship between Sampson and Pantelides went back to the early sixties, when Pantelides was Nicosia police chief and helped to cover up murders committed by Sampson.[114] EOKA B section leader and Cyprus army major Andreas Avgoustis was appointed military advisor at police headquarters. Andreas Rigas, Head of KYP in the time of Georgadjis, was appointed Nicosia police chief. Stavros Stavrou-Syros was made military advisor to Rigas. In Limassol, Chrysanthos Anastasiades was appointed chief of police, and Michael Kalogeropoulos-Diacos military advisor. In Famagusta, police chief Kyriacos Fessas cooperated with the coupists and retained his position. Kikis Constantinou became military administrator of the town. In Paphos, Dimos Zenios was made police chief, with Georgios Raftis as his advisor. In Larnaca, Pieris Zintilis was appointed chief of police, with Cyprus army captain Andreas Papapetrou as his advisor. In Kyrenia, Mamas Christodoulou was appointed chief. Georgios Georgiades was made Head of KYP, with

---

110 *Ibid.*
111 Clerides, *op. cit.*, vol. 3, p. 99.
112 Bitos, *op. cit.*, p. 200.
113 *Eikones* magazine, *art. cit.*
114 Droushiotis, *EOKA - Η σκοτεινή όψη*, p. 378.

Andreas Menzis as his deputy. In reality, the Head of KYP was the advisor Costas Ioannides.[115]

On Thursday 18 July, Sampson gave a press conference in Nicosia, flanked by the Director of the Press and Information Office of the coupist government, Spyros Papageorgiou[116] and Foreign Minister Dimis Dimitriou.

In a written speech that he read out to journalists, Sampson made no mention of *Enosis*, which had been the founding aim of EOKA B and its activities. On the contrary, he claimed that the coup was a result of the rage of the people and of the enlisted young men of Cyprus. He pledged to respect all international agreements and treaties that the Republic of Cyprus had committed itself to, and gave assurances that the intercommunal talks would continue. "It has already been announced that the President of the House, Mr. Glafcos Clerides, is continuing as negotiator."[117]

On the same day, journalists were taken to various places where fighting had taken place and were allowed to take photographs, while on 19 July only those newspapers supporting EOKA B were in circulation.

---

115 *Eikones* magazine, *art. cit.*

116 On the day of the coup, Papageorgiou was in Athens. Ioannides called him to his office and entrusted him with the Public Information Office. Papageorgiou, Spyros Arotis, Stelios Christides and other members of EOKA B who had fled to Athens, all returned to Cyprus on 16 July on a special Olympic Airways flight.

117 Papageorgiou, *Μακάριος*, p. 282.

10. From Coup to Invasion

On 15 July 1974, America's Cyprus Task Force (CTF), which coordinated communications related to the Cyprus crisis, convened at the State Department. The Washington Special Action Group (WSAG), which formulated policy concerning the crisis, also met. The WSAG consisted of the deputy Ministers of Defence and of Foreign Affairs, the Director of the CIA, and the Head of the Combined Armed Forces General Staff and the members of the National Security Council (NSC). The President of the NSC was Secretary of State Henry Kissinger. With the Watergate scandal in full swing, Kissinger was effectively standing in for President Nixon (who would ultimately resign on August 8) in matters of foreign policy.

A few hours only after the coup in Cyprus, the Head of the Cyprus Desk at the State Department, Tom Boyatt, acting on behalf of the Cyprus Task Force, drew up a memorandum, proceeding to the first comprehensive assessment of the situation on the island. The memorandum was signed by the Head of the Europe Department, Arthur Hartman, and was submitted to Kissinger on the afternoon of 15 July. Considering the coup to be successful and Makarios dead, Boyatt outlined the following basic dangers:

1. Civil strife among Greek Cypriots and the spreading of conflicts, with attacks against Turkish Cypriots.
2. Intervention by the Soviet Union through the convening of the Security Council, on the pretext that Greece had abolished the independence of Cyprus.
3. The immediate and harsh reaction of Turkey, including military intervention, in response to any move by Ioannides or the Greek government that would imply that the coup was the first move towards *Enosis*.

Boyatt considered most worrying those aspects of the crisis related to Soviet and Turkish reactions. He noted that the stance adopted by the United Sates towards the Russians and Turks would depend on the reaction from Washington to the Greek government's involvement in the coup against Makarios. Boyatt proposed three alternative policies that the United States could implement against Greece:

1. Not to make any move at all, with the risk of being accused of de facto support for the Greek coup.
2. To attempt to re-establish the status quo in Cyprus, making it crystal clear to Ioannides that America was opposed to his actions on Cyprus. To ask him to withdraw the Greek officers and to allow the restoration of the Cyprus government. Boyatt considered that, if they were to choose this strategy, the most likely response of the Greek government would be to ignore the United States.
3. To attempt to restore constitutional order in Cyprus by threatening Greece with sanctions, such as cutting off US military aid and diplomatic ties. According to Boyatt, this choice entailed the risk of a significant change in relations with Greece, and the probable loss of the military installations that the US maintained in the country.

Of these three alternatives, Boyatt proposed that the most feasible was the second, and in the event that this strategy failed, he suggested examining the possibility of sanctions.[1]

Boyatt felt American interests would best be served by the restoration of the legitimate government in Cyprus. And given that at that time Makarios was believed dead, the only

---

1 Arthur Hartman to Secretary (Kissinger), "Greek Army Coup on Cyprus", NARA, Records of the Executive Secretariat - Briefing Books, 1958-76, Lot 75D146, Cyprus, 17 July 1974, Department of State, Action memorandum, 15 July 1974.

way this could be achieved was for the presidency to be assumed by the legitimate successor, President of the House of Representatives Glafcos Clerides, and by the promulgation of elections within 40 days.

When it turned out that Makarios was alive, Boyatt proposed his immediate restoration. This proposal was discussed at the Southeast Europe Desk of the State Department, and was presented to Kissinger. According to the Head of the Turkey Desk, Robert Dillon, Kissinger had never had much liking for Makarios and "was pleased at his removal". Dillon added that Kissinger "liked the situation, and as for us, he saw us as low grade bureaucrats without imagination, unable to seize opportunities". Then Kissinger for the first time made the suggestion that Clerides succeed Makarios. Boyatt told him that "Clerides is a brilliant man, but was not the solution".[2]

At the same time Britain was also seeking the immediate restoration of Makarios. Foreign Minister James Callaghan sent a message to Kissinger, setting out three prerequisites for a joint handling of the crisis: he refused to accept Sampson; he demanded the removal of the Greek officers from the National Guard; he insisted on the return of Makarios.[3] In his message to Kissinger, Callaghan made it clear that the nine member states of the European Economic Community concurred with Britain's position. "We considered that the ideal solution would be the return of Makarios. It remains to be determined whether this can be achieved through diplomatic means," he stated. To Kissinger's question as to how this could come about, Callaghan replied the United States should exert pressure on the Greek government over the National Guard officers, because the immediate restoration of Makarios was the only way to prevent Turkish intervention in Cyprus.[4]

The Washington Special Action Force that convened on 16 July in the operational planning room in the White House basement, avoided taking decisions on the handling of the Cyprus crisis, because the situation concerning Makarios was fluid: "The most important new factor related to events in Cyprus is that Makarios is alive, and this further complicates the picture of yesterday's coup," the report states, and continues: "His intentions and capabilities in putting up substantial resistance to the developments will determine also the response of the United States."[5]

Kissinger had already decided on the political neutralisation of Makarios and gave instructions to State Department spokesman Robert Anderson to avoid statements that would be binding on the United States as to the question of the recognition or not of Makarios as the legitimate President of Cyprus. Thus, to journalists' repeated questions as to whether the United States recognised Makarios or Sampson, he answered: "The situation is fluid, and no question of recognition arises."[6]

One of the first moves by the State Department was to send telegrams to the Athens and Ankara embassies, which informed the governments of Greece and Turkey that the United States condemned the situation, that they supported Cyprus' independence and the existing constitutional arrangements, and urged calm and self-restraint so as not to put in jeopardy vital Western interests.

---

2 Robert S. Dillon, interview with Charles Stewart Kennedy, 17 May 1990, Association for Diplomatic Studies and Training (ADST), Oral History Collection.

3 Henry Kissinger, *Χρόνια ανανέωσης* [Years of Renewal] (Athens: 'Nea Sinora' – A.A. Livani, 2000), p. 229.

4 *Ibid.*

5 Memorandum for the President from Brent Scowcroft, "The Cyprus Situation – Today's WSAG Meeting". NARA, NPMS, NSC, Cyprus/Greece, 16 July 1974.

6 "Department press briefing – Cyprus", telegram 154133, Department of State, 17 July 1974.

The instructions given to Athens ambassador Henry Tasca were that he should meet Ioannides immediately and make it clear to him that the United States continued to consider Cyprus an integral, sovereign and independent state, and that all its actions would be based on this fundamental principle. It also called on Tasca to warn Ioannides that the United States "cannot ignore any action whatever on the part of the Greek government to change the political and constitutional framework of the island". The message also mentioned that the United States supported a peaceful solution to the Cyprus problem through intercommunal talks, "that aim at securing satisfactory guarantees for the safety of the Turkish Cypriot community". Finally, it called on the Greek government to show self-restraint and not to provide an opportunity to foreign powers in the area (the Soviet Union) to exploit the situation at the expense of Western interests.[7]

Tasca handed the message to deputy Foreign Minister Constantinos Kypraios, while he entrusted the contact with Ioannides to the latter's liaison with the CIA. The CIA man visited Ioannides on 16 July and read Kissinger's message to him. Reacting, "the Brigadier literally exploded, jumped up, took a step backwards, overturned a table, broke an empty glass and swore crudely". He began to lash out against Kissinger, stating that one day "he makes speeches about non-intervention in the internal affairs of Greece and a few weeks later the American government says that it is 'in line with the above principles' and threatens to intervene". Ioannides added, whatever happened in Cyprus, "I shall be held responsible. If I withdrew the forces [from Cyprus] former politicians would accuse me of handing the island over to the communists. One day the American government will realise that on 15 July 1974 Cyprus was saved from falling into Communist hands."

Concerning the substance of the message conveyed by the US envoy, Ioannides said that neither Greece nor the Greek Cypriots were demanding *Enosis*, that the Turkish government had probably accepted the developments in Cyprus and that the Turks were aware that it was an internal Greek Cypriot matter.

Then he went on to say that everyone should forget about Makarios being an international figure. "Makarios had become a corrupt, homosexual priest, depraved, a torturer, a sexual deviant and the owner of half the hotels on the island." He alleged that, to maintain his position and continue his activities, Makarios was willing to "sacrifice 70 per cent of the Greek Cypriot population [only 30 per cent belonged to AKEL] and the whole of the anti-communist Turkish Cypriot population." Ioannides subsequently maintained that the coup had been instigated by the Greek Cypriots, who "begged the mother country for an opportunity to move against Makarios" and claimed that he had helped "only afterwards, when he was confronted by *faits accomplis*".

At this point in the discussion, Tasca's envoy interrupted Ioannides and told him unequivocally: "With the outbreak of the coup coming only 24 hours after he [Ioannides] had informed the United States of the probable overthrow of Makarios, this was very difficult for anyone to believe." This caused a second outburst of fury from Ioannides, who "again exploded, waving his hands, overturned the same table, smashed another glass and swearing, stated that he had neither planned nor organised the coup".

Ioannides said Makarios had already lost the game, that the Greek Cypriots had kicked him out, that the National Guard and the Greek officers had helped their nationalist brothers, and that the only resistance now was in Paphos. The American envoy asked Ioannides if Makarios might still be alive. He answered in the affirmative, "but who cares? Now he

---

[7] For Ambassador from the Secretary, "Cyprus coup", NARA, Records of the Executive Secretariat - Briefing Books, 1958-76, Lot 75D146, Cyprus, 17 July 1974, telegram 152379, Department of State, 15 July 1974.

has no power and nobody who believes in the principle of non-intervention in the internal affairs of sovereign states will help him, not even the Russians unless the Turks ask them, and the Turks don't care." Replying to a question as to how far the Greeks were in direct contact with the Turks, Ioannides replied: "We haven't bothered the Turks; we have not proclaimed *Enosis*. The Turks agree that the 'great thorn in the side' (i.e. Makarios) has vanished. I am not in contact with the Turks."

He later expressed the view that Greece and Turkey could sit down together at some stage in the future to talk over, and solve, their differences. The Greeks, according to Ioannides, would even be willing to set up a joint company with Turkey for the discovery of oil deposits in the Aegean and to share the profits from its exploitation.[8]

In Nicosia, Sampson's Foreign Minister Dimis Dimitriou, who maintained very friendly relations with the Americans, went to the US embassy on 16 July to explain why he had accepted a ministry, and to get advice.[9] Ambassador Roger Davies received him, but made it clear that the visit was a private one, because he was still accredited to Makarios. Dimitriou also had a meeting with Chargé d'affaires Lindsay Grant, who pointed out to him that the regime's only chance was to convince the Turks that they would not touch their enclaves in Cyprus. Then he went to the Turkish quarter, showing himself disposed to meet the Turkish Cypriot leader, Denktash. In reality, he sat and waited but Denktash would not receive him.[10]

American ambassador Roger Davies, in a telegram to the State Department, in which he described the development of the situation in Cyprus, came to the conclusion that the United States should consider the possible recognition of the new regime. Davies reported that the National Guard had almost the entire island under its control, with the exception of Paphos, and that the nationalists were either complying with the orders of the Greek officers, or were remaining neutral. According to Davies, probably the false news item broadcast by CyBC that Makarios was dead contributed to this. In his note, the American ambassador characterised as very significant the stance adopted by the Speaker of the House Clerides, who appeared to have consented to continue to offer his services as interlocutor in the intercommunal talks. Clerides' decision was announced by CyBC on the evening of 17 July. Clerides says the announcement was made at the instigation of the Greek advisor at the intercommunal talks, Michalis Decleris, and that he accepted "in order to soothe Turkey and prevent a possible invasion".[11]

Davies speculated that Sampson's regime would move against the communists, and that these would resist with all the forces at their disposal. He considered internal instability very likely, and termed depressing the long-term prospect of a divided community being governed from Greece through Sampson. Whatever happened, he considered that the regime would gain control of the island for an unspecifiable period of time. Davies proposed that, if there was no Turkish military intervention, and if the Sampson regime imposed its control, the United States should not exclude the possibility of recognising it, under conditions leading to an effective relationship with it.[12]

---

8 Tasca to Secretary of State, "Cyprus coup: Meeting with general Ioannides", telegram 4528, Athens, 16 July 1974.
9 Robert S. Dillon, interview with Charles Stewart Kennedy, *op. cit.*
10 *Ibid.*
11 "Με προειδοποίησαν αι Η.Π.Α." [The U.S. Warned Me], *Phileleftheros*, 13 July 1975.
12 Davis to Secretary of State, NARA, NPMS, NSC, Cyprus/Greece, telegram 1446, Nicosia, 17 July 1974.

In Turkey, the armed forces were put on alert immediately after the coup, and significant troop movements were observed on the southern coast facing Cyprus. On the evening of 15 July, Turkey's National Security Council (NSC) convened and discussed the situation in Cyprus. The NSC's suggestion, as described by Mehmet Ali Birand, was that Turkey had no option but to intervene militarily in Cyprus, invoking article 4 of the Treaty of Guarantee of the constitution of the Republic of Cyprus. According to article 4, Britain, Greece and Turkey guaranteed the independence and the territorial integrity of Cyprus and had the right to intervene jointly, or, if this was not possible, unilaterally, with a view to restoring the status quo that had resulted from the London-Zurich Agreements, if the latter were overturned.[13]

The arguments Turkey would use were that Greece had intervened militarily in Cyprus, that at a later stage she would proclaim *Enosis* and that this would irrevocably harm Turkish strategic interests in the eastern Mediterranean. Turkey revived the old theory of being 'encircled', which it had introduced into Greco-Turkish relations in 1955, according to which enemies surrounded her and the only outlet was towards the Mediterranean. Further, she would raise the question of security for the Turkish Cypriots, especially after Sampson's assumption of the presidency. The Turkish government decided to invoke immediately the Treaty of Guarantee and to consult with Britain as the other guarantor power. At the same time, however, she would proceed with preparations for a unilateral intervention. The military assured the National Security Council that they would be ready to begin landing operations in five days, namely, on Saturday, 20 July.[14] At 1pm on 16 July, the Council of Ministers met in Ankara, to be briefed by Prime Minister Bulent Ecevit on the National Security Council's proposal. The Council of Ministers gave its approval at 2.30pm, Ecevit signed the relevant decree an hour later, and handed it to the generals. Preparations for an invasion of Cyprus had officially begun.[15]

On orders from Kissinger, the US ambassador in Ankara, William Macomber, asked for a meeting with Ecevit to sound out his intentions. After many attempts, Macomber managed to meet the Turkish Prime Minister on 17 July. The Turkish government's evaluation, as recorded by Macomber, was as follows:

- It considered the coup to have been instigated by Greece.
- It did not expect a proclamation of *Enosis*, and believed that Athens would prefer to have two votes at the United Nations, while maintaining one foot in NATO and the other in the Non-Aligned Movement.
- It did not accept that the coup was an internal Cyprus problem, but saw it as an international question that involved the violation of agreements to which Turkey was a party and guarantor power.
- It considered the situation created unacceptable, and warned that if an acceptable one was not restored, it would intervene militarily on the island.
- If the intervention was deemed essential, it would not be delayed longer than four days, because the later it occurred, the more bloodshed there would be.

Ecevit raised the question of weak cooperation with Greece within NATO, while announcing to Macomber that he would be leaving immediately for London for consultations

---

13 Constitution of the Republic of Cyprus, Part XIII – Final Provisions, Article 181.

14 Mehmet Ali Birand, *Απόφαση – Απόβαση* [Decision – Landing] (Athens, Ioannis Floros Publications, 1984), pp. 28-34.

15 *Ibid.*, pp. 35-36.

with the British government, which had already given a positive answer to the relevant Turkish demand.

Ecevit explained to the American ambassador the basic aims of Turkey, which were:
* The restoration of the constitutional government of Cyprus. By this he meant the return of Makarios to his position of leader of the government; if this was not feasible, his successor should be appointed through the established constitutional procedures. Later the demand for Makarios' reinstatement was withdrawn.
* The Greek National Guard officers were to leave the island
* A secure sea corridor was to be created for the Turkish Cypriot community. As was clarified later, the Turks were demanding an extension of the enclave north of Nicosia towards the Kyrenia coast, to be used in the event of an intervention by Turkey.

Summarising his position, Ecevit told the American ambassador that the new Cyprus regime was unacceptable to Ankara and that if the above goals were not implemented through diplomatic means, Turkey would intervene militarily. He added, however, that if the new regime remained in power, Turkey could halt the military intervention if it secured the sea corridor as a guarantee for the Turks living on the island.[16]

Forty-eight hours after the coup, the situation was as follows: the Sampson regime was in full control, the Turkish government was preparing an invasion of Cyprus, and Ioannides was totally unaware of the critical nature of the situation. With this in mind, American diplomats Boyatt, Dillon and Erdman, as members of the Cyprus Task Force, attempted a full evaluation of the situation and prepared a memorandum containing proposals on how the United States could handle the crisis: initially, they referred to the main goal of American policy – to avert an internationalisation of the crisis resulting from Greco-Turkish conflict, or complications in US-Soviet relations. The then made a detailed analysis of the Cyprus situation. They pointed out that the coup was clearly an intervention by Greece in Cypriot internal affairs and that the entire operation "had the approval, if not the operational involvement, of strongman Brigadier Ioannides". They also referred to Sampson. They called him "an irrational, psychopathic and dangerous opportunist, whom the Turkish Cypriots called the 'Butcher of Omorphita' on account of the barbarous assaults carried out by him against their community during the 1963-4 crisis". Consequently, there could not be a more dangerous development in Cyprus than that of the Sampson regime remaining in power. To the question of whether the Turks might accept a puppet government in Cyprus, with a form of de facto *Enosis* behind a facade of independence, the authors of the memorandum replied in the negative.

The three diplomats also highlighted reliable CIA information that the Turkish army was in a state of alert and that the 39th Division was in a port on the southern coast and ready to go into action. On the other hand, intelligence reports from Athens said Ioannides completely underestimated Turkish intentions and did not think of making any kind of reassuring noises. The analysis concluded there was no possibility of Greco-Turkish understanding, that the situation in Cyprus was extremely precarious and that the problem was being internationalised at a frenzied pace on account of the mobilisation of the United Nations and of the interest shown by the Soviet Union. With all this in mind, the three diplomats warned, "Turkey, after exhausting all its obligations to compromise, in consultation

16 Macomber to Secretary, "Cyprus coup: Amb – primin meeting", NARA, NPMS, NSC, Cyprus/Greece, telegram 5629, Ankara, 17 July 1974.

with the British, is very likely to engage in unilateral military operations against Cyprus, during the next 24-48 hours".

The memorandum set out four options for the US to deal with the situation:

1. Strategic acceptance: recognition or some degree of acceptance of the Sampson regime. This would satisfy the Greeks and neutralise the communists, but – contrary to what Ioannides believed – it would provoke military intervention by Turkey, would lead the Greeks into conflict, would create instability in the region and would provide the Soviet Union with an opportunity to get involved.
2. Strategic non-recognition: the United States would refuse to recognise Sampson, would publicly proclaim that it recognised the legitimate government of Makarios and would probably recall its ambassador from Cyprus.
3. Constitutional strategy: the exercise of pressure on the Greeks to restore legitimate government to Cyprus through diplomatic demarches, and under the threat of Turkish intervention. For example, the United States could impose an embargo on arms sales to Greece. In the framework of this strategy, Turkey would have to be convinced that international demarches were under way to install a broader-based government in Cyprus, and that a military intervention was needless and counter-productive. According to the Task Force analysis, different tactics could be employed, such as: reinstatement of Makarios as president; support of a government under the moderate Clerides, his constitutional successor; proclamation of elections under the supervision of the United Nations.
4. Strategy of a Greek withdrawal: the exercise of pressure on Ioannides unilaterally to withdraw the Greek officers from Cyprus, something that would negate Turkey's arguments in favour of an invasion. The analysis said Ioannides was adopting a tough stance and playing a rough game, but after pressure from the United States, Britain, Turkey and the Soviet Union, he could not but comply. This strategy is described as similar to that which was implemented in 1967 and which resulted in the withdrawal of the Greek Brigade from Cyprus. The analysis pointed out that from the moment that there was no other country on which Ioannides could depend for security and for the purchase of arms, he needed the US much more than the US needed him.

All the above options were aimed at averting conflict. However, in the event that US intervention failed and Turkey invaded, Greco-Turkish conflict was certain, in which case the memorandum suggested an alternative strategy needed to be implemented, with a different approach and goals.[17]

Of the four options suggested by the State Department diplomats, Kissinger chose the constitutional strategy with the Clerides option. However, while this solution had been proposed with a view to averting conflict, Kissinger decided to implement it only after Turkey had intervened militarily on the island.

Kissinger's policy was based on the following reasoning: Turkey considered that the Greek coup in Cyprus had created a *fait accompli* that fundamentally upset the balance of forces on the island, and that the only way to restore balance to the situation was a second *fait accompli*, creating equal strength. Kissinger accepted this position, and the United States would tolerate Turkish military intervention without serious objection.

---

[17] Department of State, Briefing Memorandum, Cyprus Task Force to Sisco, "Cyprus. Analysis and Alternative Strategies", NARA, Records of the Executive Secretariat – Briefing Books, 1958-76, Lot 75D146, Cyprus, 17 July 1974.

Naturally, this would carry the two serious dangers that the United States most feared: a probable Greco-Turkish war and the extension of the Soviet Union's influence in the eastern Mediterranean. Kissinger had solutions ready to face these dangers. As soon as Turkey unleashed its assault on Cyprus, the United States would try to persuade Ioannides not to go to war with Turkey. From the evidence so far available, it seemed unlikely Ioannides would comply. There was therefore an alternative scenario that involved his overthrow, so that Greece could be governed under controlled conditions. After Turkey had created 'a de facto equality' by occupying part of Cyprus, the United States would implement its 'constitutional strategy'. That is, Clerides would replace Sampson. Clerides would then negotiate an overall solution to the Cyprus problem with Denktash, one that would satisfy all interested parties. The banishment of Makarios, apart from freeing Clerides' negotiating position, would also neutralise the risk of Soviet involvement. In all past crises, Makarios had been accustomed to handling Turkish threats through successful diplomatic manoeuvres, basing himself chiefly on the support he received from Moscow. For this reason, Makarios' neutralisation formed the main axis on which American policy was based.

On 17 July 1974, Kissinger decided to send a diplomatic delegation to Europe to handle the Cyprus crisis. At its head was Assistant Secretary of State Joseph Sisco, and the delegation included Boyatt, Dillon and other State Department officials as well as some from the Defence Department. According to Kissinger, this delegation would combine four aims: "to overturn the Athens-inspired coup in Nicosia; to reverse the increased danger of intervention by the Turks or, if it was not possible to block this, to limit its consequences; to coordinate with Britain as one of the guarantor powers; and to keep the Soviets at bay."

According to Kissinger, Sisco "received instructions to outline a proposal that we baptised the 'constitutional solution' – 'constitutional' because it would elevate Glafcos Clerides, President of the Cyprus Parliament under Makarios, to the office of President for a period of six months. After this time, elections would be held, in which Makarios could freely participate. In the intervening period, there would be negotiations for a new communal arrangement between the Greek and the Turkish population."[18]

Even if Sisco's brief was to try to avert the invasion, this was unlikely because Kissinger had not given him any means to do so, such as the threat of cutting off American aid to Turkey or the mobilisation of the Sixth Fleet. "You are sending me on a weak mission," Sisco told Kissinger as he was leaving for Europe.[19] Under these conditions, the burden of Sisco's mission was transferred to two parameters:

1. To persuade Britain to abandon its policy of support for Makarios.
2. To convince/force Athens not to go to war with Turkey once the invasion had taken place.

An indication of where matters were heading is provided by the contents of a memorandum of the National Security Council that Kissinger's very close associate, Harold Saunders, submitted to him on the eve of the Sisco mission to London. According to its contents, the view prevailing in Washington was that Makarios was considered finished and the question was how Sisco, in the discussions he would have in London with the Turks and the British, would handle the matter. Turkey, out of ulterior motive, and Britain with more decisiveness, raised the question of Makarios' restoration.

---

18 Kissinger, *op. cit.*, pp. 234-235.

19 Ivar-André Slengesol, "A Bad Show? The United States and the 1974 Cyprus Crisis", *Mediterranean Quarterly* 11, no. 2 (2000), pp. 96-129.

According to the Saunders memorandum, "the only obstacle to the return of Makarios to power is the insistent and combined reaction of Ioannides, Sampson and their supporters. This has to be taken into consideration when searching for a solution, but it has no legal underpinning." The U.S., therefore, had written off Makarios, and considered his reinstatement not feasible, due to the Junta's refusal. On the other hand, a solution had to be found that had an element of legitimacy: "We must try to negotiate a compromise solution. The logical constitutional choice is Clerides as President." Such an arrangement should come about after negotiations with Greece within the framework of the London-Zurich Agreements. "There must also be a commitment concerning a new attempt at an intercommunal agreement on the Cyprus issue."

What would happen, however, if the Greeks refused to cooperate in the removal of the Sampson regime? The Saunders memo set out two options:

"a) Theoretically, there is the possibility that will be suggested by some [the British proposal] for the United States to force Greece into talks. This seems impossible to achieve, and in the event of failure the United States will be the scapegoat.

b) The other possibility is the tacit Anglo-American connivance at a Turkish military intervention. Most people's picture of such a move is a Turkish invasion of Cyprus, on a broad front. As I understand it, the main Turkish plan is to drop about 3,000 parachutists to secure Turkish control over the Kyrenia, Nicosia and Famagusta areas, and to expel the 50,000 Greek Cypriots to another part of the island."

According to the memorandum, the Turkish intervention could have two results: "first, the partition of Cyprus ('double *Enosis*') or, secondly, an agreed intercommunal solution, other than partition, which at some stage would be followed by the withdrawal of Turkish forces."[20]

The policy put forward by Kissinger, and which he later imposed, is contained in the above paragraph. The operation described by Saunders is nothing less than the first round of the 'Attila' military operation. And while, according to the memorandum, it was proposed that this option was to be implemented in the event of the Ioannides regime refusing to negotiate a constitutional solution, Kissinger did not allow Sisco to negotiate the Clerides solution before the Turkish military intervention. Kissinger offered support to Ioannides and Sampson until Turkey intervened.

This is confirmed by a telegram sent by undersecretary of State and trusted associate of Kissinger, Robert Ingersol, to the American embassies of countries involved in the crisis, as well as to important European allies of the United States. The telegram was sent in light of the Sisco mission to Europe and gave instructions to the embassies as to the tactics they were to observe. The basic point of the telegram was that Makarios was to be neutralised, with the argument that, if he was not, there would be an increased communist danger. "Although Makarios is de facto President of Cyprus, there is another de facto regime on the island, which has imposed full control," stated Ingersol, pointing to the danger of Soviet involvement in the event the United Nations passed a resolution demanding Makarios' return under the threat of sanctions. "The West will refuse to comply, and the Soviets will rush in to fill the vacuum. The return of Makarios to Cyprus under these preconditions would only succeed in broadening Soviet influence in the Mediterranean and that of the communists in Cyprus."

---

20 Memorandum for Secretary Kissinger, from Harold Saunders, 17 July 1974, "Where Are We on Cyprus?", NARA, NPMS, NSC, Cyprus/Greece.

Referring to the position taken by Turkey in favour of Makarios' restoration, Ingersol wrote in his note that her demand to strengthen her strategic position on the island "would have no value from the moment that Makarios would return under these preconditions". Makarios would be unwilling to appear to be "a satellite of Turkey" and "would seek for support from outside, probably from the communists, so as to balance the Turkish position". For this reason, "we must warn" the Turks to take a more long-term position and recognise that the present stance may be very detrimental to their interests.

As to the position adopted by Britain, who also supported the reinstatement of Makarios, Ingersol wrote that upon examining her present course of action, Britain "will have to admit that there is the possibility that Makarios cannot be reinstated through political means, and to recognise the fact that she has not the means of achieving such a thing in any other way."

Concerning Greece, Ingersol said Makarios' return was anathema to the Ioannides regime. The return of Makarios could be achieved only with the removal of the Sampson regime and the departure of the Greek National Guard officers. "If Makarios were reinstated under these conditions, the influence of Athens in Cyprus would lessen and the subsequent weakening of the balance of forces would tend to make Makarios depend more on the communists and the Eastern bloc."

Ingersol added that the Sampson regime was unacceptable to the Turks, to the international community, as well as to the United States. "Despite this, it is now in power and we believe that it would not be wise to demand the removal of Sampson before an alternative solution is found." Further, the United States considered it would be wrong for them to adopt any stance concerning the Greek National Guard officers, because in this way the balance of forces on the island would be upset and the communists would take advantage. Ingersol also stated it was important for the friends and allies of the United States to understand that any attempt to overthrow the Ioannides regime would allow Soviet involvement in the eastern Mediterranean, would provoke Turkish reactions, and the situation could become unpredictable and out of control, with catastrophic consequences for Western interests.

Finally, Ingersol gave instructions to the recipients of the telegram to avoid expressing public opinions that would be binding on the United States. "We view the restoration of Makarios as unlikely and we do not accept the Sampson regime," he stated, adding, however, that the question should not be allowed to solidify in favour of one or the other, but that conditions should be created "for the development of an agreed compromise solution, which would permit the continuation of constitutional arrangements, concerning internal as well as external aspects."[21] And, of course, these conditions would be created by the Turkish military intervention.

On the afternoon of 17 July 1974, the epicentre of developments concerning the Cyprus crisis had moved to London. Makarios had arrived there from Malta in the morning; in the afternoon, Ecevit came from Ankara and in the evening Sisco from Washington. The simultaneous presence of Makarios and Ecevit in London gave rise to the false news that the two men had met. The anti-Makarios press even reported that the two had lunched together over cutlets. According to Andros Pavlides, who was then working for the CyBC, the propa-

[21] Ingersoll to embassies in Nicosia, London, Paris, Bonn, Athens, Ankara, NATO, UN, "Policy considerations in Cyprus situation", NARA, NPMS, NSC, Cyprus/Greece, telegram 156312, Department of State, 18 July 1974.

ganda officer of the coup, Athanasios Liaskonis, who at that time controlled the state radio and television, had fabricated the news.[22] Constantinos Panayiotakos, in his book *Cyprus, a Dossier of the Great Betrayal*[23], even writes that the meeting took place on 17 July and was attended by British Prime Minister Harold Wilson.[24]

On the afternoon of 17 July, Makarios met with the British Prime Minister and with Foreign Minister James Callaghan. As Makarios later stated, both told him emphatically that the British government would continue to recognise him as the legitimate President of the Republic of Cyprus and "they expressed very hostile comments concerning the coupists".[25] The British government at that time supported Makarios' reinstatement. In fact, it sent a message to the Greek government, calling it to withdraw Greek troops from Cyprus, as had happened in 1967 after the Kophinou incidents. According to the British proposal, the withdrawal of the officers could be carried out using as pretext the replacement of Greek Military Contingent forces, which had already been arranged for 18 July.[26]

The British Prime Minister informed Makarios of his government's initiative to request the withdrawal of those Greek officers that had taken part in the coup, and for the restoration of constitutional order in Cyprus. However, this initiative would depend on the position adopted by the United States. Washington, however, took a different line. Assistant Secretary of State Joseph Sisco, who was expected in the British capital, would outline a very different policy on the Cyprus crisis.

A few hours after their meeting with Makarios, Wilson and Callaghan met the Turkish delegation at the Prime Minister's residence. Ecevit read out a written note setting out his country's position, according to which the new Cyprus regime was unacceptable. He maintained there had been a significant upset of the balance of forces on the island and informed London of his country's intentions to make use of its constitutional rights in Cyprus. In fact, he requested from the British to allow the Turkish army to enter Cyprus through the British Bases. Wilson replied to Ecevit that the establishment of the Bases was clearly defined. "There is no possibility of Turkish troops landing there. We do not share the view that the Treaty of Guarantee gives Britain the right of intervention."[27] Wilson agreed that Sampson had to be removed, and claimed, "all measures for a return to the old order have not been exhausted". Ecevit, according to Mehmet Ali Birand, told Wilson that things were becoming more difficult with each passing hour. "Sampson must be removed and a new order must prevail. The balance has been totally disturbed. We are determined to ensure the security of the Turkish community. For this reason, Turkey must be provided with an outlet to the sea." The British proposed that a delegation from Greece be invited to London to discuss the situation, but the Turks disagreed, considering such a thing to be a waste of time.[28]

In view of Sisco's imminent arrival, Wilson asked Ecevit to postpone his departure from London for one day, so as to attend a tripartite meeting to discuss the problem with

---

22 Pavlides, *op. cit.*, p. 793.

23 In his book, Panayiotakos whitewashes Ioannides and presents Makarios as the brains behind the coup, saying that he knew when it would take place and "was already half way to Paphos (if not already there), when fire rained down on the empty Presidential Palace".

24 Constantinos Panayiotakos, *Κύπρος - Ο φάκελος της μεγάλης προδοσίας* [Cyprus – The Dossier of the *Great Betrayal] (Athens: Philippotis Publications, 1986), p. 60.*

25 *To* Vima, art. cit.

26 The Greek and Turkish forces were replaced every six months. On 16 July, the troopship *Lesvos* left Greece to take fresh Greek forces to Cyprus and to take the departing ones back.

27 Birand, *op. cit.*, p. 64.

28 *Ibid.*, p. 62.

the United States. Ecevit refused. Nevertheless, he extended his stay so as to meet Sisco at the Turkish embassy, alone.

The next day, Callaghan had another meeting with Ecevit, at which he informed him that the British government had undertaken an initiative to invite the Greek government to send a delegation to London for consultations. Callaghan also sounded out Ecevit as to how far Turkey would be satisfied with the removal of Sampson and the reinstatement of Makarios or Clerides. According to Birand, Ecevit replied that the only condition that Turkey would impose was its physical presence on the island, namely, the landing of troops.[29]

Ecevit had two meetings in London with Sisco, in which the Turkish Prime Minister demanded outright partition of Cyprus. The then Head of the Cyprus Desk at the Turkish Foreign Ministry, Edjmel Baroutdjou, wrote in his memoirs that, in his opinion, the Ecevit-Sisco meeting was crucial. "The Americans had been persuaded, in the course of these London meetings that they should not repeat the mistakes made ten years earlier, not to send another Johnson letter."[30] In 1964 President Lyndon Johnson had sent a message to Turkish Prime Minister Ismet Inonu, calling on him not to invade Cyprus.

At the conclusion of the second meeting, Sisco asked Ecevit to give him in writing the conditions that Turkey was laying down to Greece for the cancellation of its invasion plans. Ecevit, according to Birand, dictated his proposals one by one: the presence of Turkish forces on Cyprus, for the creation of a balance and for the security of the Turkish community, has to be accepted. Sampson has to be replaced immediately, the Greek officers withdrawn, and an area with an outlet to the sea for the Turkish Cypriots has to be recognised, as well as the creation of some mechanism to control the entrance-exit to the island."[31] The American envoy departed immediately for Athens, to negotiate Ecevit's conditions with the Greek government. The two men agreed to meet again in Ankara on the afternoon of the following day, 19 July, to continue consultations in the light of the Greek reactions.

At the same moment, Makarios was on a flight to the United States to address the United Nations Security Council. His aim, repeating the tactics he had employed in similar crises in the past, was to internationalise the question through the United Nations, exploiting his personal influence within the Non-Aligned Movement and the support of the Eastern bloc.

The Security Council first addressed the Cyprus situation at its 1,780th meeting, on 16 July, at the request of Cyprus representative Zenon Rossides. The Council accepted Makarios' request to speak before the body and invited him to take part in the debate that was fixed for 19 July. It further decided that Makarios would participate in the debate as the President of Cyprus and that the country's representative at the United Nations continued to be Rossides.[32]

As pointed out by the US permanent representative at the Security Council, John Scali, any attempt to call into question Makarios' credentials as legitimate President of Cyprus would have failed, given the make up of the body. According to Scali's evaluation, this situation could have changed only if the Sampson regime's authorities had appointed some

---

29 *Ibid.*, p. 81.

30 Edjmel Baroutdjou, "The Cyprus Peace Operation and its Aftermath", series of articles published in *Cumhurriyet* from 17 July 1989. Translated into Greek by the Central Intelligence Agency of the Republic of Cyprus.

31 Birand, *op. cit.*, p. 79.

32 Rosalyn Higgins, United Nations Peacekeeping, Documents and Commentary, 4. Europe 1946-1979 (Oxford: Oxford University Press, 1981), p. 240.

representative who would be physically present in New York and would request the Secretary General to present him with his credentials as Rossides' replacement.[33]

Almost immediately, Sampson appointed lawyer Loukis Papaphilippou as the new regime's permanent representative at the United Nations. UN Secretary General Kurt Waldheim was informed of the appointment by telegram from the coupist regime's Foreign Minister, Dimis Dimitriou. After an intense process, Papaphilippou, at the head of a seven-member delegation, left for Athens; from there, they flew on a plane chartered from Olympic Airlines to New York. It was flight OA 411, leaving Athens at 12.15 and reaching New York at 16.30 local time on 19 July. Initially, Olympic Airways staff were reluctant to accept the members of the Cyprus delegation without visas, and the US embassy in Athens had to step in to give its approval.[34] The US government granted Papaphilippou and his escort entrance visas, "avoiding the question of whether they were formally 'representatives' of the Cyprus government".[35] Papaphilippou was also offered police protection.

Upon arrival in New York, Papaphilippou sent a letter to Waldheim, asking him to accept his credentials as the permanent representative of Cyprus, by the 20 July, "so I may address the Security Council on behalf of my government". The request for accreditation was rejected and Sampson's Foreign Minister, Dimis Dimitriou, was informed. The Security Council decision read: "Zenon Rossides, who was accredited by Archbishop Makarios, Head of the Cyprus State, is considered to be the Cyprus representative in the present debate."[36] Makarios addressed the Security Council on 19 July. In his speech, he accused the Greek regime of open interference in the internal affairs of Cyprus. "It was an invasion, which violated the independence and sovereignty of the Republic. And the invasion continues just as long as there are Greek officers in Cyprus. The results of this invasion will be fatal for Cyprus, if there is no return to constitutional normality and if democratic freedoms are not restored." In his speech, Makarios called on the Security Council "to employ all ways and means that it has at its disposal so as to reinstate the democratic rights of the people and restore constitutional order without delay". Then came the most controversial part of Makarios' speech: "The events in Cyprus are not an internal matter concerning the Greeks of Cyprus. The Turks of Cyprus are also affected. The coup by the Greek Junta is an invasion, and all the people of Cyprus are suffering from the consequences of it, Greeks and Turks."[37]

This reference by Makarios was interpreted as an invitation to Turkey to invade Cyprus, while some considered this speech to be the main cause of the invasion. In his book *Decision: Invasion*, Turkish journalist Mehmet Ali Birand puts extracts from Makarios' speech in inverted commas and attributes phrases to him that do not exist in the text of the speech that circulated in the official minutes of the United Nations; such phrases included: "The Greeks have invaded Cyprus and are much more dangerous than the Turks."[38] Furthermore, in anti-Makarios newspapers at the time, Makarios was arbitrarily attributed the phrase: "I call upon the guarantor powers to intervene."

In reality, Makarios' speech did not in the slightest affect the way things turned out. As he was addressing the Security Council, in Cyprus it was between midnight and daybreak

---

33 Scali to Secretary of State, "Possible appearance of Makarios and Rossides before Security Council", telegram 2465, USMISSION UN, 17 July 1974.
34 Ingersoll to Sisco, "Situation Report No. 6", telegram 156314, Department of State, 19 July 1974.
35 Tasca to USMISSION UN, "Coup regime reps travel to New York", telegram, Athens, 19 July 1974.
36 Higgins, *op. cit.*, p. 240.
37 Makarios address to the UN Security Council, S/PV 1780, pp. 7-21.
38 Birand, *op. cit.*, pp. 80-82.

of 20 July, and the Turkish fleet was approaching the northern shores of the island, while the decision to invade had clearly been taken before 15 July. Nevertheless, by calling Greece's intervention an invasion, Makarios did strengthen Turkey's legal claims. On the other hand, since he had decided to internationalise the Cyprus issue and to take it to the United Nations, he had no other choice but to accuse Greece of invading. If he handled the coup as an internal Cyprus affair, he would not have been able to request the gathering of the Security Council and would not have been able to seek its assistance in restoring constitutional order to the island.

As he was in the United States, Makarios sought a meeting with Kissinger. After moves by Ilias P. Dimitrakopoulos, the Democratic Senator William Fulbright invited Makarios to visit Washington as President of Cyprus. Dimitrakopoulos submitted a radical proposal to Fulbright so as to avert the danger of a Turkish invasion: Makarios would send an invitation to the Sixth Fleet to carry out a good will visit to all Cyprus ports. Fulbright was the Chairman of the Senate Foreign Affairs Committee and had a very good personal relationship with Kissinger. On 17 July, he telephoned Kissinger and asked him to meet Makarios and to encourage him to send an invitation to the Sixth Fleet. The latter was rejected, but Kissinger did, however, accept to meet Makarios on 22 July.[39] He gave written instructions to the State Department press spokesman, Robert Anderson, to announce the visit, but to avoid committing himself on the question of whether Makarios was recognised as President of Cyprus. Thus, in reply to a journalist's question as to whether Kissinger would meet Makarios as President or as Archbishop of Cyprus, Anderson said: "He will meet with Archbishop Makarios on Monday."[40]

In the meanwhile, Ecevit returned to Ankara at daybreak on 19 July, made straight for the General Staff and was briefed on preparations for the invasion of Cyprus. All was ready for the military operation, which had been codenamed *Attila*. The troops had already embarked on their ships and were waiting for the order to set sail. The landing was planned for first light on the following day, 20 July 1974. The fleet slipped anchor from Mersin harbour at 9.30am.[41] At ten, Ecevit summoned the Council of Ministers and informed them on the talks he had in London and on the conditions he had set Greece, through Sisco. At around midday he sent Sisco a telegram through the Turkish embassy in Athens, informing him that his conditions to Greece had been approved by the Council of Ministers. Subsequently, he invited him to come to Ankara for talks in the afternoon, or at the latest in the early evening of that same day. Sisco replied that he was continuing his talks in Athens and that he would arrive in Ankara as soon as possible, the same evening.[42] Ecevit was in a hurry to conclude his consultations with Sisco before dawn on 20 July.

In Athens, Sisco sought a meeting with the Junta leadership to discuss Ecevit's conditions. He knew, however, that it would be exceptionally difficult to persuade the Greek government to accept such conditions. Thus, before beginning his contacts, he drew up an alternative plan of action, which he would implement in the event that he would have to go to Ankara empty-handed, and he submitted it for Kissinger's approval.

Sisco's plan was based on a "constitutional strategy" which the United States had adopted, and was as follows: he would commit himself to Ecevit to go to Washington and

39 Christopher Hitchens, *Cyprus* (London: Quarter Books, 1984, p. 88.
40 Department press briefin – Cyprus, telegram 157255, Department of State.
41 Birand, *op. cit.*, p. 93.
42 Sisco to US Embassy Ankara, "Message from Turkish Prime Minister", NARA, NPMS, NSC, Cyprus/Greece, telegram 4633, Athens, 19 July 1974.

propose to the President and the US Secretary of State that an initiative be undertaken with the Greek government, aiming at the restoration of constitutional order on Cyprus through the assumption of the presidency by Clerides. Subsequently, an attempt would be made to find an agreed solution to the Cyprus problem that would satisfy Turkish demands. At most, Sisco proposed an American initiative to impose a Greco-Turkish arrangement on the Cyprus issue, thus avoiding conflict. In fact, he prepared a draft Greco-Turkish agreement, which stated as follows: "The governments of Greece and Turkey have had a meeting, basing themselves on the Treaty of Guarantee, and have agreed the following:

1. The independence and territorial integrity of the Republic of Cyprus and the security and prosperity of all its citizens are better served by a return to the previously agreed constitutional arrangements.
2. In pursuance of this goal, they agree that paragraph 2 of article 44 of the Constitution of the Cyprus Republic [he is referring to the succession of the President of the Republic by the President of the House of Representatives, in the event that the former is prevented from carrying out his duties] will have full effect as from ... 1974.
3. In addition, the parties agree that the intercommunal talks that are aiming at the concluding of an agreed solution to the Cyprus problem must restart according to the provisions that the parties accepted after the suggestion of the Secretary General of the United Nations on ... 1972. The intercommunal talks are without terms or preconditions, and the parties have the possibility of bringing up whatever matter may promote the prosperity of the people of Cyprus.
4. The governments of Greece and Turkey will take immediate measures to remove any threat to each and to Cyprus."[43]

To proceed with his plan, Sisco placed before Kissinger the following prerequisite: "I have to have from you an assurance that Turkey will undertake no military action against Cyprus or Greece for as long as my suggestion is being considered by Washington." Sisco wrote to Kissinger that, taking into consideration the contents of his talks with Callaghan and Ecevit in London, he had reasons to believe that "the Clerides solution would be very attractive to the Turkish Prime Minister".[44]

In Athens, Sisco sought a meeting with Ioannides, but the regime referred him to the Foreign Minister. After several hours, a meeting was arranged at 5pm with Prime Minister Adamantios Androutsopoulos and deputy Foreign Minister Constantinos Kypraios. Finally - without notice and to Sisco's surprise - Ioannides and Bonanos also attended the meeting.

Foreseeing Kissinger's reactions to his plan, Sisco followed the initial instructions he had been given and did not raise the 'Clerides solution' with his interlocutors. The US envoy described the situation as tragic and urged Athens to make some move to defuse the crisis. "If you do not do something we shall have war, and this is a war you will lose," he said, and asked his interlocutors to give him some indications of compromise, which he could take to Ankara and on which he could try to build some compromise formula. Then, according to Boyatt, who was present at the meeting, Ioannides launched into an emotionally charged - though not incomprehensible - description of Byzantine history, of the struggle against the Ottoman Turks and of the capture of Constantinople. "We had really got into

---

43 Sisco to Secretary of State, "Discussions re Cyprus Crisis", NARA, NPMS, NSC, Cyprus/Greece, telegram 4625, Athens 19 July 1974.

44 Sisco to Secretary of State, "Suggested strategy on Cyprus", NARA, NPMS, NSC, Cyprus/Greece, telegram 4624, Athens 19 July 1974.

trouble, because this man had lost contact with the rest of the world and all the power was concentrated in his hands. He gave us nothing," said Boyatt.[45]

Despite this, Sisco wrote in his telegram to Kissinger describing the outcome of the talks that, "the Greeks have begun to realise how serious the situation is and how equally serious it would be if I went to Ankara empty-handed". The regime empowered Sisco to convey the following proposals to Ankara:

1. Greece accepted to send a delegation to London for consultations with the British government.
2. She agreed to exert her influence with the Cyprus government for the taking of practical measures aimed at strengthening the role of the United Nations, the effective control over ports and airports and the securing of the change in the Greek and Turkish military contingents.

"What I have secured is not enough, but at least I have something in my hands," Sisco wrote to Kissinger. "I made absolutely no progress on the subject that most interested the Turks. Specifically, they are not willing to give the Turkish community access to the sea and to some port or ports, under the supervision of the United Nations." According to Sisco, the Greek government "viewed the suggestion as some form of separatism or partition (which it is), and consequently rejected it politely, but firmly". Sisco also wrote that due to Athens' refusal to accept the Turkish condition regarding an "outlet to the sea," he had not even brought up the proposal that Ecevit had made about partition, so as not to discourage them from accepting to send a representative to London for consultations.[46]

After concluding his contacts in Athens, Sisco could see that things were leading to a complete impasse and that the Turkish military intervention was now inevitable. In his telegram to Kissinger, he insisted upon his proposal for the 'Clerides solution', as a last chance attempt to prevent Turkish military intervention. "I believe that it will be necessary for me to promote yesterday's suggestion of mine, which concerns constitutional arrangements (the 'Clerides solution'), so I can attempt to secure a commitment from the government of Turkey that she will not intervene militarily. Finally, I have the distinct impression that whatever happens with this situation, the Turks see it as the ideal moment to achieve a long term aim of theirs through military intervention, specifically, double *Enosis*."[47]

Kissinger utterly rejected Sisco's proposal in his reply: "We have to remain as flexible as possible and not proceed with the Clerides suggestion until we make the interested parties recognise by themselves that a compromise solution serves their own interests." Kissinger instructed Sisco not to make use of the draft Greco-Turkish agreement he had prepared, while deterring him from asking Ecevit for a grace period to take his suggestion to Washington: "The Secretary of State does not wish you to commit yourself in any way as regards your returning to Washington at this moment," he wrote. Neither did Kissinger comment on the condition that Sisco had set: that he personally commit himself that Turkey would not undertake any action against Cyprus as long as consultations were under way. On the contrary, his instructions were that Turkey was to feel no pressure from the United States. "The Secretary of State wishes that you show sympathy and understanding for Turkish anxieties in your approach to Ecevit, and avoid creating any sort of feeling in Turkey

---

45 Boyatt, presentation at FSI, *op. cit.*

46 Sisco to Secretary of State, "Discussion with GOG leaders", NARA, NPMS, NSC, Cyprus/Greece, telegram 4658, Athens 19 July 1974.

47 *Ibid.*

that we are letting them down. We must make them feel that we are consulting with them as a friend and an ally."[48]

Sisco therefore left for Ankara on a mission that made no sense. He arrived on 19 July at 10.45pm. Ecevit was in a meeting of the National Security Council, which was discussing the operation against Cyprus. After a long wait in the antechamber to the Prime Minister's office, Ecevit received Sisco and those accompanying him at 1.45am on 20 July.

Following Kissinger's instructions, Sisco was reassuring towards Ecevit. He assured him that the United States did not feel they had ever left Turkey exposed. "We know that on some occasions there may have been disappointment [he was referring to 1964, when the US prevented a Turkish invasion]. The Turks may have felt that they were the ones who were sacrificed and that they did not achieve satisfactory results. We appreciate this. We wish to continue to fulfil our obligations as friends and allies."

After this soothing introduction, Sisco began to brief Ecevit on the results of his contacts in Athens. He said the Greeks were ready to "discuss, negotiate and enter into a dialogue", but at the same time in the event that a Turkish military intervention takes place, "they are prepared to fight".

Sisco told Ecevit that the United States wanted to avert a situation that would harm everyone's vital interests, and which would result in damage to NATO and advantage to the Soviet Union. "Athens shares the same apprehension. The Greeks are fanatically anticommunist and fear the Soviet Union."

Sisco went on to outline to Ecevit American policy concerning the official Turkish position, that is, that Turkey would intervene using its rights provided for under the Cyprus constitution as a guarantor power, so as to restore constitutional order and consequently to reinstate Makarios. Sisco told Ecevit "a pro-Makarios intervention would not serve the interests of Turkey". Sisco informed Kissinger in a note about his talks with Ecevit, "I believe that I made crystal clear our views regarding what could be called the 'Makarios solution', which for the Turks is no better than the 'Sampson solution'." Subsequently, he introduced into the discussion the 'Clerides solution'. Referring to the talks he had had in Athens, he said: "Within the framework of seeking a dialogue, they [the Greeks] stated that they desire the independence and territorial integrity of Cyprus. Secondly, they are warmly supportive of the intercommunal talks. Thirdly, and I have wasted quite a lot of time on this, we discussed two broad categories of themes – constitutional arrangements and territorial ones, security and other similar topics."

Basically, Sisco proposed to Ecevit that they negotiate a solution with Greece that would satisfy the constitutional and territorial demands of Turkey on Cyprus. Nevertheless, Ecevit's reaction was again negative. He said that, despite the fact that the Greeks were "prepared to negotiate", and that this "was something new", this "did not constitute great progress since it came after they had taken control through violent means".

Equally negative was Ecevit's reaction to the proposal that Clerides should undertake the presidency: "He asked: if Sampson leaves and Clerides takes over, who could firmly state that what happened under Makarios would not happen under Clerides?" According to Sisco, Ecevit repeated what he had told him in London, that "Makarios was not a problem". He said that "he certainly had not shed tears over his depature – he did not have brotherly feelings towards him". If Makarios were a political realist, he said, he would accept "the

---

48 Ingersoll to Sisco, "Your conversation with Ecevit in Ankara", NARA, NPMS, NSC, Cyprus/Greece, telegram 157127, Department of State, 19 July 1974.

helping hand that Turkey was extending". Ecevit again stressed that Turkey "would not make any special effort to bring Makarios back to Cyprus."

Ecevit made it clear to Sisco that Turkey was not interested in any negotiations with Greece before military force had achieved some sort of balance in Cyprus. He said that in substance the coup had brought about *Enosis*, that "the Greeks are already there" and "are trying to negotiate with Turkey from a position of strength". For this reason, according to Ecevit, "if the Turks were to negotiate, they would not do so until Turkish strength equals that of Greece". Later, Ecevit entered into a long historical retrospective on the Cyprus issue and complained about the stance of the United States, about the fact that on two occasions, in 1964 and 1967, it had prevented Turkey from invading Cyprus. "This time, Turkey alone will take the decisions that concern her, and will not listen to the United States," he said.

After this, Sisco asked Ecevit for a short break to consult his associates. "During the break, all members of my staff agreed that the situation was hopeless and the invasion was only two hours away," he wrote to Kissinger. When negotiations resumed, Sisco asked Ecevit to delay any decision for 48 hours, so that he would have the opportunity to go to Athens to convey some other proposal. Ecevit said in reply "not only days, but hours are crucial". If the Greeks had good will, they would have responded to the proposals he had made them, he said. "But they are people accustomed to violence and the only thing they understand is violence." Sisco told him that he was prepared to propose some practical measures, but needed 48 hours' grace, upon which Ecevit replied that he had some practical measures to propose to him regarding the balance of forces on the island. "If I telephoned the Greeks and told them to allow the Turks to land on the island, that would balance the situation."[49]

At 4am, while the Americans were still in Ankara, Ecevit telephoned US ambassador William Macomber to inform him that the Turkish invasion of Cyprus had begun. This, naturally, did not come as a surprise to anyone.

---

[49] Sisco to Secretary of State, "Sisco/Ecevit meeting, Saturday, July 20", NARA, NPMS, NSC, Cyprus/Greece, telegram 4742, Athens, 21 July 1974.

11. Turkey invades Cyprus

From July 18, the coupist National Guard leadership had sought approval from Armed Forces Headquarters in Greece to begin implementing a mobilisation plan, but the response from Athens was discouraging: "Do not proceed to mobilise, make no moves that could provide a pretext for Turkey to invade. Self-restraint."[1] Colonel Georgios Poulos later testified that, after his contact with the Armed Forces HQ, the leader of the coup, Georgitsis, told those present at the National Guard General Staff in Nicosia that the Turks were carrying out naval exercises after getting approval from NATO, that the US Assistant Secretary of State Sisco had assured Greece that Turkey would not attack, and that the National Guard had to show self-restraint.[2]

On 19 July, foreign news agencies published the news that Turkey had begun preparations for an invasion of Cyprus. Turkish morning papers, anticipating events, wrote that the landing fleet was already off Cyprus' coastal waters. It was probably a trick by the Turkish General Staff, so the government would be committed in the public eye and not be able to back down, no matter what pressure it came under. In reality, the fleet set out at 10.30am. The trip to the northern coast of Cyprus would last 20 hours. The first small landing craft was expected to arrive about 5.30 in the morning of 20 July. The General Staff allowed the fleet to be photographed as it set sail. The BBC broadcast scenes in its afternoon television news bulletin at 5.30pm.

Information concerning an imminent invasion of Cyprus reached the island through foreign radio broadcasts and spread throughout the island by word of mouth. Around midday it was whispered that in Famagusta clashes were under way between Greek and Turkish Cypriots. In Nicosia, shops began to close and people withdrew into their houses. The Sampson regime, in an attempt to limit panic, assured the public that nothing was afoot. Late in the afternoon, CyBC broadcast an announcement by Attorney General Criton Tornaritis that spreading rumours was a criminal offence punishable by imprisonment.[3]

Turkey had 106 landing craft at her disposal, but in the first wave of landings only 11 took part, accompanied by torpedo boats, tank-carrying ships and other escort vessels. The remainder were either kept in reserve in Mersin to bring new forces to Cyprus, or were destined for the Aegean in case Greece entered the war. By the onset of the invasion, Turkey had transferred 70 per cent of its forces to her borders with Greece.[4]

In 1974, Turkey had the largest NATO army in Europe. She had 453,000 men under arms, of which 365,000 served in land forces, 40,000 in the navy and 48,000 in the air force. Her arms were of American origin and were fully up to date. She had 1,500 medium M-47 and M-48 tanks and M-8 armoured vehicles, 1,000 armoured M-49 trucks, 200 self-propelling machine guns, anti-tank missiles, etc. The navy had 19 anti-torpedo boats, 17 submarines and gunboats, 11 torpedo boats, four tank ships, 106 landing craft, 67 auxiliary and other vessels. The air force had 292 aircraft, among which were F-4E, F-104G, F-100D, F-84F Phantoms, and others.[5]

Forty thousand troops took part in the operation against Cyprus. Turkey used the 39th Division, which had been formed after 1964 exclusively for use in an invasion of Cyprus; a

---

1 Sergis, *op. cit.*, p. 313.
2 Greek Parliament, *op. cit.*, p. 106.
3 Papademetris, Panayiotis, Petrides, *op. cit.*, vol. 15, p. 80.
4 Adrian W. Burke, "The Turkish invasion of Cyprus: The forerunner of operational maneuver from the sea", *Marine Corps Gazette*, Vol. 3, Issue 3 (March 2000), pp. 81-89.
5 Sergis, *op. cit.*, p. 246.

regiment of marines, a brigade of parachutists and a commando brigade reinforced the 39th and the navy and air force backed up the landing force. The Special Warfare Department acted as the general coordinator of the operation, with General Kemal Yamak at its head.[6]

The Cypriot National Guard, on the other hand, was equipped with ageing weapons, mainly of Russian origin, remnants from World War II. It had 35 outdated T34 tanks, 45 armoured BTR troop carriers, 20 100mm artillery guns and 60 smaller calibre machine guns. It also had at its disposal 45 British Marmon Harrington armoured reconnaissance cars, 20 Bofors anti-aircraft guns and other lighter weapons. The troops were supplied with Lee Enfield rifles No.4, commonly known as Martinis, also leftovers from the Second World War.[7] The transport of troops, the towing of guns and the moving of supplies depended on pre-war vehicles, which had been withdrawn as unsuitable from the British army in the 1940s. Cyprus had no air force, while the navy was armed with five Russian torpedo boats. These means were more than enough for carrying out a coup, but scarcely so to line up against a massive and impressively organised NATO army, equipped with all the means needed for modern warfare.

According to the operation plan drawn up by the Turkish General Staff, the assault on Cyprus would start with a massive bombardment of National Guard military installations, the aim being completely to disable the island's defences. Seaborne force would then land on the coast west of Kyrenia. At the same time, transport aircraft would drop large parachutist forces on the Turkish enclave north of Nicosia, to back up Turkish Cypriot and Turkish Contingent units, and deal with any action by the National Guard. The reinforcement of the enclave would also be carried out with commandos, who would be transported to the Agyrtas area, on the southern slope of the Pentadactylos range, their mission being to move towards the northern coast and join up with the Kyrenia bridgehead. The Turks' goal was create a bridgehead in the first 24 hours on the Kyrenia coast, to occupy the town, to link the harbour with the main Turkish Cypriot enclave north of Nicosia and to take over the capital's airport.[8]

In the invasion plans drawn up by the Turks since 1964, the bay of Famagusta was the designated landing area. Morphou bay had been the second choice, and finally the coast north of Kyrenia. Famagusta was considered the most suitable area for a landing, because in the old town near the shore there was a Turkish enclave with a large population, which adjoined the largest port in Cyprus. After its occupation, the port was earmarked for use in strengthening the landing forces. Kyrenia was just the opposite. It was an inaccessible fort, given the natural layout of the surrounding Pentadactylos range. Most of the National Guard's heavy guns, and especially the artillery, were placed in such a way as to face outwards from Pentadactylos and overlook the shoreline. Along the northern coast of Cyprus were two lines of artillery batteries, one near the shore and one on the northern slope of the Pentadactylos, which could strike at landing craft in the event of an invasion. However, the Turks chose to land in Kyrenia because they were aware that hardly any National Guard forces were there.[9] As the Commander of the 39th Division, Bedrettin Demirel, writes, the Turkish General Staff knew that National Guard units were spread out across various parts

---

6 Baroutdjou, *art. cit.*

7 Sergis, *op. cit.*, p. 246.

8 Burke, *art. cit.*

9 *Ibid.*

of Cyprus. "The main landing areas (sea and air) were left weakened by the Greek Cypriots," he reports.[10]

Indeed, to carry out the coup, the National Guard General Staff leadership had stripped Kyrenia's defences and reorganised all those grouped National Guard units that disposed of heavy weapons.

The 190th Anti-tank Artillery Unit, which was based in Acheiropiyitou Monastery on the northern coast of Cyprus, and whose mission was to hit enemy craft in the event of an invasion, had been moved on 16 July to Nicosia to strengthen the forces used in the coup. It only returned to base on 18 July.[11]

The 182nd Plain Artillery Unit, which was based at Vosporos, east of Kyrenia, was moved on 16 July to Nicosia and remained there until the next day. On the morning of 15 July, the Unit put five trailers at the disposal of the 33rd Commando Unit, so the latter could move to Nicosia. Worn out, these vehicles returned to base on the evening of 19 July.[12]

The 183rd Plain Artillery Unit had its base in the Myrtou area, on the northern edge of the Pentadactylos range. On 15 July, it put its trailers at the disposal of the 281st Infantry Battalion for its transfer to Nicosia, and then to Paphos in the hunt for Makarios. These vehicles returned to the unit in a terrible condition on 20 July at 3.30am.[13]

The 187th Plain Artillery Unit that was based at Athalassa, but whose artillery range extended as far as the shores of Kyrenia, was also sent to Paphos from the 16th to the 17th July. Returning, it left two guns behind due to mechanical failure. On 20 July, five trailers from the unit were immobilised due to mechanical breakdown suffered during their move to Paphos.[14]

Two of the three National Guard Commando Units were also based in the Pentadactylos range. The Commando Forces were among the best trained and equipped units. From 10 July, the 32nd Unit was transferred to Nicosia from its base at Ayios Chrysostomos in the Pentadactylos range.[15]

The 33rd Unit was transferred to Nicosia on 15 July from Bellapais, on the northern slope of Pentadactylos. On 17 July, it was ordered to move to Paphos. Subsequently, it returned to Nicosia and undertook the security of the airport.[16]

The National Guard had one Mechanised Infantry Regiment (MIR), the 286 MIR, which was based in Kokkinotrimithia. According to the Cyprus Defence Plan, this regiment was designated for action at landing points. On 15 July, the regiment was transferred to Nicosia, took part in the assault on the Archbishopric and subsequently patrolled the city, overseeing the implementation of martial law. On 18 July, the battalion established itself on the grounds of the Pancyprian Athletics Association in the centre of Nicosia, where it was when the invasion occurred.[17]

The solitary National Guard Tank Unit (23rd Medium Range Tank Unit), also based in Kokkinotrimithia, had a similar experience. The unit's tanks were used in the coup as the

10 Bedrettin Demirel, "The Roads that Lead to War", memoirs of the Turkish General published in serial form in *Cumhurriyet* from 17 July 1989. Translated into Greek by the Press and Information Office of the Republic of Cyprus.

11 Andros Kyriakides and Renos Prentzas, *Όταν ξεκίνησαν τα τανκς* [When the Tanks Got Going] (Nicosia, 1976), p. 331.

12 Bitos, *op. cit.*, p. 212.

13 *Ibid.*

14 *Ibid.*, p. 213.

15 *Ibid.*, p. 211.

16 *Ibid.*

17 Sergis, *op. cit.*, p. 344.

main attack force against the Presidential Palace and other government installations. On 20 July, out of the total 35 tanks, 27 were in Nicosia, assuring the safety of the coupist regime.[18]

The 251st Infantry Regiment was based at the point where the Turks chose to carry out their landing. The battalion disposed of five T-34 tanks, which were on secondment from the 23rd Medium Range Tank Unit, for use in the event of an invasion. Both the battalion and the tanks were used on 15 July to carry out the coup in Kyrenia. The tanks fired on the town's Bishopric and occupied the police station. During the attack on the Bishopric, the cavalry captain, second lieutenant Stavros Achilleos, was wounded by the battalion's second in command, Major Alexandros Maniatis, who fired at him for hesitating to carry out his orders.[19]

Another battalion earmarked for use in the event of a landing by Turkish forces in Kyrenia was the 281st Infantry Regiment, based in the Diorios forest area on the western tip of the Pentadactylos range. This battalion was transferred to Nicosia on 15 July and was used during the coup. On 16 July it was ordered to transfer to Paphos in the hunt for Makarios. On the night of 18/19 July, it returned to Nicosia and remained in Athalassa.[20]

Apart from the wear and tear of men and machines during the first five days of the coup, the National Guard had lost considerable ammunition, given over to EOKA B irregulars. In the Limassol area, the 4th Supreme Tactical Command had exhausted all its reserves of ammunition.[21] There was also a great deal of useless firing. A typical example was the case of EOKA B irregulars in the company of a National Guard column travelling from Nicosia to Paphos, through local roads and forest areas. They fired in the air continually, from the moment they started off at dawn until their arrival in the evening.[22]

The National Guard had therefore left the island's coastlines completely undefended, to the extent that in the Kyrenia area Turkish reconnaissance detachments landed unnoticed on the eve of the invasion. One such detachment was spotted and put out of action by the National Guard at Vavyla, east of Kyrenia. On the shore, the rubber boats used to transport them were found.[23] Another reconnaissance unit was seen landing on the shore in the Pente Mili area by a farmer, who was accustomed to spending the night on his land.[24] One such reconnaissance detachment found the artillery emplacements empty, and occupied some of them.[25]

At 9.15pm on 19 July, the Early Warning Station radar of the Cyprus Naval Administration at Cape Apostolos Andreas spotted six boats in formation heading towards Famagusta bay. Four of these were merchant vessels, with the Turks using the merchant fleet as a decoy to lure the National Guard into moving its forces towards Famagusta.[26] About a half an hour later, eleven more ships were spotted by the radar, heading for Cape Kormakitis in northwestern Cyprus. This was the real landing fleet.

The National Guard leadership was at the National Guard General Staff HQ following developments. The leader of the coup, Brigadier Georgitsis, was carrying out the duties of the Commander of the National Guard after the National Guard Commander, General

---

18 *Ibid.*, pp. 316-317.
19 Stavros Achilleos, interview with the author.
20 Sergis, *op. cit.*, p. 342.
21 Bitos, *op. cit.*, p. 217.
22 *Ibid.*, p. 218.
23 Sergis, *op. cit.*, p. 318.
24 Kyriakides and Prentzas, *op. cit.*, p. 341.
25 Bitos, *op. cit.*, p. 311.
26 Demirel, *art. cit.*

Georgios Denisis, had opposed the coup, and been summoned to Athens on 13 July. The day after the coup, Denisis was ordered to return to the island, but refused and submitted his resignation. The Junta then appointed Georgitsis as his replacement.[27]

As he reported in his later deposition, Navy Chief Vice Admiral George Papayiannis had gone to Georgitsis' office and briefed him on the Turkish fleet's movements. "The Chief of National Guard General Staff, in my presence, immediately telephoned the Armed Forces Headquarters on a direct line, which we had had put in four days earlier. Afterwards, he told me to continue the observations, and that at Armed Forces Headquarters they had told him that it was probably an exercise."[28] At about 2am on 20 July the six ships sailing towards Famagusta Bay made about turn and headed for Turkey. The information was again conveyed by Georgitsis to Armed Forces Headquarters, only to receive the answer that "this was confirmation it was an exercise". But by 4am, the other 11 craft had arrived 15 miles off Kyrenia. "From this hour onwards, continual reports were sent to the Armed Forces Headquarters, without, however, getting any reactions or orders from them to us," states Papayiannis. At 4.30am, the landing fleet halted 10 miles from Kyrenia, outside Cyprus territorial waters. "This was referred to the Armed Forces Headquarters. No response whatsoever."[29]

Even at that moment the National Guard General Staff did not order National Guard units to put into action the emergency plan, to empty the army camps and move to their dispersal points. Thus, almost without exception, the invasion found units at their camps and soldiers fast asleep. One of the exceptions was the Greek Contingent, which had been informed in time about the imminent invasion. Lieutenant Colonel Georgios Kourtis of Greek KYP went to its camp and informed its commander Colonel Nicolaides. One hour before the onset of Turkish operations, Nicolaides put the Greek Contingent on the alert and gave the order for the dispersal plan.[30]

At dawn, 4.45am, the Turkish assault began with aerial bombardments of military installations on the northern shores, the Pentadactylos range and in the Nicosia area. The Greek Contingent camp was bombed, as was the artillery camp in Athalassa and the airport. The Turkish air force did not waste a single bomb to destroy the camp usually housing the T-34 tanks and troop carriers in Kokkinotrimithia, because they knew it was empty and that the tanks were in Nicosia.

While the air force was bombing, the landing craft moved nearer to the shore. In Kyrenia harbour, were two Russian-made torpedo boats. The naval commander ordered them to sail out "to check out the ships, and if they are spotted by them, to attack the landing fleet".[31] The torpedo boats set out from Kyrenia harbour a little after 5am to carry out what was effectively a suicide mission. Within 15 minutes, a plane fired a rocket into the first torpedo boat and put it out of action. The captain turned back towards land to save his crew. Within five minutes the boat sank. Its crew jumped into the sea and managed to swim ashore. The second torpedo boat continued on its course, arriving within two miles of the Turkish landing fleet, when it was hit by an anti-torpedo shell and sank. Of its 10-man

27 Petros Arapakis, *Το τέλος της σιωπής* [The End of the Silence] (Athens: 'Nea Sinora' – A.A. Livani, 2000), p. 184.
28 *Ibid.*, p. 185.
29 Sergis, *op. cit.*, p. 291.
30 *Ibid.*, p. 305.
31 *Ibid.*, p. 295.

crew, only one survived, swimming ashore despite being seriously injured. They were the first casualties of the Turkish invasion.[32]

At 6.05am in the Gonyeli–Mandres area, 12 transport planes began to drop parachutists. One hour later, the transport of commandos, supplies and materiel began, with more than 80 helicopters landing in the Agirtas area.[33] The transport aircraft and helicopters were moving to and from Turkey completely unmolested. During the first crucial hours not a single anti-aircraft shell was fired at them. As Georgitsis later testified, the National Guard General Staff had asked the Armed Forces Headquarters for "artillery to be made available so as to strike at the parachutists", and received the answer: "self-restraint".[34]

The first landing craft were completely undisturbed in their approach to the shore. Initially, five small craft tried unsuccessfully to swarm onto the shore at Glikiotissa, two miles west of Kyrenia; it was rocky, however, and for this reason they abandoned the attempt and sailed parallel to the shore, seeking a more suitable landing spot. The artillery units in the area could have hit the landing craft when they were out at sea or when they drew up on the shore. The 198th Battery of Mountain Artillery, which was positioned on the Prophitis Elias heights of Pentadactylos, could have fired salvoes against the bridgehead from the beginning of the landing. "Not a single shell was fired at it."[35]

The Turkish landing detachment began to go ashore at Pente Mili at 7.15am, with a delay of one hour and 45 minutes to its programmed time, under cover of naval bombardment, "unhindered for two or more hours, without meeting any resistance from the National Guard. Not a single shot was fired against them."[36] The first landing forces consisted of 1,500 men from the 6th Regiment of Marines, 15 M 47 tanks and 15 M113 troop carriers.

The Turkish invasion caught Sampson's government completely by surprise, totally unprepared and incapable of reacting. Cyprus awoke to the terrifying sound of Turkish warplanes, but did not know what was happening. An hour and a half after the bombing had begun, CyBC was still broadcasting normal programmes (morning gymnastic exercises in this case), while Turkish Cypriot Bayrak Radio had been playing martial music from 2am. At 6.30am, CyBC finally broke off its programme and began broadcasting martial music, and later on it began calling all citizens able to bear arms to hurry and join National Guard units.

At the General Staff HQ, the coupist leadership of the National Guard was watching helplessly from Georgitsis' office window as Turkish paratroops dropped into the Turkish enclave. General Staff Officer Yiannakodimos was in continuous contact with Armed Forces Headquarters in Athens through a hot line set up for the needs of the coup, and was asking for instructions to issue an order to resist. Since the order was being delayed, he held the telephone receiver outside the window so his superiors in Athens could hear the explosions from the Turkish air strikes, to persuade them it was an invasion and not an exercise.[37] Vice Admiral Nicolopoulos, naval intelligence officer at the Armed Forces Headquarters in Athens, through whom were routed all messages concerning the activities of the Turkish fleet, testified that at about 6am, as intelligence officer in charge, he urgently addressed General Bonanos and asked him to order the dispatch of the Greek fleet's ships.

---

32 *Ibid.*, p. 296.
33 Burke, *art. cit.*
34 Constantinos A. Skiadopoulos, *Πόλεμος στην Κύπρο* [War in Cyprus] (Athens: Eleftheri Skepsi, 1989), p. 32.
35 *Ibid.*, p. 325.
36 *Ibid.*, p. 322.
37 Arapakis, *op. cit.*, p. 182.

"He gave me the following tragic answer: 'The Turks are attacking Cyprus and we are Greece.'"[38]

The Greek military leadership's indifference infuriated the National Guard's Chief of Staff, who "slammed down the receiver in a rage, and, addressing the officers present, said: 'Those guys up there haven't got a clue, give the order to defend ourselves with all means available'."[39] The National Guard finally issued an order to repel the invasion over two hours after it had begun, and without the approval of the Armed Forces Headquarters in Greece. The order from Greece was finally conveyed verbally to the National Guard General Staff one hour later, at 8.15am.

In the meantime, the first troop movements by the National Guard ended in disaster. The 281st Infantry Regiment, which had been moved to Nicosia for the coup from the western tip of Pentadactylos where it was based, was in Athalassa on the morning of 20 July. The regiment was ordered to return to its base in Panagra in full daylight. En route, it was spotted by the Turkish air force outside Kontemenos village and was decimated. Remnants of the regiment reached their destination in disarray on the afternoon of 20 July.[40]

The same fate befell the 286th Mechanised Infantry Regiment, which left the Pancyprian stadium in Nicosia where it was stationed to make its way to the Kyrenia landing points following the Nicosia-Kontemenos-Panagra-Karavas road. The column consisted of 24 BTR personnel carriers, out of the 34 possessed by the regiment. In Kontemenos a lorry of the 281st Infantry Regiment, which had been destroyed three hours earlier by Turkish warplanes, blocked the village road. The first platoon of the regiment, which was an advance column, was bottled up in the village. The column's vehicles, all grouped together, were spotted by a couple of Turkish fighters. They destroyed six BTRs and two or three other vehicles.[41] The regiment's commander, Lieutenant Colonel Georgios Boutos, was seriously injured in the air raid and later died in hospital. Suffering heavy losses, the regiment arrived at Karavas at 4pm on 20 July.[42]

The Turks had landed in territory overseen by the 190th Anti-tank Artillery battalion, based in Acheiropiyitou Monastery on the northern coast of Cyprus. This brigade was responsible for the shore batteries along the length of the coast, from Pachiammos to Karavostasi. According to one soldier, who asked why no guns were placed in the batteries, an officer replied: "We won't be shooting because they (the Turks) won't either."[43] Despite the fact that the regiment was mobilised and that 49 people joined it, neither guns nor uniforms were issued. The commander of the battalion, Major Dokos, apparently stated, "all these are Makarios supporters. They'll turn the guns on us."[44]

Finally, when the trumpeter sounded the alarm at 4.15am, the troops hurried to move the guns to the batteries. The battalion's mission was to establish one battery near the shore, in the Panagra area west of Kyrenia, one in the area where the landing took place at Pente Mili, and one at the beginning of the Karpass Peninsula. Of the 18 artillery pieces in the Brigade's possession, only 12 left the camp at 5.15am, towed by vehicles of 1940 vintage. The remaining six were transferred later, because there were no trailers. The commander

38 *Ibid.*, p. 201.
39 *Ibid.*, p. 185.
40 *Ibid.*, p. 343. Also, Bitos, *op. cit.*, p. 257.
41 Sergis, *op. cit.*, p. 344.
42 *Ibid.*, p. 346.
43 Kyriakides and Prentzas, *op. cit.*, p. 342.
44 *Ibid.*, p. 332.

and some soldiers remained in the camp. When airplanes appeared over the camp, Dokos ordered: "Don't fire unless they fire first."[45] At that moment a plane dived and machine-gunned an army camp in Pentadactylos. "Don't worry. They're blanks (...) they are firing to frighten us," he told his men.[46] There were warehouses in the camp with large reserves of ammunition and weapons, which were destroyed when they were continuously strafed by the air force from 5am until 10.30am.

In the meanwhile, the artillery brigade heading for the Panagra area placed its guns in firing position without any hindrance.[47] The other two, which were heading towards Kyrenia, fell into an ambush set by reconnaissance units that had taken over their battery positions from the evening of 19 July. The Turkish ambushers surprised the first artillery brigade, took its four guns as plunder and its men as prisoners – they are still missing persons to this day. The men from the following artillery brigade, faced with the danger of being taken prisoner, abandoned the guns and escaped on foot towards Pentadactylos.

The other artillery unit in the Kyrenia area was the 182nd Plain Artillery Battalion. The brigade was ordered to move to its rallying point in the Pentadactylos. It left its camp, leaving behind two guns that were immobilised through mechanical failure. On the way it lost another two, this time due to the breakdown of two trailers that had been sent to Paphos during the coup. In total, it lost four of the 12 guns it had before reaching the rallying point at 8.30am. In the meantime, the commander of the battalion had abandoned it and later turned up at the National Guard General Staff.[48]

With Turkey unleashing its assault on Cyprus, the National Guard was falling to pieces. As later emerged, the National Guard General Staff had no serious plan for facing a Turkish invasion. Georgios Grivas drew up the first Cyprus Defence Plan (codenamed 'Aphrodite One') in 1964, when he was commander of the Supreme Military Defence Command, Cyprus. Grivas did not have a reputation as a capable staff officer, and on the two occasions when he planned and executed larger scale military operations in Cyprus, he was a resounding failure. The first was the attack on the Kokkina-Mansoura enclave in 1964, and the second was that against the Turkish Cypriot enclave in Kofinou-Ayios Theodoros in 1967. Apart from its possible operational weaknesses, the 'Aphrodite One' plan depended on the presence of a full Greek division of 10,000 men and heavy weapons. At the beginning of 1968, when the division left, the National Guard General Staff made readjustments to the plan, covering the gap created with regiments of reserves. Thus, the defence of Cyprus was based to a great extent on the successful mobilisation of reserves. In the specific instance, as Georgitsis himself admitted, "mobilisation was a total failure", because it did not occur before the Turkish invasion.[49]

Despite the operational weaknesses of the anachronistic Cyprus Defence Plan, the National Guard General Staff had no choice but to do its best to implement it in order to repulse the Turkish invasion. According to 'Aphrodite One', in the event that Turkey were to transport forces to invade Cyprus, the National Guard General Staff had to declare the mobilisation of its own forces in time "to mop up the internal situation on the island *before* or *during* the repulsion of the landing and with the Nicosia-Agirtas enclave as a priority".[50]

---

45 *Ibid.*, p. 334.
46 *Ibid.*
47 Sergis, *op. cit.*, p. 325.
48 *Ibid.*, p. 309.
49 Greek Parliament, *op. cit.*, p. 57.
50 *Ibid.*, p. 58.

Further, the National Guard would attempt to repulse the landing detachments, with the support of a squadron of F-84F planes, two torpedo boats and a submarine that the Armed Forces Headquarters of Greece would put at its disposal, based upon a reinforcement plan for the defence of Cyprus in the event of invasion, codenamed 'K'. According to the 'K' plan, the F-84F planes would be provided to Cyprus "for a 'once and for all' attack on the landing forces".[51] Since their flying range was limited, after the operation they would land in Cyprus, Rhodes or a neighbouring country. The submarine would be situated in time in Cyprus territorial waters, so as to attack the landing fleet from below the surface. The Greek Contingent "would be kept in reserve and would compose the main counterattacking force against any bridgehead that might be formed (...) on the night of D-Day+1," in this case, the night of 20 to 21 July.[52]

It does not take a military expert to realise the defence plan was totally ineffective due to its failure to take into account Turkey's overwhelming military superiority. When it was drawn up in 1964 - and even when it was revised in 1968 - Turkey hardly had any landing craft. The building up of landing craft began after Turkey's failure to invade in 1967 during the Kofinou operations. Within five years, Turkey had built over 100 landing craft. This development was completely ignored by the commanders of the National Guard. The National Guard General Staff hatched dozens of plans for the assassination or overthrow of Makarios through a coup, and used the greatest part of National Guard forces to destabilise Cyprus internally, while scarcely concerning itself at all with external dangers.

Despite the terror that the imbalance of forces with Turkey ought to have created, the National Guard General Staff hatched an aggressive plan, 'Aphrodite Two', which provided for a surprise attack on the Turks and mopping-up operations against the Turkish Cypriot enclaves across Cyprus. In contrast with 'Aphrodite One', which would be implemented in the event that the Turks took the initiative, 'Aphrodite Two' would take place at the instigation of the National Guard General Staff. The main effort would be directed at wiping out the Nicosia-Agirtas enclave, and the Greek Contingent would be used as the main attack force.[53]

In July 1974, the initiative was entirely in the hands of the Turkish army, which established a bridgehead in Kyrenia even before the National Guard could announce mobilisation. The General Staff should therefore have implemented 'Aphrodite One'. That is, using the infantry units that the plan provided for, supported by tanks and artillery, it should have tried to contain the first landing, while waiting for naval and air support from Greece. Then the Greek Contingent, the only concentrated and battle-worthy reserve force, would attempt a night counterattack to destroy the enemy bridgehead.

The Greek Contingent was made up of 1,200 men. Half of these had replaced those who had completed their service on 19 July, as part of the six-month rotation of forces. The new men were brought to the island on board the troopship *Lesvos*, which sailed into Famagusta harbour, put ashore the fresh troops, took on board the decommissioned ones, and set sail for Greece. Each time there were such replacements, large quantities of ammunition were brought to Cyprus to top up National Guard reserves. This time, however, the ammunition was not unloaded from the *Lesvos* and was taken back to Greece, after an order issued by Bonanos, and conveyed to Cyprus by Lieutenant Colonel Farmakis, who arrived on the island especially for this purpose.[54]

---

51 *Ibid.*
52 Bitos, *op. cit.*, p. 254.
53 *Ibid.*, p. 260.
54 Arapakis, *op. cit.*, p. 217.

A successful counter-attack and destruction of the bridgehead on the evening of 20 July to 21 July was the only serious danger confronting the Turks during the first stages of the invasion. "Our greatest fear was the failure of the first wave of our landing forces through the intervention of the enemy's aerial and naval forces," wrote Bedrettin Demirel, the commander of the 39th Division. "The National Guard had no strong air force or navy. However, it could have been reinforced from Greece."[55]

Yet at such a critical moment, instead of using the Greek Contingent as planned in 'Aphrodite One', the National Guard leadership implemented 'Aphrodite Two' and on the morning of 20 July ordered mopping-up operations against the Turkish enclaves. The Greek Contingent was ordered to attack the Nicosia-Agirtas enclave from the northwest, with the support of tanks, which were ordered to move to the Contingent's camp on the morning of 20 July. Only 13 of the 27 tanks in Nicosia reached the Greek Contingent's camp, the rest remaining at various points in the city to provide security for the regime.[56] Three tanks stood outside the Central Prisons until 10am on 20 July, guarding the thousands of imprisoned Makarios supporters.[57] Of the 13 tanks that reached the Contingent's camp only seven were used in the fighting. The rest, having suffered wear and tear during the coup, remained in camp. According to Georgios Serghis, who studied the reports of the officers who took part in the Cyprus operations, the Greek Contingent's morning attack, "badly planned, without preparation, and poorly executed, could not even be termed an aggressive reconnaissance".[58]

At the same time, the 251st Infantry Regiment in Kyrenia, despite the shock from being bombed, managed to regroup some of its forces and moved with two platoons against the Turkish bridgehead. Of the five tanks that were seconded to the regiment, four were used. The other broke down as it was leaving camp. At about 10am, the commander of the regiment, Pavlos Kouroupis, ordered the attack on the bridgehead,[59] with the remnants of the artillery unit on Pentadactylos joining the battle. As the Turkish forces had gone ashore without meeting any resistance, they were all massed together and devoid of any cover in the landing area; they were taken by surprise and suffered significant losses. As the eyewitness Constantinos Papaellinas, who was in his country residence 200 metres from the landing point, describes, "the Turks were mown down in dozens before our very eyes... The area filled with blood and writhing human bodies. It was obvious that they had not expected to be attacked."[60]

Despite the counter-attack, by midday Turkish ships had managed to land all the men and supplies that they contained and returned for Mersin. The detachment that had landed, using personnel carriers, attempted to broaden the bridgehead and to march on Kyrenia, but was beaten off by a company of the 251st Infantry Regiment. Throughout the afternoon of 20 July there was no significant fighting in the bridgehead area, with only a sporadic exchange of fire.[61] At the end of the first day of the invasion, Turkey had managed to land 6,000 men in Cyprus.[62]

---

55 Demirel, *art. cit.*
56 Sergis, *op. cit.*, p. 366.
57 Bitos, *op. cit.*, p. 212.
58 Sergis, *op. cit.*, p. 378.
59 *Ibid.*, p. 326.
60 Kardianos, *op. cit.*, p. 64.
61 Sergis, *op. cit.*, p. 334.
62 Burke, *art. cit.*

On the evening of 20 July, the Armed Forces Headquarters in Athens – despite the fact that it had not put into action Plan 'K', which provided for reinforcement by naval and aerial forces from Greece – gave the order to the National Guard to wipe out the bridgehead "as a priority, and at any cost".[63] The National Guard General Staff entrusted this mission to the remnants of the 281st Infantry Regiment and the 286th Motorised Infantry Regiment – which had been hit that morning by the Turkish air force in the area of Kontemenos village – as well as to some reserve regiments that had not managed to muster completely (some of them never mustered). The attack was launched at 2am on 21 July, uncoordinated and with no artillery support. At sunrise at 4.39am, the Turkish air force again went into action and the detachments buckled into defensive positions. The counter-attack ended with no chance of success.[64]

According to 'Aphrodite One', this operation should have been carried out by the Greek Contingent, which instead was ordered to carry a new assault on the Nicosia-Agirtas enclave. The greatest part of the units of the Greek Contingent and the National Guard were employed for this operation.[65] In the enclave were seven infantry regiments,[66] while in the first 24 hours it was reinforced by 3,000 parachutists and commandos from Turkey. The balance of forces was 6:1 in favour of the Turks. Despite this, Greek troops managed to penetrate the enclave and arrived within two kilometres of Gonyeli. As Birand writes, that evening the Turks lived through difficult moments, with the General Staff anxiously waiting for daylight, so the Turkish air force could enter the fray.[67] Dawn found the Turks holding their positions, despite the heavy losses they had incurred. In the first light of day, the air force began to pound the Greek positions, and the Greek Contingent was forced to retreat.

The same fate was suffered in the attack carried out on the enclave from the east, in the Boghazi corridor, by commando detachments, which had been transferred from Nicosia - where they were during the coup – to the Pentadactylos area. "The operations [of the commando forces] achieved limited success because here also the attacking force was smaller in number than those defending. Moreover, infantry should have consolidated in the daytime (21 July) the ground gained by the detachments on the night of 20/21 July. But no such forces could have been found, given the mistakes committed by the General Staff," Ioannis Bitos writes.[68]

On the morning of 20 July, attacks were carried out on Turkish enclaves in the rest of Cyprus, both by organised National Guard units as well as by reservist regiments made up of members of EOKA B. One such regiment was the 203rd Reservist Regiment, whose commander was EOKA B cadre Michael Kalogeropoulos-Diakos. It attacked the Limassol enclave and put it out of action. An EOKA B reservist regiment also mopped up the Larnaca enclave. Extremist EOKA B leaders, acting indiscriminately, attacked insignificant enclaves and isolated Turkish villages and brought them under their control.

In Paphos, the troop carrier *Lesvos*, which was carrying the decommissioned Greek Contingent troops back to Greece, also got involved in the operation to wipe out the town's Turkish Cypriot enclave. When the invasion began, the *Lesvos* was sailing in open waters off Limassol. Its captain Eleftherios Handrinos received an order to put the troops ashore at

63 Bitos, *op. cit.*, p. 269.
64 Sergis, *op. cit.*, p. 355.
65 Bitos, *op. cit.*, p. 269.
66 Sergis, *op. cit.*, p. 255.
67 Birand, *op. cit.*, pp. 151-154.
68 Bitos, *op. cit.*, p. 255.

Paphos. The *Lesvos* anchored off Paphos at 3pm and with small boats put ashore the 450 men that it was carrying. The operation was complete by 5pm. The 4th Supreme Tactical Command also asked the captain of the *Lesvos* to provide back-up with its guns in the operation against the enclave. Handrinos accepted, and in the space of one hour the guns of the *Lesvos* had fired about 900 shells at the Moutalas settlement. Afterwards, it set sail for Greece.[69]

In contrast with the southern and western enclaves, which were mopped up, other such operations failed. The most powerful enclave, that of Nicosia held firm, despite initial gains made by its attackers. The Jaous enclave merely shrank to about half of its size. That of Galinopornis held firm, as did those of Famagusta, Louroujina, Kokkina and Limnitis.[70]

The attacks against the enclaves were the most serious error committed by the National Guard General Staff, and had grave military and political consequences, equal in degree to those of the coup. According to Ioannis Bitos, the National Guard General Staff "divided its efforts three ways (against the Nicosia-Agirtas enclave, where the Greek troops attacked, the Boghazi-Kotsa Kayia corridor, and against the Kyrenia bridgehead). In this manner, nowhere did the National Guard have sufficient forces, resulting in failure in all three attempts."[71] The attacks on the enclaves, most of which were in built-up areas, made all the Turkish Cypriots rally round Turkish troops. Bitos, in his book *From the Green Line to the Two Attilas*, which is based on confidential service reports of officers serving in Cyprus in the summer of 1974, attributes the assaults on the Turkish Cypriot enclaves to a mix-up. "The National Guard General Staff (...) confused the plans and implemented Aphrodite Two in its most unfortunate variation."[72] Nevertheless, the then head of the National Guard General Staff, Michael Georgitsis, who executed the coup plan so impeccably, is unlikely to have committed such a serious mistake as to confuse such clear plans. As the former commander of the 3rd Supreme Tactical Command, which was in charge of organising the defences in the Kyrenia area, he would have been informed in detail about the defence plans, and was unlikely to have committed such a gross blunder. In reality, the attack on Turkish Cypriot enclaves was a pre-planned operation. The British journalist Harry Gibbons publishes in his book, *The Genocide Files*, extracts from documents found in army camps occupied in 1974 by the Turkish army, according to which there was a plan with the nickname 'Hephaestus 1974', which was described as an internal security operation and provided for mopping-up operations against Turkish Cypriot villages. According to Gibbons, documents linked to the 'Hephaestus' plan bear the signatures of Michael Georgitsis and Charalambos Chios, commander of the 5th Supreme Tactical Command, based in Morphou.[73]

Gibbons, however, is a recruit of the Turkish propaganda machine. In his book, which was published and is distributed free of charge by the Denktash regime, he attempts to interpret these documents in such a way as to back up with evidence the Turkish scenario concerning a wider plan for the genocide of the Turkish Cypriots, in which the National Guard, the Makarios government and the Greek Cypriots as a whole are all involved.

Actually, the 'Hephaestus' plan began to be conceived from March 1974, at the same time as the hatching of the coup plan 'Aphrodite Three'. Georgios Serghis, who studied the army archives, and spoke with officers who took part in the events, says 'Hephaestus' was

---

69 Sergis, *op. cit.*, p. 397.
70 Bitos, *op. cit.*, p. 242.
71 *Ibid.*, p. 260.
72 *Ibid.*
73 Harry Scott Gibbons, *The Genocide Files* (London: Charles Bravos Publishers, 1997), p. 408.

part of 'Aphrodite Three'.[74] The elaboration of the 'Hephaestus' plan took some months. For the Morphou area, Charalambos Chios sent his final orders to the commanders on 3 July: "Units are to proceed with the necessary adjustments to the plans that concern their operational sectors, and return them to me by 10 July 1974."[75]

The Turkish assault on Cyprus not only took Nicosia by surprise, but Athens too. As soon as Turkey's National Security Council had given the green light for the invasion, the Greek ambassador was summoned to the Turkish Foreign Ministry and informed. The Greek ambassador conveyed the message to Foreign Minister Constantinos Kypraios, and he in his turn briefed Prime Minister Androutsopoulos. Both sought out Ioannides, but could not find him and so turned to his confidant, Charalambos Palainis, who eventually found him as day was breaking and notified him by telephone that the Turks were landing in Cyprus. "He was stunned: 'Surely,' he said, 'The Turks can't be in Cyprus; who told you this?'" According to Palainis, from that moment onwards, Ioannides was "like a man who learns something that he never, ever expected, such as his child betraying him, say, or something shocking or tragic".[76]

The regime's leadership gathered early in the morning. At about six in the morning, they were joined by US ambassador Henry Tasca and Greek-speaking Lieutenant Colonel Evert Marder. Tasca met with all the high-ranking members of the regime, including Ioannides, and attempted to persuade them not to react militarily to the Turkish invasion. Bonanos writes that Tasca told him: "Chief, Sir, don't go to war and I promise to stop the Turks."[77] Ioannides then entered Bonanos' office and argued with Tasca, telling him that Greece demanded an immediate ceasefire from the Turks, and the immediate withdrawal of Turkish forces from Cyprus, or else "we shall proclaim *Enosis* and declare war on Turkey".[78]

The regime convened a meeting of the Supreme National Defence Council, also known as the War Council, for 8am. At 7am, the chiefs of the services, Galatsanos, Papanikolaou and Arapakis gathered in Bonanos' office for a preliminary meeting. At the end of the meeting, Joseph Sisco and his entourage entered the room unannounced. The American Assistant Secretary of State had just arrived from Ankara and had rushed to Armed Forces HQ (also known as the Pentagon) to persuade the military leadership not to react the Turkish invasion, maintaining Greece would lose the war and get involved in adventures. According to Petros Arapakis, Chief of Naval Forces, Ioannides reacted angrily to Sisco's advice. He had rushed to Bonanos' office on hearing of Sisco's arrival. "Clearly shaken, he got up and shouted: 'you cheated us. We shall declare war'."[79]

Ioannides' outburst is considered proof of the assurances he had received from the United States that Turkey would not react to the coup against Makarios. In fact, as Ioannides' close confidant Palainis testifies, the CIA had advised the leadership of the Armed Forces not to take any military precautions as this would provoke Turkey. Palainis recalls that on the eve of the invasion there was a constant flow of information about Turkish military movements, but Ioannides brushed aside any suggestion of reaction.

---

74 Georgios Sergis, conversation with he author.
75 Gibbons, *op. cit.*, p. 414.
76 Charalambos Palainis, interview with Alexis Papahelas, broadcast by Mega Greece on 5 June 2001.
77 Bonanos, *op. cit.*, p. 242.
78 Tasca to Secretary of State, "Cyprus coup", NARA, NPMS, NSC, Cyprus/Greece, telegram 4664, Athens, 20 July 1974.
79 Arapakis, *op. cit.*, p. 146.

"Ioannides used to say that there wasn't going to be a Turkish invasion of Cyprus. If Greece were to mobilise troops, however, this would then provide a pretext for Turkey to invade." According to Palainis, Ioannides quoted assurances received from the United States, with whom he was in contact through the Greek-American CIA agent Petros Avrakotos.[80] The Head of the Armed Forces Georgios Bonanos adopted the same position. According to Arapakis, Bonanos continually assured that there would be no Turkish reaction, that there was no reason for anxiety and that no preparations or action was required, nor was it permitted.[81]

After the row between Sisco and Ioannides, the American delegation withdrew from Armed Forces Headquarters. At about 8am the War Council began meeting. As the Greek Parliament's Committee on the Cyprus File later learned, at the meeting, which was attended by a large number of officers "many slogans in favour of war, *Enosis* etc. could be heard". Ioannides, however, said: "We shall announce that we shall implement the *Enosis* of Cyprus with Greece, but we shan't do it, just saying this to frighten the Turks, to show them our determination."[82] Finally, the War Council decided to proclaim a general mobilisation, to make recourse to the UN Security Council and to recall the Greek ambassador from NATO headquarters in Brussels. What was not decided was an immediate assault on the Turkish landing expedition. As Arapakis writes: "the war council did not want an attack on enemy troops."[83]

After the meeting, Bonanos again received US ambassador Tasca and briefed him on developments. The Americans now began directly consulting the Head of the Armed Forces, by-passing the government, which was under Ioannides' thumb. The dictator was not only no longer useful, he was becoming dangerous. The Americans thus withdrew their confidence in him and imposed their policy through Bonanos. The Head of the Armed Forces had long-standing contacts with Tasca, as well as with the Greek-speaking colonels Evert Marder and Frank Athanson. The latter – who was of Greek-American origin and served in the Joint US Military Aid Group, Greece (JUSMAGG) – asked Bonanos to install an echelon of the American embassy at Armed Forces Headquarters so as to follow the situation from close up.[84]

Through JUSMAGG, the CIA exercised effective control within the Greek army and organised and funded anti-communist activity in the country. Corresponding channels of intervention also existed in Turkey. General Kemal Yamak, Head of the Special Warfare Department,[85] handled the general coordination of the Turkish invasion of Cyprus. Yamak was present in all the bodies that shaped Turkish policy. He linked with the Foreign Ministry through the Head of the Greece and Cyprus Desk, Edjmel Baroutdjou.[86] In this way, the United States had access to developments in both Greece and Turkey and could control the overall situation.

In cooperation with his British counterpart James Callaghan, Kissinger undertook an initiative to find a political compromise in Cyprus, based on the new *fait accompli* created on the ground. In effect, the US was promoting the 'constitutional solution' that they had

---

80 Palainis interview with Alexis Papahelas.
81 Arapakis, *op. cit.*, p. 175.
82 Greek Parliament, *op. cit.*, p. 110.
83 Arapakis, *op. cit.*, p. 187.
84 Bonanos, *op. cit.*, p. 252.
85 Baroutdjou, *art. cit.*
86 *Ibid.*

agreed before the invasion, which provided for the restoration of constitutional order in Cyprus, with the appointment of Clerides as president. Within the framework of this policy, Britain called for a conference of the guarantor powers in London and sent invitations to Greece and Turkey to take part.

The US undersecretary of State Robert Ingersoll informed Sisco that Callaghan now supported the US plan for the Clerides solution. "Callaghan recognises that the return of Makarios is very unlikely, and accepts our view that we should put all our efforts into an agreed solution, in which Clerides would play an important part."[87]

The US ambassador in Nicosia, Roger Davies, had been in contact with Clerides since 19 July.[88] In the course of these contacts, Clerides submitted some ideas to the Americans. In a note, Ingersoll asked Davies to meet Clerides again and make it known to him that "we are in agreement with some of his ideas". He added that he was especially concerned that Clerides should know that "in no circumstance should he resign from the office of President of the House of Representatives".[89] This was because Washington wanted to legitimise a Clerides presidency. According to the constitution, the President of the House succeeded the elected president if he died or was in any way unable to exercise his duties.

Kissinger also was in contact with Clerides through ambassador Davies between 19 and 20 July. At daybreak on 20 July, when the Turkish invasion had already begun, the US ambassador sent Kissinger the following message: "I have contacted Clerides and conveyed your message, for which he is very grateful. He will not take any action until the situation is clarified."[90] The precise content of Clerides' consultations with US diplomats is not known, as the relevant telegrams are not included in the documents of the Kissinger archives, which have been declassified. Clerides himself, in his four-volume work, *My Deposition*, devotes just a few lines to the background to Sampson's succession. Nevertheless, it is obvious that the consultations were linked to the question of Clerides taking over as president, in the framework of a broader Greco-Turkish agreement.

On the morning of 20 July, Kissinger sent a telegram to the US ambassador in Ankara, Macawber, giving him instructions to meet immediately with Ecevit and convey to him the "extremely emphatic view of the United States", that the Turkish military intervention in Cyprus would have very serious consequences on the Alliance and would put in jeopardy the security of the "free world". Macawber conveyed to Ecevit the following message from Kissinger: "Now that what has happened has happened, the most pressing is to restore peace and stability to the region". To this end, the United States was ready in advance to support a "constitutional solution" and the restoration of the balance of forces that had prevailed before the coup. "In our opinion, the only road to restoring a constitutional government is through the legitimate succession of Clerides. No other solution is possible, or accepted, by the Greeks." According to Kissinger's message, Ecevit, in talks with Sisco, showed he was not especially concerned with who should be the leader of the Cypriot state; for this reason, "Sisco is on his way to Athens to propose the Clerides solution to the Greeks".[91]

---

87 Ingersoll to Sisco, "Cyprus", NARA, NPMS, NSC, Cyprus/Greece, telegram 157947, Department of State, 20 July 1974.

88 "Με προειδοποίησαν αι Η.Π.Α." [The U.S. Warned Me], *Phileleftheros*, 13 July 1975.

89 Ingersoll to Sisco, "Cyprus: Glafcos Clerides", NARA, NPMS, NSC, Cyprus/Greece, telegram 157921, Department of State, 20 July 1974.

90 Davies to Secretary of State, "Cyprus: Glafcos Clerides", NARA, NPMS, NSC, Cyprus/Greece, telegram 1553, Nicosia 20 July 1974.

91 Ingersoll to Mocomber, "Cyprus", NARA, NPMS, NSC, Cyprus/Greece, telegram 157937, Department of State, 20 July 1974.

Ingersoll sent a similar message to Tasca in Athens for him to convey to Gizikis, while it was explicitly mentioned that a copy be given to Ioannides. The message stated that the events in Cyprus had brought the Atlantic Alliance close to the most serious crisis in its history. "It is not the time for us to seek the causes of this tragic situation. We must deal with the facts."

For this reason: "We address you as allies so that we can prevent the situation worsening further, and we can unite in our endeavours to arrive at an agreed solution. The only forces to gain from further quarrelling will be those of the communists, who will see the situation as an opportunity to gain benefits they never before dreamed of obtaining."

Further on, Ingersoll said that Britain, as a guarantor power, had summoned the governments of Greece and Turkey to sit down at negotiations in order to find a peaceful solution to the problem. "I give you my assurances that the United States of America will put all her powers at the disposal of these talks in order to secure a just and stable balance in Cyprus."[92]

Ingersoll sent yet another message to Sisco, that he should meet the Prime Minister and Foreign Minister of Greece, and seek the acceptance of the 'Clerides solution'. "It is probable that Ecevit rejected the Clerides proposal at the beginning because he saw it as a possible obstacle to the Turkish military intervention. However, now that the Turks have intervened, he has told you that he does not especially care about who will be the President of Cyprus. Under these conditions, we believe that there is still a possibility, albeit a faint one, of attempting the 'Clerides Solution' one more time."

As to the arguments he would use, Ingersoll suggested to Sisco: "You should tell the Greeks that, since they bear a huge part of the responsibility for what happened, we expect them to understand that, if they are not prepared to accept changes in the territorial integrity and structure of Cyprus, then they must join with the United States, Britain and Turkey in finding a constitutional solution to the Cyprus problem. As we see it, only Clerides provides an acceptable alternative solution and we are prepared to the support this proposal to Turkey."[93]

Meanwhile in Athens, with the War Council still in session, alternate Foreign Minister Constantinos Kypraios summoned Sisco to the Foreign Ministry and read him a text in which Greece demanded that Turkey immediately cease military operations and concentrate all the troops it had landed in Cyprus on Turkish Cypriot enclaves by 2pm.

Sisco told Kypraios that the United States wanted the immediate cessation of hostilities in Cyprus and for Greece and Turkey to meet in London to negotiate a constitutional solution. He told him these were the instructions he had received and that the US would work towards an urgent implementation of these two aims. "In the eyes of the world, Greece, wrongly or rightly, has a certain responsibility for this situation. With the exception of the US, she is isolated. Neither the US nor Greece wish to give the Soviet Union the opportunity of fishing in these disturbed waters," Sisco told Kypraios, adding that he had received instructions from the President to stop the bloodshed, to begin the negotiating process and to pressure the Greek government into not initiating military action that would render his initiative futile.

Sisco then consulted with Kissinger by telephone and worked with Kypraios on drawing up a new text for Greece's proposal to Turkey for a ceasefire: "The Turkish government

---

92 Ingersoll to Tasca, "Presidential Message to Gizikis", NARA, NPMS, NSC, Cyprus/Greece, telegram 157945, Department of State, 20 July 1974.

93 Ingersoll to Sisco, "Cyprus", NARA, NPMS, NSC, Cyprus/Greece, telegram 157939, Department of State, 20 July 1974.

agrees to cease all war activity immediately and not to land other weaponry, ammunition, military materiel or personnel on the island. The government of Turkey agrees that by ... hour, all the Turkish forces that landed on Cyprus from 5.45am on 20 July will be concentrated in the Turkish enclaves. Greece and Turkey agree each to send a representative to London to enter into talks between the guarantor powers, in the spirit of the London-Zurich Agreements."[94]

Turkey was unlikely to agree to such a text, but for Sisco this proposal was a good start to gain precious time. After assuring Athens that he would make every effort to persuade Ankara to accept the Greek proposal, he asked the Greek government to show self-restraint and not to undertake any military action whatsoever, so as to facilitate his mission.

Sisco asked for permission from the Turkish authorities to fly to Ankara. Seeking to exploit the advantage gained from landing forces in Cyprus, Turkey was working to achieve all the military goals it had set itself before accepting any ceasefire. Citing security reasons, Sisco's request was rejected, upon which the American envoy ordered his pilot to take off from Athens and while in flight simply to inform the Turkish authorities that he was heading for Ankara.

One hour after his arrival, Sisco met with the Foreign Minister and then with Ecevit. As he wrote in a telegram to Kissinger, he wasted no time on courtesies but went straight to the substance: "I told him that immediately after the last conversation we had, a short while before the operation against Cyprus began, you gave me instructions to go to Athens and meet with the Greek leadership. While talking to them I had in mind continually that which Ecevit had requested from the United States, specifically, to use our influence to persuade the Greeks 'not to shoot'."

Referring to what he had heard from the Greeks, Sisco told Ecevit that they had started the discussion by threatening to declare war and proclaim *Enosis* unless the Turks withdrew immediately. But, "the United States government has persuaded the Greeks to postpone the declaration of war for a while". However, "they will not wait long". It was of the utmost importance for Turkey, the United States, NATO and the future stability of the region that "operations cease and dialogue begins", he insisted.

Sisco then handed Ecevit a copy of the Greek ceasefire proposal. Ecevit replied that from the moment a military operation began, it couldn't simply be halted immediately. "Certain objectives have been set, and they must be achieved," he said. Ecevit made it clear to Sisco that nothing could be done that evening and that the next day he would meet with the generals and the Council of Ministers to discuss his proposal. He said he was "a mere politician and could not decide alone on Turkey's behalf".

Sisco raised his voice: "I told Ecevit that he had asked the United States to allow Turkey to act in her own way (rather than pressure the Turkish government into not fighting, as in 1964), that he had asked the US to put pressure on Greece not to get involved in hostile activity, and that he had said that, since the Turkish forces were achieving a balance with those of Greece in Cyprus, the Turkish government would be prepared to initiate a dialogue with Britain and the Greeks in the spirit of the London-Zurich agreements. All this has come and gone. We supposed that Ecevit was speaking on behalf of Turkey and we expected that Turkey would agree to a ceasefire before the Greek government took hostile action."

---

94 Sisco to Secretary of State, "Cyprus", NARA, NPMS, NSC, Cyprus/Greece, telegram 4667, Athens, 20 July 1974.

Sisco told Ecevit the US had the right to expect that he "would keep his word and will do as he said". If Turkey "does not respond positively to our approach, the most serious consequences could blight the close relations between the United States and Turkey, including American military aid."

According to Sisco's note, his reference to the fact that the US had fulfilled all its promises to Turkey and the threat of severance of military aid shocked Ecevit, who promised he would have an immediate meeting with the military and the Council of Ministers, and that he would meet with him again later that same night.[95]

In Cyprus, within the bridgehead, the situation for the Turkish troops was desperate. Their goal – the occupation of Kyrenia and the link-up of the landing group with the Nicosia-Agirtas enclave – had not been met. The detachments that had landed had no contact with the General Staff in Turkey. The troops were exhausted after the sea journey, and had had no sleep or food for almost 48 hours. The summer heat was unbearable and they were facing a serious dehydration problem. On the evening of 20 July, their commander, Colonel Karaoglanoglu, was killed by a mortar shell and morale took serious blow. Furthermore, information had reached the Turkish general staff that Greek troops were landing in Paphos. Turkish Cypriot fighters holed up in Paphos castle had observed the landing of Greek Contingent troops from the *Lesbos* and sent the information to TMT headquarters. When the troop ship began to fire on Moutalos, the Turkish Cypriots sent a message to their command in Nicosia that "Greek warships are carrying out a landing in Paphos. They are firing on us with machine guns. If we do not get help in a short while, we shall surrender". The Turkish Nicosia command replied: "Defend yourselves for a few more hours. We are seeing to the provision of effective air support."[96]

On the morning of 21 July, the Turkish General Staff ordered the commanders of the anti-torpedo boats *Kotsiatepe*, *Antatepe* and *Tsiakmak*, which were off the northern coasts of Cyprus, to sail to the Paphos region to cut off the "Greek landing fleet". Later, Turkish airplanes carrying out reconnaissance flights off Paphos, mistook the Turkish ships for Greek ships that had hoisted the Turkish flag as a trick. Believing Greece had mobilised forces to defend Cyprus, and taking into consideration the adverse condition of the landing group, Turkey decided to negotiate a ceasefire that would give her plenty of time to regroup her forces. The Turkish Foreign Minister called Sisco to his office and delivered a written proposal from Ecevit, saying Turkey was prepared to implement the UN Security Council resolution of 20 July that called on the parties involved to observe a ceasefire. "As soon as the United States government gives us an assurance that Greece will honour and observe the ceasefire, as provided for in the resolution, I shall convene the Council of Ministers to take a decision on this matter," Ecevit's proposal said. Turkey was setting one more condition: "This time, as a demonstration of good will on their part, we would wish the Greek warships heading for Cyprus to direct their course far from the island and avoid entering waters that we have declared to be 'a danger zone' around Cyprus." Sisco informed Kissinger in Washington and Tasca in Athens of the Turkish demands. He then left for Athens to negotiate the ceasefire agreement with the Greek government.[97]

As soon as he received the call from Sisco, Tasca went unannounced to Prime Minister Androutsopoulos' office, briefed him on the Turkish proposal and asked for assurances that

---

95 Sisco to Secretary of State, "Cyprus", NARA, NPMS, NSC, Cyprus/Greece, telegram 5745, Ankara, 20 July 1974.

96 Sergis, *op. cit.*, p. 397.

97 Sisco to Secretary of State, NARA, NPMS, NSC, Cyprus/Greece, telegram 5753, Anakara, 21 July 1974.

Greek ships would either keep their distance from Cyprus, or would return. He also conveyed to him the Turkish threat that if the ships entered the danger zone, they would be sunk.[98]

Androutsopoulos conveyed the message to the military, and at 10.25am he rang Tasca to tell him the Greek government agreed to the ceasefire. He proposed, in fact, that it come into force in half an hour, at 11am. As to the ships, "their course to Cyprus will be halted at the time of the ceasefire". According to Androutsopoulos, "the Greek government will not issue any order to the armed forces to revise or abandon their plans". After this warning, Androutsopoulos told Tasca "in private" that there were no Greek ships anywhere near Cyprus.[99]

Tasca informed the US ambassador in Ankara, Macomber, that Greece accepted the conditions of the agreement. Macomber hurried to the Prime Minister's office and told Ecevit that Greece agreed to an immediate ceasefire, accepted the British invitation for talks in London and consented to a change in course of its ships that were sailing to Cyprus. The Turks, however, had no faith in the assurances given by the Greeks. Ecevit told Macomber the Greeks were making fools of both Turkey and the United States, and that "the Greek flotilla was ready to disembark in Cyprus". He also said "the Turkish army has been authorised to open fire on the ships as soon as they reach the point of no return," and that this "would occur at any time".[100]

At the same time news arrived in Ankara of the message that Ioannides had conveyed to Sisco, namely that there was no Greek fleet sailing towards Cyprus. "If the Turks see Greek ships in the danger zone around Cyprus, tell them to sink them," was the precise message.[101] In the presence of Ecevit, Macomber phoned Kissinger and briefed him on what the Turkish Prime Minister had told him. Macomber then handed the receiver to Ecevit, for him to talk to Kissinger in person:

"Ecevit: We have a problem. We doubt the reliability of Greece. The word of honour of Ioannides is a joke. We have now figured out what the joke is behind his words. He said that we could fire on any ships bearing Greek flags. His ships are bearing Turkish flags!

Kissinger: Well, nobody can blame you if you sink your own ships.

Ecevit: No, Dr Kissinger, they are not our own ships. They are Greek ships. They are Greek ships bearing Turkish flags.

Kissinger: Yes, Mr Prime Minister, but you can sink them if they are not your ships but are flying Turkish flags.

Ecevit: They are using two tricks. We are NATO allies and the Greek pilots know our codes. They speak Turkish, and call our pilots in Turkish using our code words. We can no longer rely on the words of Greece.

Kissinger: What is it that you want? I know you are an intelligent man – I know that from the days of Harvard. With all due respect, I cannot take this. This can go on for six weeks on this basis.

98 Tasca to Secretary of State, "Cyprus: GOG Informed of GOT readiness to accept ceasefire", NARA, NPMS, NSC, Cyprus/Greece, telegram 4720, Athens, 21 July 1974.

99 Tasca to Secretary of State, "Cyprus", NARA, NPMS, NSC, Cyprus/Greece, telegram 4722, Athens 21 July 1974.

100 Macomber to Sisco, "Cyprus Coup", NARA, NPMS, NSC, Cyprus/Greece, telegram 5763, Ankara 21 July 1974.

101 *Ibid.*

Ecevit: They say that they want an armistice. It has become obvious that they want to exploit the ceasefire to mass troops on the islands. The Greeks must cease these methods.
Kissinger: What methods should they cease?
Ecevit: They say that they are ready for a ceasefire. They have already shown us the tricks that they will use to violate the ceasefire.
Kissinger: Are you telling me that you will not accept a ceasefire?
Ecevit: We will accept a ceasefire.
Kissinger: Today?
Ecevit: We are in the middle of discussing the problem now."[102]

At 3.50pm on 21 July, the Director General of the Turkish Foreign Ministry informed the United States embassy that the Turkish air force had just bombed three Greek ships.[103] The *Kotsiatepe* was sunk, and 54 of its 230-man crew drowned. Israeli and British ships in the area picked up the survivors. The remaining two Turkish anti-torpedo boats suffered serious damage.

While Turkey was blackmailing Greece with the threat of sinking the "Greek landing fleet", to dissuade her from joining the fray, Ioannides was trying to blackmail the United States. On 21 July, at 7.30am, during the routine meeting of the military leadership, the decision was taken that, if the bombings did not cease within an hour, the Greek government would announce at 10am its withdrawal from NATO and declare war on Turkey. Alternate Foreign Minister Constantinos Kypraios phoned Tasca with the information. The American ambassador, considering this to be a very serious development, asked for an urgent meeting with Gizikis, who saw him immediately. Gizikis told Tasca that the withdrawal from NATO would be announced at 10am and that at midday the Prime Minister would speak on the radio and television to explain to the Greek people why Greece was taking this step. He continued by stating that they had taken this decision to free themselves from their contractual obligations to NATO. As soon as this freedom was achieved, Gizikis told Tasca, "Greece would be free to take whatever decisions it considered vital to its national interest". The US ambassador warned Gizikis that the withdrawal from NATO would isolate Greece and would have negative repercussions on the US attempt to negotiate a ceasefire. He also asked for time to inform the President and the Secretary of State before Greece announced such a serious decision.[104] It is not known what steps the US took, but the announcement to withdraw from NATO never took place. Shortly after, the Council of Ministers unanimously rejected the proposal. According to Bonanos, the Interior Minister, former Army Chief Vasileios Tsoumbas, played a leading role in this decision.[105]

The regime's plan to withdraw from NATO was linked to its decision to activate 'Plan K' and send forces to Cyprus. On the morning of 21 July, Ioannides called a meeting with Gizikis, Bonanos, Androutsopoulos and Defence Minister Latsoudis, and announced to them his decision to send reinforcements to Cyprus and involve Greece in the operations.

---

102 Kissinger, *op. cit.*, p. 240.

103 Macomber to Secretary of State, "Cyprus Coup", NARA, NPMS, NSC, Cyprus/Greece, telegram 5778, Ankara, 21 July 1974.

104 Tasca to Secretary of State, "Cyprus - Ambassador's meeting with president Ghizikis", NARA, NPMS, NSC, Cyprus/Greece, telegram 4716, Athens, 21 July 1974.

105 Bonanos, *op. cit.*, p. 268.

Bonanos accepted, but with the proviso that the Services' Chiefs would agree. Immediately afterwards, he summoned the chiefs of the three armed services – Navy, Army and Air Force – as well as their deputies, and informed them of the decision.[106] According to Arapakis, all the chiefs expressed grave reservations as to the chances of winning a war with Turkey, while invoking the dangers the country would face from the north. During those days, various Western sources, with the contribution of Greek KYP, misled the Junta with false information of a significant deployment of Warsaw Pact forces towards the Greco-Bulgarian border.[107]

Thus, the chiefs of the services, taking into consideration the "threat" from Bulgaria, the tactical situation in Cyprus, the capabilities and intentions of Turkey, and mainly the threat of the Turkish armed forces (army and navy), which were concentrated in the Izmir region, refused to give their consent.[108]

Bonanos accepted their views without hesitation: "We cannot, therefore, declare war," he stated, and he intended to inform Ioannides and Gizikis. As Bonanos writes, he had already come to the decision that "Greece would only get involved in a war with Turkey as a result of the latter attacking her at some point of our ethnic territory. Under no circumstances, except those involving an insult to our national honour, would I have been disposed to involve the country in the adventure of a war."[109] Bonanos did not consider Cyprus to be a part of the Greek ethnic territory and thus the invasion did not wound national pride. Before the invasion, however, the Junta had justified its intervention in Cyprus with the theory of the national centre, according to which Athens was the centre of Hellenism, and Nicosia, as a province, had to obey, since Greece could not remain idle in the event of Turkish intervention

After the meeting was over, Bonanos ordered the deputy chiefs to withdraw, and remained alone with Arapakis, Papanicolaou and Galatsanos. The four of them had a lengthy discussion, which lasted until 1pm and concluded with the decision to free themselves from Ioannides. According to Arapakis and Bonanos, at that meeting there was a tacit agreement to hand over power to the politicians.[110] This was the "Generals' Coup".

Arapakis writes that after the generals' meeting was over, Bonanos asked him to stay behind and ordered him to recall the two submarines that were on their way to Cyprus, on the grounds that the Aegean islands had to be covered. Arapakis sent a signal to the submarines *Glafkos* and *Nireus*, which halted their course for Cyprus and turned back. When they received the signal, the *Glafkos* was 140 nautical miles from Kyrenia and 130 from Rhodes, while the *Nireus* was 164 from Kyrenia and 100 from Rhodes.[111]

While Arapakis was giving this order, the Turkish follow-up force or second landing operation, had already set sail from Mersin and was heading for Cyprus. At the head of the landing detachment was the Commander of the 39th Division, Bedrettin Demirel.[112] The detachment was made up of 500 men, while the transport craft were carrying another 15 tanks, as well as fuel for the 15 that had gone ashore the first time and had used up their stocks. The follow-up force was to arrive in Cyprus in about 20 hours. General Demirel's task was to regroup the Turkish forces that were squeezed into the bridgehead, to occupy

106 Arapakis, *op. cit.*, p. 221.
107 Sergis, *op. cit.*, pp. 470-473.
108 *Ibid.*, p. 473.
109 Bonanos, *op. cit.*, p. 268.
110 Arapakis, *op. cit.*, p. 235, and Bonanos, *op. cit.*, p. 271.
111 *Ibid.*, p. 211.
112 Demirel, *art. cit.*

Kyrenia and to march on the interior. At the same time, the Turkish forces that were in the Nicosia enclave were to move towards the coast to link up with the bridgehead.

To facilitate the landing of the follow-up force, the Turkish air force and anti-torpedo boats from the sea were to strike at Greek Cypriot villages on the northern slope of Pentadactylos relentlessly from 5pm until sunset. At the same time, transport planes and helicopters continued to drop parachutists and move commandos for the further strengthening of the enclave.

On the evening of 21 July, Gizikis called the generals to his office. With Ioannides also present, they discussed sending air and naval reinforcements to Cyprus. The generals probably did not yet feel powerful enough openly to disagree with Ioannides. Nevertheless, they invoked security problems and refused to approve the involvement of the air force and navy in the Cyprus crisis.[113] Finally, the generals decided to send an infantry regiment, a commando regiment and one of medium tanks. The Armed Forces Headquarters requisitioned the vehicle ferry *Rethymnon*, which took on board the 537 Infantry Regiment and a regiment of tanks, as well as approximately 500 Cypriot volunteers, mainly EOKA B supporters, who were organised into four companies under the former Commando Commander, Colonel Papapostolou. The *Rethymnon* set sail from Piraeus for Cyprus on the evening of 21 July.

On the same evening, Greece airlifted a regiment of commandos using 15 NORATLAS planes. The operation ended in total failure. The aircraft were identified as Turkish by the National Guard, which opened fire with anti-aircraft batteries. The mission's first aeroplane was shot down by friendly fire a little before it landed at Nicosia airport. Four members of the crew and 28 commandos were killed. Only one survived.

The decision to send reinforcements, however, was of little real substance. The generals, who had agreed from midday to rid themselves of their dependency on Ioannides, were already working with Sisco. The American envoy returned from Ankara on the evening of 21 July and went directly to Armed Forces Headquarters, where, at 11am, he met Bonanos and Arapakis, who had just returned from the meeting with Gizikis and Ioannides. As Sisco mentioned in his telegram to Washington, Bonanos was worried about the delay in securing a ceasefire, and asked Sisco to continue his efforts, "before it is too late". "I am convinced, more than ever before, that he (Bonanos) is a true man of peace, and that he will continue to pursue a policy of moderation," Sisco wrote to Kissinger.[114]

Sisco left military headquarters and went to the US embassy, where he consulted with Kissinger by telephone. The instructions he received were to secure a ceasefire at any cost. Kissinger phoned Ecevit and persuaded him to accept the agreement. Subsequently, he informed Sisco that Ecevit accepted in principle the US proposal for a ceasefire, to take effect from 4pm the following day. "I attempted to convey this promise to the Greek government, but it was impossible to find anyone. I sought the Prime Minister, the Foreign Minister and Ioannides," Sisco wrote. He eventually communicated with Bonanos, who told him there was no cause for worry as he would find them in the morning.[115] At 1.50, Sisco communicated with Arapakis, who was at Armed Forces Headquarters. The Navy Chief, after securing some form of political cover from Foreign Minister Kypraios, negotiated with Sisco the text of the truce agreement that would come into effect the next day.

---

[113] Arapakis, *op. cit.*, p. 235.

[114] Sisco to Secretary of State, "Conversation with GOC officials", NARA, NPMS, NSC, Cyprus/Greece, telegram 4756, Athens 22 July 1974.

[115] *Ibid.*

While the generals were working out the ceasefire agreement, Ioannides was trying to impose his decision to send forces to Cyprus. Sampson's coupist government, which was at National Guard campaign headquarters, was also pressing for Greek reinforcements. It was situated in a mineshaft that had been converted into a command post by the British during World War II, in the Malounda area west of Nicosia. Sampson and his minister, Pantelis Dimitriou, a personal friend of Ioannides, were in continuous contact with Armed Forces Headquarters in Greece and were making desperate appeals for help.

Finally, information reached National Guard General Staff that it had been decided to activate plan 'K'. The Greek air force was to destroy the bridgehead, and the navy would sink the landing fleet. From the morning of 22 July, CyBC radio began to broadcast slogans such as: "Greeks of Cyprus, the great hour has arrived!" and "Our national dreams, our age-old aspiration, will now be fulfilled!" "We knew that at 11am our submarines and aeroplanes, coming from Athens, would hit enemy forces. It is for that reason that, from the morning, the radio spoke of the fulfilment of our national aspirations," Nicos Sampson recalled.[116]

At the same time, Georgitsis, the leader of the coup, asked Sampson to prepare a proclamation of *Enosis*: "In the name of God and men, and of the sacrifices of Cyprus Hellenism for freedom, I declare the union (*Enosis*) of Cyprus with the Mother Country. The eternal aspirations and the ideals of our people find their fulfilment at this historic moment. Long live the united nation."[117] As Sampson was writing the *Enosis* proclamation, 80 dots appeared on the radar screen. "Then we all ran to the radar screens and saw the Turkish helicopters approaching the bridgehead. Very soon they seemed to land. A few minutes later, another 80 appeared, then others. We made urgent telephone contact with Athens. Bonanos again expressed the opinion that we were telling lies so as to trap Greece and force her into a war with Turkey."[118]

Sampson then contacted Gizikis by telephone, accusing Bonanos and making a desperate appeal for help. "I shall do what I can to get you help. Hang in there!" Gizikis replied.[119] Five minutes later, National Guard Headquarters was told by Athens that Greek Phantoms had taken off from Crete and were flying towards Cyprus. Papageorgiou, who was present, describes the frenzied enthusiasm that followed, with embraces, kisses and cries of: "Our planes are coming! Long live Greece! Long live *Enosis*!"[120] The Phantoms, however, had not taken off. At 11.07, Air Force Chief Papanicolaou gave the order for 12 planes to take off, but two minutes later Bonanos ordered Papanicolaou to cancel the order.[121]

At the same time, the Turks were undertaking their second landing operation under General Demirel. The landing fleet this time consisted of five anti-torpedo boats and frigates, many landing craft, three merchant vessels and other auxiliary ones.[122] The landing started at 8am and lasted several hours.

After the successful second landing, the escort of anti-torpedo boats extended their fire south of Ayios Georgios up to the Pentadactylos, laying the ground for the drive towards Kyrenia. The Turks acquired an overwhelming superiority over the National Guard, and

---

[116] Kardianos, *op. cit.*, p. 190.
[117] *Ibid.*, p. 191.
[118] *Ibid.*
[119] *Ibid.*, p. 192.
[120] *Ibid.*
[121] Greek Parliament, *op. cit.*, p. 103.
[122] Sergis, *op. cit.*, p. 482.

began to march on the town, meeting with no real resistance. "Their greatest mistake was not having the guts to engage us in close combat. As we approached, they retreated or accepted to be made prisoners,"[123] General Demirel writes in his memoirs. In reality, there were no longer any forces capable of putting up any substantial resistance. The Turks had 30 M48 tanks, two regiments of artillery, many personnel carriers and 2,500 men, with air and naval support. In contrast, the National Guard had suffered the loss of its five T34 tanks, had no effective anti-tank defence and absolutely no air cover. At 11.34, the first Turkish tanks appeared at the edges of Kyrenia. The town was almost empty, its inhabitants having abandoned it to seek a secure refuge at the Abbey of Bellapais, on the northern slope of the Pentadactylos. The fall of Kyrenia caused a psychological shock at National Guard General Staff headquarters in Malounda. Ioannides' lackeys were still pressing Armed Forces Headquarters in Greece, desperately seeking help. At 12.24, the order was again issued for aircraft to take off from Crete to bomb the Turkish landing forces. Only two minutes later, Bonanos again intervened and revoked the order, invoking the danger from the north.[124]

At the same moment, Arapakis again ordered the submarines sailing to Rhodes to change course and head for Cyprus. Twenty-four hours later, he recalled them again. The transport ship *Rethymnon* suffered the same fate. By midnight of 22-23 July, the ship had come to within 100 miles of Cyprus. Zoulias, its captain, then received a signal from Armed Forces Headquarters, which stated: "Hurry and land the detachments in Rhodes, which is under attack from the Turks." The captain carried out the order and ordered its course to be changed for Rhodes. When the *Rethymnon* reached Rhodes, it landed the 537 Infantry Regiment, then continued to Piraeus, where the Cypriot volunteers disembarked. At Rhodes they noted that there was no military activity, and the soldiers serving there were going for walks along the shore.[125] Later, Bonanos, in his report to Averoff, took responsibility for revoking the orders for the reinforcement of Cyprus: "the Naval (submarines) and Air Force reinforcements did not get involved in the Cyprus struggle because it was judged that their involvement would be the cause of war between Greece and Turkey".[126]

Through his lawyer Georgios Alfantakis, Ioannides charged the generals with treason for having refused to implement his decision that Greece should enter the war and strike the second wave of landing forces with the air force and navy. Some argue that Greek intervention could indeed have wrecked the Turkish landing fleet.[127] So convinced was Ioannides' entourage of the positive outcome of a Greco-Turkish war that Constantinos Panayiotakos maintains that a historic opportunity to take Constantinople was lost: "Throughout eastern Thrace there were but token Turkish forces. That is to say, the advance of our army as far as Constantinople would – for the first time – have been merely a military stroll!" In fact, Panayiotakos sketches a scenario according to which "the brave Brigadier P. Papadakis (former Chief of Staff of the National Guard) passed over the Evros (the river marking the border between Greece and Turkey) and, with patriotic enthusiasm marched about 30 kilometres (without firing a shot) inside Turkish territory, even capturing some wandering Turkish soldiers." According to Panyiotakos, the "advance" on Constantinople was halted through the intervention of the Commander of the Third Army Corps, General

123 Demirel, *art. cit.*
124 Sergis, *op. cit.*, p. 506.
125 Greek Parliament, *op. cit.*, pp. 102-103.
126 Arapakis, *op. cit.*, p. 204.
127 Panayiotakos, *Κύπρος*, pp. 67-68.

Ioannis Davos, who, "with a revolver to his head, forced Papadakis to return to his base".[128] This incident is not confirmed by any reliable source. The only episode recorded at the Evros was of the Turks firing four artillery shells, which fell near Soufli railway station, without any retaliation from the Third Army Corps.[129] However, Davos' cooperation with the generals at Armed Forces Headquarters in weakening Ioannides is a fact. According to Edjmel Baroutdjou, head of the Cyprus Desk at the Turkish Foreign Office in 1974, Ankara was aware of the generals' activities.[130]

The military battle for Cyprus had been lost before the Turkish invasion even began. The military situation as it had shaped up on account of the coup was impossible to reverse. The Americans, who had carefully guided events, utterly precluded the possibility of a Greco-Turkish flare-up and imposed their decisions on the Junta leadership. "On the morning of the invasion, the allied NATO administrations, through their permanent representatives, as well as ambassador Tasca, urged self-restraint and avoiding a Greco-Turkish conflict. After intense American pressure, the government has also adopted a similar policy concerning the avoidance of general involvement," Bonanos said in a later report submitted to Averoff.[131]

Greece's self-restraint was not imposed on the Greek government at the last minute, as Bonanos reports, but long before the onset of the invasion. From 1 July 1974 – a mere 20 days before the Turkish invasion – Bonanos issued an order addressed to the Chiefs of the Armed Forces that stated: "Reasons of National Policy impose the obligation to avoid any kind of provocation to Turkey. Strict orders are to be issued to this effect by existing administrations. There is to be not the slightest deviation allowed on this matter."[132]

At 4pm on 22 July, the National Guard put the truce into effect. In any case, it had no reserves with which to offer any real resistance. The Turkish forces, on the contrary, continued their operations, given that the goals they had set themselves for the first phase of the invasion had not yet been achieved. They had occupied Kyrenia, but the landing forces had not yet joined up with the Nicosia enclave, nor had they taken Nicosia airport. At 4pm, at the same time as the ceasefire was supposed to come into force, the Head of the invasion forces General Demirel ordered the advance on the interior. Turkish tanks started out in procession from Kyrenia and headed for the Nicosia enclave, with General Demirel at their head. He had placed on his tank a Greek Cypriot reservist lieutenant, who had been taken prisoner, to show him the way to Boghazi, where the Turkish forces had their headquarters.[133]

---

128 *Ibid.*
129 Sergis, *op. cit.*, p. 481.
130 Baroutdjou, *art. cit.*
131 Arapakis, *op. cit.*, p. 205.
132 *Ibid.*, p. 174.
133 Demirel, *art. cit.*

Brigadier Michail Georgitsis (second from right), to whom Ioannides entrusted the conduct of the coup.
To his left is naval commander Papayiannis and to his right is Lieutenant-Colonel Kokorakis.
The photo was taken at the National Guard General Staff on July 15, after the coup had taken place.

The Presidential Palace in flames.

Plate 20

The toughest resistance to the coup came from men of the Presidential Guard defending the Archbishopric.

Nicos Sampson (wearing shirt with large checks) and the staff of Machi greet the tanks heading for the Presidential Palace.

Sampson as president of the coup government makes his way to a press conference at the Press and Information Office.

A tank stands guard outside the Lycavitos police station in Nicosia.

Plate 22

On the morning of 20 July, the National Guard's tanks were lined up in the Hilton area of Nicosia, providing security for the coup leadership.

Despite watching Turkish parachutists falling from the sky from the window of the office of the General Staff commander, the coupist leadership of the National Guard awaited instructions from Athens before ordering a counter-attack.

41. Turkish forces land undisturbed on the beaches of Cyprus.

Limassol's Turkish Cypriots were rounded up and detained at the city's stadium.

Plate 24

A Turkish tank and soldiers at Kyrenia harbour.

Despite the cease-fire agreement, Turkish forces continued to advance and to occupy Greek Cypriot villages.

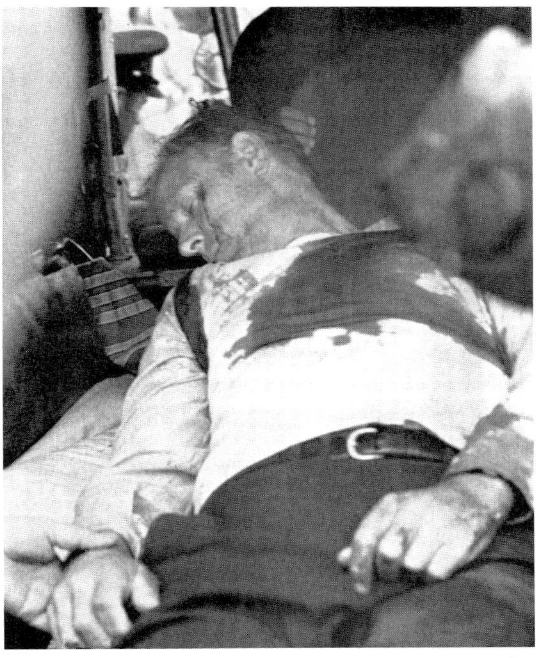

Glafcos Clerides with a gas mask outside the American embassy in Nicosia, where he had gone in an effort to calm public emotions.
Thousands of demonstrators attempted to burn down the US embassy.
The US ambassador to Cyprus, Roger Davis, was killed by shots fired from among the demonstrators.

Plate 26

After the cease-fire agreement, Turkey kept landing reinforcements in Cyprus, leading to fears that it was planning the total occupation of the island.

The delegations of the three guarantor powers during the first Geneva conference.

Hunted down by Turkish forces, civilians fearing for their lives
abandon their homes in their bare feet.

Turkish forces open a mass grave at Santalari village.
The massacre at Santalari was yet another alibi handed by EOKA B to the Turks.

Plate 28

Using whatever means they could, Greek Cypriots fled their homes and lands, as Turkey carried out its ethnic cleansing plans.

The return of prisoners and the agony for those who had not come back.

One third of the Greek Cypriot population (160,000 people) became refugees.

Plate 30

The talks between Clerides and Denktash at the Ledra Palace, though nominally addressing humanitarian issues, ended up touching on the substance of the Cyprus problem.

On 7 December 1974, Makarios returned to Cyprus through the British Bases. He was brought by helicopter from Akrotiri base to Nicosia.

Makarios addresses the crowd from the balcony of the Archbishopric,
still in ruins from the coup.

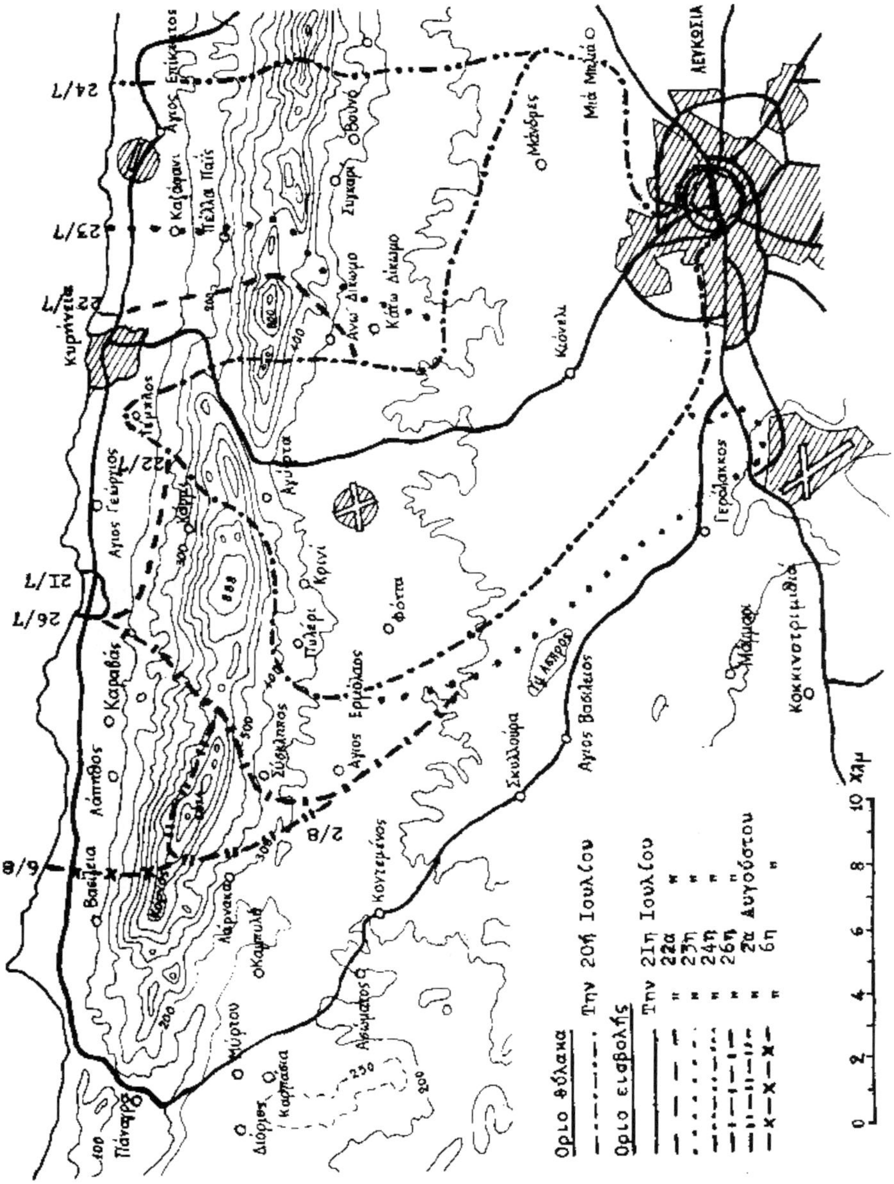

Map showing the first phase of the Turkish invasion. The dates indicate the different phases of the Turkish advance.

A diagram showing the Turkish advance towards Famagusta during the second phase of the invasion.

Plate 34

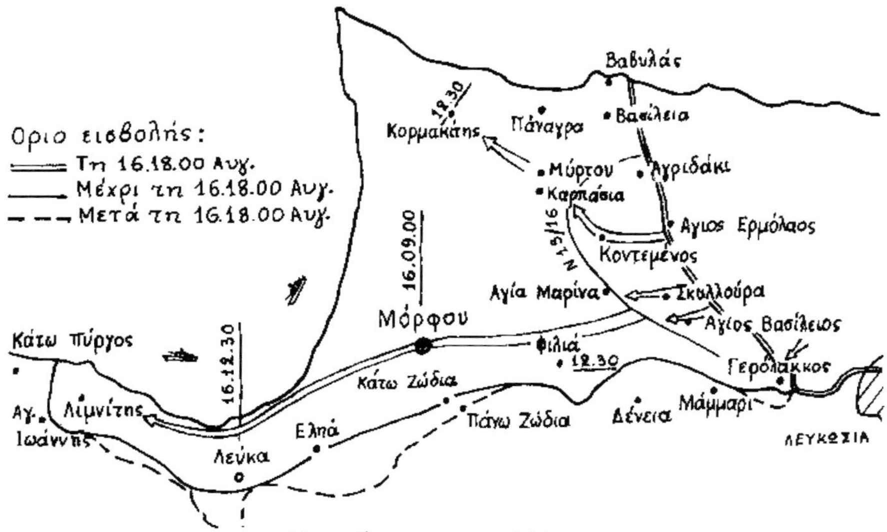

Η προέλαση προς τη Μόρφου

Diagram showing the Turkish advance towards the Morphou district.

12. A chance for diplomacy

Once the cease-fire agreement had been reached, the process of dismantling the Junta began in Athens. The regime could not withstand the weight of the Cyprus tragedy and was on the verge of collapse. The generals, who had weakened Ioannides, were negotiating the handover of power to the politicians. The United States set in motion such developments as would secure the continuity of Greece's policy of restraint towards Turkey, and the imposition of a solution to the Cyprus problem based upon the new realities that had been created.

In concert with the US, Britain had already extended an invitation to Greece and Turkey to send their representatives to Geneva on 24 July, to participate in a conference of the guarantor powers to discuss the Cyprus crisis. In view of this diplomatic initiative, there was a pressing need for a civilian government in Greece. On the morning of 23 July, the generals gathered in Bonanos' office to discuss developments. The heads of the three services, Galatsanos, Arapakis and Papanicolaou, also attended, the latter agreeing that the process of political change should begin immediately. A second meeting of the generals followed in Gizikis' office, discussing how best to handle Ioannides. Gizikis invited Ioannides to the meeting, briefed him on their decision and asked for his cooperation. Although Ioannides' reaction was negative, he pledged to conform: "Sirs, I do not agree since my perceptions are different; however, as five are in agreement, I withdraw and request that the Head of the Army grant me a two-day leave of absence." The generals asked him to promise not to attempt any move within the ranks of the army. "OK, I promise not to," he replied, and left.[1]

At two in the afternoon, Gizikis called various political representatives to his office for a meeting. Former prime ministers Panayiotis Kanellopoulos, Gerogios Athanasiades-Novas, Spyros Markezinis and Stephanos Stephanopoulos were all invited, as were former ministers Georgios Mavros, Evangelos Averoff, Petros Garoufalias and Xenophon Zolotas. Averoff tabled a proposal that Constantinos Karamanlis should be recalled from self-imposed exile in Paris to form a government. His proposal did not enjoy support from the other politicians. Finally, it was decided that Panayiotis Kanellopoulos, who had been the last prime minister of the country before the coup of 21 April 1967, should undertake the duties of Prime Minister. Georgios Mavros would be Deputy Prime Minister. The meeting broke up, and a new one was fixed to take place at Armed Forces Headquarters at 8pm, in which Kanellopoulos would come forward with his government for the swearing-in ceremony.

As the other politicians were leaving, Averoff pretended he was going to the toilet and stayed in Gizikis' office. In collusion with Arapakis, he again put forward his proposal for Karamanlis to take power. After consultations with the generals, they agreed to ignore the decision just taken and to summon Karamanlis instead. From Gizikis' office, Averoff phoned Karamanlis in Paris and proposed that he return immediately to Greece to be sworn in as Prime Minister. After talking with Gizikis and the other generals, Karamanlis accepted. At 4.30pm, Averoff phoned Kanellopoulos to announce to him that another decision had been taken, and that they were awaiting Karamanlis' arrival from Paris to form a government.[2]

---

1 Arapakis, *op. cit.*, p. 306.

2 *Ibid.*, pp. 312-314.

Karamanlis arrived in Greece in the early hours of 23 July in the personal aeroplane of the French President, Valéry Giscard d'Estaing, and at 4.30am was sworn in as prime minister in Gizikis' office. Kanellopoulos could not hide his irritation and refused to take part as Vice-President in the government of national unity formed by Karamanlis, invoking his need for rest. "If it was necessary for me to form a government, I would have done it yesterday. Though tired, I would have felt it an obligation. But for me to enter a government now as someone else's assistant, this has tired me a lot," he stated.[3]

It would be naïve to think the decision to call on Karamanlis had been taken at the last minute. In reality, Averoff had been negotiating his return with the Junta since 1970, when he made himself the 'bridge' between the regime and the political establishment for the restoration of parliamentary democracy. Through third parties, Averoff was in contact with both the Papadopoulos and the Ioannides regimes.[4] The high point of this initiative was when he sent Gizikis a note on 19 April 1974, in which he commented on the situation in Greece and urged the regime to adopt a "clearly anti-communist and anti-Papandreou constitution".[5]

Karamanlis himself had parallel contacts with the Americans, having never come out publicly against the dictatorship, while from 1969 seeking Washington's support to return to Greece as Prime Minister. During those years, Greek American tycoon Tom Papas, who had powerful contacts with the White House and the CIA, also promoted Karamanlis. Papas put forward the Karamanlis solution through US ambassador Henry Tasca, who in fact put his name forward in November 1973 for the post of prime minister in the Ioannides regime.[6]

Karamanlis, therefore, was the ideal choice. The equivocal stance he had adopted towards the Junta, and the presence of Averoff as "bridge builder" in the new government – as Minister of Defence – created a climate of trust among the generals, whose cooperation was seen as essential, both to weed out Ioannides and ensure a smooth transfer of power, as well as to maintain the policy of restraint against Turkey. In exchange for their cooperation, the generals received assurances they would suffer no consequences for their actions during the dictatorship. For this reason, not one of the generals who had played leading behind-the-scenes roles in the Junta was prosecuted, either for the dictatorship, or for the Cyprus coup, or for the failure to react to the Turkish invasion. Gizikis remained President of Greece until 17 December 1974, when caretaker president Michael Stasinopoulos replaced him. Together with Gizikis, Air Force Chief Papanicolaou was decommissioned with the title of honorary Air Marshal. Bonanos was decommissioned on 19 August 1974, together with Army Chief Galatsanos, who was succeeded by Ioannis Davos, one of the group of generals that had cooperated in the sidelining of Ioannides. Arapakis was kept on as Navy Chief until January 1975, and when he departed he was conferred the title of honorary Admiral.

---

3 Constantinos Karamanlis, *Αρχείο - Γεγονότα και κείμενα* [Archive – Events and Documents] (Athens: Ekdotiki Athinon, 1996), vol. 8, p. 16.

4 Detailed reference in Makarios Droushiotis, *Eleftherotypia* (Athens) 27.7.2001, "Tom Papas plots the return of C. Karamanlis", based on material from the US National Archive.

5 Tasca to Secretary of State, "Caramanlis and Averoff - their position", NARA, NPMS, NSC, Cyprus/Greece, telegram 5311, Athens 1 August 1974.

6 Makarios Droushiotis, *Πώς ο Κίσινγκερ επέβαλε πρόεδρο τον Κληρίδη* [How Kissinger Imposed Clerides as President] (Nicosia: Archeio/5, Diafaneia, 2001), p. 101.

In Cyprus, matters were less complicated. As President of the House, Clerides was constitutionally the legitimate replacement for Makarios. At midday on 23 July, Clerides was informed by Dimis Dimitriou, Foreign Minister in the coupist government, that Sampson was prepared to step down and that Athens had given its approval for him to take on the presidency. Shortly after, Clerides met Sampson at the Foreign Ministry, and in the presence of the National Guard leadership, the process of succession was agreed. Clerides was sworn in as President by the dethroned Bishop of Paphos, Gennadios, despite the fact that the constitution did no provide for the president to be sworn in, but rather confirmed before the House of Representatives. Sampson addressed the people, announcing his resignation and the handover of the presidency to Clerides, invoking his experience as a negotiator given the imminence of the Geneva conference. In his message, Clerides thanked Sampson for granting him the opportunity to make use of his experience in the negotiations on the Cyprus issue that were about to begin.[7]

The assumption of the presidency by Clerides was received by public opinion with relief, because it restored constitutional order and raised hopes that Turkish military operations might now be contained. With the exception of the EDEK party, Clerides had the support of the whole political leadership. In fact, even before he took on the presidency, AKEL had sent their deputy Hambis Michaelides to Clerides' house to hand him a written statement from the party requesting him to take it on.[8] In an announcement circulated on 24 July, the political bureau of AKEL's Central Committee greeted Clerides' assumption of the presidency as a "hopeful development in the political sphere", noting that "the handling of the extremely serious difficulties created by the coup and the Turkish invasion demand the unity, compassion and united efforts of the entire population".[9]

From New York, Makarios also accepted the assumption of the presidency by Clerides, on the understanding that he would be acting president for a brief period of time until he himself returned to Cyprus. However, Clerides saw his role in a completely different light. In the first press conference he gave after assuming his duties, he stated that the constitution allowed him to form policy on his own initiative and that he would not "act on the orders of anyone",[10] clarifying that he saw himself as a caretaker president with the responsibility of ensuring "that democratic elections are held within a certain period of time". As for the future of Makarios, he stated that he would have the right to stand as a candidate, and consequently "whether he would continue to hold the office of President or not would depend on the decision made by the people of Cyprus".[11]

Makarios replied to Clerides in comments to British journalist Charles Foley, who met him in New York on 28 July: "Mr Clerides," said Makarios, "is my constitutional replacement, empowered to take routine decisions when I am absent from the island, as has previously occurred. He may not change policy or appoint new ministers, while I, even when abroad, am able to do both."[12] Makarios told Foley that elections would be held only when his term of office expired in three years' time, at which time he would not stand for election and would devote himself to Church matters. "At this point, I should be happy to

---

7 Papageorgiou, *Μακάριος*, pp. 295-297.
8 Papademetris, Panayiotis, Petrides, *op. cit.*, vol. 15, p. 163.
9 *Ibid.*, p. 160.
10 *Ibid.*, p. 171.
11 *Ibid.*, p. 157.
12 *Ibid.*, p. 170.

give Mr Clerides my full support in presidential elections, and he will win. If I do not support him, he will not win."[13]

It was clear the two men had totally different perceptions concerning the handling of power during the most critical phase of the Cyprus crisis. Makarios, on the one hand, considered Clerides to be acting president with limited duties until he himself returned to Cyprus, while Clerides saw himself as acting President with unlimited powers.

Later, Clerides said that he had only accepted to be sworn in by Gennadios, spoken about elections and avoided taking a clear position on Makarios' return in order to appease the coupists, who remained in control of the situation. "As soon as I felt some security, I said that Makarios was free to return. If I had stated that from the moment I took office, they would have toppled me too," he said.[14]

Despite this, Clerides was subjected to harsh criticism, mainly from the President of EDEK, Vassos Lyssarides, who accused him of tolerating the coupists and failing to disarm EOKA B. He even termed his regime a "follow-on coup". Clerides gave his reply to Lyssarides two years later, when the question was discussed in the House in July 1976: "And you, Mr Lyssarides, wanted me – while standing among the ruins, without army, without police – to arrest and disarm thousands of armed men that were wandering freely about on the island. I did not arrest them, Mr Lyssarides. That is true. I admit this. But you have the duty and obligation to admit another more important fact. I disarmed them without shedding blood, Mr Lyssarides."[15]

Although Clerides' claims are persuasive, the diplomatic background of the period makes it clear that he had taken the political decision to go along with Kissinger in his attempt to sideline Makarios. According to diplomatic correspondence between the State Department and US embassies in Nicosia, Athens and Ankara, Clerides was in contact with Kissinger through ambassador Roger Davies, and would brief him on the policy he would follow. Occasionally, he would even inform Davies of replies he planned to give reporters over the status of Makarios.[16]

What Clerides told his first press conference concerning elections and Makarios, as well as the positions he set out on the issue of his powers as President of the Republic, was identical to the suggestions that Davies had submitted to Kissinger, with a view to assisting Clerides in imposing himself against Makarios. Immediately after Clerides' swearing-in, Davies had sent a telegram briefing Kissinger, who replied: "Given this development, I want you to understand that you should be extremely friendly to Clerides and that you should continue to establish effective communications and contact with him, stopping just a shade short of recognition." In the same telegram, Kissinger asked the ambassador, as a matter of urgency, to conduct an evaluation "concerning the balance of political forces on the island", comparing the political positions of Makarios with those of Clerides.[17]

In his evaluation, Davies proposed the immediate recognition of the Clerides government and the implementation of the provisions of the Constitution for the promulgation of elections. Davies believed Clerides had a good chance of winning the elections, even against Makarios. "He is an ideal president from our standpoint, because of moderate

---

13 *Ibid.*

14 *Ibid.*, p. 159.

15 *Ibid.*, p. 162.

16 Davies to Secretary of State, "Clerides role as head of government", NARA, NPMS, NSC, Cyprus/Greece, telegram 1681, Nicosia, 23 July 1974.

17 Kissinger to Amembassy Nicosia, "Your Approach to Clerides", NARA, NPMS, NSC, Cyprus/Greece, telegram 159994, Department of State 23 July 1974.

political orientation" and "because he is the Greek Cypriot likely to be able to negotiate successful arrangements with the Turks." According to Davies' analysis, "it would be most important for Greece to make it clear that the 'motherland' endorses Clerides, and for Ankara not to convey non-approbation, which could be the kiss of death, but rather the clear signal that Clerides offers the best prospect of avoiding war". Davies concluded his report by writing that in the final analysis, the Clerides presidency during the critical weeks that would follow "is the best hope of making a real solution which will head off a Greco-Turkish war. This alone achieves our key purpose."[18]

In another telegram, Davies referred to the question of Makarios' return to Cyprus, spurred by a conversation with Dimis Dimitriou, who told him that all Greek Cypriots, except AKEL and Lyssarides supporters, "are already saying that if Makarios comes back, blood will flow again and there will be civil strife on the island, and Greek will be fighting Greek again". Davies wrote in his telegram that "the present government, including Clerides, are convinced that Makarios' return, if it is soon, would be a disaster here" and that time was needed for tempers to cool, and for the island to return to some form of normality. According to Davies, Clerides had communicated to Karamanlis his anxieties about Makarios' possible return, as did Dimis Dimitriou to Bonanos, putting pressure on them so that Makarios would put off his return for at least three months. Bonanos agreed, while Karamanlis asked for time to think it over.[19]

Clerides complained to Davies about statements by Greek vice President, George Mavros, who came out in favour of Makarios' immediate return. Davies informed Washington, and Kissinger sent a telegram to Athens, instructing Tasca to meet Karamanlis and ask him "not to make any special effort to support Makarios and his early return to Cyprus".[20] Karamanlis had reservations about clashing with Makarios, perhaps on account of his rivalry with Mavros, but Evangelos Averoff called the Cyprus ambassador in Athens Nicos Kranidiotis, and told him "the early return of Makarios will be catastrophic for Cyprus".[21]

Kissinger also turned to Ankara, asking Ecevit to support the Clerides solution. On 23 July, the US ambassador in Ankara, Macomber, conveyed to Ecevit Kissinger's view on the next steps to take on the Cyprus issue. Kissinger's analysis was based on the policy of the "constitutional strategy", namely, the assumption of the presidency by Clerides and the solution of the problem through Greco-Turkish talks. Ecevit handed his views to Macomber in writing, adding some verbal comments. Ecevit told Macomber that Turkey did not have any personal objection to Clerides, although they knew that, during the inter-communal talks, "he had been ardently following Makarios' policy of attempting to turn Cyprus into a state completely dominated by the Greek Cypriots". Subsequently, Ecevit raised the question of the legitimacy of the Cyprus Republic. "The regime of Cyprus had ceased to be constitutional a long time ago," he said. "Mr Clerides' assumption of office as acting president is, no doubt, a relatively satisfactory development, in view of the fact that as President of the House of Representatives he is entitled to this position." Despite this, Ecevit considered that this development was not enough for a "return to real constitutionality" in

18 Davies to Secretary of State, "Clerides' Succession", NARA, NPMS, NSC, Cyprus/Greece, telegram 1663, Nicosia 23 July 1974.

19 Davies to Secretary of State, "Cyprus", NARA, NPMS, NSC, Cyprus/Greece, telegram 1723, Nicosia 24 July 1974.

20 Ingersoll to Davies, "Cyprus", NARA, NPMS, NSC, Cyprus/Greece, telegram 162101, Department of State 25 July 1974.

21 Tasca to Secretary of State, "Cyprus: Conversation with defense Minister Averoff", NARA, NPMS, NSC, Cyprus/Greece, telegram 5046, Athens 26 July 1974.

Cyprus. "As long as a government and administration which strictly fits to the constitutional pattern does not exist, it has to be admitted that there will be no 'President' or 'government' of Cyprus which can be recognised as legitimate representatives of Cyprus."[22]

While Kissinger, behind the scenes, was promoting Clerides as the only acceptable president of Cyprus, from New York (where he was staying), Makarios was trying to assert his authority over Clerides. Through the Greek Foreign Ministry, he sent Clerides instructions about the steps he should take, and indicated he should request a meeting with Denktash through the permanent representative of the Secretary-General of the United Nations in Cyprus, proposing to him the immediate implementation of the Zurich solution, including the clauses of the Constitution that the Greek Cypriot side considered to be unworkable, and that the Turkish vice-president, ministers, members of the House of Representatives, police and civil servants, should all return to their positions.[23]

Clerides responded to Makarios' suggestion, and asked for a meeting with Denktash, which took place the same day at the official residence of the vice-president of the Republic, in the Turkish quarter of Nicosia. The representative of the Secretary-General in Cyprus, Weckman Munoz, accompanied Clerides, as did the Commander of UNFICYP General Prem Chand. After listening to Clerides' proposal, Denktash replied this was a matter that had to be discussed with the Turkish government. He told him he would be going by helicopter to Ankara, and that he would reply within three to four days. Denktash eventually gave his reply through the UN Secretary-General's representative, stating: "The Turkish government could not countenance a return to the London-Zurich Agreements," which "for 10 years the Greek Cypriots have been refusing to implement (…) with the claim that they were unworkable."[24] Furthermore, Turkey claimed that the assaults by the Greek Cypriots on the Turkish community had demonstrated that the Zurich Agreements did not furnish adequate protection for the Turkish Cypriots.

On the pretext of ensuring security for the Turkish Cypriots, while in fact exploiting the military advantage it had gained, Turkey had already passed on to the next stage of its campaign, the creation of a unified Turkish Cypriot zone. Thus, despite the ceasefire agreement, it continued its aerial bombardments and the landing of forces on the Kyrenia coast.

On the evening of 23 July, the Turks mobilised forces towards Yerolakos village, west of Nicosia, with a view to occupying the airport. These moves rang alarm bells in London, since, according to the Treaty of Establishment, the British had rights concerning the use of Nicosia airport installations, and were opposed to their occupation by the Turks. In Nicosia, UN special representative Weckman Munoz telephoned the US ambassador and informed him that the situation at the airport was becoming alarming and that the Turkish commander was threatening to take over his installations, which were defended by only 70 United Nations troops.[25]

The continued Turkish offensive and its approach towards the Nicosia area caused panic in the civilian population. Clerides phoned the US ambassador and told him there were

---

22 Macomber to Secretary of State, "Cyprus - political future", NARA, NPMS, NSC, Cyprus/Greece, telegram 5860, Ankara 23 July 1974.

23 Clerides, *op. cit.*, vol. 4, p. 38.

24 *Ibid.*, p. 39.

25 Davies to Secretary of State, "Turkish violations of ceasefire", NARA, NPMS, NSC, Cyprus/Greece, telegram 1678, Nicosia 23 July 1974.

signs of a fresh, general offensive by Turkish forces and called on Washington to intervene to ensure respect of the ceasefire.[26] Clerides also turned to Athens for assistance, where Kanellopoulos, in his capacity as caretaker Prime Minister, still ignorant of the manoeuvrings to ensure the return of Karamanlis, contacted Kissinger in Washington, and told him that the information from Cyprus suggested the Turks were preparing to occupy Nicosia. And if such a thing were to take place, his government would have no choice but to resign or go to war. "No government could survive such an event," he told him. Kissinger contacted Ecevit, who assured him that Turkey had no intention of attacking Nicosia. Kissinger passed the message on to Kanellopoulos.[27]

Despite Ecevit's assurances, Turkey continued to build up forces across the territory it occupied. Early in the morning of 24 July, the American General Galloway, following instructions from Defence Secretary Schlesinger, contacted the deputy chief of the Turkish General Staff General Ersoz and expressed his deep anxiety concerning the possibility of a new military offensive in Cyprus, something that would have consequences on the attempt to impose the ceasefire agreement. "Action of this kind could make it very difficult for a new Greek government and could force it to take actions which it might otherwise not have considered," he told him. General Ersoz replied that he did not personally know of any major operations by the Turks that day, and that both sides were breaking the ceasefire agreement. At the same time, the US ambassador in Ankara Macomber communicated with Ecevit and forcefully conveyed to him the US position that Turkey should not come into conflict with the United Nations, nor attempt to occupy Nicosia airport. Ecevit repeated his categorical assurances that under no circumstances would Turkish troops attack British or other UN forces, and that the Turkish General Staff had sent the relevant orders to Turkish officers in Cyprus.[28] Despite this, at about midday, the Turkish ambassador in Nicosia informed his government that "Turkish forces will take Nicosia airport in two hours' time". Turkish operations were raising the danger of a clash between Turkish troops and UN forces, since UN Secretary-General Waldheim had given instructions to UNFICYP to resist any attempt by Turkish troops to take control of the airport.[29]

At 3pm, Kissinger again phoned Ecevit, raising the comments by the Turkish ambassador in Nicosia. Ecevit told him once again that, "in no event would Turkish troops mount an offensive against UN forces".[30] Subsequently, Kissinger spoke with Callaghan, who told him London had information that tanks and infantry were preparing to move on the airport. Kissinger informed him of the assurances Ecevit had given him. Callaghan said he too had received such assurances, but was not so reassured.[31] The Americans again took up the matter with Turkey. Ambassador Macomber spoke on the telephone with Ecevit, who told him the airport would remain under Turkish control, but that respect would be shown to the rights of the British. "We are sending specific instructions 'to our people in

---

26 Davies to Secretary of State, "Cyprus: Clerides fears further Turk military action", NARA, NPMS, NSC, Cyprus/Greece, telegram 1680, Nicosia 23 July 1974.

27 Kissinger to embassies in Ankara, Athens, Nicosia and London, NARA, NPMS, NSC, Cyprus/Greece, telegram 160114, Department of State 23 July 1974.

28 Macomber to Secretary of State, "Cyprus - situation at Nicosia airport", NARA, NPMS, NSC, Cyprus/Greece, telegram 5896, Ankara 24 July 1974.

29 Kissinger to embassies in Ankara, Athens, Nicosia and London, NARA, NPMS, NSC, Cyprus/Greece, telegram 161223, Department of State 25 July 1974.

30 *Ibid.*

31 *Ibid.*

Nicosia' to this effect," Ecevit assured him.[32] Ecevit's comments complicated the situation yet further, as he was under the false impression the airport was already in the hands of the Turks.

Eventually, Turkish invading forces cancelled their plans to capture Nicosia airport, which has remained to this day under the control of the United Nations. However, Turkey's failure to implement the ceasefire agreement seriously undermined the efforts to bring together the guarantor powers in Geneva. Greek Foreign Minister Georgios Mavros informed the American and British ambassadors that the Greek government was convinced the Turks were preparing to attack in Nicosia, irrespective of the way the airport question was dealt with, and for this reason refused to go to Geneva.[33] The US ambassador in Athens, Henry Tasca, worried about Greece's probable reaction to Turkey's continuous ceasefire violations, suggested that the US should have recourse "to a convincing threat of force" as the only credible form of pressure against Ankara. The best way to get the message across, Tasca argued, was "through the appropriate deployment of the US Sixth Fleet".[34]

Addressing Kissinger personally, Tasca pointed out the danger of Greece being destabilised, and of Karamanlis' authority being called into question by the generals. "Brigadier Ioannides is still in Athens with his supporters, the majors and captains. I believe that we had better hypothesise that, if the army chiefs are persuaded that in reality Karamanlis has nothing better to offer than the government he replaced, the alternative solution of a political government might completely be called into question. In this case, there is the probability that we shall see very rapid deterioration in the relations between Greece and Turkey, such as the withdrawal of Greece from the Atlantic Alliance."[35]

Eventually, Callaghan managed to convince Mavros to go to Geneva for the conference of the guarantor powers, which began on 25 July. However, in Cyprus the situation remained the same, with the Turks reinforcing their forces undisturbed. As the Geneva conference began, Turkish tank-carrying ships approached Kyrenia and landed tanks and a large number of troops. Clerides once more contacted the US ambassador and protested at the Turkish reinforcements, arguing, "the Turkish plan is clearly to extend the geographic area of control".[36]

Fearing that Turkey's continued military activities in Cyprus would destabilise Greece, US Under Secretary of State Ingersoll addressed himself to the American ambassador in Ankara Macomber, telling him to make the following points to the Turkish government, discretely:

(a) The Turkish government has successfully made its point that the intervention in Cyprus was to create a balance of forces favourable to Turkey.

(b) Any breaking of the ceasefire and further large-scale introduction of troops and equipment into Cyprus, as the Geneva conference is now under way, would not be conducive to the successful outcome of negotiations.[37]

---

32 Macomber to Secretary of State, "Cyprus - situation at Nicosia airport", NARA, NPMS, NSC, Cyprus/Greece, telegram 5897, Ankara 24 July 1974.

33 "Cyprus Ceasefire", NARA, NPMS, NSC, Cyprus/Greece, telegram 161724, Department of State 25 July 1974.

34 Tasca personal for the Secretary, "Potentially grave Turkish violations of Cyprus ceasefire", NARA, NPMS, NSC, Cyprus/Greece, telegram 4967, Athens 24 July 1974.

35 *Ibid.*

36 "Cyprus Ceasefire", NARA, NPMS, NSC, Cyprus/Greece, telegram 161724, Department of State 25 July 1974.

37 *Ibid.*

The Americans also made demarches to Athens. However, in contrast to its approach to Ankara, where persuasion was the tactic of choice, in Athens the Greek government was submitted to intense pressure to enter into compromise, with America squarely laying the blame for the crisis on Greece, as the one that had provoked Turkey through the coup. In his telegram to Tasca, Kissinger gave instructions as to the approach he should adopt in his dealings with the Greek government: "We hope the Greeks will carefully consider the damage which has been done in the past 10 days, not only in terms of alliance relationships, but also in terms of the potential for Soviet meddling in the eastern Mediterranean." In his instructions to Tasca, Kissinger said Athens should exploit the opportunity of the Geneva Conference and work "toward a viable, and hopefully durable, settlement of the Cyprus problem, while at the same time restoring the somewhat battered Greek-Turkish alliance relationship".[38]

American diplomacy considered the ostracism of Makarios to be an essential prerequisite for the success of their policy. Addressing the Greek government through Tasca, Kissinger clearly outlined the criteria that the President of Cyprus should fulfil: "This person will emerge from a consensus of Greece and Turkey and, of course, the Cypriots themselves, and provided the Soviets have had no hand in the selection. We particularly want to avoid any confrontation between Greeks and Turks over personalities." Although in his note Kissinger states that he neither opposed nor supported Makarios or Clerides, he made it clear that the choice that would be made would have to be an arrangement that seemed best suited to protect America's interests. "We will want to be sure that the person who emerges is well aware that his emergence is due in large part to our support and that of the Greeks, and that this support was not just a free ride."[39]

Tasca met Karamanlis on 26 July and told him America's policy on Cyprus on the basis of his instructions from Kissinger. Karamanlis told Tasca the immediate problem was the continued violation of the ceasefire, and that there could exist no climate of cooperation until the Turks halted operations. "Without American intervention we cannot avoid conflict. Wishes and hopes and recommendations are not enough," said Karamanlis. Tasca said his government was doing what it could for the truce to be observed, and promised to convey his anxieties to Washington. Karamanlis added that US efforts to make the Turks comply must succeed within 24 hours "or there could be no talks in Geneva".

As to the question of Makarios, Karamanlis told Tasca that the Greek government had been in touch with the Archbishop, who was in the United States and wished to go first to London and then to Geneva. "He [Karamanlis] believed the Greeks had persuaded him to go only to London, and asked that the US should seek to persuade Makarios not to go to Geneva". In the telegram that Tasca sent to Kissinger, he commented on Karamanlis' words: "I take these remarks to mean that the Greek government fully appreciates the prospective trouble-making potential of Makarios in the present delicate circumstances."[40]

That same day, Tasca had a telephone conversation with Averoff, who told him that if the Turks continued to land forces in Cyprus, the Greek military would recommend that Greece should do the same. He clarified that he himself disagreed with this option, while pointing out to Tasca the danger that Greece was facing from the north. According to Tasca's telegram back to Washington, Averoff thought that if Greece and Turkey fought,

---

38 *Ibid.*

39 Kissinger to Tasca, "Cyprus", NARA, NPMS, NSC, Cyprus/Greece, telegram 161369, Department of State 25 July 1974.

40 Tasca to Secretary of State, "Ambassador's conversation with prime minister Karamanlis", NARA, NPMS, NSC, Cyprus/Greece, telegram 5048, Athens 26 July 1974.

there would be a wider war within 24 hours, including the prospect of Soviet intervention to support a Bulgarian move to the sea.

As to the question of Makarios, Tasca repeated to Averoff what he had told Karamanlis, "stressing the need for flexibility in Geneva and the dangerous internal situation that could evolve on the island if Makarios were pushed to the forefront". Averoff agreed and had told the Cypriot ambassador in Athens exactly the same thing. "In fact, Averoff appeared to agree with our views on Makarios."[41]

In the message that Makarios sent Clerides on 23 July 1974, concerning the steps he should take as acting President, he asked him to turn to the Soviet ambassador in Nicosia, Sergei Astavin, and seek diplomatic support. Clerides met Astavin on 26 July and asked that his country lend its support in the United Nations Security Council, so that Turkey would be obliged to respect the ceasefire agreement. News of Astavin's meeting with Clerides was transmitted from Athens to Kissinger, who immediately sent the following message to Nicosia ambassador Roger Davies via Ingersoll: "You should see Clerides as soon as possible and tell him that we have received word from sources in Athens that he has requested Soviet support. We want him to know that we believe this to be a serious mistake, which can only complicate an already difficult situation. (...) Clerides should understand that Soviet involvement can only force us into positions which, under other circumstances, we would not take."

In his message, Kissinger said he was in contact with Ecevit and Karamanlis, in an effort bring about a strict observance of the ceasefire agreement and the continuation of the Geneva Conference between the three guarantor powers for a solution of the problem. Kissinger expressed his "sympathy" for the suffering people of Cyprus and said that he appreciated the difficult position in which Clerides found himself, but "we must emphasise to him [Clerides] that Soviet involvement in the Cyprus crisis will inevitably make that crisis more difficult to resolve and in no way serve the interests of his people".[42]

Davies met with Clerides at 6pm on 27 July, and conveyed to him verbatim what was contained in the telegram. Clerides responded that, given the situation the previous day, he had contacted the Soviet Union's ambassador Astavin and asked for Soviet diplomatic support so that Turkey would be obliged to adhere to the ceasefire agreement. Davies told Clerides that he thought the involvement of the Soviet Union would have the most serious complications, especially in Cyprus and Greece. He told him that if his initiative became known, it would cause a disturbance from the right wing, not only in Nicosia but also in Athens, where hard-liners were still in place. "Furthermore, the Turks had in part justified their military action as essential to prevent the rise of communist influence on this island, which is vital to Turkey's national security." He also told him "the Turks could seize on this development as a propaganda plum. (I thought Clerides paled somewhat during this part of our discussion)."

Davies told Clerides the United States did not have the absolute power to force governments to do its bidding, and that if it took a tougher stance against Turkey this could well disrupt relations between the two countries, to the incalculable disadvantage of all in the area. However, Davies said that the US did command considerable influence, and that this was being used to convince the Turkish government that restraint was in its long-term

41 Tasca to Secretary of State, "Cyprus: Conversation with defense minister Averof", NARA, NPMS, NSC, Cyprus/Greece, telegram 5099, Athens 26 July 1974.

42 Ingersoll to Davies, "Cyprus", NARA, NPMS, NSC, Cyprus/Greece, telegram 163905, Department of State 27 July 1974.

interests. Davies urged Clerides to have confidence and be patient. "I recognised that yesterday, when the rumour that the Turks would take Nicosia last night brought a mass exodus to the hills, must have been particularly trying."

Davies went on to tell Clerides that, "obviously, the primary Soviet interest now would be establishing a basis for insisting on the withdrawal of the British forces, whose presence on Cyprus had just two days ago been shown to be helpful. (He was referring to the British intervention that had prevented the Turkish army from occupying Nicosia airport.) Given the position of Cyprus some 40 miles from Turkey and hundreds from Greece, do you perhaps feel that it would be in the interest of the Greek Cypriots to provide a basis for an international demand for a British withdrawal?" Clerides replied that the British presence was the best possible insurance for the Greek Cypriots, and that withdrawal would leave them hostage to Turkish military power. He said he deeply appreciated Kissinger's concern and could accept the points made. "I could assure you most categorically that there will be no further appeal to the Soviets nor contacts seeking support. It is likely that the Soviet ambassador will ask to see him to bring Moscow's response. In this event, he will listen and politely disengage," Davies reported back.[43]

In his book, *My Deposition*, Clerides provides a completely different version of his appeal for Soviet support. He says he asked Astavin to convey to his government an invitation from Cyprus to send troops, and that he was ready to put Cypriot territory at their disposal for the creation of a Soviet military base on the island. According to Clerides, Astavin conveyed the proposal to his government and in a few days received the answer that "the Soviet Union would be prepared to intervene only if this were to occur in conjunction with the United States".[44] Yet in contrast to his later recollections in his book, Clerides told a meeting of political parties on 15 August 1974 that he had asked the Soviet Union for military assistance, but had received no reply.[45]

The reality is that there was no possibility of the Soviet Union becoming militarily involved in the Cyprus crisis. Despite the diplomatic support it gave the Cyprus Republic, Moscow accepted that Cyprus belonged to the Western sphere of influence, and did not react to the Turkish invasion. The Turks had informed Moscow of their invasion plans, maintaining that their operation would aim at restoring the independence of Cyprus. And an independent state, with whatever limitations, was for the Russians preferable to its being united to a NATO member state.

Despite the fact that the Cyprus crisis favoured the Soviet Union, weakening the southeastern flank of NATO, Moscow offered Cyprus diplomatic support, as it had done in the past. This was mainly due to Makarios' personal influence in the Non-Aligned Movement, with which Moscow frequently formed a majority in the United Nations General Assembly. The eastern bloc and the Non-Aligned Movement formed the backbone of Makarios' initiatives for the internationalisation of the Cyprus problem through the United Nations. However, in this case, the Americans neutralised Makarios and completely limited the Soviet Union's role in the Security Council. America's stance irritated Moscow, which was attempting to make Cyprus break away from the framework of NATO. On 28 July, it issued a diplomatic note to Ankara, in which it protested at the increase in foreign forces (it avoided using the term 'Turkish') in Cyprus. The note also protested the attempt to marginalise Makarios, and stated that, despite the assumption of the presidency by

---

43 Davies to Secretary of State, "Cyprus", NARA, NPMS, NSC, Cyprus/Greece, telegram 1842, Nicosia 27 July 1974.

44 Clerides, *op. cit.*, vol. 4, p. 42.

45 Papademetris, Panayiotis, Petrides, *op. cit.*, vol. 15, p. 212.

Clerides, power was still in the hands of the coupists. The note also mentioned that "the harsh intervention in the internal affairs of the Cyprus people aimed at the establishment of a military occupation of the island and at its dismemberment," and warned that "this situation can no longer be tolerated".[46]

At the same time, the Soviet delegate at the Security Council, Jacob Malik, was unsuccessfully attempting to get his country off the sidelines to which the West had confined it. Malik initially exercised the veto and subsequently abstained from approving the Security Council's Resolution 355, which called on the Secretary-General to take action to implement the ceasefire in Cyprus.

On the morning of 29 July, Clerides again met with US ambassador Roger Davies, who briefed him on Malik's attempt to upgrade the Soviet role in the Cyprus crisis through a demarche in the Security Council. Davies made it clear to Clerides that Cyprus was not to encourage the Soviet Union to get involved. "If the Soviets inject themselves into the situation via this route, the whole US perception of, and policies towards, the problem could change," he warned. Clerides told him he had no communication with Cyprus representative Zenon Rossides, who was clearly getting instructions from Makarios. "If Rossides is making common cause with the Soviets, it was not at the behest of anyone in Cyprus," said Clerides, who, according to Davies, believed "that a Soviet involvement in negotiations would be catastrophic, and for this reason the Geneva Conference had to be kept going until it resulted in an agreement between Athens and Ankara".[47]

In Geneva meanwhile, the conference of guarantor powers continued. British Foreign Secretary James Callaghan, who presided over the conference, attempted to achieve agreement on a declaration of basic principles for the solution of the Cyprus problem. Greece proposed that Turkish forces withdraw to the territory occupied on 22 July, and respect the ceasefire. Turkey demanded an *a priori* commitment by Greece to a federal solution on the basis of geographical division, that Greek forces should vacate the Turkish Cypriot enclaves, and the defining of a 10km-wide buffer zone between the occupied territory and the one controlled by the Cypriot government. The Turkish proposal required an evacuation of 40 Greek Cypriot villages lying within this zone.[48]

One of the more important points in the declaration being drawn up was the one that referred to the Turkish invasion forces. The Turks would not accept anything that would bind them to withdrawal by a certain date, bringing the conference to the brink of collapse. In an attempt to salvage the process, Callaghan sought the intervention of Kissinger, who was exercising telephone diplomacy from Washington. Kissinger was pressing Greece to make concessions to Turkey, saying there was no other way of preventing the advance of Turkish troops. However, Georgios Mavros, who hesitated to undertake such a heavy responsibility and be burdened with the political cost of compromise, threatened to withdraw from the conference. Kissinger phoned Karamanlis on the evening of 26 July, asking him to do whatever necessary to keep the talks alive. At 4am on 27 July, Tasca visited Karamanlis and handed him a letter from Kissinger, in which the latter expressed "sympathy and commiseration" over the tragedy befalling the people of Cyprus, and assured him that he would do what he could to help the parties reach a "just and honourable" solution. "However, we are making these attempts discreetly because we

---

46 *Ibid.*, p. 190.

47 Davies to Kissinger, "Meeting with Clerides", NARA, NPMS, NSC, Cyprus/Greece, telegram 1932, Nicosia 29 July 1974.

48 Karamanlis, *op. cit.*, vol. 8, p. 45.

believe that they have a greater chance of success if they are carried out far from the public glare." After recognising that the actions of the Turkish government were making matters difficult for Karamanlis, Kissinger wrote that he was trying to persuade Turkey to accept the implementation of the truce. "I shall keep you informed of these attempts, which do not cease to be intense and determined as they come from myself. But Greece will have to keep to a moderate course and understand that the Turkish government feels not merely that it is not responsible for the events that sparked off this crisis, but, on the contrary, that it is a victim of them."

Kissinger wrote to Karamanlis that the first objective was the stabilisation of the situation in Cyprus, and then the establishment of a procedure in Geneva that would restore "a just and honourable peace for all the people of Cyprus". Kissinger finally urged Karamanlis to take advantage of the opportunity given by the Geneva process. "The most important point is that the Geneva talks should not be broken off, because if we lose the opportunity that Geneva now offers, it may not present itself again until more lives are lost, other properties destroyed, and the position of our common enemy is reinforced."[49]

When Karamanlis had read the letter, he told Tasca that what Kissinger promised "was not enough" and declared that the Turks "could be stopped by only one of two methods, either by direct military intervention by the US and/or the UK, or by the dispatch of the Greek fleet with men and supplies to Cyprus". He told him that Greece had rights in Cyprus based on the London-Zurich agreements, and noted with some bitterness that five days after the Turkish government had accepted the ceasefire resolution, it was continuing to violate it. "At one point the Prime Minister likened the Turks to 'gangsters', and suggested that the Turks' intention was to 'humiliate' the Greek people, and quoted the proverb, 'you can defeat your enemy, but you cannot humiliate him'."

Karamanlis also stated that if the present situation were allowed to continue, the Greek delegation would be unable to remain in Geneva, describing the talks as a mockery because Turkey had neither good faith nor good will. Tasca responded by saying that Kissinger fully understood his difficult position, but "the maintenance of the Geneva talks was far preferable to military confrontation". Tasca turned the discussion towards the variety of interests involved, "including the strong Soviet presence in the eastern Mediterranean, and the presence of the armies of the Warsaw Pact countries to the north," and emphasised the importance of the "integrity of the southern flank of NATO to the defence of the West against Soviet communism and damage which could be wrought to it by a breach between two members of its southern flank". Finally, Tasca urged Karamanlis to do everything in his power to keep the talks going in Geneva. "He then for the first time moderated his position and assured me that he would follow the suggested course of action to the degree possible."[50]

Meanwhile in Cyprus, Turkey continued to violate the ceasefire. According to American estimates, by 28 July, the Turks had landed about 200 tanks and 20,000 troops. The Turkish reinforcements were so great that they aroused fears in Nicosia that they even aimed at occupying the whole of Cyprus. These fears grew after statements by Ecevit that "Turkish troops will not be bound either in their movements on the island nor in reinforcement efforts" and that "they have no intention of being so bound until the political problems of the island are solved".[51] Similar views were expressed by Foreign Minister

---

49 Karamanlis, *op. cit.*, vol. 8, pp. 36-37.

50 Tasca to Kissinger, "Comments of PM Karamanlis on Secretary's letter and general views on current crisis", NARA, NPMS, NSC, Cyprus/Greece, telegram 5109, Athens 27 July 1974.

51 Tasca to Kissinger, NARA, NPMS, NSC, Cyprus/Greece, telegram 5134, Athens 28 July 1974.

Gunes in Ankara, upon which Mavros again threatened to walk out of the conference in Geneva and return to Athens.

The Greek government turned to British Prime Minister Harold Wilson, pointing out to him that his country, as a guarantor power, had the obligation to intervene with its military forces to prevent possible Turkish occupation of the whole island. Karamanlis ordered military commanders to be on the alert, while sending a letter to Ecevit via the Greek embassy in Ankara, stating that "unless troop movements to the island cease and Turkish forces remain in place, the government of Greece will exercise its rights of intervention under the London-Zurich agreements".[52]

That same evening, Averoff hurried to Tasca's house and informed him of all the developments, stating that "the military commanders are for war with Turkey," and that "there is renewed pressure for Greece to leave NATO," both from the military and from civilian components in the Greek government. Tasca told Averoff it was of the greatest importance for the Greek government "to exercise restraint" and that "reaction with force could only complicate the present conflict to a catastrophic point". He also told him "Mavros leaving Geneva would be a colossal blunder in terms of Greece's world position, as well as for dealing effectively with the concrete Cyprus crisis". Tasca noted back in a telegram that he was convinced that "Karamanlis and Averoff are striving to the greatest degree possible to maintain a position of restraint and moderation, but they are clearly coming under increasing pressure to take some action to protect what they consider vital Greek national interests".[53]

On 29 July, acting president Glafcos Clerides and American ambassador Roger Davies discussed the impasse in Geneva and the danger of the conference collapsing if Mavros waled out in protest at Turkish intransigence. Davies said that Clerides had told him that Mavros feared that in the fast moving situation in Athens, his own personal political fortunes might be impaired, and for that reason he was anxious to return. "Furthermore, Mavros, because of his political aspirations, would be most reluctant to identify himself with substantial concessions to the Turks, which any realist would recognise must be made."

As Clerides told Davies, he had had a telephone conversation with Averoff in which both agreed that Mavros had to be told to remain in Geneva. Later, Clerides also spoke with Karamanlis, who said that since Clerides and Averoff were in agreement, he would send orders to Mavros to stay in Geneva.

Clerides believed the Turks wanted to move from a ceasefire agreement to a second phase conference, which would be based on the 1960 accords and would seek to achieve the structuring of two separate administrations on the island, a solution which he personally agreed with, but which was not acceptable to Athens. According to Davies, Clerides lamented "that Athens still does not appreciate the fact that Turkish military power – always a potential, and now invoked by the Greek coup on the island – has changed the entire ballgame".

Clerides had proposed to Davies that Cyprus be represented in the second phase talks by a single government, with himself as President and Denktash as Vice-President. Thus, Clerides appeared prepared to concede provisional status rather than de facto status to Turkish Cypriot authority, pending an agreement on the restructuring of the Constitution. To a question of Davies as to whether this formula "would not raise the Makarios vs Clerides

52 *Ibid.*
53 *Ibid.*

issue", he "smiled and noted that Ecevit seemed to be moving away in his press conference of Sunday from his previous position of indifference to Makarios' return, to one supporting negotiations including both Clerides and Denktash".[54]

Clerides told Davies that, to prevent Soviet trickery and for Cyprus to be brought out from the present chaos, the Geneva Conference had to succeed. If there were signs of it breaking up, he suggested, via Davies, that Kissinger should make a flying trip to Ankara and Athens to provide the basis for pragmatic negotiations "recognising Turkish security interests and the basic rights of both peoples of Cyprus".[55]

Later that same day, Mavros spoke on the phone with Clerides and informed him that Callaghan was working on a compromise formula that would refer to a phased withdrawal of Turkish troops from Cyprus. Clerides informed Davies, who made the following remark in a telegram he sent to Washington: "The clear message from Clerides is that a compromise is preferable to allowing the talks to fail. We suspect, though Clerides did not indicate, that the Mavros call to Clerides was intended to elicit support for a compromise on the above lines."[56]

As Clerides appeared disposed to enter into the great compromise, Makarios, from the United States, tried to convey his own uncompromising position. On 29 July, he met Kissinger in Washington. According to information obtained by the Greek embassy, Kissinger's views on the questions raised by Makarios were as follows:

- His return to Cyprus was a matter for the Cyprus people.
- For reasons of wider political convenience, the Americans were avoiding public condemnation of the Turkish intervention or a demand for the withdrawal of Turkish troops.
- They supported the independence and territorial integrity of Cyprus, but did not any longer make mention of a unified state, as in the past.
- To Makarios' challenge to take a position against Turkey for not respecting Security Council resolutions, Kissinger merely observed that the United States would do what it could to bring about a peaceful solution.[57]

Makarios also handed Kissinger a memorandum with five conditions for a political solution to the Cyprus problem, appealing to him to convey it to the Turkish government. Kissinger sent the note to his ambassador in Ankara, Macomber, with the instruction to hand it over at a low level, and to explain that he was doing it merely because he had promised to do so. Makarios' proposals were as follows:

1. Full implementation of the operative part of the Security Council resolution of July 1974.
2. Talks between the guarantor powers for a lasting solution of the Cyprus problem.
3. The basis of the talks will be the 1960 Constitution.
4. If no agreement is reached in the talks, then the 1960 Constitution should be considered to be in force as a whole. Only with the agreement of the parties concerned will it be possible to change any provisions of the Constitution.

---

54 Davies to Kissinger, "Meeting with Clerides", NARA, NPMS, NSC, Cyprus/Greece, telegram 1932, Nicosia 29 July 1974.

55 *Ibid.*

56 Davies to Secretary of State, "Geneva conference", NARA, NPMS, NSC, Cyprus/Greece, telegram 1968, Nicosia 29 July 1974.

57 Karamanlis, *op. cit.*, vol. 8, p. 38.

5. A committee consisting of representatives from Greece, Turkey, the United Kingdom, and Greek and Turkish Cypriots, under the chairmanship of a representative of the Secretary-General of the United Nations, is to take the necessary practical measures for the normal return to the constitutional regime of 1960 and the dissolution of 'de facto' situations.
6. A mixed special police force of Greek and Turkish Cypriots, with the participation of United Nations police, is to take the necessary practical steps for the disarming of all those bearing weapons illegally.

Makarios' memorandum included a further note, which read: "It would perhaps be advisable if Greece and Turkey would decide to withdraw the Greek and Turkish contingents stationed in Cyprus under the Treaty of Alliance, although the treaty should still be valid. We must not forget that the presence in Cyprus of these two contingents was one of the main factors which contributed to the beginning of the intercommunal troubles in 1963, by training illegal groups and providing them with arms."[58]

Kissinger also sent a copy of Makarios' proposals to Athens, as well as to Nicosia, with instructions to Davies to note down any comments by Clerides. Davies handed the document to Clerides, who after reading it made the following remark: "Makarios is badly out of touch with reality."[59]

On July 30, the foreign ministers of Greece, Turkey and Britain reached agreement on a statement of principles for a solution to the Cyprus problem. The three ministers agreed on a new meeting, to begin in Geneva on 8 August, with the participation of Greek and Turkish Cypriot representatives.

According to Edjmel Barountdjou, before the signatures were appended to the declaration, "the three guarantor powers Britain, Turkey and Greece agreed on the side-lining of Makarios". In connection with this verbal agreement, Mavros had made the following statement: "We have to act in such a manner that only Glafcos Clerides represents the Greek Cypriot community at the second Geneva conference." Turkish Foreign Minister Turan Gunes responded in a similar way, saying "only Rauf Denktash represents the Turkish Cypriots". Callaghan agreed with both, stating that at the second Geneva conference "Clerides represents the Greek Cypriot community and Denktash that of the Turkish Cypriots". Barountdjou writes that the aim of these statements was "to prevent Makarios, the main culprit in the Cyprus tragedy for so many years, from exploiting a final opportunity".[60]

The text of the Geneva Declaration included the following basic points:

- The hostile parties are to stabilise their positions at the point that existed at 22.00 hours Geneva time on 30 July.
- A security zone is to be set up between the territories occupied by the Turks and those controlled by the Cyprus Republic, the extent of which will be agreed at a later time with the cooperation of the United Nations.
- All the Turkish Cypriot enclaves that were under the control of Greek and Greek Cypriot forces should be immediately evacuated. The enclaves are to come under the

---

58 "Makarios' proposals", NARA, NPMS, NSC, Cyprus/Greece, telegram 166128, Department of State 31 July 1974.Kissinger to embassies in Athens, Ankara and Nicosia.

59 Davies to Secretary of State, "Makarios' proposals", NARA, NPMS, NSC, Cyprus/Greece, telegram 2093, Nicosia 2 August 1974.

60 Baroutdjou, *art. cit.*

protection of the Peacekeeping Force of the United Nations and to maintain their own police and security forces.
- There is to be an exchange of prisoners under the supervision of the Red Cross.
- Measures should be worked out for the phased reduction of forces, weapons, munitions and other war materiel from the Cyprus Republic.
- Talks will begin on 8 August with the participation of representatives of the Greek Cypriot community, for negotiations concerning the new constitutional regime of Cyprus.
- Ministers have agreed upon the existence of two police administrations in Cyprus, those of the Greek and Turkish Cypriot communities.[61]

The Geneva declaration was a triumph for Turkish diplomacy, since none of its points were negative for Turkey. Turkish troops were not named, while the general reference to the "phased reduction of forces" in Cyprus was anything but binding on Turkey. There was no mention of the termination of reinforcements of Turkish forces, which, despite the ceasefire agreement, were continuing without interruption.

Barountdjou called the agreement a precious document, which confirmed the acceptance of Turkish demands. "The most important of all, Greece accepted the presence of Turkish troops on the island for an undetermined period of time, even after the working out of a solution. We celebrated the signing of the agreement of the first Geneva conference with champagne. After the signing of the agreement, we returned to Ankara. The public received Gunes and the members of the delegations as heroes. Turan Gunes became the 'conqueror of Geneva'."[62]

The international community hailed the Geneva Declaration as a positive development towards the peaceful solution of the crisis, and placed particular emphasis on the reference to the ending of military operations. Makarios, also expressing his satisfaction concerning the ceasefire agreement, was not satisfied by the entire content of the agreement, however. "In its most important part, that which refers to the withdrawal of Turkish forces from Cyprus, the agreement is very vague," he said.[63]

---

61 Papademetris, Panayiotis, Petrides, *op. cit.*, vol. 15, p. 188.
62 Baroutdjou, *art. cit.*
63 Karamanlis, *op. cit.*, vol. 8, p. 45.

13. Partition by Force

With a second round of Geneva talks looming, Kissinger started a new round of behind the scenes diplomacy, aimed at reaching a political solution that would satisfy Turkish demands for a federal solution based on two territorially distinct regions, with the Turkish zone taking up 34 per cent of the island. Moreover, the United States felt that, for such an agreement to be reached, it remained essential to neutralise Makarios as a political force.

Makarios, however, firmly intended to remain centre-stage, planning to go from New York to Geneva to take part in the conference as President of the Republic of Cyprus. The Americans turned to Karamanlis, asking him to persuade Makarios to change his mind. Karamanlis sent Makarios a letter, saying the Greek government believed the Archbishop's presence in New York was essential, both because it was the seat of the United Nations as well as because he would be able to influence the United States government, which had the decisive say in the issue. In the letter dated 2 August, Karamanlis pointed out in an indirect but clear manner the dangers his possible insistence would entail: "The Archbishop should take into consideration that at this moment Turkey is speaking from a position of strength."[1] Makarios replied immediately, expressing his desire for cooperation with Athens, and assuring that he would bear in mind the difficult position in which the Greek government found itself. However, after urging Karamanlis to convey his thoughts directly to him, even if these might cause him displeasure, he declared himself ready to assume full personal responsibility if withdrawal from the talks proved necessary. Makarios concluded his letter with a clear warning: "The Archbishop will not underwrite an arbitrary action of Turkey, even if the Turks were to occupy the entire island."[2]

In the end, Makarios decided not to go to Geneva, but left New York and established himself in London. For entirely different reasons, the Americans discouraged Clerides also from taking part in the conference. Wishing to shield him from the heavy responsibility involved in compromise, they advised him to remain in Nicosia and send a representative to Geneva. This conflicted with the views of Greek Foreign Minister Georgios Mavros, who wanted Clerides to sign whatever agreement was reached. He therefore telephoned him on 2 August and told him that he absolutely had to take part in the conference.

Clerides, who was unwilling to leave Cyprus, invoked the danger of internal destabilisation, pointing out that EOKA B was still in control of things. In fact, Clerides told US ambassador Roger Davies that in a meeting he had on 1 August with a senior EOKA B delegation, they had warned him that, "if he were to make any attempt to allow Makarios to return, they would blow Cyprus out of the water". Commenting on Mavros' insistence that Clerides should take part in the conference, Davies wrote in his report that "Athens seemed not to realise that if he [Clerides] left, there was nobody who could balance the forces that were threatening to push the Greek Cypriot area of Cyprus into chaos and turmoil".[3]

Clerides discussed the question of who would represent Cyprus at the Geneva conference with the Head of the Europe Desk at the State Department Arthur Hartman, who in those days was visiting Ankara, Athens and Nicosia as Kissinger's personal envoy ahead of the second round of talks in Geneva. In a meeting in Nicosia on 5 August, Hartman handed Clerides a personal letter from Kissinger, "which he read with evident satisfaction".

---

1 Karamanlis, *op. cit.*, vol. 8, p. 51.

2 *Ibid.*

3 Davies to Secretary of State, "Makarios's proposals", NARA, NPMS, NSC, Cyprus/Greece, telegram 2093, Nicosia 2 August 1974.

Hartman told Clerides that Kissinger felt strongly that he was "the right man in the right job to handle the present situation in Cyprus". He also expressed the support of the United States "for the moderate stance he had taken in the past and his evident sense of realism".

Concerning Greek Cypriot representation at the Geneva conference, Hartman told Clerides "his political skills and presence could not be spared from Cyprus". For that reason, Kissinger, "as his political advisor", did not recommend that he go to Geneva. "Before I could finish explaining your rationale, Clerides did it for me. He said that he had exactly the same thought. If he went to Geneva, he would be made to assume a responsibility which would weaken him at home," Hartman wrote to Kissinger in a telegram. "On the other hand, the others in the Greek Cypriot community would not go without him. Mavros was pressing him to go, but at the same time Mavros would not take any of the responsibility for unpalatable decisions in Geneva. Karamanlis and Averoff appeared more realistic, but Mavros did not want to sully his political reputation by being the one to mention a federal (or cantonal, as Clerides prefers) solution."[4]

Later, in a discussion after a working dinner, Clerides told Hartman of two other reasons why he should not to go to Geneva. The first was connected with his decision to reshuffle the government formed by Sampson, and the second was the arrival in Cyprus of Efthimios Karayiannis, the new Commander of the National Guard at the head of a first group of Greek officers to replace those that had played a leading role in the coup. Clerides feared the extreme elements might interpret this as the first step towards the restoration of Makarios, and that this group might react before officers loyal to Karamanlis could clip their wings. According to Hartman, Clerides "is suspicious of Makarios and (...) believes that a solution must bar his return". For this reason, he is thinking that he should "go to Geneva just for the opening day and then return immediately". In the same meeting, according to Hartman, Clerides "raised the spectre of the Soviet Union capitalising on the continued presence of Turkish forces, which they would portray as a violation of the UN resolution. This would attract the support of the communists, the left generally and pro-Makarios forces on the island." Reacting to this scenario, Hartman cautioned Clerides that "he should understand that whoever plays with the Soviets will lose our support". He also told Clerides that "the solution to the Cyprus question could only come about in the context of better relations between Greece and Turkey, and that this was not a result that the Soviets could help bring about".[5]

The next stop on Hartman's trip was Athens, where he met with Karamanlis to hand him a letter from Kissinger. The US Secretary of State put forward the need for unity to be restored to the alliance, and expressed his intention to help Greece in the defence of her interests. He also wrote that the role of the United States would be more effective "if based on a realistic appraisal of the interests of all parties" and asked him tell Hartman his views on the long-term possibilities of an "honourable settlement". "I do not have a crystallised view on the nature of such a settlement because I remain convinced that the final solution will have to be developed realistically, through the consensus of all the interested parties," Kissinger concluded.[6]

It became obvious that the US was seeking a solution based on the realities that had been created by the invasion, and the satisfaction of the Turkish demand for a federal solution on the basis of territorial partition. Clerides appeared to be willing to accept this settle-

---

4 Hartman to Secretary of State, "Cyprus", NARA, NPMS, NSC, Cyprus/Greece, telegram 2176, Nicosia 3 August 1974.

5 *Ibid.*

6 Karamanlis, *op. cit.*, vol. 8, p. 53.

ment, but support from Athens was essential. Hartman told Karamanlis that in the talks he had had in Nicosia, Clerides "referred vaguely to a cantonal or federal solution". Repeatedly, however, he emphasised that Clerides was politically very weak and that, "for the promotion of his idea in Geneva, there is a clear need for support from the Greek government".

Hartman thought the involvement of the Soviet Union had to be prevented at all costs, and linked the Soviet interest with Makarios' insistence on returning to Cyprus. "Why, otherwise, do the Russians want Makarios to come back to Cyprus? As for the Archbishop, he should put off his return to the island, at least for the foreseeable future, because doing so would bring on civil unrest and probably a pretext for an expansion of the Turkish presence."[7]

Karamanlis assured Hartman that the Greek government was driven by good will to find a solution. "However, no government or state is able to accept humiliation. Turkey is heading in this direction, and if she persists, Greece will be obliged to go to extremes." Karamanlis warned Hartman that if Turkey continued to violate the ceasefire in Cyprus, Greece would not go to Geneva, and if she were present, would not be able to remain. Finally, he told him to assure his government that he would make every effort towards an honourable solution. "I am not, however, able to accept humiliation. I shall handle the matter in all seriousness and in no way demagogically." To convince him of his sincerity, he told him that when he returned to Greece and the people expected to hear him speak about the Cyprus question, he had avoided even mentioning Cyprus. "Because I did not want to aggravate an already heavy atmosphere. I repeat to you that we expect you to exercise influence on Ankara, because there is the key to the solution."[8]

Ankara, however, was discussing nothing less than the evacuation of the northern part of Cyprus by all Greek Cypriots and its surrender to Turkey. Hartman was informed of Turkey's policy in the meeting he had in Ankara on 5 August with Prime Minister Bulent Ecevit, Foreign Minister Turan Gunes and Defence Minister Hassan Isik. During that meeting, as Hartman reported back to Washington, the Turks set out, without providing details, a proposal for resolving the Cyprus problem, which they described as "a necessary surgical operation". The substance of the proposal was "the creation of a large territorial zone for an autonomous Turkish Cypriot community, within the framework of a single independent Cyprus," with a federal system of administration. After pressure from Hartman, Ecevit promised that if Athens accepted his suggestion "then the phased reduction of Turkish forces could begin".

Hartman pointed out that Turkey should take care not to appear to impose a solution on Greece or to humiliate the new government. "This could lead to a change of regime and swing either to the left, with Communists dominating the new government, or to the right, with a new military combination."

Ecevit and his ministers retorted that they too wished to remain in power, that they too had serious problems with their own public opinion. They said that the decision they had taken to accept the ceasefire and stop the advance of the Turkish army, when the army could easily have occupied much more than 30 per cent of the island, should be recognised and appreciated by Greece, the United States and Turkey's other friends.

After making extensive reference to the history of previous Cyprus crises, Ecevit said that this time Turkey, by sending its army to the island, was introducing an "innovation"

---

7 *Ibid.*, p. 54.

8 *Ibid.*

into the equation. "Turkey is determined to use the new realities thereby created so as to bring about a lasting solution. Two autonomous administrations had been created by 'natural forces', which are also pressing the Turkish Cypriots to congregate in one geographic area on the island."

Ecevit and his ministers repeatedly told Hartman that the 1960 constitution and the London-Zurich agreements were dead, except for the role of the three guarantor powers. Within this framework, they hoped to work out a solution along the lines that they proposed. They indicated that they were prepared to negotiate with Greece on the size of the Turkish Cypriot geographic zone and the modalities of creating new arrangements for two autonomous administrations, preferably within the framework of the three guarantor powers that had been established during the recent Geneva talks.

Briefing Kissinger on his discussions with the Turks, Hartman admitted that the US had offered cover to Turkey in its invasion of Cyprus: "I said that our actions since the onset of the latest Cyprus crisis should have demonstrated clearly to Ecevit and his ministers the sympathy and understanding which Turkey enjoys from the United States government (...). I promised to convey the views expressed by Ecevit and his ministers to you. I said that we would study them carefully, and provide frank views we thought would be useful in private. They could be sure that whatever we had to say to them would be our real position, that if we had any recommendations to make they would be made in an effort to be as helpful as possible, and we would not make suggestions which could not be achieved."

Concluding, Hartman told Kissinger that Ecevit and Gunes were effusive in their reiterated praise for him personally, and for the role which the US government had played in the recent crisis. "However, it is clear to me that, despite all this, he will continue to press us very hard for our support of his substantive position and our assistance in selling this to the Greeks."[9]

When Hartman returned to Washington on the eve of the second Geneva conference, he suggested to the State Department that "probably a separation of both communities is necessary".[10] He also reported that two autonomous administrations existed on the island and would continue to exist regardless of constitutional arrangements. From this, Under Secretary of State Joseph Sisco and the US observer in Geneva, William Buffum, concluded that Turkey's strengthened position on Cyprus provided the key to resolving the dispute. "A premature withdrawal of Turkish invading forces, they argued, was neither feasible nor in the US interest."[11]

Because Turkish withdrawal had to be part of a new arrangement that would assure greater security and autonomy for the Turkish Cypriots, the officials recommended to the Secretary of State a "federal" solution, similar to that sought by Turkey, with a gradual reduction of Turkish forces as stability returned. "The enhanced Turkish position on the island and the growing Greek Cypriot willingness to make concessions suggested that the scheme might succeed."[12]

Under these conditions, the second Geneva conference began on 8 August with the participation of the foreign ministers of the three guarantor powers. Clerides also took part from 10 August, as did Denktash. According to the UN Secretary-General, Kurt Waldheim,

---

9 Hartman to Secretary of State, "Cyprus", NARA, NPMS, NSC, Cyprus/Greece, telegram 6176, Ankara 5 August 1974.

10 Slengesol, *art. cit.*

11 *Ibid.*

12 *Ibid.*

who had separate meetings with the three foreign ministers, Turkey from day one made crystal clear its intentions "to resort to military might to succeed in her aim: the creation of two territorially and ethnically separate regions, with autonomy for each".[13]

One of the provisions of the first Geneva declaration had called for the evacuation of Turkish Cypriot enclaves by National Guard troops and EOKA B irregulars. Despite the fact that there was a genuine attempt to abide by this provision, the process was halted as a result of Turkey's continual violation of the ceasefire. Citing the non-evacuation of the enclaves, Turkish Foreign Minister Gunes told the UN Secretary-General that his country was no longer bound by the truce and demanded the immediate creation of a Turkish Cypriot region on the northern coast of Cyprus, which would include 34 per cent of the island's territory.[14] The Greek side's response, with which British Foreign Secretary James Callaghan agreed, was that the evacuation of the enclaves was interlinked with the ceasefire and the halt of Turkish advances. From 30 July when the Geneva declaration was signed until 8 August, Turkey had occupied a further 30 square kilometres, increasing the territory under occupation to 430 square kilometres.

After fruitless discussions that lasted four days, the United States and Britain undertook a joint diplomatic initiative to persuade the Greek delegation to come closer to the Turkish positions so as to salvage the conference. On 12 August, Callaghan asked for a meeting with Clerides at which he proposed to him to issue a joint declaration with Denktash that would state that "they agreed that it was necessary fundamentally to review the governmental system in the Cyprus Republic",[15] so the two communities could peacefully co-exist. Callaghan presented Clerides with a draft statement, which stated that the two sides agreed to the "establishment of a system based upon the existence of two autonomous administrations within common borders, under the leadership of a central government".[16]

The same day, Callaghan summoned Clerides and Denktash to a joint meeting to discuss the draft of the joint declaration. At that meeting, according to a note of Greek Foreign Minister Mavros, Clerides unofficially submitted to the Turkish side a plan for a federal solution, which provided for:

a. The preservation of the bi-communal character of constitutional order in Cyprus.
b. The distribution of powers and authority between the central government and the autonomous community administrations.
c. The preservation of the presidential system.
d. The definition of territorial areas, within which the Greek and Turkish community administration would exercise power and authority.[17]

Denktash received the Clerides plan with hesitation, and subsequently submitted his own plan, which provided for:

a. The preservation of the bi-communal nature of the state.
b. The creation of two federal states, with absolute control and autonomy within their territorial boundaries.
c. The cession of 34 per cent of Cyprus territory to the Turkish Cypriot state, north of the Nicosia-Famagusta line.

---

13 Karamanlis, *op. cit.*, vol. 8, p. 75.
14 *Ibid.*
15 Clerides, *op. cit.*, vol. 4, p. 65.
16 *Ibid.*, p. 66.
17 Karamanlis, *op. cit.*, vol. 8, p. 76.

d. Subject to agreement on the final constitutional structure of the Republic, the two autonomous administrations would undertake full administrative procedures within their home territories.[18]

Denktash's plan was discussed at a meeting of the Greek delegation and was unanimously rejected. Typically, Mavros stated that such a document could not be signed, and that "it were better for Cyprus to go to war and be conquered rather than it sign and be a party to its own enslavement".[19]

In the meanwhile, as a result of Kissinger's behind the scenes diplomacy, Turkey accepted to submit a plan for a federal solution, which provided for the creation of several Turkish Cypriot cantons instead of a single territorially unified area. On the evening of 12 August, Gunes summoned the Greek delegation to a meeting, and handed them the new Turkish proposal. The Turks conveyed to the Greek delegation in coercive fashion that, if they did not appear at the meeting, they would break off the talks and would be free to take action.[20] At the meeting, Gunes submitted the Turkish plan, according to which the Turkish Cypriots would be ceded a large territory between Nicosia and Kyrenia, and six smaller zones that would add up to 34 per cent of the territory, so as to make up the autonomous Turkish Cypriot administration. Gunes set the condition that the main Turkish Cypriot autonomous zone be evacuated by the National Guard in not less than 48 hours from the day of the signing of the declaration. Order, security and the administration of the district would all be undertaken immediately by the Turkish Cypriot administration.[21]

That same evening, Callaghan pointed out to Clerides that it would be helpful if he himself submitted some proposals for a cantonal solution, based on the following principles:

a. A need for a radical review of the Constitution;
b. A need for cooperation between the two communities;
c. The bi-communal character of the Cyprus state;
d. Acceptance up to a point of the principle of communal autonomy;
e. A need for a central government;
f. A grouping of Turkish villages for administrative reasons.[22]

Clerides drew up a proposal on the basis of these principles and discussed it with Callaghan in the presence of Mavros. The British Foreign Secretary was not satisfied with its contents, because its points "did not go far enough and were not likely to salvage the conference from certain collapse".[23] Callaghan warned Clerides that as soon as the conference's proceedings were halted, "the Turkish forces would advance and great bloodshed would follow". According to Callaghan, if the Turkish advance was to be prevented, the Greek side had to make additional concessions and accept an agreement concerning a separate Turkish Cypriot area that would comprise 20-30 per cent of the Republic's territory.[24]

Clerides replied that even if he agreed to territorial separation, he would not be in a position to impose such a solution on Cyprus, because 90,000 people would be affected, there would be an enormous wave of refugees and very large amounts of property would be lost. Callaghan agreed, but observed that the Greeks would be in a better position if the

18 *Ibid* and Clerides, *op. cit.*, vol. 4, p. 68.
19 Clerides, *op. cit.*, vol. 4, p. 69.
20 Karamanlis, *op. cit.*, vol. 8, p. 79.
21 Clerides, *op. cit.*, vol. 4, p. 71.
22 *Ibid.*, p. 72.
23 *Ibid.*, p. 74.
24 *Ibid.*

solution was an agreed one, rather than that the area demanded by the Turks be taken by conquest.[25]

Callaghan told Clerides and Mavros that he was in contact with Kissinger, and that the "United States was not about to exercise the slightest pressure on Turkey to prevent any further advance of Turkish forces", unless there were further concessions. Callaghan consulted with Kissinger by telephone, and there followed a conversation between Kissinger, Mavros and Clerides. Kissinger advised them to accept the condition concerning the cession of 20-30 per cent of territory to the Turkish Cypriots. He promised that in such a case the United States would use its influence to prevent any further move by the Turkish forces.[26]

In the effort to promote his plan, Kissinger contacted Karamanlis at 4am on 23 July through US ambassador Tasca. Kissinger sent Karamanlis a written note urging him to make concessions, taking into consideration the new realities prevailing on Cyprus, in fact, putting the blame on the Greek side: "My view from the beginning has been that only through the consensus of the parties will an arrangement emerge that we can all support. It must be an arrangement that all the parties involved consider to be one safeguarding their interests. There are, naturally, new realities in Cyprus that arose in part due to the previous Greek government."[27]

In his reply, Karamanlis highlighted the arrogant behaviour of Turkey and the ultimatum with which Gunes submitted his proposals to the Greek delegation in Geneva, and said the problem was no longer in Athens but in Ankara. "Greece is not being provocative, but if she finds herself faced with the dilemma of war or humiliation, she will necessarily choose war!!" he told Kissinger, pointing out that the United States should put an end to the tactics of advice and good wishes and exercise real pressure on Turkey.[28]

Late in the afternoon of 13 August, the Geneva conference came together in plenary session. Gunes again tabled as an ultimatum the two Turkish proposals, that of Denktash and his own, and in both cases the total amount of Turkish territory had to amount to 34 per cent. "Two territorial zones have to be created. One for the Greeks and one for the Turks. The name of the system does not matter. We could call it regional or cantonal. I shall call it federal," he said.[29]

Gunes asked the Greek delegation to take a position on the principle of the proposed solution. "The Greek government stated that it recognises Archbishop Makarios as the legitimate president of the island. If we come to an agreement, does the Archbishop have to give his consent? And what if he does not agree? For this reason, I want us to decide this evening, immediately, on the principle. We must roughly determine the territory and I propose a total area of 34 per cent. If there are to be many districts, let us at least define the boundaries of one and the names of the rest. I have prepared a plan, which I shall submit to you," he said, and handed them a map of Cyprus with the six Turkish cantons marked on it.[30] Gunes said that all the outstanding issues were negotiable, except the principle of territorial separation. "I would ask you next to take a position. Do you accept or reject the plan?"

---

25 Karamanlis, *op. cit.*, vol. 8, p. 80.
26 Clerides, *op. cit.*, vol. 4, p. 74.
27 *Ibid.*, p. 79.
28 Karamanlis, *op. cit.*, vol. 8, p. 80.
29 *Ibid.*, p. 81.
30 *Ibid.*

Clerides said that Turkey's position until then had been for a federal solution, and that it was now for the first time raising the question of territorial separation. For that reason, he asked for 36-48 hours to study the proposal. At that moment, a message from Kissinger came to Gunes. Taking the floor, he said: "Since Mr Clerides said that my proposals are new, I shall read out a message of Mr Kissinger in which he states that he knows about the Turkish proposals, and recognises the need for increased protection for the Turkish Cypriots."[31] In his message, Kissinger said "the United States believed that the position of the Turkish Cypriot community demanded significant improvement and protection," and that "there was a need for it to have a greater degree of autonomy." Also, that "diplomatic means have not been exhausted" and for this reason the United States "would consider any recourse to military action as unjustified". Gunes concluded by saying that his proposals had been made known to NATO and the countries of the EEC.

In reply, Clerides said: "Does he [Gunes] not think that he should communicate them to us also? We are not a colony of the US or NATO. I am not prepared to accept that, because Mr. Gunes had consultations with third parties, I have to accept his plan."[32]

Faced with the impasse that had arisen, Callaghan proposed that the talks be suspended for 15 minutes, during which he consulted with Kissinger by telephone. With Kissinger's consent, Callaghan asked Clerides to sign a statement saying he was willing to go to Cyprus with the aim of carrying out a "favourable examination" of the ideas concerning territorial separation. Clerides said he was not prepared to go that far. He could, however, agree to go to Cyprus with the aim of examining "carefully and with an open mind" the various proposals.[33] When proceedings resumed, Gunes repeated his ultimatum. The dramatic dialogue between the leading players, a little before the collapse of the procedure, was as follows:

Gunes:	Are you ready to agree that a line beginning from Famagusta and going through Nicosia forms the boundary of the two territories? This line will be defined later, in view of the cantons that will probably be established. In total, the Turkish Cypriot territory will amount to 34 per cent. This area will be handed to the Turkish Cypriot administration within a reasonable time frame, and a security zone will be created between the two areas...
Clerides:	... I am prepared to examine without prejudice and very carefully Mr Gunes's views, and to reply within 48 hours.
Gunes:	Do you accept or not?
Callaghan:	The reply of Mr Clerides is clear. He will examine your proposals and will answer within 48 hours.
Mavros:	Our position is clear. We do not have the right to impose a regime on the island. As long as the two communities are in agreement, the Greek government will not raise any objections.
Clerides:	I ask Mr Gunes: is he trying to tell us that the Conference has failed because I asked for a suspension of proceedings for 48 hours?
Gunes:	No, but it is a tactical manoeuvre intended to delay matters. In my opinion, the work here has been accomplished.[34]

In reality, Turkey had the second Attila plan ready. A copy of the plan was found in the possession of a Turkish colonel captured in a Turkish tank in the Pentadactylos on 5

31 *Ibid.*, p. 82.
32 *Ibid.*
33 Clerides, *op. cit.*, vol. 4, p. 85.
34 Karamanlis, *op. cit.*, vol. 8, p. 83.

August.[35] The only thing lacking for its implementation was the completion of military preparations. On 13 August, the last day of the conference, Ecevit sent the Turkish delegation in Geneva the following message: "Turan Gunes's daughter visited me. I told her she can travel. Tell that to Turan Gunes ". As Edjmel Baroutdjou states, this was the coded message to Gunes that the military preparations had been completed and that he had to lead the conference towards collapse, so that the next phase of the Turkish invasion could begin.[36]

Turkey already had in Cyprus an army corps headquarters, two divisions (28th and 39th), a brigade of parachutists, the 39th commando regiment, the 6th regiment of Marines and a regiment of tanks from the 5th Armoured Brigade. In all, Turkey had concentrated in Cyprus 40,000 troops, 160-200 M48 and M47 tanks, 200 M113 personnel carriers and 120 guns of both 105mm and 155mm calibre. The forces were supported by the Turkish air force, which flew unmolested over Cyprus.[37]

According to the action plan of Attila 2, the 39th Division, reinforced by tanks and personnel carriers, would advance to the Mesaoria plain and would end up in the Turkish enclave of Famagusta. Subsequently, the 28th Division would advance on the plain of Morphou and would reach the Limnitis enclave.[38]

Against Turkish armour, the National Guard had absolutely nothing to deploy. In his report to the Armed Forces Headquarters in Greece, dated 29 July, Georgitsis described the situation as follows: "Units have reached the verge of dissolution, there have been serious cases of units' self-destruction that are taking on the aspect of a revolt. If there is a delay in signing the ceasefire agreement, the dissolution will be total, the troops and population will turn against the Greek officers, and against Greece generally."[39]

In Athens, in a meeting at Armed Forces Headquarters on 13 August shortly before the collapse of the Geneva conference, the military leadership agreed it was impossible to put up any resistance in the case of a Turkish advance, and that "the only possible solution in the case of a general Turkish offensive was to retreat, while maintaining contact".[40]

At 4.55am on 14 August, one and a half hours after the collapse of the Geneva talks, the Turkish air force began to bomb Cyprus relentlessly. The bombing continued until 9am, when the 39th Division broke out of Gonyeli to the east. After breaking the defensive line of the National Guard at Mia Milia, the Turkish tanks, with infantry in their rear, advanced in two directions along the length of the new and old Famagusta roads. National Guard units broke up of their own accord, with the troops throwing away their weapons and dressing in civilian clothes for fear of falling into Turkish hands in uniform.

While the Turkish army advanced, Athens followed the developments helplessly. Karamanlis ordered the forming of a division to send to Cyprus, but the unwillingness of the generals, the disintegration that was taking place within the Armed Forces, and the fear of the war extending to the Aegean, did not allow the dispatch of military forces to the island. In a proclamation to the Greek people, Karamanlis stated that to confront the Turks in Cyprus "was impossible both because of the distance as well as because of the known *faits accomplis*. And it was not possible to carry this out without risking a weakening of the

---

35 Clerides, *op. cit.*, vol. 4, p. 75.
36 Baroutdjou, *art. cit.*
37 Sergis, *op. cit.*, p. 570.
38 *Ibid.*, p. 573.
39 Greek Parliament, *op. cit.*, p. 148.
40 Karamanlis, *op. cit.*, vol. 8, p. 85.

defences of Greece herself."[41] The Greek government, to maintain its prestige abroad, decided that Greece should withdraw from the military wing of NATO.

The distance from Nicosia to Famagusta could be covered in just a few hours, but the Turks were in no hurry to reach their destination, giving time to the Greek Cypriots to abandon their villages, within the framework of a broader scheme of ethnic cleansing that they were beginning to implement. The Greek Cypriots, most of them farmers, loaded whatever they could of their belongings into their cars and tractors, and became refugees. In many cases, those who had not managed to flee were executed on the spot, while several thousand were taken prisoners. Among those in the vanguard of the Turkish advance were TMT Turkish Cypriots, who showed the way and indulged in looting. "We saw that the abandoned houses had been searched, their stuff thrown into the streets and the cars had been pushed and overturned into the rivers, or into fields or swimming pools."[42]

The testimony is that of the Commander of the 39th Division, General Demirel, who describes in his memoirs the scenes he faced in the abandoned Greek villages: "The doors of the houses were wide open. The stuff inside, such as food, clothes etc. were abandoned. There were also children's food, cooked food, fruit that had been cut and half consumed... the bedrooms and the living rooms had been abandoned just as they were. It was impossible not to feel pain when faced with such situations."[43]

At 5.30pm, the first detachment of the 39th Division entered the Turkish enclave in the old town of Famagusta. The rest of Famagusta was not part of Turkish occupation plans. However, the town was emptied of its inhabitants, the Turks found it abandoned and 24 hours later occupied it.

The same scene was repeated in the western part of Cyprus, where the 28th Division advanced on 15 August, and by 9.30am on the following day occupied Morphou, reaching Lefka by midday. All other areas, with the exception of Ayios Pavlos west of Nicosia, where there was substantial resistance from the Greek Contingent and National Guard units, surrendered to the Turks without a fight. After occupying about 35 per cent of Cyprus, the Turks declared a ceasefire. This they again violated, advancing their forces to a point where they touched on the borders of the British bases in the eastern part of Cyprus so as to make the Attila line stand out, throughout its length, to their advantage.

Clerides says the Turks had agreed on the Attila line in advance with the Americans. He cites as an example the case of Athienou village in the Larnaca District, which borders the line. The inhabitants went to him and asked whether they should abandon their village or not. He told them to wait a while. "I contacted Roger Davies and he told me to tell them not to leave. The Turks stopped outside their village. It had been agreed for them to go as far as there."[44] Finally, 36.3 per cent of Cyprus came under Turkish control. The Republic of Cyprus retained control of 60 per cent of the island, while 3.7 per cent became a demilitarised zone.

When Clerides returned to Cyprus from Geneva, the Turkish advance was still under way. On 15 August, he called a broad-based meeting to be attended by the entire political leadership, the Bishops (dethroned or not), former ministers, deputies and other elements. At the meeting, Clerides entered into an extensive briefing concerning the Turkish demands for a federal solution based on territorial zones. He referred to the support Turkey enjoyed,

---

41 Papademetris, Panayiotis, Petrides, *op. cit.*, vol. 15, p. 219.
42 Demirel, *art. cit.*
43 *Ibid.*
44 Glafcos Clerides, interview with the author, Nicosia, 12 July 2001.

mainly that of the United States and to a lesser extent from Britain; he informed them that he had asked for military assistance from the Soviet Union, but had not received a formal reply, and he explained Greece's inability to offer any substantial help to Cyprus. Afterwards, he invited views on the following crucial questions:

1. When the Turkish forces complete the occupation of the territory provided for in the Attila plan and ask for negotiations, what answer should I give?
2. If I reject negotiations, the Turks have the opportunity to take over the whole island. What is to be done?
3. Would it not be preferable for me to negotiate with little probability of the Turks accepting less territory than 34 per cent and with the likelihood of securing guarantees for those Greeks that will reside in Turkish areas?[45]

In simple language, the question that Clerides was posing was: to what extent should he accept or reject a plan of partition, with the hope of some territory being returned and taking into consideration the threat of all Cyprus being occupied. He invited those present to adopt a position on this question, requesting them to avoid references to the past, to avoid bitterness and for them to be brief, because – as he put it – "time is pressing". The main opinions expressed were as follows:

The Secretary-General of AKEL Ezekias Papaioannou called the plans unacceptable, but committed himself to giving his party's views in writing. The next day, an AKEL delegation handed Clerides a memorandum containing its positions: it suggested the return of Makarios, the formation of a government of national unity, and an international campaign to seek support for a solution of the Cyprus problem based on the principles of international law.

The president of EDEK, Vassos Lyssarides, referred extensively to the causes of the invasion, proposed outright rejection of the Turkish demands, and suggested a diplomatic struggle after first restoring constitutional order through the return of Makarios.

The president of ESEA, Georgios Vasiliades, proposed rallying round Clerides and a struggle in the unoccupied areas to avert an expansion of the Turkish forces. "Our most powerful weapon is our honour, and with this we must fight through the United Nations."

On the part of the Church, the first to speak was the Bishop of Paphos (later to become Archbishop Chrysostomos), who said that there could be no acceptance of the Turkish plans, and that use had to be made of the prestige of Makarios in order to handle the crisis. Former Bishop of Paphos Gennadios, who spoke as locum for the Archepiscopal throne, said that it would be "preferable for there to be a holocaust rather than accept the plans" and his associate Stavros Papagathangelou asked that "we declare *Enosis* with Greece so that Greece assumes its responsibilities".

The *Enosis* of the two thirds of Cyprus with Greece was supported also by the former president of the Greek Communal Assembly Constantinos Spyridakis, with the remainder of the island to be considered under occupation. Nicos Sampson suggested that all lend a hand to Clerides so he could face the situation.

Finally, no decision was taken and Clerides, calling an end to the meeting, made the following statement: "I shall do the duty demanded of a Greek. If I make a mistake, may God forgive me. I take full responsibility, which I shall soon announce. If I do not sign any plan for a solution I shall be accused of irresponsibility and opportunism. If, on the other

---

[45] Papademetris, Panayiotis, Petrides, *op. cit.*, vol. 15, p. 212.

hand, I do sign I shall probably be accused of being a traitor and a national cheapskate. I shall do what I believe will best serve the national interest."[46]

Citing the immediate danger of the occupation of the whole of Cyprus, Clerides was prepared to accept the compromise that he had rejected in Geneva, and to agree to a federal solution based on a territorial zone and the cession of between 30 and 34 per cent of territory to the Turks. However, before taking this step, the support of the Greek government was essential. This question was to be discussed in Athens on 23 August.

With Clerides' visit imminent, the British government on 20 August delivered a memorandum to the Greek government, which contained its views on the Cyprus problem. Britain believed that "if the Greek government was prepared to consider a solution based on the principle of two regions, then Mr Clerides also would be prepared to do so. Furthermore, in Mr. Callaghan's personal opinion, President Makarios would probably not be against such a solution."[47]

Clerides went to Athens accompanied by Tassos Papadopoulos and Minister of Finance Patsalides. On the agenda, apart from Cyprus developments, was the question of economic assistance to Cyprus. On the Greek side, Prime Minister Karamanlis was joined by Foreign Minister Mavros and Defence Minister Averoff. As emerges from the minutes of the meeting, Clerides came out in favour of accepting federation with a territorial foundation. "Any diplomatic moves etc. will not help us to avoid a federation based on territorial separation. Are we prepared to accept this solution? At this moment everyone is urging us to accept it. For example, the Americans promise support, but only if the basis of the solution is federation."[48]

The views of Clerides conflicted with those of Mavros, who represented the "rejectionist" tendency within the government of national unity in Greece. In fact, with elections looming on 17 November, he did not want to be identified with any kind of compromise on Cyprus.

Clerides said in the meeting that he had not had the courage to accept the territorial basis in Geneva. "I was remiss, being fearful of public opinion. Let us not repeat this," he said and asked the Greek delegation: "who will take responsibility if all of Cyprus is occupied?"

Karamanlis, as well as Mavros disagreed with Clerides that there was a real danger of the whole island being occupied. But Clerides insisted that "the Turks were halted by the American factor" because they preserved a hope that the Greek Cypriots might negotiate. "We have to give an indication of what we are willing to accept," he said.[49]

Ultimately, the final decision, as set out by Karamanlis, was the following:

- Insistence on the return of the refugees to their homes under conditions of safety, and the return of the Turkish troops to the positions they occupied on 9 August, at the start of the second Geneva conference.
- With the above pre-conditions, a dialogue could begin, without excluding the possibility of examining a federal solution on a territorial basis, on the condition that there would be no exchange of populations.[50]

---

46 *Ibid.*, p. 213.
47 Karamanlis, *op. cit.*, vol. 8, p. 113.
48 *Ibid.*, p. 121.
49 *Ibid.*, p. 122.
50 *Ibid.*, p. 126.

At the end of August, UN Secretary-General Kurt Waldheim visited Nicosia, Athens and Ankara, exploring the possibility of opening talks to solve the crisis. According to Waldheim's briefing of the Greek government, Clerides was prepared to accept federation of the two communities on a territorial basis, while negotiating the powers of the central government, but without the exchange of populations. As for Denktash, Waldheim merely determined that he was not free to decide on anything without the assent of the Turkish government. The position of Ankara, as Ecevit explained to Waldheim, was that the Turks should be ceded 30 per cent of the territory. The return of occupied land would be the subject of negotiations, while the return of refugees could be allowed as part of a general settlement. He also discussed the reduction of Turkish forces, but under the condition that first those Turkish Cypriots living in the south would be allowed to transfer to that part of the north that was controlled by the Turkish military.[51]

Waldheim came to the general conclusion that the conditions were not yet suitable for talks for a solution of the problem. He managed, however, to succeed in initiating talks between Clerides and Denktash over humanitarian issues. The first meeting took place on 26 August at the Ledra Palace Hotel in the demilitarised zone of Nicosia. The first subject raised was that of the exchange of prisoners, with the cooperation of the International Red Cross. According to the arrangement that was agreed, the Greek Cypriot prisoners whose villages were under Turkish occupation would have the right to choose to go to their homes or to the area under the control of the Cyprus Republic. The corresponding Turkish Cypriots, most of whom came from the southern parts of Cyprus, could choose to return to their villages or go to the occupied area. When the exchange of prisoners began in mid-September, only 164 Greek Cypriot prisoners, whose families remained in the occupied areas, chose to go to their villages. The Turkish army did not allow any of the discharged Turkish Cypriots to go to their houses in the south. Thus, a serious social problem was created, with the Turkish Cypriot men in the north, and their wives and children in the south.

Makarios was mostly in agreement with Clerides' evaluation that the Turkish invasion had changed the situation, and that the acceptance of a federal solution was unavoidable. However, he set preconditions such as a strong central government, the return of a large amount of territory and the right of refugees to return to their homes. In contrast with Clerides, who was ready to accept the Turkish condition concerning the acceptance of territorial federation before starting the talks, Makarios was not prepared to sacrifice the principle before making sure of the exchange.

Makarios discussed the new conditions that had been created in the Cyprus problem with ambassador Michalis Dountas in New York. As the ambassador wrote in a note to Karamanlis, Makarios told him that he was in favour of the continuation of "a diplomatic struggle following aggression, which is one through persistence and determination, *not* one through the force of arms, and of the utmost exploitation of all the means available". However, he had no illusions as to what could be achieved. Recognising the new realities that had been created in Cyprus, he believed that the objective aim of a diplomatic struggle "can be none other than the aspiration to limit the extent of territory controlled by the Turks". He told him that he considered the acceptance of federation on a territorial basis unavoidable, but efforts had to be made so that the central power should be shaped in such a manner as to protect Greek interests. And yet, Dountas noted in his telegram, the Archbishop would not rejoice in this agreement. He would blame the dictatorial regime. He

[51] Karamanlis, *op. cit.*, vol. 8, p. 130.

would not react, however, or do anything that would cause hardship to Prime Minister Karamanlis; nor would he do anything that could even be interpreted as torpedoing the agreement.[52]

The different approaches of Makarios and Clerides weakened the latter's position, as much internationally as domestically. There was a public mobilisation in Cyprus in favour of Makarios' immediate return. The EDEK newspaper *Ta Nea* conducted a press campaign in favour of the immediate restoration of constitutional order. The campaign for the return of Makarios provoked the reaction of EOKA B, which was in full control of the internal situation. According to Clerides, 7,500 police weapons had disappeared during the coup, taken by members of EOKA B.[53] Clerides describes a scene in which three men in police uniform entered his office in the Public Information Office without warning, and pointing to the revolvers hanging from their belts, warned him not to take any measure in favour of the return of Makarios.[54] However, the moves for Makarios' return gathered pace. The strongest such came from a movement founded in Limassol called the National Rally. It organised a massive demonstration in Limassol on 1 October, the biggest ever to take place in the town, demanding Makarios' immediate return. A rally had already taken place in Paphos, while one was planned for Larnaca and a national one for Nicosia. The huge popular response to these rallies caused anxiety in the American embassy, which attempted to stop them. As recalled by one of the leaders of the National Rally, Menelaos Kanakis, diplomat James Williams tried to persuade them to stop their moves in favour of Makarios, with the argument that the return of the 'Castro of the Mediterranean' would not be helpful to the Cyprus issue.[55]

Clerides also made contact with the National Rally, summoning a delegation to Nicosia, where he asked them not to proceed with further moves, as they could be exploited by Turkey to occupy all of Cyprus. Clerides assured them categorically that as soon as conditions were ripe he would himself call on Makarios to return and the organisers agreed to cancel the Larnaca and Nicosia rallies.[56]

Clerides writes in his memoirs that the Makarios supporters "were putting about the unacceptable rumours that I was ready to accept the partition of Cyprus and that, precisely for this reason, it was necessary for Makarios to return as soon as possible to head off such a development".[57] To a certain degree, these views were endorsed by Makarios himself, who was in New York for the General Assembly of the United Nations. In an interview to Eric Rouleau of *Le Monde*, who asked him about the position adopted by Great Britain on the Cyprus crisis, he said it had been friendly, but passive. "Perhaps the British wish to negotiate with someone like Mr Clerides, whose position of compromise in the present negotiations is much appreciated in London and elsewhere."[58]

In reaction, Clerides informed the Greek government that he would resign on 3 October. On 27 September, Karamanlis sent a telegram to Mavros, who was also in New York, pointing out to him the impossibility of coming to a stable understanding between the

---

52 *Ibid.*, p. 114.

53 Papademetris, Panayiotis, Petrides, *op. cit.*, vol. 15, p. 164.

54 Clerides, interview with the author.

55 Kanakis made these allegations on Radio Proto on 2 November 1994, and they were published in the press the following day. The comments were made on the occasion of the visit to Cyprus of James Williams, who had been appointed as State Department Co-ordinator for Cyprus.

56 Menelaos Kanakis, interview with the author, Nicosia, 21 December 2000.

57 Clerides, *op. cit.*, vol. 4, p. 134.

58 Makarios interview with Eric Rouleau, reprinted in *Παγκύπρια Πορεία Αγάπης Αρχιεπισκόπου Μακαρίου Γ* [Pancyprian March of Love of Archbishop Makarios III], annual edition no. 8, p. 151.

Greek government, Clerides and Makarios, and he authorised him to convey to Makarios that, if the required harmony could not be restored between the latter two, he would be compelled to declare publicly that the position taken by the Cyprus leadership made the handling of the national issue impossible. "Mr Clerides has decided to resign on the coming Thursday 3 October, because he cannot take responsibility for a repeat civil war in Cyprus between supporters of Archbishop Makarios and his opponents. In a situation of the utmost gravity, the Archbishop will bear the heaviest historic responsibility, not only to Cyprus, but to the whole Greek nation, if he does not avert the threatened tragic development," Karamanlis wrote in his telegram.[59]

Karamanlis called on Makarios publicly to support Clerides. Makarios responded positively, and in a public statement, he said that the time of his return to Cyprus would be decided by himself. "Nobody is blocking my return, and consequently, there is no reason for arguments and rallies related to this subject." He asked the people to show solidarity with Clerides, who "has my trust in the political negotiations he is carrying out, and has my warm support".[60] Karamanlis, AKEL, and the House of Representatives all issued a declaration of support for Clerides, who withdrew his intended resignation.

Having secured public support from Makarios, Karamanlis and the Cyprus parliament, Clerides' talks with Denktash on humanitarian issues began to touch on more substantial aspects of the problem. Before discussing the constitutional future, and citing humanitarian reasons, Denktash insistently demanded that the thousands of Turkish Cypriots in the south be allowed to move to the occupied north. Several thousands Turkish Cypriots, who had taken refuge in British base areas in Limassol, were living in tents in temporary camps set up by the British. Moreover, the attacks on the enclaves during the first phase of the invasion had created a feeling of insecurity and a wave of Turkish Cypriots fleeing to the occupied area. All this, together with the hope that in the rich north they would find prosperity, prompted the Turkish Cypriots to leave their homes and escape in any way they could to the occupied territories. As it turned out, the transfer of the Turkish Cypriot population to the occupied part of Cyprus was inevitable, and only a swift agreement on the constitutional future of Cyprus that would assure the return of refugees to their homes could have stopped the creation of two ethnically 'cleansed' areas in Cyprus.

The only power that was in a position to exercise effective pressure on Turkey for a swift solution was the United States. The American government, and Kissinger in particular, came in for intense criticism from Greek expatriates in the United States for the complaisance it showed for the Turkish assault on Cyprus. On 20 September, the US Senate approved by 64 votes in favour, and 27 against, the cutting off of US military assistance to Turkey. The House of Representatives also took the same decision on 24 September, with 307 votes in favour, and 90 against. Initiatives by Congress (Senate and House combined) came into conflict with the stance adopted by Kissinger, who maintained that implementation of the decision would harm American efforts at mediation. President Ford used his veto and there was finally a compromise between Congress and government to implement the decision from 10 December, if by then Turkey had continued to strengthen its forces in Cyprus and to violate the ceasefire agreement.

Kissinger, under the weight of the pressure exerted by Congress, undertook a personal initiative and prepared to visit Turkey. In the framework of his initiative, he met Turkish Foreign Minister Gunes, who was still in New York for the proceedings of the UN General

---

59 Karamanlis, *op. cit.*, vol. 8, p. 171.
60 Clerides, *op. cit.*, vol. 4, p. 135.

Assembly. Kissinger asked that Turkey make certain gestures, so as to open the way for a political solution of the Cyprus problem, and submitted to Ankara a package of proposals, which included the following points:

- The withdrawal of a certain number of troops from the island;
- The opening of Nicosia airport to international air traffic;
- The opening of Famagusta port to international shipping;
- The opening of the Nicosia Industrial Area in Mia Milia to the Greek Cypriots;
- The acceptance by Turkey of the return of a certain number of Greek Cypriot refugees.[61]

According to the Head of the Cyprus Desk at the Turkish Foreign Ministry, Haluk Bayulken, his ministry opposed the return of refugees. Turkish policy was to reduce the number of Greek Cypriot enclaved persons to the minimum "for reasons of national security". Instead of this, the Turkish Foreign Ministry proposed some territorial concessions along the ceasefire line. Kissinger assured Ankara that, in exchange for these gestures, it would have the consent of Athens to a bi-zonal federation.[62]

Kissinger's visit to Ankara was fixed for 8 November. On 2 November, the United Nations General Assembly approved resolution 3212 on Cyprus, which supported the return of refugees to their homes under conditions of security, the withdrawal of foreign troops and the beginning of negotiations between the parties involved. The resolution was approved unanimously and was voted on by 117 countries, including Turkey. The vote by Turkey was seen as a consequence of US pressure, given Kissinger's impending visit to Ankara.

In Cyprus, apart from humanitarian issues, Clerides and Denktash behind the scenes began to discuss the substance of the Cyprus problem. The Turks insisted on their demand for a bi-zonal federation on the basis of territorial zones, as a fundamental prerequisite for them to accept the beginning of talks.

On 7 November, after meeting with Denktash, Clerides spoke of Cyprus developments at a public gathering at Argo Gallery in Nicosia. Many people, including foreign journalists, hurried to hear him make his first public speech on the Cyprus issue since the Turkish invasion. After clarifying that he was not speaking as acting President of the Republic but in a private capacity, Clerides said, "Any thought of a solution emerging that is based on a unified state is out of touch with reality, since Turkey will not accept this basis, given that she has created a 'de facto' situation on the island. Since the state will not be a unified one, then the solution will be based on a federation. Those who tell the people that it is possible to achieve a solution on the basis of a unified state are misleading the people, and are not telling them the truth."[63]

In his speech, just 24 hours after the adoption of resolution 3212 by the UN General Assembly, which Makarios termed a success, Clerides said: "Whoever believes that the United Nations can deliver a solution to the Cyprus problem is, according to me, politically naïve."[64]

Clerides' speech, made just three days before Kissinger's planned visit to Ankara, was effectively a commitment to Turkey's demand for a bi-zonal federation on the basis of territorial areas. Predictably, Clerides' stance sparked angry political reaction. Makarios

---

61 Baroutdjou, *art. cit.*

62 *Ibid.*

63 Papademetris, Panayiotis, Petrides, *op. cit.*, vol. 15, p. 254.

64 *Ibid.*, p. 255.

supporters now openly accused him of undermining Makarios' efforts at the United Nations, and pointed out that just 24 hours earlier Denktash had announced his decision concerning the drawing up of a constitution for the federated Turkish Cypriot state he proposed to create. In reply, Clerides released to the press a statement attributable to "reliable political sources", which maintained that: "Whoever claims that through Cyprus talks it is possible for a solution to arise other than that of a federal state with some territorial basis, is mocking the people."[65] The Turkish Cypriot press hailed Clerides' statements, while Denktash called them "realistic and constructive" and observed that if the Greek Cypriot leadership – i.e. Makarios – "had operated with the same realism in 1964, Cyprus would be a prosperous country."[66]

However, just as Clerides took the momentous step of publicly adopting territorial federation, Kissinger's initiative with Ankara collapsed before it even began. Only 48 hours before the planned visit, the National Salvation Party of Erbakan, which was part of the governing alliance, withdrew its support for Ecevit, on account of differences concerning the American proposals for Turkey to make gestures on the Cyprus issue.

On 7 November, Ecevit resigned as Prime Minister. The country remained without government and entered a period of political instability. Kissinger informed the Greek government through Greek ambassador Bitsios that "the resignation of Ecevit finally removed the last chance for a productive visit. It is probable that further progress can only be made when the political situation in Ankara is clarified."[67]

On 23 November, Clerides met Makarios in London for the first time since the coup. Clerides writes in his memoirs that he decided to visit Makarios in London to brief him first hand on the situation in Cyprus, on his talks with Denktash and his views concerning the aims and demands of Turkey.[68] However, in an interview with the author, Clerides said that the objective of his trip to London had been to persuade Makarios not to return to Cyprus, so that he could take the responsibility for a compromise solution. "I told him: look, Your Beatitude, there will be tough negotiations and whatever the solution arrived at, it will not be one that an Ethnarch can put his signature to. You are the Ethnarch. I am a politician, which is different. His answer was that he would return to Cyprus,"[69] which he eventually did, on 7 December.

Before that, however, Clerides returned to the island, where, on 25 November, he held his final meeting with Denktash before Makarios' return. According to a note from Clerides to Karamanlis, Denktash told him, in the presence of the UN representative in Cyprus, Weckman, what he thought of Makarios' decision to return:

"If his Beatitude, on his return to Cyprus, or before his return, makes statements that he will not accept a federal solution on a territorial basis, even cantonal, or says that he does not recognise the partnership of the two communities, or if he adopts the position that the Turkish Cypriots form a minority and not an ethnic community, or states that he will not permit the Turks to be transferred to the northern part unless the refugees are allowed to return to their homes, then as a first step the Turkish side will refuse to negotiate with the Greek one.

---

65 "Αποκλείεται γεωγραφική ομοσπονδία" [Geographic Federation Ruled out], *Ta Nea*, 9 November 1974.
66 *Ibid.*
67 Karamanlis, *op. cit.*, vol. 8, p. 231.
68 Clerides, *op. cit.*, vol. 4, p. 140.
69 Clerides, interview with the author.

"As a second step, the Turkish army will proceed to transfer the Turks from the south to the north without the use of force, unless there is resistance, in which case Turkey will use both naval and air forces, as well as the army, while at the same time the Turkish forces will cut off the town of Nicosia."[70]

Denktash's blackmail brought results, since that meeting saw the first agreement for the transfer of populations on humanitarian grounds. The transfer of the entire population of the village of Tochni to the occupied territories was agreed upon. Basically, it consisted of women, children and old people, since EOKA B extremists had murdered all the men. This transfer was the blueprint for the massive transfer the following year of all the Turkish Cypriots to the Turkish occupied north.

Before the Turkish invasion, 180,000 Greek Cypriots and 44,000 Turkish Cypriots had lived in the part of Cyprus that was now under occupation. Another 71,000 Turkish Cypriots had lived in the southern part of the island. They now moved to the north. By the end of the second invasion, 160,000 Greek Cypriots had already abandoned lands now under occupation, while the remaining 20,000 stayed enclaved in the Karpass region on the easternmost tip of the island. Towards the end of June 1975, one year after the invasion, the Turks forced most of those in the Karpass to abandon their homes and transfer to the areas still under control of the Cyprus government. At the same time, they brought 60,000 colonists from Turkey. As the years have passed, the number of Turkish settlers has increased, until they are now in a majority.

On 29 November, Makarios arrived in Athens. He was to stay there for a week and on 6 December to return to Cyprus. Clerides also went to Athens from Cyprus. At a two-day meeting of the Greek and Cypriot leadership, the further handling of the Cyprus issue was discussed. On the Greek side, Karamanlis, Mavros, Averoff and Nicosia ambassador Dountas took part, while the Cypriot side was represented by Makarios, Clerides, Ioannis Christofides, Tassos Papadopoulos, Spyros Kyprianou and ambassador to Athens Nicos Kranidiotis.

The first meeting took place on 30 November, when all the crucial issues concerning the next steps on the Cyprus problem were raised. "We could not ignore reality," said Makarios, who ruled out the possibility of expelling the Turks by force. Makarios conducted an extensive analysis of the options available, with a view to finding a compromise solution, given Turkey's demand for a solution on the basis of territorial federation, and posed the dilemma as to how far it was in the interests of the Greek Cypriots to put their signature to a compromise solution in exchange for 10 per cent of the territory, or for the Turks to continue to hold on to 40 per cent without a signature. According to Makarios, the problem was Turkey's refusal to clarify its intentions. "If we say we accept in principle a federation on a territorial basis, they will start bargaining and our position will not be an enjoyable one. They are telling us to accept in principle, and discuss the rest later."

Analysing the options available, Makarios commented:

1. Concerning a viable federation, namely, a federally structured state without transfers of population: "Once, the Turks were demanding this, and we refused. Critics are right, but Mr Clerides could not accept this solution without my consent, and I could not accept this because I feared a coup."
2. Concerning a geographical federation with cantons: according to Makarios, this solution would have the advantage of more powers for the central government. "If the Turks tell us the size of the cantons we would be in a position to think it over."

---

[70] Karamanlis, *op. cit.*, vol. 8, p. 237.

3. Concerning a geographical federation into two zones: "I do not wish us to sacrifice the principle before knowing all the Turkish demands."

Makarios estimated the Turks were willing to give back certain areas, but that they would do so within a framework of negotiation, and expressed the expectation of a swift liberation of Famagusta and Morphou, something that would diminish the refugee problem. Although he ascribed considerable responsibility for the Turkish invasion to Kissinger in person, he judged that only with his help could there be a way out. "Only Henry Kissinger can make soundings, exert pressure and persuasion on the Turks so that they state what the minimum is concerning the concessions they are prepared to make, so that we know their intentions."[71]

Clerides said that the maximum the Americans could offer was to prevent the Turks from taking any further military action against Cyprus and to persuade them to make certain concessions. "They want a federation on a territorial basis, and in fact, with two zones. So do the British. The Russians are not prepared to take action to force the Turks out of Cyprus."[72] Clerides suggested an acceptance in principle of a federation on a territorial basis, arguing that maintaining the existing situation in Cyprus only favoured Turkey, while invoking the danger of the occupation of the entire island.

Karamanlis stressed the utter inability of Greece to offer military assistance to Cyprus. He said the army was disorganised, the country was facing serious economic difficulties, while the international climate was not at all favourable to Greek interests. In the discussion that followed, Makarios said that any line taken could not achieve progress, given the government crisis in Turkey. "If we accept geographical federation with two zones as the only solution, there will be reactions in Cyprus, which will probably give Turkey the opportunity to take measures at our expense." Makarios said the multi-zonal solution could be accepted, one with a strong central government and many Turkish Cypriot cantons, without the upheaval of a transfer of populations.

"Clerides: I respect the views of His Beatitude, but I completely disagree. His Beatitude has employed the argument that there is no Turkish government, but precisely because there is no Turkish government there is danger. We shall not avoid accepting a bi-regional solution, even if in the first phase we have to start from the multi-regional federation, which I doubt if Turkey will accept. Whoever puts his signature to this solution is politically finished. I haven't heard a single argument that we do not accept federation but we are just putting off taking a decision. We have to decide, because otherwise I cannot continue negotiating with Mr Denktash. Someone else will have to take over. (…)

Christofides: I agree with Mr President as to the inability of Greece to offer military assistance to Cyprus. I also agree with what Mr President said of the international factor. I believe that we are at the eleventh hour. The more we neglect the subject, the more the situation hardens within the 40 per cent of Cyprus. We must begin immediate negotiations in Cyprus based on a federation with a territorial basis. Our objectives must be: 1) either many cantons, 2) or fewer cantons and, 3) our retreat into two regions. (…)

Karamanlis: If we accept federation with many cantons, will the Turks start talking?

71 *Ibid.*, p. 240.
72 *Ibid.*, p. 241.

Clerides:	I believe that for them to initiate a dialogue, they set as a precondition our recognition a bi-regional federation or a large canton in the northern part and between one and two smaller ones, again in the north, as well as the transfer of Turkish Cypriots from the south to the north.
Karamanlis:	The contacts you had were on whose initiative?
Clerides:	On that of the Secretary-General concerning humanitarian issues. The Turks asked that we accept a geographical federation as a basis for them to enter into further discussions. When I told them that we could discuss, taking geographical federation as one of the solutions, then the Turks brought up the question of whom they were discussing with.
Karamanlis:	Was there unwillingness to discuss?
Clerides:	Yes, given that we have not accepted the basis. The Turks will not entertain a solution with many cantons. They want a bi-regional solution with a large canton of about 18 per cent and one or two cantons of about 7 per cent each.
Makarios:	What is to happen concerning the population?
Clerides:	They will permit a return to Morphou, Famagusta, Larnaca, and I believe that if they have an effective majority in the northern canton they will probably accept the return of refugees to it.
Makarios:	You have said that whoever signs will have to sacrifice himself. What would be the value of an agreement that would not be acceptable to the people of Cyprus, considering that it is not easily persuaded?
Clerides:	Today the refugees are not interested in a solution to the Cyprus solution, and the only thing they want is to return to their homes.
Makarios:	They will not return.
Clerides:	They will return. There is even a possibility that a certain number will return to Kyrenia.[73] (...)
Makarios:	I do not agree with the second and third line of Mr Christofides. We must insist on multi-regional federation. If we accept a bi-zonal federation, it will be a mistake. We shall stick to a multi-federation and Mr Clerides will continue his negotiations. In the meantime, Kissinger will carry out his soundings as to whether the Turks will tell Clerides that they will not entertain multi-regional federation but a bi-regional one. Then, Mr Clerides will also know what is the extent of this, because if we accept from the beginning a bi-regional federation, we are on a slippery slope downwards. If I have to choose between the 40 per cent held by the Turks and the 28 per cent that we shall probably end up with, I prefer that they keep the 40 per cent even against our will, rather than that they hold 28 per cent with our consent.
Averoff:	Is your position fixed?
Makarios:	Yes.
Karamanlis:	We have to start talking. A dialogue is sought by him who has the problem, and in the present case that is us. At the latest, we have to start talks in 10 days or a month, because after 2-3 months nobody will care about the Cyprus problem.
Makarios:	It would be a mistake to sacrifice the principle before we know where we are heading. My reply to Mr Averoff is that, between 40 per cent against

[73] *Ibid.*, pp. 245-246.

our will and 28 per cent with our signature, I prefer the 40 per cent. If Kissinger or whoever tells us that a multi-regional federation is unacceptable, then we have to talk again about our future position.

Karamanlis: We must not repeat the mistakes of the past. You must define your objective in advance.

Makarios: Our objective is a multi-regional federation.

Averoff: If that fails?

Makarios: We meet again.

Karamanlis: I accept. And I shall exert pressure on the Americans.[74] (...)

Clerides: Your Beatitude, if we follow your line, we cannot negotiate on the extent (of territory).

Karamanlis: In both cases the extent will be equally limited, in my opinion, to 25 per cent.

Kyprianou: I am in favour of multi-regional federation, without giving it that exact name.

Clerides: If you do not know whether you have the right to accept, then the dialogue ceases.

Makarios: What stops you from probing? The worst will be sacrificing the principle while not knowing the line to follow..."[75]

Finally, Makarios imposed his view, and Clerides insisted for the instructions he should follow to be given to him in writing, which is what happened.

The return of Makarios was postponed for a day, to give time to the journalists that accompanied him to arrive by ship on the island, since there was no communication by air. Makarios finally returned to Cyprus on 7 December by aeroplane, via the British base of Akrotiri. He went to Nicosia by helicopter, where 250,000 people greeted him. "I was considered dead. Here I am, alive," he said, addressing the crowd from the balcony of the archbishopric that had been ruined during the coup. "I am happy to be back in Cyprus. But I am sad because Cyprus is no longer the fair and prosperous island it was until the criminal coup of 15 July. It is a place of ruin."[76] In his speech, Makarios proclaimed reconciliation and proffered an "olive branch" to the instigators of the coup. "I shall not refer to the cause of the division, because I do not wish to reopen wounds of the past, which I would prefer to be healed. (...) I offer to all an amnesty and remission of sins, in the hope that the desired harmony and unity of our people will follow."[77]

As to the policy he would pursue on the Cyprus problem, he avoided making any statement, except for the commitment that "in no case will the Greek Cypriots be prepared to recognise and accept *faits accomplis* established through military operations." In his speech, Makarios attempted to bring down to earth all those people who had greeted him with so many hopes and expectations: "I do not wish to make promises that I probably will not be able to keep. My only promise is that I shall do my utmost and leave no stone unturned for a solution of the problems, within the bounds of the possible, and for a vindication of your hopes."[78]

Makarios avoided making any reference to Clerides, who was standing at his side. Later, he issued a written statement, in which he said: "I would like to express my deepest

---

74 *Ibid.*, pp. 246-247.
75 *Ibid.*, p. 247.
76 Papademetris, Panayiotis, Petrides, *op. cit.*, vol. 15, p. 277.
77 *Ibid.*, p. 279.
78 *Ibid.*

gratitude to Mr Glafcos Clerides for what he has achieved as acting President of the Republic". Ten days later, Makarios gave written instructions to Clerides to call Denktash for talks to arrive at a solution of the Cyprus problem. The first Clerides-Denktash talks began in Vienna, in January 1975. Up to the present day (2002), they are still talking…

Bibliography

Material from the Central Intelligence Agency (Kentriki Ypiresia Pliroforion – KYP) of the Republic of Cyprus, author's personal archive

KYP report, entitled "Προετοιμασίαι και δημιουργία προϋποθέσεων αφίξεως Γρίβα εις Κύπρον, συνωμοτικαί και άλλαι πολιτικαί δραστηριότητες, έργα και ημέραι Χουντικών αξιωματικών, ματαιωθέν πραξικόπημα Φεβρουαρίου 1972 και πραξικόπημα Ιουλίου 1974" [Preparations and creation of conditions for the arrival of Grivas to Cyprus, conspiracies and other political actions, activities of Junta officers, the thwarted coup of February 1972 and the coup of July 1974]. The report is entirely based on evidence gathered from intercepted telephone conversations.

Transcripts of intercepted telephone conversations.

Written notes based on intercepted telephone conversations.

Audio tapes of intercepted telephone conversations.

Reports on the activities of the Grivas movement and actions of EIOKA B.

Collections of documents from the National Archives of the United States of America. (National Archives of Research Administration - NARA), Maryland.

Record Group 59, Central Foreign Policy Files, 1970-1973, Cyprus. Referred to in footnotes as: NARA, RG59, CFPF, 1970-1973, Cyprus.

Record Group 59, Central Foreign Policy Files, 1970-1973, Greece. Referred to in footnotes as: NARA, RG59, CFPF, 1970-1973, Greece.

National Archives of Research Administration (NARA). Records of the Executive Secretariat - Briefing Books, 1958-76, Lot 75D146, Cyprus, 17 July 1974.

National Archives of Research Administration (NARA). Nixon Presidential Materials Staff (NPMS). Files of the National Security Council (NSC). Country Files, Cyprus/Greece, Boxes 592-595. Referred to in footnotes as: NARA, NPMS, NSC, Cyprus/Greece.

Collections of documents from the electronic archive of the historical section of the U.S. State Department. Series entitled 'Foreign Relations of the United States'

1945-1950, Emergence of the Intelligence Establishment, *http://www.state.gov/www/about_state/history/intel/index.html*

1958-1960, Vol X, Part 1: Eastern Europe Region; Soviet Union; Cyprus, *http://dosfan.lib.uic.edu/ERC/frus/frus58-60x1/index.html*

1964-1968, Cyprus; Greece; Turkey, *http://www.state.gov/r/pa/ho/frus/johnsonlb/xvi/*

Association for Diplomatic Studies and Training (ADST).
Oral History Collection

Boyatt, Ambassador Tom, "Advocacy and Dissent within the System", presentation at FSI September 30, 1992 made to incoming classes of Foreign Service officers, which deals with Cyprus and his difficulties with the Secretary of State.

Crawford, William R., Interview with William Moss, 12 March, 1991.

Dillon, Robert S., interview with Charles Stuart Kennedy, 17 May, 1990.

Grant, Lindsay, interview with Charles Stuart Kennedy, 31 January, 1990.

Select Committee on Intelligence, U.S. House of Representatives

Pike Report, published in *The Village Voice*, 16 February 1976, special supplement, "The CIA Report the President Doesn't Want you to Read. Cyprus: Failure of Intelligence Policy"

Henry Tasca, interview with Jack Bush, U.S. intelligence agencies and activities: Committee proceedings. Select Committee on Intelligence, U.S. House of Representatives, part 4.

Testimonies to the Committee on the 'Cyprus File' of the Cyprus House of Representatives of the Republic of Cyprus.

Ioannou-Psomas, Nicos, 14 December, 1999.
Koshis, Nicos, 11 January 2000
Lyssarides, Vassos, 11 February, 2000.
Tombazos, Georgios, 16 November, 1999.

Interviews with the author

Azinas, Andreas, Nicosia, 28 March, 2001.
Carousos, Georgios, Athens, 13 June, 2000.
Christides, Stelios, Athens.
Chrysafis, Chrysafi, Nicosia, 25 November 2001.
Clerides, Glafcos, Nicosia, 12 July, 2001.
Demetrakopoulos, Elias P., Washington, 30 June, 2001.
Kanakis, Menelaos, Nicosia, 21 December, 2000.
Kalogeropoulos, Diakos, 15 March, 2001.
Lagodontis, Georgios, Athens, 10 March, 1996.
Loizia, Vaso, Nicosia, 2 April, 2002.
Lyssarides, Vassos, Prodromos, 21 August, 2001.
Malas, Dionysios, Paphos, 21 October, 2000.
Papadopoulos, Tassos, Nicosia, 27 August, 2001.
Papaphotis, Photis, Limassol, 17 January, 2001.
Salatas, Eftichios, Nicosia, 29 November 2000.
Soteriou, Panicos, Limassol, 2000.

Television Interviews

Carousos, Georgios, interview with Demetris Andreou, CyBC1 television channel, 16 July 1994.

Palainis, Charalambos, interview with Alexis Papahelas, Mega Greece, 5 June 2001.

Eyewitness testimonies

Athanasiades, Spyros, "TMT", series of articles carrying the first-hand testimonies of protagonists in the establishment and subsequent activities of the TMT. Translated from Turkish sources and published in *Agon* newspaper in Nicosia between 6 June and 12 December 1997.

Baroutdjou, Edjmel, "The Cyprus Peace Operation and its Aftermath", series of articles published in *Cumhurriyet* from 17 July 1989. Translated into Greek by the Press and Information Office of the Republic of Cyprus.

Bedrettin Demirel, "The Roads that Lead to War", memoirs of Turkish General Demirel pubished in serial form in *Cumhurriyet* newspaper in Istanbul from 17 July 1989. Translated into Greek by the Press and Information Office of the Republic of Cyprus.
Tremeseli, Mehmet Ali, serialised testimony to *Ortam* newspaper, 20-27 April, 1992. Translated into Greek by the Press and Information Office of the Republic of Cyprus

Articles and Research

"Operation Gladio, Statewatch", *http://users.westnet.gr/~cgian/gladio.htm*
"Staying Behind: NATO's Terror Network", *Fighting Talk*, 11 (London: May 1995).
"The War against the People: the Contra-Guerrilla. Turkey's 'Cointelpro' Scandal", *ANTIFA Info-Bulletin*, translated from *Kurtulus* weekly, *http://www.ozgurluk.org/contrind/brochu/part1.html*
Agee, Philip, "Ο 'νέος αμερικανικός παράγοντας' και η 'συγκαλυμμένη δραστηριότητα' της CIA στην Ελλάδα" [The 'New American Factor' and the 'Hidden Activities' of the CIA in Greece] in *Anti* (Athens: May 1997).
Burke, Adrian W., "The Turkish invasion of Cyprus: The forerunner of operational maneuver from the sea", *Marine Corps Gazette*, Vol. 3, Issue 3 (March 2000), pp. 81-89.
Celik, Serdar, "Turkey's Killing Machine: The Contra-Guerrilla Force", *Kurdistan Report*, 17 (February/March 1994)
Ertugrul Kurkcu, "Turkey. Trapped in a Web of Covert Killers", *Covert Action Quarterly*, 61 (Washington: Summer 1967).
Fernandes, Desmond, and Ozden, Iskender, "United States and NATO Inspired 'Psychological Warfare Operations' against the 'Kurdish Communist Threat' in Turkey", *Variant*, 12 (Glasgow: Spring 2001).
Komisar, Lucy, "Turkey's Terrorists: a CIA Legacy Lives on", *The Progressive* (Madison, Wisconsin: April 1997).
Lee, Martin A., On the Trail of Turkey's Terrorist Grey Wolves, *The Consortium*, http://www.consortiumnews.com/archive/story33.html
Slengesol, Ivar-André, "A Bad Show? The United States and the 1974 Cyprus Crisis", *Mediterranean Quarterly* 11, no. 2 (2000), pp. 96-129.

Books

Agee, Philip, *Inside the Company: CIA Diary* (New York: Stonehill Publishing Company, 1975).
Agee, Philip, Wolf, Louis, *Dirty Work: The CIA in Western Europe* (London: Zed Press, 1978).
Azinas, Andreas, *50 χρόνια σιωπής* [Fifty Years of Silence], volumes 1 and 2 (Nicosia: 2001).
Athanasiades, Spyros, *Φάκελος Τ.Μ.Τ.* [The T.M.T. File], (Nicosia, 1998).
Athanasiou, Andreas, *Ο άγνωστος πόλεμος Αθηνών – Λευκωσίας* [The Unknown War between Athens and Nicosia] (Athens: Tzionis Publications, 1989).
Alexandrakis, Menelaos, Theodorakopoulos, Byron, and Lagakos, Efstathios, *Το Κυπριακό 1950-1974, Μια ενδοσκόπηση* [The Cyprus Problem 1950-1974, an Examination] (Athens: Elliniki Evroedotiki, 1987).
Ali, Ihsan, *Τα Απομνημονεύματά μου* [Memoirs], (Nicosia, 1980).
Androutsopoulos, Adamantios, *Η μαρτυρία ενός πρωθυπουργού* [A Prime Minister's Testimony] (Athens, 1993).

Arapakis, Petros, *Το τέλος της σιωπής* [The End of the Silence] (Athens: 'Nea Sinora' – A.A. Livani, 2000).

Ball, George W., *The Past Has Another Pattern*, (New York: W.W. Norton & Company, 1982).

Barker, Dudley, *Grivas - Portrait of a Terrorist* (London: The Cresset Press, 1959).

Birand, Mehmet Ali, *Απόφαση – Απόβαση* [Decision – Landing] (Athens, Ioannis Floros Publications, 1984).

Bitos, Ioannis G., *Από την πράσινη γραμμή στους δύο Αττίλες* [From the Green Line to the two Attilas] (Athens, 1997).

Blum, William, *Killing Hope: U.S. Military and CIA Interventions Since World War II* (Monroe, Maine: Common Courage Press, 1995)

Bonanos, Grigorios, *Η αλήθεια* [The Truth] (Athens, 1986).

Bouloukos, Aris G., *Υπόθεση Ασπίδα* [The 'Shield' Case] (Athens: O. Typos A.E., 1989).

Byford-Jones, W., *Grivas and the Story of EOKA* (London, Robert Hale Limited, 1959).

Charalambopoulos, Charalambos, *Περιμένοντας τον «Αττίλα»* [Waiting for 'Attila'] (Athens: Estia, 1992).

Christodoulou, Miltiades, *Η πορεία μιας εποχής* [The Course of an Era] (Athens: I. Floros, 1987).

Christodoulou, Nitsa, Μακάριος - Ένα προσωπικό ημερολόγιο [Makarios – A Personal Diary] (Published illegally without the author's permission).

Clerides, Glafcos, *Η κατάθεσή μου* [My Deposition], volumes 1-4 (Nicosia: Alithia, 1988-1991).

Crawshaw, Nancy, *The Cyprus Revolt* (London: George Allen & Unwin, 1978).

Deane, Philip, *I Should Have Died* (New York: Atheneum, 1977).

Droushiotis, Makarios, *EOKA - Η σκοτεινή όψη* [EOKA – the Sinister Side] (Athens, 1988).

Droushiotis, Makarios, *Η 'εισβολή' της χούντας στην Κύπρο* [The Junta's 'Invasion' of Cyprus] (Athens: Stachi, 1996)

Droushiotis, Makarios, *Πώς ο Κίσινγκερ επέβαλε πρόεδρο τον Κληρίδη* [How Kissinger Imposed Clerides as President] (Nicosia: Archeio/5, Diafaneia, 2001).

Filias, Vasilis, *Τα αξέχαστα και τα λησμονημένα* [The Unforgettable and the Forgotten] (Athens: Papazisi Publications, 1997).

Foley, Charles, and Scobie, I. W., *The Struggle for Cyprus* (Stanford, California: Hoover Institution Press, 1975).

Gibbons, Scott Harry, *The Genocide Files* (London: Charles Bravos Publishers, 1997).

Grivas-Dighenis, Georgios, *Απομνημονεύματα Αγώνος ΕΟΚΑ 1955-1959* [Memoirs of the EOKA Struggle, 1955-1959] (Athens, 1984).

Grivas-Dighenis, Georgios, *Χρονικόν Αγώνος ΕΟΚΑ 1955-1959* [Chronicle of the EOKA Struggle, 1955-1959] (Nicosia, 1997).

Higgins, Rosalyn, *United Nations Peacekeeping, Documents and Commentary, 4. Europe 1946-1979* (Oxford: Oxford University Press, 1981).

Hitchens, Christopher, *Cyprus* (London: Quarter Books, 1984).

Holland, Robert, *Britain and the Revolt in Cyprus, 1954-1959* (Oxford: Clarendon Press, 1998).

Ioannides, Christos P., *Νεο-οθωμανικός ιμπεριαλισμός, 1955-1995* [Neo-Ottoman Imperialism, 1955-1995], (Athens: Karatzias/Trochalia, 1995).

Karamanlis, Constantinos, *Αρχείο - Γεγονότα και κείμενα* [Archive – Events and Documents] (Athens: Ekdotiki Athinon, 1996).

Kardianos, Dionysios, (Spyros Papageorgiou), *Ο Αττίλας πλήττει την Κύπρο* [Attila Strikes in Cyprus], (Athens: G. Ladia publications, 1976).
Katris, Yiannos, *Η γέννηση του νεοφασισμού στην Ελλάδα* [The Birth of Neofascism in Greece] (Athens: Papazisi Publications, 1974).
Kissinger, Henry, Years of Renewal, (New York: Simon & Schuster, 1999).
Koumoulides, John T.A. (ed.), *Cyprus in Transition 1960-1985* (London: Trigraph, 1986).
Kranidiotis, Nicos, *Ανοχύρωτη πολιτεία, Κύπρος 1960-1974*, [The Undefended State, Cyprus 1960-1974] (Athens: Estia, 1985).
Kranidiotis, Nicos, *Δύσκολα χρόνια* [Difficult Years] (Athens: Estia, 1981).
Kyriakides, Andros, and Prentzas, Renos, *Όταν ξεκίνησαν τα τανκς* [When the Tanks Got Going] (Nicosia, 1976).
Loizides, Savvas, *Άτυχη Κύπρος* [Unlucky Cyprus] (Athens: Bergadis Publications, 1980).
Makarios III, Archbishop of Cyprus, Άπαντα [Complete Works] (Nicosia: Archbishop Makarios III Foundation), volumes A-ID.
Markezinis, Spyridon V., *Αναμνήσεις 1972-1974* [Recollections, 1972-1974] (Athens: Sp. V. Markezinis editions, 1979).
Mahlouzarides, Panayiotis, *Κύπρος (1940-1960)* [Cyprus (1940-1960)] (Nicosia, 1985).
O'Malley, Brendan and Craig, Ian, *The Cyprus Conspiracy*, (London: I.B. Tauris, 1999).
Ozgur, Ozdemir, *Η Κύπρος στη ζωή μου*, [Cyprus in my Life] (Athens: Kastaniotis Publications, 2000).
Palamas, Christianos Xanthopoulos, *Διπλωματικό τρίπτυχο* [Diplomatic Triptych] (Athens: Ekdoseis ton Filon, 1979).
Panayiotakos, Constantinos, *Στην πρώτη γραμμή αμύνης...* [On the First Line of Defence...] (Athens, 1979).
Panayiotakos, Constantinos, *Κύπρος - Ο φάκελος της μεγάλης προδοσίας* [Cyprus – The Dossier of the Great Betrayal] (Athens: Philippotis Publications, 1986).
Pancyprian March of Love of Archbishop Makarios III, annual edition no. 8.
Papademetris, Panayiotis, Petros Petrides, *Ιστορική Εγκυκλοπαίδεια της Κύπρου, 1878-1978* [Historical Encyclopaedia of Cyprus, 1878-1978], volumes 10-14.
Papageorgiou, Spyros, *ΑΚΕΛ το άλλο ΚΚΕ* [AKEL, the other KKE] (Athens: G. Ladia Publications, 1984).
Papageorgiou, Spyros, *Από την Ζυρίχην εις τον Αττίλαν* [From Zurich to Attila] (Athens: G. Ladia Publications, 1980).
Papageorgiou, Spyros, *Αρχείον των παρανόμων εγγράφων του κυπριακού αγώνος 1955-1959* [Archive of Unofficial Documents of the Cyprus Struggle, 1955-1959] (Nicosia: K. Epiphaniou Publications, 1984).
Papageorgiou, Spyros, *Μακάριος - Πορεία διά πυρός και σιδήρου* [Makarios – the Path through Fire and Brimstone] (Athens: Ladia Publications, 1967).
Papageorgiou, Spyros, *Τα κρίσιμα ντοκουμέντα του Κυπριακού (1959-1967)* [Critical Documents of the Cyprus Problem], volumes 1-3(Athens: G. Ladia Publications, 1983).
Papagos, Leonidas, *Σημειώσεις 1967-1977* [Notes 1967-1977] (Athens: Goulandri-Horn Institute).
Papahelas, Alexis, *Ο βιασμός της ελληνικής δημοκρατίας - Ο αμερικανικός παράγων, 1947-1967* [The Rape of Greek Democracy – the American Factor, 1947-1967] (Athens: Estia, 1997).
Paralikas, Demetris, *Ι.Δ.Ε.Α. και Α.Σ.Π.Ι.Δ.Α. (ρίζες και πλοκάμια), 1944-1974* [I.D.E.A. and A.S.P.I.D.A. (Origins and Spread), 1944-1974] (Athens, 1978).

Parliament of Greece, *Πόρισμα της Εξεταστικής Επιτροπής για τον «Φάκελο της Κύπρου»* [Findings of the Investigative Committee on the 'Cyprus File'] (Athens: Eleftheri Skepsi, 1989).
Pavlides, Andros, *Φάκελος Κύπρος* [The Cyprus File] (Nicosia, 1982).
Psycharis, Stavros. P., *Τα παρασκήνια της Αλλαγής* [In the Wings of Change] (Athens, 1975).
Sarris, Neoclis, *Η άλλη πλευρά* [The Other Side], volume 2, books I and II, (Athens: Grammi Editions, 1993).
Sergis, Georgios P., *Η μάχη της Κύπρου* [Cyprus' Struggle] (Athens, 1996).
Simpson, Christopher, *Science of Coercion: Communication Research and Psychological Warfare, 1945-1960* (New York: Oxford University Press, 1996).
Simpson, Christopher, *Blowback: America's Recruitment of Nazis and Its Effects on the Cold War* (New York: Weidenfeld & Nicolson, 1988).
Skiadopoulos, Constantinos A., *Πόλεμος στην Κύπρο* [War in Cyprus] (Athens: Eleftheri Skepsi, 1989).
Laurence, Stern, *The Wrong Horse - The Politics of Intervention and the Failure of American Diplomacy.* (New York: Times Books - Quadrangle, 1977).
Tahsin, Arif, *Η άνοδος του Ντενκτάς στην κορυφή* [Denktash's Rise to Power] (Nicosia: Archeio/4, Diafaneia, 2001).
Venizelos, Costas, and Ignatiou, Michalis, *Τα μυστικά αρχεία του Κίσιντζερ* [Kissinger's Secret Archives] (Athens: A.A. Livani, 2002).
Vlachos, Angelos, *Δέκα Χρόνια Κυπριακού* [Ten Years of the Cyprus Problem] (Athens: Estia, 1980).
Vlachos, Angelos, *Μια φορά κι ένα καιρό ένας διπλωμάτης..., τόμος Δ (Γενικός Πρόξενος)* [Once Upon a Time a Diplomat..., vol. 3 (Consul General)] (Athens: Estia, 1986).
Weintal, Edward, Bartlett, Charles, *Facing the Brink* (New York: Charles Scribner's Sons, 1967).

Anonymous and collective publications

Η τρομοκρατία εν Κύπρω, Το ημερολόγιον του Γρίβα [Terrorism in Cyprus, the Diary of Grivas] (Nicosia: Government Printing Works, 1957).
Πώς φτάσαμε στην ΕΟΚΑ [How we got to EOKA] (Nicosia: Archeio/3, Diafaneia, 2000)
Η ζωή και το έργο του Γεωργίου Γρίβα Διγενή [The Life and Works of George Grivas Dighenis], proceedings of conference held in Nicosia, 1995
Ο άγνωστος πόλεμος της Χ [X's Hidden War], Athens.
Constitution of the Republic of Cyprus, (Nicosia: Government Printing Office, 1960).

Newspapers and Magazines

Cyprus

Newspapers: *Alithia*, *Asirmatos*, *Ethniki*, *Gnomi*, *I Machi*, *Mesimvrini*, *Ta Nea*, *Patris*, *O Phileleftheros*, *I Simerini.*
Magazines: *Eikones*, *O Kosmos Simera.*

Greece

Newspapers: *Apogevmatini*, *Eleftherotpia*, *Ethnikos Kyrikas*, *I Kathimerini*, *Ta Nea*, *To Vima.*
Magazines: *Anti*, *Panorama.*

USA

Newspapers: *New York Times*, *The Village Voice*, *Washington Post.*

Index

Makarios Drousiotis is a journalist and writer from Cyprus. He is the Nicosia correspondent of Greek newspaper *Eleftherotypia* and a columnist for the Nicosia newspaper *Politis*.
He has published a number of books on recent Cypriot history (1945-1974), based on research in private and public archives in Cyprus, Greece, the United States and Great Britain.

www.makarios.ws
makarios@makarios.ws

Books in Greek by Makarios Drousiotis

1989: ***In Denktash's Jails***, Nicosia
Personal account of my arrest and detention by the Turkish army while on assignment, covering a buffer zone demonstration by women in Nicosia.

1994: ***From the National Front to EOKA B***, Nicosia.
Covering the 1968-1972 period of turmoil in Cypriot history and the action of the 'National Front' and 'EOKA B' terrorist organisations.

1996: ***The 'invasion' of the Greek junta in Cyprus***, 'Stahi' publishers, Athens.
New edition of the above book, with the addition of further material.

1998: ***EOKA, The dark side***, 'Stahi' publishers, Athens.
An account of the actions of the Cypriot organisation EOKA during the Cypriot uprising against British colonial rule (1955-59), the establishment of the Republic of Cyprus in 1960, and the actions of the 'para state' during the first years of independence.

2002: ***EOKA B & CIA***, Alfadi, Nicosia.
The result of 12 years of research into the period 1947-1974 in Cyprus, including the foundation and activities of the EOKA B organisation and the coup against President Makarios on 15 July 1974. It also includes an extensive introduction, which is concerned with the American presence in Greece, Turkey and Cyprus during the period 1944 -1974.

2002: ***1974, The Turkish Invasion of Cyprus***, Alfadi, Nicosia, 256 pages.
The backstage of the Turkish invasion in Cyprus. From the coup d'état to the invasion and the events that followed until December 1974.

2005: ***The First Partition,*** *Cyprus 1963-1964*, Alfadi, Nicosia.
The Greek Cypriots' attempt to amend the constitution of the bi-communal Republic of Cyprus. The fight between Greek and Turkish Cypriot underground organisations, which resulted in the collapse of the 1959 agreements, upon which the Republic of Cyprus was established.

2005: ***EOKA, the dark side***, published in Turkish.

Essays by Makarios Drousiotis

1999: ***'S-300 and other modern myths'***, Diaphania Publications, Nicosia.
Refers to the crisis in relations between Cyprus and Turkey (1997-1999), which was sparked by the Cypriot government's decision to deploy Russian anti-aircraft missiles on the island.

2000: ***'1619 sins'***, Diaphania Publications, Nicosia.
A critique of the handling of the humanitarian problem of "missing persons" as a result of the Cypriot tragedy of 1974.

2005: ***The constriction of reality and the mass media of Cyprus***, IKME, Nicosia.
The obliteration of opposing opinion through defamation: the case of President Papadopoulos' accusations that his political opponents were financed by the United States and the United Nations. (Published in Greek end English. Available on the web: www.makarios.ws)

Documentary:

2005: ***The Ambient Atmosphere***
Based on the essay "The constriction of reality and the mass media of Cyprus". In Greek with English subtitles. Available on the web: www.makarios.ws.